EXPERTISE AND INNOVATION

EXPERTISE AND INNOVATION

Information Technology Strategies in the Financial Services Sector

ROBIN FINCHAM

JAMES FLECK

ROB PROCTER

HARRY SCARBROUGH

MARGARET TIERNEY

ROBIN WILLIAMS

CLARENDON PRESS · OXFORD

1994

Oxford University Press, Walton Street, Oxford OX2 6DP

Oxford New York
Athens Auckland Bangkok Bombay
Calcutta Cape Town Dar es Salaam Delhi
Florence Hong Kong Istanbul Karachi
Kuala Lumpur Madras Madrid Melbourne
Mexico City Nairobi Paris Singapore
Taipei Tokyo Toronto
and associated companies in
Berlin Ibadan

Oxford is a trade mark of Oxford University Press

Published in the United States
by Oxford University Press Inc., New York

British Library Cataloguing in Publication Data
Data available

Library of Congress Cataloging in Publication Data
Expertise and innovation : information technology strategies in the
financial services sector / Robin Finchman . . . [etc.].
Includes bibliographical references and indexes.
1. Financial services industry—Data processing. 2. Financial
services industry—Technological innovations. 3. Financial services
industry—Great Britain—Data processing. 4. Expert systems
(Computer science) I. Fincham, Robin.
HG173.E973 1994   94–22033
332.1'0285—dc20
ISBN 0–19–828904–9

1 3 5 7 9 10 8 6 4 2

Typeset by Datix International Limited, Bungay, Suffolk

Printed in Great Britain
on acid-free paper by
Bookcraft (Bath) Ltd., Midsomer Norton, Avon

Preface

Over the past decade the potential of information technology to change the way firms do business has been widely acknowledged. The precept that 'IT provides competitive advantage' has given rise to much discussion of the need to include these technologies within corporate strategies. However, the strategic management of information technology has raised more questions than it has provided answers. The failures of costly acquisitions have received as much public airing as the commercial successes and have highlighted a range of social and technical difficulties in planning, designing, and implementing such new technology. Novel and uncertain systems are not easily fitted to business needs. Nor is it sufficient to delegate development to technical specialists since a wide range of suppliers, top management, computer specialists, and the managers and staff who use the systems are involved—each articulating their requirements in terms of their own knowledge and experience.

In this research we set out to study these strategic processes and early on formed the view that the role played by expertise would be crucial. The management of expertise, and the problems of splicing different (and sometimes competitive) forms of expertise, are currents that run through the entire study. This obviously includes technical or computing expertise, but given the complex interactions between players in most large-scale projects the diverse skills of business functions are also of central importance. During the period of research, in the late 1980s, these issues loomed especially large in the financial services sector. High levels of investment in information technology in these industries coincided with rapid changes in commercial practices which were accentuated by earlier deregulation. The sector, which has been a site of large-scale information system developments from the earliest days of commercial computing, presented an ideal opportunity to study processes of technological and organizational innovation.

The research group itself was based in Edinburgh,[1] and it was funded by the Joint Committee of the Economic and Social Research Council and the Science and Engineering Research Council under its initiative on 'The Successful Management of Technological Change'. We are very grateful to the Joint Committee for its support, and in particular for recognition of the importance of a multi-disciplinary approach. For this was a collaborative project involving researchers from a variety of backgrounds—in the social studies of technology

[1] The research team and their affiliations were: James Fleck (Business Studies), Rob Procter (Computer Science), Robin Williams (Research Centre for Social Sciences) and Margaret Tierney (Research Fellow), all at Edinburgh University, Robin Fincham (Management and Organization) at the University of Stirling, and Harry Scarbrough (Industrial Relations and Organizational Behaviour) at Warwick University.

and technology management, computer science, industrial sociology, organization theory, and business strategy. Doing the research, and writing this book, meant combining these different subject areas and approaches. Indeed, this amounted to a challenging project of our own in the management of expertise in parallel with the ones we were studying.

Bringing together the disparate approaches and modes of analysis of six people was necessarily a protracted process in which one thing seemed evident: no single framework adequately covered the scope of these issues. But while there was no simple synthesis of approaches, we believe that a much enhanced understanding of the dimensions of expertise did emerge from the work of the group. This was a challenging, often difficult, but ultimately rewarding process in the course of which we engaged in debates in our own disciplinary fields and attempted to reassess existing approaches; we sought to develop the concept of expertise to enhance understanding of the firm and its sectoral context, the character of information technology, and the methods by which technologies are designed and implemented. Our objective throughout was to develop a properly integrated account and as far as possible to draw our different voices together. While total integration no doubt remains some way off, and, indeed, is probably not achievable in practice, we believe the expertise focus has provided a conduit between some quite different fields of study all of which have important contributions to make in understanding the organizational aspects of strategic innovation.

Contents

List of Figures

List of Tables

Abbreviations

APACS	Association of Payment Clearing Systems
ATM	Automated Teller Machine
BACS	Banks Automated Clearing System
BSP	Business Systems Planning
CASE	Computer-Aided Software Engineering
CHAPS	Clearing House Automated Payments System
CIM	Computer-Integrated Manufacture
CPM	Computer Planning and Management
DBMS	Database Management System
DP	Data Processing
DSS	Decision Support System
DTI	Department of Trade and Industry
EDI	Electronic Data Interchange
EFTPOS	Electronic Funds Transfer at Point-of-Sale
4GL	Fourth-Generation Language
HOBS	Home-and-Office Banking System
IS	Information Systems
ISDN	Integrated Services Digital Network
IT	Information Technology
JSD	Jackson System Development
JSP	Jackson Structured Programming
LSDM	Learmouth and Burchett Management Systems System Development Method
MIRAS	Mortgage Interest Relief at Source
MIS	Management Information System
O&M	Organization and Management
PC	Personal Computer

SDM	Structured Design Methodology
SIB	Securities and Investment Board
SOP	Study Organization Plan
SRO	Self-Regulation Organization
SSADM	Structured Systems Analysis and Design Method
SWIFT	Society for Worldwide Inter-Bank Financial Telecommunications

1

Expertise and Innovation

INTRODUCTION

This is a study of information-technology-based innovations in the particular setting of commercial computing in the retail financial services industry. The empirical material we draw on contains much industry- and technology-specific detail; and certainly one objective of the study is to explore how software is produced in large-scale commercial projects, as well as the patterns of change in industries like banking and insurance. However, the study also attempts to answer some more fundamental questions.

The research is based on cases spanning an industrial sector, and we have used this breadth of material to explore sectoral parameters. It is widely accepted that organizational processes alone cannot account for the knowledge inputs into innovation. We are therefore interested in how sector-level constructs influence and contribute to the development of innovative projects. Our main focus of interest, however, lies with the expertise involved in these processes. While experts have traditionally been a self-regulating form of labour, in complex activities where expertise is distributed across many occupational groupings new uncertainties arise. In particular what are the managerial problems of handling divergent forms of expert knowledge? Expertise itself we believe provides a unifying focus for understanding innovation.

Many have linked the radical and transforming power of information technology (IT) to patterns of change in industrial society, particularly the rise and fall of occupational groupings. Around 1 per cent of the total working population in Britain work in information systems (IS) and related functions; these groups have grown by 20 per cent since 1985 and are expected to continue to outpace growth in the labour force as a whole (Skills and Enterprise Briefing 1991). The investment in IT that has produced these changes also continues to rise. The current level of about 4 per cent of GNP in the advanced economies is set to double over the next ten years (Coombs 1992). Such figures support the view of industrial society as a new type of 'knowledge economy', involving vast increases in information-based work. Reich's (1993) influential thesis, for example, suggests that old ideas of nationally-based economies are unlikely to be the basis of successful future economic policy; economic activity itself is now constituted differently. He puts forward a new occupational division of labour based on service, routine, and symbolic categories. The last are the knowledge workers. They dominate in new and growing industries and are beginning to develop distinctive social traits. An industry like financial services, which is highly information intensive, is a mirror of such trends.

On their own, however, numerical trends are merely suggestive. As Kumar's (1978) seminal critique of the post-industrial thesis pointed out, literal notions about the impact of knowledge are too simple. The existence of so-called new knowledge élites says little about the power that attaches to them or the uses to which knowledge is put. The nature of industrial and occupational change is better gauged by examining technological innovation at the level of business organization. Here changing occupational structures create contradictory pressures on management; power tends to gravitate away from hierarchical management and towards the possessors of specialist knowledge, as myriad specialist knowledge groups seek to control different functional areas.

On the other hand, the potential of IT makes it imperative for management to pursue a unified, strategic approach to the design and use of technologies. In the uncertain settings of disorganized capitalism, firms increasingly have to compete in turbulent market and operational conditions (Lash and Urry 1987). A premium is placed on the integration of design, delivery, and marketing of products, though many organizations still find it difficult to fit technological opportunities to their business strategies. In order to absorb uncertainties they have increasingly had recourse to forms of specialized knowledge.

Crucial questions still revolve around the nature of technical expertise. There has been a 'skills crisis' in commercial computing almost from its inception, such has been the demand for labour to develop information technologies (Buckroyd and Cornford 1988). But the employment of 'experts' does not eliminate the problems faced by firms. The recruitment of experts solves some problems, but it complicates decision-making and raises fresh challenges. The specialist groups introduced into decision-making tend to offer diverse and potentially conflicting prescriptions for business success. New groups brought in to absorb uncertainty will possess varied priorities and ways of evaluating change, and may pursue their own interests within distinctive occupational and organizational settings. Experts also open up other innovative possibilities. They create new areas of uncertainty for firms making it hard for managements, given their own relative lack of specialist knowledge, to respond to the potential on offer.

Thus firms cannot simply acquire new types of expertise; they must identify and combine the knowledges appropriate for diagnosing and solving the problems that confront them. This book is about the work of understanding the potential and limitations of specialist groups, mediating among them, and co-ordinating their efforts—tasks that comprise the *management of expertise*.

A Framework for Research

The study then examines the management of expertise as a critical moment in the appropriation of technology. In order to give it a somewhat wider context we begin with literature on the management of innovation. This has often sought to establish correlations between innovation, organization structure, and the technological and market environment. Following classic research like that of Burns and Stalker (1961), the search has been for organizational arrangements best suited to different technological environments and most likely to foster innovation. Mainstream studies of innovation, like that of Rothwell (1986), conjure a sequence of iterative steps through which technical knowledge becomes transformed into operational systems. Initial phases of idea generation and conceptual definition give way to product development and pilot production, and finally to full production and marketing. Emphasis is on the smoothing of information flows between functions that perform these tasks.

However, this approach tends to focus on the structural relationships between contingencies and says little about the processes by which innovations are developed or the roles which different groups play. The relative neglect of sectoral and occupational influences, and of the contested nature of the processes under consideration, make this a poor model for understanding innovation. In addition, the positive theory of knowledge implied tends to define variables, like technology and structure, and establish correlations between them. But there seems little real evidence that actors have access to such objective knowledge. We must query notions that markets and technology operate as immanent forces, and see instead their existence through the knowledge which actors have of them.

The implications of this mean a blurring of the distinction between organization and environment. This appears in a more fragmented, nuanced form, seen through the now competing now complementary knowledges of the sector constructed by different groups and networks. Emphasis on the social construction of the sector also modifies our view of management strategy. The picture of senior managers scanning the environment and acting on the best available information gives way to more negotiated images of management action. Much the same applies to the concept of technology. One concern of this research is to explore the use of IT in achieving the integrative functions needed in organizations. But it is necessary to go beyond conceptions of technology as little more than hardware or artefacts plus a set of instrumentalities. It is better to see technology at different levels of social action, from specialist know-how through an architecture of generic designs, to the crystallization of knowledge as specific applications (Scarbrough and Corbett 1992).

In this framework of analysis a number of considerations stand out: the need to privilege knowledge and process over structure, the importance of power, and the distributed nature of modern IT skills.

As Teece (1987) has suggested, it is the organization's knowledge base, not its structures or systems, that constrains performance. The privileging of knowledge over structure contrasts a stable and predictable environment with the pressures posed by more turbulent and discontinuous settings. In the former, the job of distributing and co-ordinating specialist knowledge could be done by compartmentalized structures—the different functions and the hierarchical distinctions between strategic and operational roles. But as new markets and technologies dissolve the regularities of organizational life, the pursuit of new combinations of knowledge becomes more important. Nor is there any objective or functionally defined structure into which IT knowledge can be slotted. Knowledge is constructed and transmitted through social processes and relations. It is not freely available but is colonized and controlled by the proliferating specialisms of the IT occupations.

The potential to subvert hierarchical relationships also points up the need for a theory of power in considering the management of expertise. The instrumental use of expertise to advance individual or group interests, or IT experts acting as technological gatekeepers to boost their own prestige, has been researched in classic studies like those of Pettigrew (1973). Equally, the role of expert practices in the construction of mundane organizational realities gives rise to the systematic nature of power and its implicit 'capillary' transmission (Foucault 1979). While this makes it difficult to disentangle expertise from power, we have been at pains to contrast the political expression of expertise with other forms. Thus our study recognizes the importance of the socio-economic validation of expertise which takes place at the level of labour and product markets, transcending organizational power.

Another constraint on the political expression of expertise is the distribution of knowledge. Rapidly diversifying occupations like computing produce expertise distributed across many groups. The technological evolution in IT has involved a move from 'data processing', providing back-room support for administration, to systems which are much more pervasive. This has had important implications for the knowledges involved in systems design and implementation. Where the automation of a clerical task might require only systems analysis and programming, the use of IT to support marketing or strategic decision-making depends on wider knowledges. A range of expert and user groups is typically involved in the design of such systems. As Friedman (1989) has argued, this places considerable stress on the relationship between IT experts and the users of the systems they develop, so that the 'user constraint' has become the key problem in current applications.

The Management of Expertise

The above framework outlines the ways in which IT expertise is acquired and transmitted through social relationships. It stresses the role of management

Strategy

Decision-Making Processes

Innovation Process

Management of Expertise

Distribution of Knowledge
Power of Expert Groups
Economic Validation of Knowledge

Expertise

Formation and Deployment of Expertise

Technology

FIG. 1.1 *The Management of Expertise*

policies and practices in innovation. But management itself is constrained by expertise and cannot be defined simply as a self-aware practice. A mutually defining relationship is suggested between the management of expertise and construction of the knowledges involved in IT projects. Figure 1.1 represents the elements of that complex of relationships.

While it is important to challenge the demarcations found in innovation studies, it is also necessary to explore the major categories which inform existing theories. The framework implicit in the above discussion attempted to achieve this synthesis by mapping out the major fields of study: strategy-making within an industrial sector, technology design and implementation, and the social formation and organization of expertise.

First, it is important to differentiate between current action and the structural context in which projects unfold. Over time, specialist knowledges become embedded in organizational regimes, and political successes at one point in time become part of the fabric of organization life. In Figure 1.1 the outer perimeter denotes the visible processes of development and implementation of projects. Over the short- or medium-term, the available expertise influences management strategy and sets limits on what developments can be attempted. In turn this conditions the design and implementation of technology as strategic choices are made about which technologies to pursue. The cycle is closed as innovation in new technologies produces incremental change in expertise that comes with the gradual development of new skills.

However, the long-term relationships between strategy, technology, and expertise—in particular the internal ordering of expertise itself—unify what are often seen as discrete categories of thought and action. The IT experts' role in innovation projects brings together strategic and technological knowledge and highlights the common social basis of divergent forms of knowledge. In this context several important concerns and working hypotheses guided our empirical research.

1. Our research bracketed strategy and technology as joint aspects of innovation, rather than viewing them as discrete variables. The interaction of expert groups in the innovation process was seen as constructing strategy and technology. Strategic and technical inputs tend to be subsumed in expertise, since, in the technical arena, management action is far removed from pure policy-making. Available technologies become a routine part of development, and diffused in the innovation process, only if they can be successfully integrated into existing operations.

2. The management of expertise needs to be viewed as the summation of cognitive, political, and economic factors which link the formation and deployment of expertise with innovation processes. Here we stress the variety of ways in which expertise is acquired and transmitted through social relations. (*a*) The distribution of skills across different expert groups produces different types of knowledge; non-formal knowledges in particular are significant given the failure of professionalizing projects among IT specialists and a continuing predeliction for localized skills. (*b*) The exercise of power through knowledge stresses how expertise defines the context of its own application. What are seen as possible (or impossible) technology choices can be shaped by expert input into strategy-making as well as day-to-day decisions. And (*c*) expertise itself is not simply the possession of technical skills; skills have to be validated on internal and external markets, via accrued reputation and the capacity of groups to define problems for which they can provide solutions.

3. Strategic practices themselves are less a top-down initiative, and more a part of the decision-making processes around IT, as expert groups themselves define the strategic context via their knowledge of the organization and wider technological environment. Expert knowledge of software process technologies and IT applications is a necessary basis of strategic choice. Thus senior management has no guaranteed role in adjudicating between the claims of expert groups.

The remainder of this chapter examines in more detail the use of strategy, technology, and expertise as research themes. This is not to detract from the role of the management of expertise as a theoretical axis. But this was not a totalizing framework able to assimilate all findings. The picture of the management of expertise unfolds progressively in the study. But before developing that discussion mention must be made of the sectoral context of the research.

The Sectoral Context

There are two distinct if related aspects of sector: first, a *descriptive* account of financial services, the separate industries that make up the sector, and the distinctive features of the Scottish part of it; and secondly, an *analytical* account of how industrial sectors influence firms within them and of the variables that operate at a sectoral level.

IT and Financial Services

The financial services sector offers particular opportunities for exploring the strategic management of technological change. The relative long-term stability of the sector has been undermined in recent years by institutional changes and deregulation. In the late 1980s, changes in markets, in the relationships between different types of firm within the sector, and in the strategies adopted affected the sector as a whole. IT played a major role in meeting these challenges and underpinned new services and operations. Yet its application created additional uncertainties about how financial services could be organized, especially with respect to the all-important customer interface. The increasingly fluid and uncertain commercial environment called for a strategic response. But this has remained evolutionary rather than revolutionary, reflecting the constraints on radical change imposed by institutional distributions of expertise.

In part this reflects the very different industries that make up the sector. This study concentrates on retail financial services, which has traditionally divided into three main arms: banking, insurance, and the building societies. More recently credit cards have formed a new part of the sector, though these are frequently a subdivision of banking. In the next chapter we look at these distinctive businesses in more detail, but for now we can note some major structural differences.

Both banking and building societies are essentially branch-based and involve similar activities of the safe-keeping of deposits, savings, and release of cash to customers. The provision of these services is closely tied up with the branch network as a means of delivery. Insurance, on the other hand, is a much more centralized business; branch networks are much more limited and products tend to be distributed through agencies like building societies and solicitors. Insurance is also a rather different type of activity; it involves finance (as much as financial service) in the sense of providing the customer with future finance for life-events (retirement, death, accident). These basic parameters are reflected in the very different skills of these industries which support activities like the calculation of risk in loan provision, the design of policies, and the provision of account services.

A critical part of the service offered is based on massive payments infrastructures, and here there has long been a close relationship between the development of financial services and the evolution of IT. Financial services was one of the earliest commercial users of IT and is currently the largest. Retail financial services in particular involve the need to process huge volumes of standardized transactions, tasks for which the early data-crunching computers were ideally suited. These early 'back-room' systems were concerned with central record-keeping and administration. Their introduction changed organizational practices—clerical staff were obliged to enter data on to coding forms for central data entry and processing—but most employees were not directly involved in using the systems.

More recently, the development of IT networks has enabled distributed access to central records and has facilitated the earlier capture of data, opening up greater choice in the design and conduct of financial activities. The possibility of further centralization, allowing the application of Taylorist models of task fragmentation and routinization to attain higher efficiency, is now matched by the possibility of integrating distributed activities and improving the quality of service. Also, growing emphasis on marketing and product cross-selling has led to the recognition of internally generated information as a strategic resource, and one worth sharing across the organization. These trends have suggested the value of redistributing tasks to the branch, the point of interface with the customer. In particular, the development of integrated databases of customer accounts has been seen as a means of converting branches into financial 'supermarkets', delivering a range of financial products; while IT networks have created new methods of service delivery like EFTPOS and home banking.

These possibilities clearly illustrate the strategic potential of IT, particularly for banking organizations (Bilderbeek and Buitelaar 1992). But many banks have experienced great difficulties in evaluating the best strategic opportunities. Some failed to recognize the strategic potential of Automatic Teller Machines, for example, initially assessing them as merely a rationalizing device rather than a new method of service delivery that would prove highly attractive to customers (Scarbrough and Lannon 1988).

Difficulties such as these could not be attributed to a shortage of skills. Most finance organizations had begun to install computers at a stage when very little software was available on the market and had large resources of in-house expertise. Rather, such problems highlighted the difficulties in deploying and managing this expertise. IT expertise was unevenly distributed within organizations; there was little familiarity with computers amongst line and top management, most of the expertise resources being segregated in large IS departments which had grown up as the keepers of internal databases. These arrangements had proved satisfactory when computing was a back-office function, but appeared less appropriate as IT began to have greater strategic implications. Thus financial organizations had to face up to the complexity of forming and implementing new policies. They had to adapt their methods of deploying technological and other forms of expertise.

Sectoral Analysis

Concern with the sector also distinguishes ours from other studies of innovation, which may be confined to a particular organization and its product-market environment. Studies by the so-called firm-in-sector school, by Whipp and Clark (1986) and C. Smith, Child, and Rowlinson (1990) (see the discussion below in this chapter), have examined leading firms in automobiles and confectionery. But these were industrial sectors in which dominant national exemplars were already established. Our research interests suggested that studying the 'focal' organization would do little justice to the complex interaction between firm and sector, which shapes strategic innovations and the forms of expertise deployed around them. As Shearman and Burrell (1987) point out, sectoral influences are likely to be more than a matter of consumer reaction or market segmentation; study of them needs to be extended to shared relationships and knowledges encompassing occupational networks and collaborating firms.

Our empirical research explores the boundaries of the sector and addresses innovations taking place across a range of firms. Though retail financial services are oligopolistic, dominant national exemplars adopted uniformly appear not to exist. We therefore explore the cognitive and political construction of the industrial sector, strategically relevant aspects of which were underpinned by expert activity. These included broad ideological programmes of the optimal ways of running organizations, the impact of regulatory context on strategic developments, the influence of networks of suppliers, producers, and consumers whose behaviour underpins the dynamics of the market, and the deployment of models of technological capability articulated by IT specialists within the sector and from external suppliers.

In this sense we were keen to develop the sector as a level of analysis in its own right. Here sectoral development is seen to exert a strong effect on the management of expertise and the generation of innovations within individual firms. In a tightly knit industry like retail financial services, many means of communication inform firms and managers about other firms' ways of doing business. The problem in focusing on such 'recipes', however, is that the metaphor suggests they are transmitted from some dominant environment. Recipes on the whole have to be followed; but we were also concerned with how firms' own resources and history caused them to interpret sectoral pressures in distinctive ways. In developing the sector as a level of analysis, the use of multiple case studies, and in particular our interpretation of strategic issues as forms of negotiation of the sector, were important points of departure.

STRATEGY

Strategic issues can be approached in different ways: the (IT) strategies of firms, the notion of strategic ITs, and the social processes by which strategic decisions are arrived at. And in the course of this account we hope to address all of these.

Certainly a concern with strategy has been central to management practice and the business literature alike, and has increasingly addressed questions of technology (Porter 1985). However, popular ideas about management strategy remain problematic as either analytical or practical guides. Knights and Morgan (1990, 1991) have pointed out that prevailing rationalistic views of strategy tend to have been informed by militaristic ideas absorbed into management theory via the American business schools. This genealogy explains where the rather heroic (but unrealistic) view of the manager as commander-in-chief came from. Such an approach suggests that information needed is objective and accessible, that managers systematically review options, and that they have the unfettered power to implement them. However, while this undoubtedly legitimizes and dramatizes the role of manager, the assumptions implicit are remote from reality.

A more influential approach has been the notion of 'strategic choice' (Child 1972). This perspective stresses the primacy of voluntaristic managerial decision-making over constraints imposed by business structure or technology. It usefully counters deterministic accounts of business and technological development by highlighting the existence of choice; but it too has shortcomings. It tells us little about the nature of the constraints or the limits of alternatives (Hyman 1987). The assertion of voluntarism tends to obscure how strategies are formulated and implemented, by glossing over the role of interest groups in the organization and tensions within dominant coalitions. Even allowing for the 'attenuation' of preferences as a result of internal resistance (Wood and Kelly 1982), strategic choice still construes strategy as the outcome of top-down decision-making. Nor does it fully address the issue of technological innovation, where extra-organizational linkages and collaboration in the development and supply of new techniques are so important. Technological innovation raises questions about managers' ability to exercise strategic choices, especially where top management is under-informed about technological capabilities and the scope for resolving business problems. The role of technical expertise in mediating the uncertainties intrinsic to innovation cannot be reduced to a simple upward provision of information and downward flow of commands. Top managers may be free to 'choose' technology, but their choice will be dependent on expert advisers and subject to political influence and control by such groups.

Rationalistic and voluntaristic approaches to strategy are inadequate, therefore, in a number of ways. They understate the difficulties faced by managers in acquiring the knowledge and information needed to develop policy on a rational basis, especially where a multiplicity of divergent assessment criteria is available. They also overlook the social nature of managerial decision-making, which patterns and constrains the planning and implementation of change. In particular, they ignore the political processes of interest articulation and accommodation that surround decision-making.

Some have recognized these issues and gone beyond narrow views of the rationality of decision-making. Knights and Morgan (1990, 1991), for example, stress the symbolic nature of strategy formation and the cultural context of the organization. They take the extreme position that strategy formation is a purely political process, involving struggles for power and the social construction of policy in the organization. Identifying certain actions as strategic is seen as an exercise of power and legitimation by which particular groups claim the high ground.

Although this view challenges normative and voluntaristic accounts, there are also problems in seeing strategy exclusively in terms of internal power relations. Such a view abandons the idea that managerial decision-making is subject to any tests of external efficacy. It sidesteps certain important questions about strategy: How does management decision-making engage with the practices of the organization? And how do decisions within the firm take into account changing technological and commercial environments? What is required is a more detailed exploration of both the cognitive and the political processes inherent in policy formation and implementation within the firm, and an examination of how these processes succeed (or fail) in dealing with the complex relationship between organization and market and technological environment. We believe that the management of expertise approach can surmount the division between political and knowledge processes, and help to answer these questions.

Strategy and Expertise

Development and implementation of corporate policies will clearly be shaped by the knowledge resources available to the organization. Knowledge, however, is not freely available as disembodied information, but is embedded within individuals and groups—with their own sectional interests and perspectives, and coloured by their location in the organization and broader occupational structures. Such knowledge and expertise is subject to various forms of independent external assessment, including an implicit economic evaluation in terms of the ability of experts to 'trade' their knowledge through labour and product markets. Differences between various management groups (arising from their functional and hierarchical location), expert groups, and other occupational groupings, are thus highlighted in terms of their knowledge resources and competences. Groups will make distinctive knowledge claims by projecting their ability to define and overcome problems faced by the organization.

Strategic practices around IT in particular thus become less of a top-down initiative; expert groups themselves help to shape the strategic context through their knowledge of the organization and its technical environments. Expert knowledge of things like software process technologies is a necessary basis of strategic choice, and top management has no necessary prerogative over technology choices nor a guaranteed role in adjudicating between the claims of expert groups.

The actual policies and practices of the organization emerge through competition between rival claims and rival visions of how the organization should proceed, as groups represent their preferred approaches and attempt to enrol others. Through accommodation and alignment, divergent perspectives may be combined, eventually allowing the formation of a dominant alliance around a particular view. This is not to equate policy formation with the establishment of consensus within the firm, however. The struggle for dominance takes place under markedly unequal circumstances in terms of power, access to resources, and legitimacy; and some groups might be excluded while particular approaches are imposed. Nor is strategy formation limited to formal policy; official strategy may be only partly realized, with fragments of the intended strategy joining emergent elements in the eventual outcome (Y. Mintzberg and Mintzberg 1988). Recognizing the gulf between formal and *de facto* policies does not mean abandoning the concept of strategy, but raises questions about the scope of strategic decision-making. The extent to which particular functions and interest groups are part of a corporate perspective and a calculus of values and goals may vary over time, and according to the circumstances of the firm. Crucially for our concerns it will also vary according to the expertise and knowledge of the parties involved.

Pettigrew (1985) has noted discontinuities in the organizational and technological development of firms. Periods of incremental innovation, conforming to established patterns and trajectories, tend to be separated by bursts of more rapid and profound change and the destabilization of existing models. The stability of corporate policies and practices is in part a product of expertise resources and 'structural repertoires' (Whipp and Clark 1986)—sets of techniques and practices possessed by management and expert groups. The maintenance of stable alliances amongst this array of groups will be a strong conservative force underpinning the selection of techniques which spell out the organization's future (Miller and Friesen 1984). However, roles and repertoires develop over time, and alliances become unstable, paving the way for realignments of interests and a redefinition of the problems addressed by strategy.

Thus an undue emphasis on processes internal to the organization may be misplaced. In attempting to explain why periods of stability give way to more radical change, the relationship with the external environment has frequently been stressed. Pettigrew's (1985) evolutionary model of organizational behaviour sees changes in external reality alter the chances of success for groups within the firm attempting a realignment of interests around a new vision of strategy.

Sectoral Influences on Strategy

The environment and market context of the organization is clearly of great importance. It constitutes a source of ideas about new approaches to organizational activity, markets, and uses of technology, and it forms the arena in which ideas and innovations are tested and evaluated. Some like Pettigrew have sought to avoid environmental/market determinism by arguing that organization members are able to articulate subjective constructs of their internal resources and the environment, thereby reserving scope for conscious manoeuvre by the firm. This model can be usefully modified by extending the relationship between firm and environment to include the flow of ideas about the nature of market challenges and the instruments available for meeting them. Similarly, the apparently objective external market context itself can be seen as ultimately constituted by the behaviours of networks of actors including, of course, experts. Behaviour may be sufficiently routinized to act as an impersonal constraint (i.e. an objective market), but in other cases firms may be able to shape and adapt local networks to their own ends.

It would be misleading, therefore, to oversimplify the relationship between the subjective internal environment of the firm and its objective external environment. Instead, we need to explore the extent to which individuals, groups, and organizations influence and even reshape their environment, at least at a local level, and are able to orient themselves to the actions of other players in the sector. This does not imply that actors have unlimited power to shape and reshape the environment. The key distinction is not between 'inside' and 'outside' organizations, or between 'objective' and 'subjective' relationships, but between the networks of interaction which are more or less amenable to local negotiation by players.

This line of enquiry is informed by the firm-in-sector approach, which itself draws on the 'product-process life cycle' of Abernathy (1978). Abernathy showed how the strategic development of firms is intertwined with the dynamics of sectors. Sectoral competition is shaped by innovations in product and process, and in turn helps to shape competencies and the 'design hierarchies' of existing expertise in firms (Whipp and Clark 1986). Such a perspective draws attention to the structural consequences of innovations, the competencies and dominant forms of expertise in firms, and the nature of the selection environment in sectors. But it does not provide a complete account of the relationship between sectoral conditions and strategy-making in individual firms. A second element of the firm-in-sector approach recognizes that strategy and decision-making do not operate in a vacuum, but are connected to the cognitive, social, and material conditions of the sector.

For example, C. Smith, Child, and Rowlinson (1990) extend the model of conditions outside the control of any organization versus managers' subjective constructs to examine how collaborative networks of actors that cross firm boundaries become channels for information about external reality. Managers seek to understand the sector by means of cognitive constructs of how organizations should operate, which tend to be shared at the sectoral level: 'Senior managers hold very similar constructs of the firm's operational dynamics which effectively furnish the rules of the game for the sector' (Child and Smith 1987: 569).

In the early stages of development of an industrial sector, a range of these strategic recipes will exist, from which managers can choose. As a sector matures, this range narrows through several mechanisms, including 'active learning' whereby firms adopt the models successfully applied by competitors. Ultimately, it is suggested, concentration leads to dominant industrial exemplars, supplemented by concentration in the supply of technologies (reducing the availability of information to user firms about alternative technical options), and results in the creation of dominant recipes for an industry. Such processes provide channels for and constraints on the cognitive autonomy of actors in the firm.

TECHNOLOGY

Technology is often regarded as exogenous to social and economic systems. Created through its own internal dynamics, technology has 'impacts' on the structure and performance of organizations. Such a technological determinist view however is widely criticized (e.g. Williams and Edge 1992) and is particularly inappropriate in our study. Banks and insurance companies have long been major users of information processing and have played an important part in the emergence of IT and of the computing industry itself.

Rather than regarding technology as independent of social and economic processes, it is necessary to explore how technological innovation is shaped by its economic, political, organizational, and cultural contexts. The management of expertise approach is central to this analysis. On the one hand, technologies represent a condensation of existing expertise; they embody various kinds of technical knowledge about scientific principles and how these can be applied for useful purposes. And on the other, their application calls for new types and combinations of expertise. The creation and use of new technologies involves processes of design, manufacture, and implementation. Transformed structures of expertise are embodied in new divisions of labour at several levels: between firms involved in the production and use of technological artefacts; within organizations where corporate structure may have to alter to accommodate the acquisition of new kinds of expertise; and in occupational structures which cut across firms and even sectors, and may involve informal networks or bodies such as professional associations.

The management of expertise approach also highlights the range of different kinds of knowledge involved in the development of complex technologies. As well as technical knowledge about the particular types of hardware and programming methods, this involves knowledge about the application context —user organizations, their ways of working, their purposes and requirements, and their industrial location (Fichman and Kemerer 1993). We emphasize the contributions of different types of 'users' (user firms, groups of managers and specialists, and the end-users of computer systems) each with distinctive resources of knowledge and experience. The development of technology is thus seen as an evolutionary process in which development continues beyond the initial design, through to implementation and use. Indeed, the implementation of complex software systems represents a key site for innovation where supplier offerings are combined and adapted to meet the exigencies of use (J. Fleck 1988).

Evolution of IT Systems

The nature of information technology has changed dramatically over its fifty-year history. The nature of the applications tackled and the social and industrial organization of the supply and development of the technology have also changed. Technical developments include the astonishing increases in memory capacity and processing power of computer hardware, changes from centralized batch-processing modes of operation to on-line distributed networks, and the continuing evolution of higher-level programming languages and software systems. Applications of IT over the same period have moved from the automatic execution of well-defined routine tasks such as account- and record-keeping, to providing information support for variable organizational activities like co-ordination and decision-making.

Friedman's (1989) authoritative overview of computer system development notes two principles of development: *elaboration*, in which technological systems become more diverse and elaborate over time; and *compensation*, the drive to compensate for developments in one area by eliminating bottle-necks created in another. The latter encapsulates what Hughes (1988) identifies as 'reverse salients' in the 'front' of technological progress. Friedman suggests that key bottle-necks in computer system development have changed over time, and that development can be periodized into three different phases according to the constraint dominant at any one time: namely, hardware, software, and user needs, successively.

During the first phase, hardware was extremely expensive and not very reliable, and most effort was devoted to using it effectively and overcoming its limitations. In the second phase, due to dramatic and sustained improvements in hardware performance and reduction in the costs of processing power, difficulties in producing software surfaced as a major problem. Cost and time over-runs and poor software reliability culminated in the famous 'software crisis' (Peláez 1988), and the focus of effort shifted to controlling and improving the productivity of software production.

In the third and current phase, software has remained an issue, but with the widespread use of personal computers and distributed systems, the chief problem of development has become the matching of computer systems to the working practices and requirements of user organizations. Considerable difficulties exist as regards communication between technical experts and business users, given the increasingly strategic rather than just operational importance of IT for the firm. Emphasis on decision-making at higher levels has meant interaction between more diverse groups of experts and managers.

This type of 'stages theory' can suggest a deterministic trajectory of development—implying that problems of previous stages have been comfortably solved and a broad front of progress through the stages established—little of which is true for commercial computing. But to be fair to Friedman he is fully aware of these problems. He stresses that constraints from 'earlier' stages emerge in newer forms, and that many organizations lag behind so-called current practice. Nevertheless, as a structural framework for making sense of computer systems development, this is extremely useful.

The Strategic Nature of IT

The computer's initial application as a rationalizing tool, employed primarily to increase the productivity of clerical and administrative labour, meant its acquisition could be justified in terms of reduced labour costs. However, after many operational successes the opportunities for simple, labour-saving applications started to run out. At the same time, the impact of new applications diffused as systems became more elaborate and distributed through the organization. More significantly, as IT moved from back-room operations to becoming an 'organizational technology' which supported extensive activities of communication and co-ordination, the goals against which IT was evaluated became more complex.

As a result of these changes, firms began to experience problems in the financial justification of new systems (Dean 1987). Evaluation criteria had to go beyond immediate cost-effectiveness to include service enhancement, process effectiveness, and flexibility—items notoriously difficult to appraise in financial terms. These developments came to a head during the 1980s, a period in which very large investments in IT were made. Between 1984 and 1990, for instance, the annual average IT budget for firms with a data-processing department of at least five staff was between £2.75 and £3 million (Price Waterhouse 1991). Though harder to justify in conventional terms, these investments were increasingly perceived as essential for the competitive viability of firms in all industrial sectors (McFarlan 1984; Porter 1985). By offering solutions for many of the challenges faced by firms in reducing lead times, improving quality, creating new methods of service delivery, and allowing new approaches to design and functioning, IT was seen as 'changing the way firms compete' and was given a central role in achieving the new vision of the lean, market-responsive organization of the 1990s (Scott Morton 1991).

But many firms failed to realize the potential of the new technologies. The problems with adoption of technologies like ATMs reflected the fact that the requirements of organizations were changing and becoming more exacting, so that previous IT applications were poor guides for development. Existing approaches to the selection, evaluation, design, and use of technology were called into question. Firms grappled with how to match technological capabilities to organizational needs and how to integrate IT policy with strategy. The lack of technological knowledge amongst top managers, and their inability to envisage potential applications, were compounded by the limited understanding of organizational methods and goals on the part of IT specialists. In this context, the management of major technological changes emerged as a key concern, with the effective exploitation of expertise at its heart.

Integrating IT with Organizational Requirements

Two important issues were identified above: the integration of IT with strategy, and the matching of technological capabilities to organizational needs. The first concerns the role of the IT function within the organization and in particular how it can help in formulating corporate strategy. Here the focus is on how managers obtain information about emerging technological opportunities and how they articulate these with organizational objectives. The second question explores the interface between technical specialists and the different kinds of users, and asks how technical expertise and users' knowledge of the sector and organization can be effectively harnessed to specify and design new systems.

Under the stable conditions in financial services up until the 1980s, a strong functional division of labour proved an adequate means of deploying computing expertise. Data-processing departments emerged in which IT specialists tended to be segregated from the rest of the organization and internal specialization was encouraged. Nevertheless, firms still found it difficult to control the performance of technical specialists, and software development was often slow and expensive (Kraft and Dubnoff 1986). A range of techniques was deployed to try to improve control. These included a horizontal and vertical division of labour within the IT function which divorced decision-making and system design from programming tasks, the application of procedures for financial accountability and performance monitoring, and the use of programming standards for system specification. Other measures were used to increase the responsiveness of the IT function. Attempts were made to bind IT specialists to central goals, for instance, by setting up IS departments as service functions with direct links between the specialists and clients in the organization. In some cases, an 'internal market' for IT services within the firm was established. In others, this was taken further and the supply of IT was completely outsourced.

With organizationally convoluted systems and the growing strategic import-ance of IT, traditional patterns of functional segregation started to break down. A wide variety of strategies for managing the IT function (as we will see later in the case studies) arose in different firms. Political relations in management tended to destabilize, and other functional groups like account-ants sometimes sought to enhance their position by taking on board the IT function and claiming special ability to map out the strategic future for the firm. Functional divisions of managerial labour were also eroded by the increasing complexity of decision-making. This led a few firms to try to incorporate IT expertise within top management. Others sought greater integration between the IT function and areas of management, attempting to assimilate IT expertise more generally within the organization.

The latter is particularly expensive in terms of the training required. Earl (1989) suggests that the minimum of two to three years of industrial experience needed by managers to acquire sufficient IT expertise is likely to be unaccept-ably high, both to the employer and to individuals contemplating their career opportunity costs. Earl anticipates the emergence of high-technique individu-als, or 'hybrid managers', able to work at the interface between the organiza-tion and its specialist functions, though the full assimilation of IT expertise is unlikely.

The range of responses highlights the openness of choices surrounding the management of IT and reflects tensions between different organizational objectives. Such contradictions are equally important in the design and implementation of IT systems and in matching these to organizational require-ments. Incorporation of inputs from users has become a major theme in systems development. Such 'user involvement' is concerned both with the straightforward exchange of information (where users provide technical spe-cialists with information about current and future system requirements) and with the negotiation of systems development. Participation may be more or less open and two-way. For example, 'end-user' involvement may be restricted to merely winning the commitment of end users to technological change by fostering a sense of ownership and familiarity with proposed changes, or it may actively encourage them to articulate their own objectives and visions of how working practices could be improved.

Whether or not there are formal mechanisms for involving users in systems design, however, they are necessarily involved when IT systems are imple-mented. In recent years it has become abundantly clear that implementation is much more than a purely technical process of installing complete designs (Swanson 1988). Rather, it is a complex learning and negotiation process in which both technology and organization are modified. In the course of implementation, available technologies are combined with crucial local know-ledge about the activities of the specific firm and sector to create a working IT system. This involves many aspects, from the selection of appropriate technological components and the use of suitable methods of evaluation, to the detailed design of the organization and working practices. In contrast to the universal or generic character of IT capabilities, implementation is contingent on the specific circumstances, traditions, and structures of expertise of the firm. These critically affect the character of the systems eventually adopted, as well as the outcomes of change. Technologies thus evolve during implementation and use, and implementation is revealed as an important site for innovation; user-led innovations in the implementation process may be incorporated into future generations of technology. Innovation itself can be seen as an iterative process, spiralling between design and implementation. This contrasts with the conventional view of technology moving from design to implementation and diffusion in linear fashion.

EXPERTISE

Ideas about knowledge, skill, and information exchange have been important in many accounts of industrial and technological development, but have been increasingly emphasized in recent times. Different literatures have conceptualized information and expertise in different ways. Early accounts (e.g. Braverman 1974) tended to adopt a functional definition of skill as related to individual abilities. Expertise was often treated as an independent variable, and a direct relationship assumed between knowledge possessed and an individual's labour market position and organizational status. More recent thinking, in contrast, has tended to see skill and skilled status as outcomes of a broader political process (e.g. Wood and Kelly 1982; Cockburn 1985). At the same time, research on the development of scientific knowledge has emphasized the provisional nature of even 'hard' scientific facts and demonstrated how claims about the veracity of knowledge are underpinned by social processes of evaluation within communities of peers, sharers of a paradigm (T. S. Kuhn 1962), or members of a 'reputational network' (Whitley 1988). Scientific knowledge is thus subject to particular institutional arrangements for articulating, validating, and rewarding knowledge claims (Barnes 1974).

Expertise as a social construct, therefore, may be defined as the capability for authoritatively applying special knowledge or skill which has been tried and proven by experience. Expertise is concerned with knowledge, but knowledge embodied in individuals and institutions, and located within particular social, political, and economic contexts. The status of 'expert' does not simply depend on knowledge or skill possessed; it also depends on individuals' and groups' ability to legitimate that status by gaining recognition for knowledge claims. This involves social and political processes within the organization and in occupational and professional networks cutting across organizations.

The Nature of Expertise

Expertise itself can be analysed into a number of cognitive, political, and economic dimensions. The knowledge content of expertise comes in different forms ranging from highly formalized theoretical knowledge—for example computer science—which constitutes the universal or generic aspects of expertise, to the more informal and tacit elements which represent experiential aspects. The need for substantial user involvement in the development of IT systems also stresses the importance of local contingent knowledge concerned with the idiosyncrasies of a firm's ways of doing things and its specific industrial relationships.

As already outlined with respect to strategy, however, it is not a straightforward matter to identify just who has the appropriate expertise, and in turbulent times many different groups will compete to offer their services and press their claims. The internal organization then provides a milieu in which the authority of one group of specialists over another will be established. This power aspect of expertise is of course never independent of other aspects. The possession of clearly appropriate knowledge is itself a valuable resource in the power plays that occur in any organization. Another crucially important resource is external legitimation—traditionally via professional accreditation, but also through the tradeability of particular forms of expertise on external (and for large organizations, internal) labour markets. The availability or otherwise of alternatives through market structures will clearly affect bargaining positions.

As well as the supply of labour, the market acquisition of expertise includes the employment of consultants, the subcontracting of bespoke systems to software services companies, and the purchase of 'condensed' expertise in the form of commodified technological artefacts—equipment and software packages. Market structures are most developed in relation to hardware, software functions such as operating systems, and relatively standard industrial applications like word-processing. Markets are far less developed for industry-specific software applications, although a shift can be detected towards the increasing involvement of external suppliers in the development of such systems. However, there are limits to how far externalization can be carried through, particularly with organizationally convoluted applications of IT. In these cases, it is difficult to acquire finished packages suitable for the particular needs of the user firm, so internal expertise is still required to assess supplier offerings and to achieve the necessary level of customization.

The complex nature of expertise makes its effective management a demanding task. This task is most immediately concerned with the deployment of the existing resources of expertise available. Some resources may be highly concentrated and compartmentalized (for example located within specialized IT departments and defined by a set of occupational categories), whereas others (for example contingent knowledge about the methods of operation of the firm) may be dispersed across a range of players, some external to the organization. The ways in which organizations deploy existing resources of expertise will of course contribute to the evolution of new bodies of knowledge. And as well as being influenced by the strategies of the user organization, expertise will be shaped by individuals and groups in pursuing their specialisms and developing their careers. Thus the management of expertise is necessarily involved with the formation of expertise, as well as its deployment, to solve outstanding problems.

Formation and Deployment of Expertise

The formation of expertise includes both its acquisition through the employment of specialists, their acquisition of skills by means of training and experience (relating to technical knowledge as well as contingent knowledge of the organization and sector), and the development of these knowledge resources through career development via internal or external labour markets. In acquiring expertise, firms have a choice between developing expertise in-house or recruiting skills from the external labour market. Each has advantages and disadvantages and will be more or less appropriate to certain kinds of situations. But companies using IT tend to place considerable reliance on the employment of technical specialists—though the level of in-house expertise varies between firms.

Finance sector organizations, in particular, have developed historically high levels of in-house expertise. This was the preferred route, partly for security reasons, and partly to enable finance organizations to fulfil their requirements for local experience of organizational working methods, technical systems, and application areas. It was an effective way of obtaining the combinations of knowledge required. In contrast, recruitment from the external labour market was an effective means of gaining knowledge of newer techniques and fostering alternative approaches to system development.

However, the specific patterns of expertise evident in an organization do not simply reflect the functional requirements for different kinds of tasks. These patterns are also shaped by the recruitment and career policies of organizations, and the 'occupational projects' of professional groups—their individual and collective strategies to acquire status and knowledge.

These considerations emphasize the importance of tradeability in validating expertise claims (e.g. through labour markets). However, even where expertise is not explicitly traded, it is still subject to indirect economic regulation, for instance through the potential for firms to acquire expertise as externally supplied artefacts. Still, there are intractable problems in establishing an appropriate price for information and expertise, particularly with respect to technical innovation, due to uncertainties in specifying in advance the tasks and satisfactory outcomes. Williamson (1975) suggests that, under these circumstances, organizations may seek to acquire expertise through 'hierarchies' (i.e. organizationally mediated arrangements) rather than markets. But, however expertise is acquired, firms are forced to rely on indirect measures of the efficacy of expertise—such as the reputation of agencies for solving problems. Reputations and information about the problems to be solved are communicated through social networks within and between organizations. Reputations themselves of course are formed, negotiated, and legitimated through political processes taking place in those same networks.

The deployment of expertise, as already noted, is closely related to its formation. Many different types of knowledge are required in the development of industrial IT systems, requiring collaboration between expert and business groups. This remains true even where IT systems or system components are acquired through the market. Collaborative networks are key structures through which expertise is deployed. Such networks have formal aspects, like hierarchical command structures, and informal communication flows. The informal collaborative networks vary a good deal between expert groups. Wide and fluid linkages are typical for those who interface between users and technical specialists, while more narrowly focused links tend to be associated with purely technical experts. Such differences arise from the means through which individuals construct their careers by obtaining information about job opportunities and developing reputations, and project their abilities in terms of which skills they choose to present and to whom.

The marshalling of such networks to link together appropriate expert and user groups is one mechanism for the deployment of expertise. Organizations can also achieve combinations of skills and knowledge to develop and implement policies in other ways. These include initiatives around the overall structure of the organization, for example, regarding the relationship between the IT function and other groups. There have also been attempts to create hybrid knowledge assemblages, both collectively through project teams comprising different specialists, and at the individual level through experts who combine in their own persons knowledge of traditionally separate areas.

We noted above that 'hybrid managers' have recently been put forward as a strategy for integrating IT with organizational requirements. This clearly has skill implications, and discussion has focused on the nature of the 'fit' between the provision of formal training and the roles adopted by IT specialists. However, debate has taken take place primarily within a functionalist perspective on skills (British Computer Society 1990). It has not been informed by any great understanding of the social processes of skill formation and deployment. The fact that this debate has occurred in relation to computing, rather than other specialisms such as personnel or marketing, is revealing of how IT specialists and their technical knowledge tend to be regarded. They are seen as 'boffins', or 'techies', who possess arcane technical skills but lack the 'people' skills of their counterparts elsewhere in the organization.

The emergence of hybrid expertise typifies evolution in the occupational and organizational divisions of labour. Requirements for hybrid expertise arise where new problem areas do not match the scope of the existing division of labour. Such incongruence may arise either in the conduct of particular tasks (i.e. within occupational categories) or in the overall arrangements for carrying out some function (e.g. where decision-making cuts across existing functional boundaries). Hybrid groups may then emerge as intermediaries between existing functional specialisms, where well defined occupational groups draw on distinct bodies of knowledge and techniques. However, deliberate attempts to develop hybrid skills are likely to fail if they address only some aspects of the formation of expertise (e.g. training) and do not take into account the ways in which expertise is acquired, validated, and rewarded—in short, the full scope of the management of expertise.

STRUCTURE OF THE BOOK

This introductory chapter has reflected the structure of the book and has set out our theoretical framework. In the next two chapters we discuss the sectoral context and our methodology, and we present the case studies. The remainder of the book is divided into three parts: Part I discusses the problematic nature of IT strategy; Part II reviews relevant aspects of the development of information technologies; and Part III develops our analysis of expertise and its management.

In more detail, in the next chapter, Chapter 2, we enlarge on the distinctive features of the financial services sector, an important industry in its own right, and one which afforded an admirable opportunity to explore the issues introduced above. Chapter 2 also deals with our methodology, and in particular how we adapted a 'comparative case method' to investigate processes of technological change. The structure of the sample and its relation to the Scottish retail finance sector are also examined. In Chapter 3 the case studies are briefly reviewed, showing how the specific themes of each case explore the nature of the management of computing expertise. This is followed by the detailed narrative accounts of the case studies, which conclude this introductory section.

In Part I we explore debates about strategy. Noting the limits of normative and rationalistic analyses of management decision-making, we show how the concept of expertise illuminates the processes of political accommodation and learning inherent in the formation and implementation of managerial policy. Strategy, however, is also about how managers assess and respond to changes outside the firm—in the technologies available, in markets, and in the competitive dynamics of the sector. Networks of information exchange between firms play an important role in the way managers understand the sector and its implications.

Part II examines the development of technology. We argue that an understanding of the industrial implications of technological change must be informed by an analysis of technologies as products of social and economic activity. Information technology represents a condensation of expertise—not only knowledge of hardware and software principles, but knowledge about the practices and purposes of the organization, and visions of how organizations and IT applications need to change to meet competitive challenges. This highlights in particular the contribution of different kinds of 'users' to successful innovation. It also reveals some of the problems that firms have in managing technological change—in integrating different kinds of expertise to formulate IT policies and design and implement IT systems. These problems have changed with developments in technological potential and in the requirements of the organizations, as IT has moved from being a productivity tool to become a vehicle for organizational communication and co-ordination.

Finally, in Part III, we explore the nature of expertise. We seek to explain how knowledge and skill become embodied in individuals and groups, with their own political objectives and subject to different kinds of economic regulation. This part brings together the themes previously developed around the management of expertise. We outline how expertise is doubly shaped: by the occupational strategies of its holders and by the strategies pursued by organizations for its acquisition, formation, and deployment. We trace the intricate and dynamic relationships between the means of legitimating skills via market-based and localized forms of knowledge. The ways in which IT experts articulate their claims to be expert and valuable to the organization are also explored. And we examine how expertise claims are presented through collaborative networks utilized by specialists in their work.

2

Context and Methods of the Study

During the 1980s the financial services sector had an impact on performance and employment in the UK economy as a whole. The sector also had a paradoxical combination of technological potential and organizational conservatism which made the management of expertise a problem of acute importance. On the one hand, it already had the highest level of investment in IT and the forecast impact of future IT use was staggering (Rajan 1984). On the other, those who joined the swelling ranks of IS workers in financial services found their employing organizations dominated by conservative professional groupings like bankers and actuaries. Strong internal labour markets and paternalist styles of management were still the order of the day.

Much of the competition between IS functions and other expert groups was expressed in the organizational shaping of innovation processes, a detailed account of which is the focus of this study. But the sector itself played an important part in defining the terrain of competition. This chapter combines a description of that sectoral context with an account of the research methodology employed in investigating our case studies. Dealing with these issues together reflects the necessity to remain aware of the sectoral context in developing research methods.

Much concern in innovation studies has focused on manufacturing. Theoretical debate tends to centre on questions of the sequencing of different stages of the innovation process (Rothwell 1986). Even in financial services firms some elements of this kind of linear development are found. In insurance, for instance, new policies are spoken of as 'products' that emerge from definite stages of development in the hands of technical staff like statisticians and actuaries. In financial services, however, the meaning and effects of product and process innovation diverge sharply from the assumptions of the manufacturing paradigm. As Scarbrough and Lannon (1989) point out, the nature of the product has very different competitive implications in a service context. Distinctions between product and process innovation are also harder to sustain, where the product is produced at the point of use and is more closely bound up with the means of service delivery.

This is obvious to consumers of financial services. Payment services, for instance, cannot be purchased at any street corner; the consumer must set up an account and enter a relation with a branch of a bank or building society. The relationship between customer and service provider frequently extends over a significant time period and may involve some uncertainty for the customer. With an insurance policy, for example, most consumers have very little real knowledge of the competitiveness of the product they are purchasing. This makes the reputability of the institution as important a criterion as the product itself.

Though our case studies focused on the retail end of financial services these underlying structural features were an important, if implicit, influence on innovation. They helped to explain the segmented forms of expertise in financial service firms and the tensions between IS experts and historically dominant groups such as bankers and actuaries. They also helped to explain the forms that innovations took. Customer database systems, for example, may seem a rather prosaic improvement in the administration of customer files. But the information nexus with the customer accounts for the powerful marketing advantages which bankers perceive in their ability to unlock stores of customer information.

RETAIL FINANCIAL SERVICES

The question of how to theorize sectoral effects will be left until Chapter 4. Here we provide a descriptive account of the industrial sector. Even in focusing on aspects of financial services directly relevant to our study, it is necessary to avoid any neat or hermetic account. Social formations underpinning sectoral evolution challenge any idea that industrial sectors have an independent existence imposed unilaterally on the firm. As Rasanen and Whipp put it: 'A sector is an accomplishment of many actors, working in several periods and with diverse logics of action. It is . . . never a completed and coherent project but a contradictory whole, the nature of which is under constant contest' (1992: 7).

Sectoral Functions and Competencies

Most of the firms in our sample dated back to the nineteenth century or earlier, the oldest, the Bank of Scotland, going back to 1695. The origins of the sector help to illuminate its underlying features. A pre-condition of the acceptability of financial practices, like money transmission, was the successful conversion of gold or goods first into promissory notes, and later into symbolic form on paper and in electronic signals. Hence trust and information are fundamental to the business. Once trust in promissory institutions allowed money itself to become a commodity, products and services were similarly freed from material constraints. Relationships, or more accurately information about relationships, became the life blood of the sector.

Products

The products of the sector are broadly defined as mobilizing savings, making investments, transforming maturities, and carrying out money transmissions

(Bain 1981). In the UK the complexity of providing and marketing such products and services has been reflected in the institutional demarcations between banks, building societies, and insurance companies. Latterly these have been supplemented, though not displaced, by various market changes; but one key factor behind a restructuring of financial products is their information-based character. Products can be readily collapsed into each other using IT, and ranges of products can be offered from a single service site.

But the malleability of services is still constrained by the need for specific product competencies and by problems of achieving sustainable advantages from IT applications. The first constraint has already been encountered by building societies seeking to extend their range to services like current accounts. The lack of appropriate systems and legacy of corporate skills caused may experiments to stagnate after an enthusiastic start and inhibited the pursuit of quasi-banking status. The second relates to the imitability of service innovations. Being intangible and non-patentable, product innovations in financial services can be copied relatively quickly by competitors—normally within six months of launch in banking and a year in insurance. None the less, success in financial services is not so much inherent in the product as in the selection of appropriate 'risks' to sell the product to, again emphasizing the importance of key competencies.

Infrastructures

Indeed, the marketing of discrete products itself depends on delivery infrastructures—branch networks, payments systems, ATM networks, viewdata and telephone systems. Once such infrastructures are in place they encourage the pursuit of economies of scope through delivery of a large range of products (via the bank branch, for example, or the cross-selling of insurance products) and also permit the bundling of different services into one generic product. Thus one of the earliest product innovations in financial services was the current account, which encompasses money transmission, savings, and loans.

The need for elaborate infrastructures is greatest where product complexity is highest. The standardized character of credit cards, for instance, means that money transmission and loans can be supported outside a bricks-and-mortar branch infrastructure. Even so, card products depend on infrastructural forms ranging from merchant acquiring and service organizations, to processing centres and the postal system.

Intermediary Functions

Another distinctive characteristic of financial institutions is the importance of intermediary functions. These include: *maturity transformation*, or exploiting the law of large numbers, where the short-term liabilities of depositors can be used to fund long-term assets; *risk pooling*, where depositors gain advantages from not bearing the risk of ultimate borrowers' defaulting, instead the financial institution bears the risk; *aggregate savings*, which serves a 'go between' function so that borrowers do not have to resort to many different savers; and *reduction in transaction costs*, where the distribution network minimizes the search costs of depositors and borrowers.

Such functions involve two-way flows of information between service provider and customer, and form the very basis of profitability. In banking, for instance, profits arise largely from the margin between the cost of attracting deposits and the return on loans and investments. The provision of the actual service is secondary and has developed out of the need to attract depositors and lenders through the provision of payment systems.

The intermediary function greatly increases the managerial complexity of the industry. Standard techniques of product costing are of limited application. In banking the costs of products are bound up with infrastructural costs and are difficult to allocate precisely. In the case of EFTPOS, for example, as Howells and Hine (1993) show, the launch of the system foundered partly because the parties (banks and large retailers like supermarkets) could not agree on processing costs. The development shifted from collaborative to competitive mode, and eventually was abandoned, as it was unclear who was getting the savings and who should cover the costs of processing. Also, the financial returns on the intermediary role mean that many services are provided free of charge. Until the mid-1980s, for example, the 'float' on current accounts, or interest derived from deposits, covered 60 to 65 per cent of costs (Howcroft and Lavis 1987). In insurance, the cost of the product cannot be known in advance; highly complex actuarial and statistical skills in underwriting are needed to provide estimates in order to set premiums. Even so, in most recent years companies have found that claims have exceeded premiums, with profitability only achieved from investment returns.

Composition of the Industry

Aside from these broad functions, it is also important to bear in mind the levels of diversity in the sector. In terms of the nature of the basic business and the skills involved, banking, insurance, building societies, and credit cards are in some respects very different industries.

While sectoral change involved no uniform trajectory, for many financial services organizations the 1980s represented a period of transition that saw exceptional levels of change and uncertainty. A tension existed between the past and future of the sector; between a legacy of institutional demarcations and the pressures to exploit new market opportunities. Banks, insurance companies, and building societies remained recognizable as members of distinctive sub-sectors, with their own product portfolios and distribution networks. Such institutional patterns continued to influence the nature of expertise in these firms, and had important implications for strategic innovation. But forces including the globalization of capital and UK deregulation were beginning to challenge long-established institutional boundaries and stimulate new interpretations of sector identity.

In order to take account of tensions between continuity and change, we first present brief accounts of the different institutional sub-sectors. Secondly, we highlight transformed interpretations of the sector which formed around new product markets, diversification, and hybrid organizational forms.

The Insurance Industry

As in other sub-sectors of financial services, insurance encompasses a variety of product markets, distribution networks, and forms of organization. In product terms we can differentiate between the general and life areas. General insurance provides cover against risks such as fire, theft, or accident, and the most usual items insured are cars and property. Life insurance is long-term in nature, and includes life and endowment policies, and other forms of investment such as pension funds. Within the distribution networks, life business is divided between 'industrial life' policies promoted and administered by a direct sales force, 'high net worth' insurance based on unit trusts, and insurance products sold through many thousands of intermediary agents such as solicitors, building societies, and accountants.

Important organizational distinctions exist between the life and general arms of the business. Life insurance firms deploy skills that reflect the long-term nature of the risk they handle, and are uniquely dominated by one specialism. Actuaries control the career structure in most life companies and occupy a high proportion of senior management positions. Life companies also tend to have highly institutionalized structures, which reflect the importance of the relationship with policy-holders rather than internal forms of integration. Thus the major business departments, such as pensions, are often run like independent fiefdoms. General insurance companies, by contrast, do not need such very specialized skills in order to model the shorter term risk they handle. Career structures tend to be more open, though organization structures are no less function-based.

Insurance companies can also be distinguished by ownership and by product specialization. In terms of ownership there is a distinction between 'mutual' companies, which are 'owned' by their policy-holders to whom profits are distributed, and the more conventional public limited companies. Many of the mutuals date back to the eighteenth and nineteenth centuries. While ownership is an absolute demarcation between firms, product specialization is relative. Although most companies can be categorized as either life or general, there are smaller numbers of 'composite' firms trading in both areas. The latter are often amongst the largest insurance firms. In 1988 the largest composite insurer, the Prudential, controlled 9.3 per cent of the total world-wide premium income of UK companies. The ten largest companies controlled 55 per cent of world-wide premium income.

In the 1980s the life sector grew most rapidly, stimulated by demand for personal pensions and unit trust products. By 1988 a total premium income of £22 billion had been achieved, of which 18 per cent was foreign business. Conversely, in the same year, the general sector, which had been squeezed by the increasing scale of underwriting losses, generated over £12 billion of which 42 per cent was foreign business. The management of investments and 'float'—the time-lag between premium payment and claims—had become vital to profitability.

While both life and general business generated a significant amount of foreign income, the UK insurance industry in common with the rest of financial services remained relatively insulated from foreign competition in its home market. The period under review came before the Single European Market and barriers to trade were still in place, not least the nation-specific web of social-welfare provisions. In this period, foreign penetration amounted to only 5 per cent by premium income. Competition in the industry was sustained, however, by the relatively low degree of industrial concentration compared with other parts of financial services.

The Building Societies

By the end of the 1980s UK building societies had a total of 45 million shareholders/depositors, 7 million borrowers, and total assets of just under £190 billion. They provided 59 per cent of mortgage loans, and 44 per cent of personal-sector liquid assets.

The building societies had emerged in the nineteenth century, when they saw themselves as having an explicitly social role: to channel the savings of small savers into providing mortgages for workers' housing. Traditionally the societies were a 'movement' not a business, they had 'members' rather than customers, and made a 'surplus' rather than a profit. Moreover, their basic business of lending, secured against property, is relatively low risk and has defined the skills base of the industry. Of course, the size and influence of building societies today means they bear very little resemblance to the friendly societies that flourished in earlier centuries. Whether they can still be regarded as truly mutual institutions in terms of their relationship with their shareholders remains questionable. However, formal mutual status did mean that building societies put greater emphasis on balance sheet growth rather than profit or surplus *per se*.

Historical constraints were also reflected in the products that building societies specialized in. These concentrated on providing mortgage finance, loans against mortgages, and collecting personal savings. Reflecting the pursuit of balance-sheet growth and non-price competition, the twentieth century saw a rapid expansion of branch networks. But as branches, assets, and customers grew there was also a steady decline in the number of societies, due to closures and more recently mergers.

Prior to the 1980s the building societies held a virtual monopoly over the supply of mortgage finance. Acting as a cartel since 1939, they continued (through the Building Societies Association) to offer a standard interest rate on investments and mortgages across member societies and to control the funds available for mortgage finance. Draper *et al.* (1988: 160) claim that until the 1980s, 'governments of different shades considered this (the cartel) politically expedient because of the sensitivities of many households' costs to mortgage interest'.

The monopolistic tendencies of the industry were challenged by the Building Societies Act 1986 which, among other things, allowed societies to abandon their mutual status and become fully-fledged public limited companies. But while one major society—the Abbey National—did pursue this option, most retained their mutual status. The Act also permitted an extension in the products offered by building societies, with the possible portfolio now including unsecured lending, chequing accounts, foreign exchange, house-buying services, and share selling. Many societies did exploit the provisions of the Act to extend their range of banking products, often by launching current accounts. However, there was little attempt to penetrate banking or corporate finance markets, and the Act itself restricted the provision of unsecured lending to the larger societies (with assets over £100 million), and even then to a maximum of £10,000. Indeed, a significant number of societies opted to focus on mortgage and savings products, only extending themselves in the area of insurance broking where high commissions could be made.

The Credit-Card Industry

Though the credit-card industry encompasses 'travel and entertainment' cards (such as American Express) and the retailer cards issued by store chains, the focus in this study is on the bank credit-card market currently dominated by the Visa and Access organizations. Unlike other financial service industries, credit cards are of a recent provenance, dating back to the launch of Barclaycard (now Visa) in 1966, and then Access by a consortium of the other major clearers in 1972. By the mid-1980s nearly 18 million bank credit cards were in circulation in the UK.

The success of such cards is based in large part on their simplicity and widespread acceptability, providing ease of use to the customer and limiting the information requirements of the product. For the provider this allows the centralization of information processing at factory units (of the kind seen in our Bank of Scotland Visa case study). These are supported by highly efficient infrastructures for acquiring and servicing merchants, and global collaborative organizations (Visa and Mastercard) to maintain international transactions. For banks, credit cards are an opportunity to build barriers to entry by adding economies of scope—their credit-scoring skills and customer information base—to economies of scale in information processing.

Of course, the simplicity of the product can also create threats to profitability. Regulatory changes and investigations by the Monopolies and Mergers Commission loosened the banks' grip on the credit-card business. As this began to happen, the simplicity of the product allowed high levels of customer mobility. This was combined with increasing ease of access to credit-card infrastructures via the opening up of the Visa and Mastercard networks and the break up of merchant acquiring monopolies. The result was a proliferation of credit cards and diminishing profitability.

The Banking Industry

Banking is the largest sub-sector of financial services in terms of employment, and like the building societies, the industry is structured around a branch network and a very visible high-street presence. By the 1980s retail banking in the UK had grown to encompass 13,000 bank branches of 21 banks taking retail deposits (i.e. less than £100,000), amounting to 45 per cent of personal-sector liquid assets. Retail bank branches—the great majority of which are operated by the 'Big Four' English clearing banks and the three Scottish clearers—offered a diverse range of services including factoring, leasing, unit trusts, credit cards, executor and trustee services, investment and tax advice, share dealing and portfolio management, and insurance and estate agency.

The branch-based nature of banking gives the industry a distinctive set of organizational dynamics. There are always potential centralizing pressures; since real cost savings come from rationalizing the enormously expensive branch structures. But branches are also the indispensable sites for service provision, and branch management is a highly influential professional grouping. Thus equally strong decentralizing pressures persist too. As S. Smith and Wield (1988) showed, the desire to apply Taylorist measures to restructuring branch networks has sometimes conflicted with the demand for service provision based on branches. Failures to resolve these tensions have led to poor choices in the design of organization structures, and a number of U-turns in policies of restructuring.

The banks have long been the most muscular and strategically adventurous part of the sector. Their links with merchant banking and history of industrial investment place a premium on skills associated with high-risk lending. As early as the 1950s and 1960s, the banks had begun to move into other finance-related areas such as factoring and hire purchase; and the 1970s and 1980s witnessed large (though ultimately often costly) incursions into overseas markets by the English clearers. The area all the banks have most successfully moved into is the mortgage market.

Despite this diversity of products and operations, the overall strategic position of the banking industry reflects the banks' control of the payments system. This is the fundamental infrastructure on which retail products and services depend. The system is operated through APACS, with all clearing banks as members, while non-clearers are able to get an agent, for instance the Cooperative Bank, to clear for them. The 1980s saw the opening up of the clearing system to a wider range of institutions. The latter groups' ability to challenge the clearers' dominance of the payments infrastructure—by offering current-account products, for instance—was another important example of sectoral change influencing the business strategies of individual firms.

The Scottish Sector

Scotland has a long history in the management and provision of financial services. The Bank of Scotland was founded in Edinburgh in 1695 only one year after the Bank of England, and the Royal Bank of Scotland was responsible for originating that most vital of banking facilities, the overdraft. With the addition of the smaller Clydesdale Bank based in Edinburgh, and the amalgamation of the Royal Bank with William and Glyns, in the period under review the three medium-sized Scottish clearing banks constituted a significant force in UK financial services. Much the same applied to the insurance sector. From the nineteenth century onwards Scotland, and especially Edinburgh, saw the growth of a number of large insurance firms. So successful were these firms that in the 1980s the assets controlled by one of them, Standard Life, had an importance to the whole UK economy. By the end of the decade this mutual life company was managing around 2 per cent of the entire UK equity market. In short, while the Scottish sector is certainly outranked by the sheer size of London as a financial centre, it is certainly a major sector in its own right and has developed a significant market presence. With three clearing banks, credit-card operations, a large crop of life offices and a few large general insurance businesses, the full range of retail banking, insurance, and ancillary activities are represented in Scotland.

Nor are the larger Scottish institutions especially dependent on the Scottish market; their activities extend throughout the UK, if not world-wide. The Bank of Scotland and the Royal Bank of Scotland, Standard Life and General Accident all generated more than 50 per cent of turnover outside the country. Through these wider economic connections, the Scottish economy benefited substantially from the 1980s' boom in financial services. In employment terms there was a 30 per cent increase during the 1986–90 period alone, such that by 1990 there were 180,000 people working in the sector (*Financial Times* Survey, 23 March 1990), making it the largest and fastest-growing employment area in the country.

Scotland's deficiency in retail financial services lies in the building society industry. The indigenous Scottish building societies have never achieved the size of their English counterparts. The building societies are nearly all 'English' companies even though their branch structures are fully developed in Scotland. In part, this reflects the regional skew of the 1960s, 1970s, and 1980s waves of building society mergers. But it also reflects social conditions, notably the lower proportion of home ownership in Scotland (40 per cent in 1984 compared with 63 per cent in England and 57 per cent in the UK as a whole). The result was that by 1985, only five building societies had their head offices in Scotland. The £244 million assets of Scotland's largest, the Dunfermline, were hardly more than 1 per cent of the assets of the Halifax, the UK's largest.

SECTORAL CHANGE IN THE 1980s

Since the Second World War, the financial services sector had grown extensively and steadily, maintaining a mature and stable character. Regulation of the different areas of business resulted in relatively rigid demarcations between sub-sectors and underpinned overall stability. Competitive pressures were restricted, not least by cartels or cartel-like behaviour in relation to interest and tariff rates; traditional methods for the operation of different services became embedded in the structure of organizations, and working practices and the knowledge they embodied became strongly professionalized for particular types of business.

During the 1980s this stability increasingly eroded, stimulated by regulatory changes and the arrival of new entrants. Both threatened the traditional demarcation between the types of institutions that make up the sector, and increasing competition ensued between firms that previously had reliable markets. Still, the sector continued to expand for most of the decade through the opening up of new areas of business—often exploiting the potential of IT—and the penetration of existing markets.

Continuing economic stagnation in the early 1990s led to a period of retrenchment, involving rationalization through branch closures and takeovers. But proliferation of the range of products and services continued. Banks came to offer mortgages, pensions, and different kinds of insurance policies, as well as traditional banking services, while standard products like savings accounts, current accounts, and policies became available in forms tailored to suit consumer needs.

As well as pursuing growth through expanding the proportion of the population holding bank accounts and life insurance, finance organizations sought to expand their existing customer base through cross-selling, and by creating packages of services configured to the needs of particular types of client. Product-cycles for financial services became shorter and internal structures and relationships in organizations came under review. Whereas there had previously been a high level of internal functional differentiation around the provision of particular kinds of service (e.g. in insurance offices, between pension, life, and general insurance policies), the shift towards new packaged products required greater interaction between functional groupings and the incorporation of new forms of expertise, notably IT and marketing.

Deregulation

Financial services is not readily comparable with most other industrial sectors; it is a central component of the overarching political and economic system in which other sectors are located. This means that regulation of the sector is an important instrument of government economic policy. The setting of interest-rate levels, for instance, is a significant determinant of the sector's profitability. It is not surprising then that the 1980s growth in the sector owed as much to specific government policies—which favoured finance over manufacturing industry—as it did to the general expansion of the UK economy. In the 1980s the numbers employed in financial services (Standard Industrial Classification: banking, finance, and insurance) boomed from 1,771,000 in 1982 to 2,435,00 in 1988. The sector's share of GDP increased from 11 to 19 per cent. Deregulation in the 1980s involved the reduction of some overt forms of state control. Various Acts of Parliament swept away some of the legal constraints on financial service activity. Their effects varied according to the industrial context, but their main features are summarized below.

The Financial Services Act 1986 and the subsequent work of SIB (Securities and Investment Board) established the so-called 'polarization principle'. This reflected the need for companies to choose between operating as independent intermediaries—with a requirement to meet rigorous standards of 'know your client' and 'best advice'—or to become 'tied' to the products of a particular company. Polarization created a particular dilemma for the insurance industry, which relied heavily on independent intermediaries. The effect of the Act also spread to the building societies, where there was a general move amongst the major players towards tied-agent status. These changes came on top of the effects of the Building Societies Act 1986, which allowed societies to adopt the structure and products of fully-fledged banking operations. Finally, a more indirect effect of government regulation was felt in life insurance with the advent of the 'portable pension' under the Social Security Act 1986. This combined with attractive incentives to individuals to opt out of the state pension scheme to give an enormous boost to the personal pensions business.

The effect of these legal changes was less to sweep away regulatory constraints than to change the scope and emphasis of regulation. Deregulation involved the widespread removal of what can be termed structural forms of regulation (Pawley, Winstone, and Bentley 1991); that is, restrictions on the type of activities that different categories of institution can carry out. However, other forms of regulation remained and were strengthened. Prudential regulation—the supervision of liquidity, capital adequacy, and solvency—was enshrined in the Banking Act 1987 under which all banks became subject to the supervision of the Bank of England. Similarly, investor protection was extended by controls on the marketing of investment products embodied in the polarization principle.

In some respects deregulation really meant more formalized regulation. In the aftermath of the Financial Services and Building Societies Acts, club-type informal agreements like the minimum commission system in insurance and the interest-rate cartel of building societies were abandoned. However, formalization did not necessarily mean direct intervention of the state. There was a greater emphasis on self-regulation by the industry. Thus different industries established Self-Regulation Organizations (SROs) under the supervision of the DTI and SIB. SROs were to formulate rules acceptable to SIB and to authorize members.

Diversification

Diversification into new geographic or product markets, by organic growth or acquisition, has long been a feature of the banking industry. But by the 1980s diversification had spread to the other sub-sectors and was part of an emergent sectoral context of service activity. In the pursuit of cross-selling opportunities, firms were seeking vertical integration into a range of hitherto discrete markets, as well as a new commercial role for their branch infrastructures. Product ranges and marketing networks were extended into many new areas. For example, all types of institutions diversified via acquisition into estate agencies as a means of marketing their mortgage products and participating in the 1980s' property boom. Diversification was also often seen as a defensive means of spreading risk and avoiding over-exposure in particular markets. Equally important was the sense of achieving a critical mass, and sufficient breadth of product range and depth of resource to exploit the intermediation opportunities created by deregulation.

This pattern had significant implications for the management of large institutions. Even the major clearing banks, which had the greatest experience of managing a diversified portfolio, encountered difficulties with the acquisitions made in this period. The Royal Bank of Scotland, for example, acquired a travel-agency chain, A. T. Mays, in 1988, with some broad intention of using it as a vehicle for the marketing of financial services, extending to the provision of information terminals in travel-agent branches. But within a few years, as its strategy shifted to Europe, the bank had divested itself of this acquisition.

While diversification demanded new strategic skills, therefore, it did not reduce the need for individual professionalisms. Indeed, as the Bank of England Annual Report (1988) suggested, one of the hidden difficulties for banks in the 1990s will be the resulting segmented organizational structures and demarcations between retail and corporate business.

Inter-Industry Competition and Collaboration

Although much of the 1980s' strategic pattern can be explained in terms of straightforward inter-firm competition, the gradual lowering of institutional demarcations also created an intermediate level of competition. At this level, the continuing distinctions between banks, building societies, and insurance companies created opportunities for direct competition and also for co-operation.

Certainly, deregulation meant that banks and building societies came closer to outright competition in this period. The banks' foray into the mortgage market was followed by some of the largest building societies developing their own current accounts. In like manner, the extension of opening hours by the major banks was matched by an extension of services in the building societies, the deployment of ATMs, and provision of direct debits and standing orders. As product competition intensified, so did the pressure on margins and costs. The advent of 'free in credit' and then interest-bearing current accounts greatly reduced the ability of the banks to recover the associated costs (around 7 per cent of current-account deposits) through transaction charges and 'float'. The abolition of bank charges alone cost Barclays £22 million in one year.

However, the stimulus of deregulation to competition was matched by the incentives to co-operation. Building societies and insurance companies, for example, had enjoyed increasingly close relationships since the introduction of MIRAS (Mortgage Interest Relief at Source) in 1983, which had encouraged endowment mortgages. These rose from 20 per cent of mortgages in 1982 to 80 per cent in 1989, providing building societies with valuable commission earnings from insurance companies, while deterring the latter from entering the retail mortgage market directly.

The polarization principle of the Financial Services Act also encouraged co-operation. Almost all the largest banks and building societies took their cue to become tied agents of particular companies. The Halifax Building Society sold only Standard Life insurance products, as did Bank of Scotland; the Woolwich Building Society sold Sun Alliance products, Midland Bank became tied to Commercial Union, and Alliance and Leicester to Scottish Amicable. By 1993, though, the situation was changing once more; building societies were coming under great pressure for the commissions they received from 'tied in' insurance premiums. Yet the strategy had been so lucrative (more than 40 per cent of mortgages had tied-in home insurance) that they were making the first moves towards developing their own insurance products.

These changes went hand-in-hand with the strategies of many insurance companies engaged in rationalizing their own distribution networks. They were placing greater emphasis on field sales staff and exploiting the use of banks and building societies as retail outlets. There was also the emergence of the no-branch company such as the Direct Line subsidiary of Royal Bank of Scotland, which exploited new communications and database technology to underwrite and market its products over the telephone.

The effect of these changes was to introduce a level of uncertainty into areas which had previously operated as cosy cartels or within well-defined institutional boundaries. While the term, financial services, had once denoted a group of cognate but highly segmented institutional forms, it was now starting to take on real meaning. Newly forged networks of actors began to open up product alliances, and hybrid forms were starting to emerge—the idea of 'bancassurance' for instance. However, this is not to say that pre-existing institutional forms were simply swept away. By and large, banks, building societies, and insurance companies kept their separate identities and adapted incrementally to the new context. New products were added to product ranges and subsidiary firms acquired in new market areas.

METHODOLOGY

Turning to the question of research methods, a discussion here is useful for obvious reasons of showing how data were collected and processed, but also because the selection of methods was intimately bound up with the nature of the sector.

Social-science research frequently has to choose between extensive and intensive approaches (Bryman 1988; Sayer 1992). Extensive large-scale surveys usually result in a lack of interpretive and processual information, while the choice of intensive research carried out on a limited scale invariably means problems of generalizing from individual cases. For the latter it is difficult to read a macro level of analysis into qualitative data, or to graft theoretical conclusions on to case-type material. Some, however, have argued for combining the two research traditions and have sought to explore the common ground between them (Bryman 1988; Crompton and Jones 1988). Organizational research in particular is well suited to composite methods. Complex processes of organizational change are best studied using a blend of data from multiple sources—such as interviews, documentary evidence, and survey data.

These considerations were influential in designing our research methodology. We wished to locate our study in its sectoral context and to gather data across the sector. This would always have been difficult, but in a sector as complex as financial services it posed acute problems. Equally, our concern with the deployment of expertise around IT innovations suggested the investigation of processual issues at an organizational level. The solution was a research design that combined case-study methods with a cross-sectional coverage of the sector. The aim was to use a discrete number of cases to serve three levels of analysis: a focus on the Scottish component of the UK financial services sector, a comparative account of Scottish financial institutions, and a focus on specific IT projects within those institutions. In the remainder of this chapter we explore each of these levels of analysis.

Scottish Focus

With the exception of building societies, Scottish financial services were of a scale whereby a discrete number of case studies in the larger financial institutions would encapsulate the sectoral dynamics that influenced strategic innovation. Of course, there are important qualifications to the notion of

Scottish financial services as a microcosm of the whole. In one sense, the idea of a Scottish sub-sector is itself a myth. The free-flow of capital means that Scottish institutions are integrated into the UK, indeed the global, financial scene. Thus the geographical locus of control ceases to be important. The contrary view highlights the specific regional identity and the cultural and political differences which mark out the Scottish sub-sector as a unique component of the UK industry. It points to the highly concentrated character of élite institutions in Scotland—many of the key decision-makers are located within the couple of square miles bounded by George Street and The Mound in Edinburgh—and the political sensitivities which have protected the commanding heights of the Scottish sector from foreign (principally English) takeover.

In our view these arguments tend to cancel each other out. Whether 'Scottishness' is defined in terms of ownership, markets, or the siting of headquarters, the features of the Scottish sector ultimately illustrate a tension endemic to financial services as a whole—that between the localized nature of social settings and the global aspirations of economic activities. As we saw above, Scottish-based institutions are well connected with broader networks of institutions and markets. Conversely, there is little doubt that important social and organizational features of the Scottish sub-sector are unique and localized. Tendencies towards geographical concentration of head offices and compact management structures differentiate Scottish institutions from more dispersed and extensive structures associated with the largest London-based firms.

While distinctive social and cultural characteristics qualify the wider validity of our findings, they do not detract from the main concerns of the research. Where there was a disproportionate economic dependency on Scotland—as for instance in the local bias of some branch networks—the effect often stimulated rather than retarded technological innovation. In innovations like remote banking, and in credit-card development, Scottish institutions were well advanced. Overall, the sample evoked a rich context of UK and local dimensions. Each case firm was a significant player in its own market and provided an organizational setting for innovation which differed little from comparable institutions elsewhere. Indeed, all our firms showed a level of IT use and innovation which was at least as advanced as the major English institutions, and in some areas probably more so.

The Sample and Case Analysis

The composition of the Scottish sector was obviously reflected in our selection of case studies. However, industrial sectors are constructed in complex ways; they have ragged edges rather than clear-cut boundaries, and internal divisions that overlap with external markets. As well as the main services, a number of outrider activities like funds management and loan finance could be considered. For Scotland, however, the key exception as we noted above was the building societies. The larger players are all English, and as IS is a head-office function for research purposes it effectively lay outside the local sector. Thus no main case studies were conducted in the building society industry, and our findings have to be qualified in this respect.

In the event, the basis of the study was provided by the three Scottish clearing banks, two large insurance companies (one from general and one from life insurance), and two credit-card operations (see Figure 3.1). While this is to some extent a compromise, it does illustrate that industrial sectors are complex constructions, and that awkward choices are perhaps inevitable for research that attempts to 'capture the sector'. We would argue that our sample of case firms did in the end provide breadth enough to encapsulate changes in perceptions across and possible convergences within financial services.

We adopted what can be termed a 'comparative case' method of analysis. At one level this simply meant using a reasonably large sample of case studies to provide the depth of the case approach, while the spread of cases allowed a degree of generalizability across the sector. Comparative case research distinctively divides up case material between an initial set of brief case studies, which familiarize the reader with the firms, and later empirical material distributed across the substantive themes of the research. This method can be extremely useful in studying processes of change where both breadth and depth in research are essential (e.g. Zuboff 1988; Walsham 1993).

Of course, even with a sample of case studies the dangers of using material selectively do not go away. The case study itself is still a story constructed by retaining some materials and 'losing' others, at the discretion of the researcher (Silverman 1985: 40). With a mass of case material used selectively one can prove almost anything—or produce what Crompton and Jones (1988: 74) call 'a kind of ethnographic salt and pepper'. However, the aim must be to avoid these pitfalls and to use empirical material in ways that are representative of the data as a whole.

In this spirit we constructed the sample of case studies to ensure a degree of 'pairing'. The unit of analysis ceases to be the individual case and becomes some 'comparative unit'—small groups of cases assembled and reassembled out of the original sample, and compared across the variables of the research. It is the clustering of case materials which effectively squares the circle between intensive and extensive methods, and allows data to be employed in an aggregative rather than selective fashion. In our group of cases a number of different points of comparison could be built in. By including all three Scottish banks, for instance, we were better able to isolate wider sectoral effects from the strategic responses specific to each bank. In the insurance and credit-card businesses, we chose firms from the two main arms of the industry. And, again, in choosing packaged processing systems we looked at two quite different cases which permitted comparisons between in-house development and subcontracting.

The Project Focus

We also built in a focus on 'strategic IT projects' which in practice meant that, in the initial contacts with firms, senior managers were asked to nominate an IT innovation that could be seen as strategic for the company. Usually after a certain amount of discussion and negotiation, in which questions of access and commercial sensitivity played a part, we were able to settle on a suitable project. These are listed together with the case firms in Figure 3.1.

The reason for the project focus was that, rather than conduct research on general aspects of a firm's IT activities, it seemed better to concentrate on concrete processes of decision-making and the development of specific systems. This reflected our concern with the management of computer-skilled staff in systems development. In addition, the project focus would also provide a sample of IT innovations which we anticipated would reveal different facets of technological change. With firms, and projects within firms, we had a kind of 'double sample' that helped to broaden the research. Of course, there was a danger that managers would feed us projects which, for whatever reasons, they would be happy to have us look at. None the less, there were distinct virtues in relying on managers' own ideas about what was and what was not 'strategic'. Strategy could be better anchored in human action and perceptions, rather than being seen as a form of planning, or what in some senses could be almost as abstract namely an 'emergent' product of interaction. As with the choice of case firms, we believed that the end-result was a balanced sample and that (as we argue in introducing the case studies below) a range of interesting and important IT projects was covered.

Data Collection and Methods

Interviews were usually held with the majority or all of the IT staff involved in a particular project. IT project teams tend to be small in size; six staff working exclusively on a single project would constitute quite a large team, even for a big organization. So it was often possible to interview the entire development group. That said, there was much variation around this norm. As already emphasized, systems developments are distributed across many groups and skills, and we made every effort to reflect this in our respondents. Thus interviews took in prominent users and groups like business analysts. We also extended the sample upwards into systems management, as well as senior managers in functions like accounting and the corporate group, seeking perspectives on IT from these quarters.

Our case material broadly covered the firm's IT activities, structures, and career patterns. But the bulk of research time was devoted to the development of the particular project and the respondent's role in it. Indeed, we anticipated that analytical issues like the overall pattern of technological change, common perceptions of problems in the sector, and IT strategies to resolve them would 'come through' in discussing the project, and that it would be better for issues to be contextualized in this way.

Open-ended interviews were carried out, structured around discussion topics. Interviews were tape-recorded and transcribed, and the case studies were written up from transcripts. Good data capture and the precise language that respondents used in talking about their work (particularly its technological aspects) were essential detail. While interviewing provided the main source of data, other methods and sources were also employed. Here too the focus on specific projects proved useful. A good deal of written material was always linked to projects—reports issued at various stages, and minutes of steering committees. Access to such material was usually forthcoming, and the material proved extremely useful in tracing the pattern of decision-making and in introducing a longitudinal aspect to research.

3

The Case Studies

Our case studies focused on banking, insurance, and credit-card companies and within these organizations on four main types of projects: large-scale branch automation systems, out-of-branch banking, bought-in processing packages, and management information systems (see Figure 3.1). There were gaps in this coverage, of course. As already discussed, one arm of financial services, the building societies, was omitted from the study. As regards individual projects, it is more difficult to spot any obvious types that were missed. Even very large institutions with in-house development capacity have only a limited number of new projects under development at any one time; and in a number of cases the project we studied was the main new activity in the research period. During our field-work we did notice a potential shift in the type of project being developed, from a kind of stand-alone medium-scale development (such as home banking) which seemed to be typical of the mid-1980s, towards much larger scale and extensive projects (like branch automation) more typical of the later 1980s. But both of these types of development are covered in the case firms. At the end of the day, the case studies did seem to provide a good cross-section of the IT activities in the sector current at the time of the research.

In addition, the projects that were chosen well illustrated the issues and problems that occur at different stages in the development process. Two of the projects we examined had been completed and were being researched in

Case institution	Project
1. Bank of Scotland	CABINET branch automation system
2. Royal Bank of Scotland	Royline corporate cash management system
3. Clydesdale Bank	Telebank remote banking system
4. Mutual Life Insurance	Customer Care database
5. Home and Auto Insurance	Management information system
6. Premier Financial Services	INDEX card-processing package
7. Bank of Scotland VISA Centre	FDR processing package

FIG. 3.1 *The Case Firms and Projects*

retrospect (Bank of Scotland VISA Centre and Royal Bank/Royline); three were nearing completion with the broad outlines already fairly clear (Clydesdale Bank/Telebank, Premier Financial Services, and Home and Auto); one was well under way but there were still crucial and highly problematic stages remaining (Bank of Scotland/CABINET), and one project was in its very early stages with hardly any development work actually undertaken (Mutual Life/Customer Care). This type of coverage is particularly important given that many of the most interesting questions concern the way in which objectives become 'rewritten' over time, under pressure of unexpected and unplanned implementation problems. Certainly the cases showed how, in different stages of development, different problems present themselves to actors: the need to define the problem and the nature of the system that is supposed to solve it, the need to mobilize support, to actually start to produce results, and so on. These different stages led to radical differences in stance adopted by actors and changes in the prominence and influence of particular actors.

The studies have been written up as ethnographic accounts with a minimum of interpretative material. As generalized accounts therefore most of the themes of the research recur in most of the cases. However, the case studies also reflect the specificity of technical change. Put simply the cases were all 'about' something and taken as a group they illustrate distinctive aspects of the development process. Thus, for instance, one case we interpreted as showing how grandiose plans can end in pragmatic conclusions (very common in the IT field!), and another the difficulty of getting a major technological change under way in a bureaucratic organization. While there are dangers in 'dramatizing' case material in this way, it can be immensely useful in linking empirical detail to theory, if clear central themes are picked out.

In this introductory section, therefore, it may be helpful to review the case studies and indicate briefly how these aspects of the development process were explored—hopefully without anticipating the case material too much or constraining readers' own interpretations.

Bank of Scotland—CABINET (Case 1)

Bank of Scotland's system of branch automation, CABINET, was a very large project by industry standards, and one which illustrated many of the central problems of managing computing expertise. The necessary involvement of numbers of user groups, the involvement of suppliers and telecoms, of steering committees and working parties, the need to bring in specialist skills not present in-house—these were all arrangements which required a complex management structure. To be sure, many of the problems inherent in this scale of development were apparent. There was no lack of politicking in the various committees, for example; and we can also see ambitious objectives being squeezed into later stages as the difficulties of implementation were driven home. None the less, we came to regard CABINET as a kind of 'norm' of IT management. On the whole, the management structures 'worked' in the sense that deadlines were met, and there was a degree of continuity in the strategic vision of the system. CABINET probably represented a very fair model of good practice in the management of this kind of large commercial system.

Mutual Life—Customer Care (Case 4)

In contrast, our other major branch automation system, Mutual Life's Customer Care project, was only in its very early stages at the time of the research. This in fact was not a case study about systems development at all; what it illustrated was the problems of initiating large-scale technological change. The insurance business in some senses is less a financial service than a form of finance based on legal contracts with clients. This tends to mean a highly fragmented organization structure, so that internal linkages needed for effecting technological innovation may be weak. In this sense, it would be to miss the point to denounce insurance companies as 'bureaucratic', as if to imply unfettered managerial choice over organizational design. Indeed, our Mutual Life case shows how difficult it proved to be to develop a strategic line and stick to it. It shows the degree of difficulty that change agents experienced in breaking through the structure of established relationships and mobilizing support for technological change, and how the possibility of the project being rewritten to stress marketing and cultural goals rather than the (nominally more difficult) technical ones seemed a real possibility.

Royal Bank of Scotland—Royline (Case 2)

Of the two out-of-branch banking systems we studied, the case study of the Royal Bank's Royline system explored the strategic nature of the thinking behind systems development. Here was an organization weighing up the market advantages of a new delivery system, against the costs of possibly undercutting its own existing systems (i.e. the classic dilemma with any new product that you may end up competing with yourself). Also examined is the essentially iterative relationship between strategy and implementation, and how this differs from many conventional interpretations of strategy. The case discovered contrasting views about the initiative for corporate cash management. One, coming from top management, reflected the almost classic market-led image of strategic thinking; the other view coming from the systems people suggested a more pragmatic rationale of development embedded in internal dynamics and business realities. Research that is sensitive to different voices in organizations is very likely to uncover the kinds of sectional viewpoints that we found in the Royal Bank—particularly given the strong motives to establish proprietary rights over large investment projects. There may be an argument for privileging the view from the top. But the study suggests indeterminacy in the decision process and develops the different versions as complex 'stories' with equal claims.

Clydesdale Bank—Telebank (Case 3)

The other out-of-branch system, Clydesdale's Telebank system of home banking, also has a strong flavour of an organization seeking very carefully to position a new product alongside competitors. Yet given the slimmer resource base of the Clydesdale, the answer they arrived at was very different from the Royal's choice of corporate cash management. Clydesdale opted for a system aimed at the personal and small business end of the market; also one with a selling-on potential and a large contracted-out component. Most importantly, however, this case illustrated how the strategic salience of a development need not be market-driven. The Telebank case was essentially about a decision-making process, and the political dimensions of the project were openly conceded by management. After having been derailed on a major project some years earlier, Telebank served as a basis from which the systems department was able to get back into contention as a large-scale developer. Thus the case presents a subtle image of organizational change. It challenges the tendency to think primarily in rationalist terms—of projects being planned and resources assembled. The Telebank case shows that objectives and means are not always related in this obvious way; new development projects present crucial opportunities for interest groups to appropriate resources and to reposition themselves effectively in the organization's power structure.

Premier Financial Services (Case 6)

We conducted three studies of bought-in systems which amply demonstrated that outsourcing presents no easy solution to the problems of managing expertise. Computer packages are in no sense ready-made systems that somehow can be merely plugged in. The processing package bought in by Premier Financial Services bore some interesting comparisons with the Clydesdale/Telebank case above. In both cases the purchase of packages meant several months of conversion programming to get the new systems running on the parent organization's mainframe. And, while some managerial problems were displaced on to supplying agencies, there remained many other problems of integration with the supplier. In both of these cases, too, a well-articulated decision-making process surrounded the system development, and political factors were close to the surface. Premier's credit-card operation needed a new processing system, and this was acquired in the midst of wider organizational restructuring which threw up a range of stakeholders.

Bank of Scotland VISA Centre (Case 7)

The other purchased system was also for a credit-card operation, yet in a sense it presented the opposite of an indeterminate decision process. The setting up of Bank of Scotland's VISA Centre was 'strategic' in almost the classic sense of an operation planned carefully from the outset, and an organizationally complex system that was smoothly and successfully implemented. To be sure, there were traces of a political process (battles over 'who gets what', and where specific functions should be sited) in the early stages of designing the Centre. Nevertheless, there seemed a striking lack of anything problematic in the management of the workforce or of expertise. One obtains a strong sense with the VISA case of the pieces being moved about on the board, and a management overwhelmingly concerned with efficiency.

Home and Auto—MIS (Case 5)

Finally, if VISA involved a strategy that manifestly had 'worked', the management information system installed by the insurance giant, Home and Auto, was much more problematic. Here was a case of an implementation phase generating all sorts of unforeseen problems, and that led to a drastic revision of the scope and nature of the project. A degree of scaling-down of IT systems is quite common, and in such cases one always has to question whether we are observing a true strategic 'failure'. In other words, what appear to be original strategic goals can often be more in the nature of objectives set deliberately ambitious by systems people in order to generate support for a project. (This kind of talking up of a project in its early stages was evident in Bank of Scotland's CABINET system, for example.) In Home and Auto some of the changes in emphasis we observed were possibly due to these kinds of manoeuvres. However, this case study was distinctive in that it provided a clear-cut example of the shift from strategy to pragmatism. Originally intended to provide common management information for the whole organization, the MIS was radically changed in favour of a staged and more 'doable' project. The difficulties of rationalizing tacit information, and of applying grandiose methodologies to real-life commercial situations, were well illustrated here.

CASE 1: BANK OF SCOTLAND'S CABINET PROJECT

This case concerns Bank of Scotland's project for a branch network. CABINET was a very large-scale, open-ended system that potentially involved a wide range of applications through on-line access to existing central databases, and in particular the ability to aggregate accounts data for individual customers. The project itself had a long history in the bank, and an understanding of the longitudinal aspects showed how this massive investment in development was intimately bound up with organizational changes in the IS function. The case study also shows how CABINET became redefined at several points in its history, as changing rationales were used to legitimate and promote the project.

Strategic Context

Bank of Scotland is a UK clearing bank headquartered in Edinburgh employing (in 1990) about 12,000 UK-wide with nearly 10,000 employed in Scotland. It controlled around 35 per cent of the Scottish market and only 2 to 3 per cent of the English, but obtained a significantly higher proportion of its profits and turnover from the English operation. This regional emphasis in their customer base is the most striking feature of the Scottish banks, and, like the others, Bank of Scotland saw gaining new custom south of the border as a main long-term objective. Up to 1985 the bank was one-third owned by Barclays, and was almost certainly dissuaded from competing seriously in England, though this share has since been bought out by Standard Life.

Like many firms in its market situation, the bank's strategic pathways were to an extent defined by the need to distinguish itself from the bigger players. Since the mid-1980s Bank of Scotland sought to retain its shape as an independent and has taken a conservative line towards policies like growth by acquisition, overseas loans, and forays into property. Sticking to their knitting has paid off. Bank of Scotland has not found its market share squeezed, as other banks have not been strikingly successful with the more aggressive strategies. As regards expanding south, the bank has argued that 'one underlying intent has been successfully to turn a supposed weakness, the lack of an extensive branch network in England, into a recognised strength' (BoS Annual Report 1990: 11). Making a virtue of necessity in this way has meant an emphasis on generating organic growth.

Bank of Scotland offered the standard product and service range of the clearing banks. Apart from retail services, the Bank of Scotland Group had subsidiaries which included merchant banking, factoring and finance, and its money transmission systems were fully automated. The bank was late introducing ATMs, however, and during the first half of the 1980s installed nearly 300 in order to catch up. This experience helped to shape attitudes towards innovation. In 1986 the bank was the first to introduce 'home and office banking', which has been progressively developed to provide a range of new products such as corporate cash management.

The bank earned a name as a technology leader which it saw as compatible with a customer-conscious style. Their advertising slogan, 'A Friend for Life', reflected this policy and considerable efforts were made to project a 'caring' culture. When it was suggested to one senior planning manager that they had chosen to expand into the English market via the technology route, she explained their approach as follows:

I hope we haven't given the impression to customers that the technology is overtaking the customer services. It's why we've adopted the Friend for Life image—to try and assure people that technology is there but working in the background. Everybody is fully committed to it being used as a delivery system and the customer services still being in the forefront.

These overarching orientations—a positive attitude towards IT, the experience of having once missed the technology boat, and an enthusiastically adopted customer-care policy—were all instrumental in the development of CABINET, the system of branch automation that is the subject of this case study.

Organizational Structures

The bank's computing function, as in most similar organizations, had been consolidated into a large and distinctive division, the Management Services Division. MSD had about 750 staff located in a well-appointed, purpose-built site on the outskirts of Edinburgh. At the time, the division was treated as a utility for the rest of the bank and did not charge out its services to branches or departments, though it did charge subsidiaries in the Bank of Scotland Group.

MSD had two main subdivisions, Systems Development and Systems Operations. Systems Operations was the larger and here most of the day-to-day DP tasks were concentrated, with several hundred clerical shift-workers on computer operations, help desks, computer liaison, and the like. Systems Operations also contained smaller groups of staff in departments like Network Control, Systems Programming, and Database Administration which had a high grade of technical skills. These sections had grown almost from nothing over the preceding few years. They reflected the growth of networking and databases, and the need to create central facilities for dealing with problems in remote locations. Among these groups a complex pattern of skills existed, which included branch-bred staff who had been given technical training; these were in sections that were primarily concerned with resolving technical difficulties for staff in the branches. There were also the 'pure-bred techies' in departments like Database Administration that had a more centralized function.

Systems Development and Systems Operations until a few years previously had been Computer Services, a separate service division. This arrangement arose because the bank had wanted to by-pass internal recruitment and grading structures in order to handle the 1970s computing labour shortages. However, the predictable problem was conflict between computing and the bank, and an inability to arrive at consensus over proposed IT developments. This came to a head in the wake of the episode over ATMs. The bank felt that the potential of this technology had been badly misjudged, and the management board asked for recommendations on how to proceed with the whole area of branch automation. Computer Services voted for teller terminals, while Management Services (which handled O&M-type work) put forward self-service banking.

What this did for the bank was highlight the problem of having two separate areas with very much overlapping responsibilities. Because we couldn't agree it meant that the bank couldn't do anything. The people at the top had no mechanism for actually making a decision. Each group made separate presentations to the board, but even that was inconclusive. I don't think they understood the arguments all that clearly, and they certainly didn't understand them well enough to be able to make a judgement. (Senior Manager, Systems Development)

The upshot was that Computer Services together with the smaller Management Services department allied with Computer Operations (and some other smaller IT functions) then became the Management Services Division, an entire new division of the bank. The outcome of the management board's decision on how to proceed with customer service automation therefore created a powerful new alliance in the bank. The structure of MSD meant that the remit of organizational change (via the O&M people) was integrated with the banner of technological change.

The existing subdivision contained two main departments: Systems Investigation (SIV—part of the old Management Services) housed the business analysts, and Systems Implementation (SIM—the old Computer Services) contained the programmers and systems analysts of the systems-development function. This structure formed the basis of the progress of work. SIV consulted with users and between users and systems developers. Knowing the language of both sides, SIV was able to make effective compromises.

The CABINET System of Branch Automation

CABINET (which stands for Customer and Branch Information Network) is a screen-based information system for branches. It was conceived as the major infrastructural change within the bank for the next decade. The rationale for the system reflected the broad trends of customer demand (an increasing volume of transactions) and an emphasis on marketing and customer service in a context of increased competition. As the Divisional General Manager explained, the use of IT to make branch work more productive had been a strategic given since the 1970s: 'There has to be a stopping-point. You can't shove the walls out any further. There are limits to the number of people you can pack in.'

Three main goals were to be met by the system. First, CABINET was billed to improve branch productivity. Computerized information held in various formats would be made accessible through a single screen. The system would also capture information beyond what was currently held, and retrieve and merge this in new ways. Secondly, CABINET would change the nature of branch work and certain key jobs. Eventually with all manual and microfiche information on customers held on databases, layers of clerical and managerial staff would find the balance of their jobs shifting towards sales-type work or narrower definitions of managerial work. Thirdly, CABINET was designed to improve the bank's competitive position in the market. Client-centred data meant that the system became a tool for analysing the customer base and for strategic marketing responses.

The technical basis of the project was the restructuring of the bank's computerized information from account-centred to client-centred databases, linked via a network management package. CABINET thus provided information on customers, not accounts as is traditional with bank databases. A screen of information would be based on single customers, showing all their accounts and the financial and marketing data that the bank held on them. Client-based information enables staff to answer customer requests directly, instead of having to hunt up information and collate it from several files. Routine enquiries would be speeded up and managerial staff would not have to delegate enquiries to clerical staff. Customer service was thus CABINET's clear focus, so the system fits very well the notion of a market-led innovation.

Initiating CABINET

The project originated and gathered support in a committee established in 1981 to report on the whole area of customer service automation. The customer services committee was itself one result of the events that led to the formation of MSD. The bank wanted a high-level group to consider the role of IT in relation to the business, and in particular to develop a strategy for the provision of information to branches. One key finding was that they had very limited detail on customers. This rather startling point appeared to originate from the market-place—they saw the Midland Bank operating a type of customer database. The committee reasoned that this would become an increasingly dominant trend but that the bank needed an even more strategic approach than the Midland's, 'something five years further down the road'.

The first major report to come out of the customer services committee saw the system being accessed directly by customers. However, the old Management Services (O&M) were prevented from getting their way on this form of self-service banking because ATMs took off, and the self-service part of the equation was incorporated into this technology.

The system of steering committees that controlled the project included, first, the Policy Committee. This oversaw the entire operation and was integrated closely with very senior management. It met infrequently once CABINET was under way, and was mainly used to brief top management. However, the Policy Committee was responsible for early decisions and set up the CABINET Working Party, the ongoing means of controlling implementation. The Working Party itself was split into subcommittees that reported to it, including security, functional specifications, suppliers, operations, and enhancement review. The real work of designing and implementing the system went on in the subcommittees. They provided the structure for monitoring feedback, imposing time deadlines, and were the forum for integration of the design and user interests involved.

Progress through the Phases

CABINET was thus intended to transform the branch from a mechanized 'procedural' office into an automated, customer-interactive 'sales' office. This was to occur through five phases of planning, development, and installation.

Phase 1 was an 'operational' stage in which the terminals were installed in branches and basic enquiry facilities set up. In Phase 2 data input would come on stream. This meant a 'quantum leap' beyond simple accessing of the database and extracting information, to inputting information and changing the database. This gave rise to many development and design problems of access control and database security. Phase 2 was also more 'organizational' in the sense that current branch work was being incorporated into screen design, including facilities like loan evaluation, mortgage processing, costing accounts, and much better statistics (e.g. regular updates on the performance of accounts). Phases 3, 4, and 5 were still some way ahead, and as yet few firm decisions had been taken. However, CABINET's scope was to extend some way beyond the automation of existing clerical tasks into more 'strategic' areas. These were to include expert systems and areas of special managerial skill like report writing and customer intelligence.

Between 1981 and 1985 the detailed planning for Phase 1 took place and, by all accounts, in these early years the project was heavily 'sold'. Systems Development managers agreed that CABINET had come to be seen in some quarters as a cure-all for all branch-to-customer and branch-to-head office relationships. Users were encouraged to be enthusiastic. MSD reports were overlaid with terms like 'marketing potential' and 'strategic advantage'. In this sense, the authorization to start anew and build a beautiful big system gave the CABINET designers the intellectual space to reinvent how the branch should operate, organizationally as well as technologically. As a Project Manager explained:

I feel quite emotional about CABINET. It's only just starting up . . . it doesn't reach its maturity until Phase 3 and we provide a true integrated information system. . . . There's a logic behind it, but it will take a long time for it to flower completely. . . . EFTPOS is exciting but you don't have control over it. You've just got to put the damn thing in. But CABINET is specifically for the bank, and we determine what it's going to be.

None the less, while still far and away the biggest project in the bank, the way that MSD regarded CABINET did become greatly scaled down. Between about 1984 and 1988 financial rectitude replaced strategic adventure. One SIM Manager, for example, who moved to CABINET in the mid-1980s, described feeling 'a little bit terrified' because of the pressure. He came to see his role as being to 'make people think more realistically in terms of what CABINET can and cannot do'. Another senior SIV Manager spoke of CABINET as a kind of magnet for strategy because of a lack of strategic thinking elsewhere in the bank.

When we were proposing CABINET we did discuss these more strategic issues. That CABINET would represent an opportunity to hold customer information, to use it for marketing purposes, to do this, to do that. And people tended to become convinced that CABINET was going to do all these things. Of course it wasn't! I have come quite clearly over the last few years to see it as just a branch terminal system. The problem is that other people's perceptions are of this global wish list.

This may well have been a timely shift for MSD. Indeed, if creating a high level of expectations was their initial aim in order to get the project off the ground, financial stability and becoming 'more realistic' was the logical next move. Designers were also soon made aware of the problems of making rapid or radical decisions through a cumbersome Working Party of over 30 members. So during 1986–7 Phase 1 was split into two phases, the development timetable was lengthened, and the Working Party was dispersed into subcommittees leaving only four to six people making decisions on any one issue.

Once terminals with query facilities began to be installed in branches there was a rush of interest from users. Feedback in the form of new ideas for future phases came in thick and fast. As one senior Branch Administration Manager pointed out, branch people had been told through Working Party reports that from the day the first terminal was installed they could have access to every single account in the bank. Somehow, though, they didn't actually 'know' this until they saw the early branches having access to information.

The sudden scramble for terminals and demand for added features when users did realize the potential of the new system was met with resistance from MSD. They had experienced difficulties enough in handling Phase 1 and now wanted to 'stabilize the situation'. They began stressing users' lack of any real knowledge base from which to 'usefully contribute to how CABINET should be built'; and as far as possible, as one Branch Manager put it, 'they deliberately chose facilities which required absolutely no input from the branch. They were there to be extracted from the mainframe. They were already on computer files.' Thus MSD was dealing with the deluge of (mostly favourable) reaction by redefining what CABINET was. As a SIM Project Manager noted, Phase 3 was up for grabs but as far as current phases were concerned: 'there are all sorts of conflicting interests, like, Can we not rewrite the back-office phase? Can we not put teller terminals in? Yes, yes, we can do all of these things! But is this what CABINET is all about? I'd just like to expand on the information base.'

Interestingly, the branch perception of this process was that 'with so many things coming forward it is getting away from block phases' towards a more continuous development. We can perhaps see reflected here branch management attempting to define the process of systems development to take more account of their own interests. This way of putting pressure on MSD meant that the branches to some extent began to set the agenda, creating expectations of 'something useful coming along every so often'.

Strategic Technology and the Marketing Culture

The decision to unite departments previously responsible for organizational and technological change into the new division gave MSD unique powers as 'strategists' for the bank. Not only was CABINET understood as a strategic technology, but this was intertwined with strong beliefs about the role of 'marketing' in systems development. An awareness of the market had been very consciously added to the armoury of MSD's technical expertise. It was a line of thinking that distinguished MSD from more cautious banking types and head-office groups like accountants. A senior SIV Manager explained how this contrasted with their original belief (the old O&M culture) that technical developments had to be cost-justified before they could be supported.

We'd said 'no' to ATMs, 'no' to teller terminals. We'd been asked to do a CBA and had done one. And it proved conclusively that they weren't cost justified. Which I think was the right answer to the question we were asked. It was just the wrong question. We couldn't cost out the *customer* viewpoint at all. We didn't consider the alternative which was to take a strong *marketing* route and extract out a general benefit from that.

Having been 'negative for too long' the marketing culture grew in strength. The constant refrain coming from MSD managers was that CABINET was a marketing tool and it was this dimension that defined it as a strategic project. For example: 'I'm conscious of the fact that I keep coming back to this marketing, but it's the driving force. You have to be there. It's staying alive. It's keeping up!' (Automation Planning Manager). 'The marketing side is more important than anything else. It's not as if we were pushed in that direction. I think it was just a view that we took—that this was the right strategic way to go' (SIV Manager). 'CABINET itself is not a product. CABINET is a strategy. It's a strategy to aggressively attack the market-place in the nineties' (Network Control Manager).

Investment appraisal criteria were less important in the initial design phase than strategic goals for improving the customer service achieved by branches. The marketing benefits of a customer database were strongly promoted by MSD. Indeed, it had been technical people who had argued that 'in the end you can't justify technology since it's inherently non-justifiable. You need it to stay in front of the market or to protect against potential loss of business. But that's impossible to measure' (Network Control Manager). CABINET was born out of this mood. The original customer services committee felt that they could afford, or even needed to take the plunge over at least one major project outside the confines of cost-benefit analysis.

We knew that if we tried to cost justify each application as it came up, we would never be able to do it, because the infrastructural costs would always be too high. We had to take a longer term marketing view and accept that we would have to implement one project that was actually not going to be cost justified. The main thing was that we chose the right project and that it took us in the right strategic direction. (SIV Senior Manager)

This more adventurous attitude towards technology was echoed in other quarters, though not in quite the same spirit. The bank's Chief Executive was acutely aware of the dilemma that projects like CABINET raised and placed it in the context of the bank's conservative approach to large-scale investments: 'The danger with CABINET is that you go down a blind alleyway from which you cannot escape. The danger of not doing it is that you go out of business.' He suggested that it was 'not always sensible' to ask whether systems like the ATM network and branch automation were cost-effective. Similarly, a senior member of the Accounting Department confirmed that CABINET was 'a strategic decision, and the cost of not doing it was more important than the cost of doing it . . . Cost cannot be an overriding concern in a strategic decision like CABINET; an awareness of cost is part of the overall thing.' Thus it was a 'political question' whether CABINET was to be governed by normal return-on-investment techniques. These were not imposed when the project was initiated, although in the development stage projects were strictly costed.

Market pressures in the form of modern retailing concepts also emanated from the branches. The manager of one of the main city branches, which had been a pilot site for CABINET, stressed that automation (and the more rational use of labour, particularly casual labour) should be used to routinize back-office functions, while trained staff should be used for selling the bank's services. Branches should be reconceptualized as 'selling shops'; and he elaborated the analogy with references to department stores and how they used their retail space to create a welcoming environment for customers.

This viewpoint can perhaps be understood as an expression of the sectional interests of branch management—who have an obvious stake in the survival of the branch network. In recent years branches have come under attack; the huge costs of a bricks-and-mortar branch network are the obvious places to make savings as financial service firms begin to retrench. Moreover, corporate moves to centralize banking services have often been accompanied by an ideas offensive against branches as the old-fashioned way to deliver banking services. Here, however, we see an alternative strategy premised on the survival of branches. The argument was that back-office functions should be centralized while 'selling' was decentralized to the branches. What were alleged as the bank's marketing problems—a lack of any real knowledge of customers and whether they want the products that banks have developed—gave a central role to the functions that only the branches can supply.

CASE 2: ROYAL BANK OF SCOTLAND AND THE ROYLINE CORPORATE CASH MANAGEMENT SYSTEM

This case is about a development at the top end of remote banking, namely a cash management system designed for corporate clients. It shows how the system reflected the parent bank's market needs, and how the bank weighed up the decision to opt for this particular product. The case also shows how top management concerns interacted in complex ways with technical and business pressures to determine the final shape of the system.

Strategic Context

Royal Bank of Scotland was the largest of the country's three clearing banks. It had about 40 per cent of the Scottish market and 3 per cent of the UK market. Since the early 1980s the bank had followed a distinctive strategic path: a pattern of growth by acquisition and merger facilitated by its size and resource base. This began with the merger with Williams and Glyn's Bank in 1982, which greatly expanded the branch system in England; and in 1986 the acquisition of Charterhouse Japhet provided a merchant banking arm. Since then have come developments in a variety of finance-related areas: the acquisition of a US banking interest, alliances and holdings in Europe (Portugal, Germany, Belgium), and in particular the alliance with Banco Santander in Spain.

This strategy has been supported by corporate restructuring. A group structure has been formed centred on a holding company, the Royal Bank of Scotland Group, and a group executive charged with policy and strategic responsibilities. The various businesses are organized into operating divisions which include merchant banking, insurance, finance and investment. The Royal Bank itself formed the banking division, by far the largest and most profitable business division. In 1990 the staff of the Royal Bank totalled 20,650 UK-wide, while the Royal Bank Group employed 23,350. Both the bank and the group are headquartered in Edinburgh.

In a sense the above strategy represents grasping the nettle of the diversifying nature of the financial services industry. Under a group structure a number of things can be achieved which might be inimical in a traditional bank. The group executive is intended to play an active strategic role; with the group division they are charged with ensuring optimal use of resources (which means taking potentially tough decisions about priority setting and migrating skills around the divisions), and they have overall responsibility for technology policy. The group executive has also brought in senior people from outside banking. This too is radical in an industry where the need for wider 'business flair' has been anticipated but few have actually made the move.

Three main strategy strands can be detected. First, the group can provide services beyond traditional banking; it has flexible strategic options and is able to exploit niche markets across Europe. Secondly, there is a strong synergy between the businesses and the clearing bank. The corporate structure is geared towards cross-selling new products, such as insurance and unit trusts, to customers of the bank using the branch network. (In 1990, for example, the group divested itself of its recently acquired travel-agent business when it was unable to cross-sell due to regulatory constraints.) Group management in particular is heavily committed to the cross-selling concept and very interested too in developing associated marketing databases. Thirdly, a bank the size of the Royal Bank might prove a tempting target for some of the European and British giants in the context of the Single European Market, so the European-wide network of alliances and holdings is designed to fend off takeovers.

The Royal Bank's domestic strategy has been to expand south of the border through its branch network. All the Scottish banks saw England as their major growth market, and branches remain the superior means of delivering services given the basis of customer awareness and identity that a branch creates. But maintaining a branch network on expensive high-street sites is a policy that only a larger bank can contemplate. The Royal Bank saw its English branch network as a crucial asset. It had opened new branches regularly, particularly in areas of new business growth like the English Midlands, and had medium-term plans to add a further ten branches. Policy towards the branch structure had been expansion in England and rationalization in Scotland.

With the other two banks we saw that technology is to some extent seen as an alternative to costly bricks-and-mortar expansion. But the Royal Bank was conscious that new services should be complementary with the branches as a delivery mechanism. For example, the new Phoneline telephone banking service was extensively piloted before being launched in June 1990 to ensure it did not compete with branch-based services. Also the Royline system of cash management (the subject of this case study) was aimed at the business sector rather than private customers, which again would mean that it did not compete with the branches. The bank was strongly focused on corporate business and viewed its major competitors as the English clearers who were also supplying cash management systems.

The Royline System and Technology Policy

The development of Royline clearly reflected general trends in delivery systems. The development of customer-based electronic banking was still at an early stage. Evidence of a lack of consumer interest—as in the USA where various remote banking schemes have netted relatively few customers for a very considerable development outlay—was balanced by success stories like the spread of remote banking in France (admittedly on the back of the heavily-subsidized Minitel system). It was important therefore not to prejudge developments: not to be overly optimistic about technical possibilities, nor to be pessimistic about current levels of customer take-up. The fact that the big four English clearers had not hitherto embarked on major home/office banking investments may simply have reflected their strategic and technological position—not wanting to create a market that new entrants, unencumbered by high overheads, might enter; and being less able to accommodate home/office banking interfaces on their massive central computer systems.

None the less, the technology was both cost-effective and good for the corporate image. The widespread conviction that home/office banking would eventually take off was reflected in pilot studies conducted by the English clearers, and the launch of phone-based home banking by firms like the TSB, Nationwide-Anglia, and Lloyds Bank. However, remote banking was not a homogeneous delivery system; it encompassed various approaches and technologies. This suggested that market segmentation and targeting would be a key success factor, and that any generalizations about the development of systems were likely to be wide of the mark.

For major players like the Royal Bank, therefore, home/office banking needed to be approached cautiously. Apart from potential conflict with the existing branch network, there were administrative costs and risks attached to the proliferation of payment systems. The costing of a system would be complex, and the very diversity of payment systems (the spread of ATMs, standing orders, etc.) might undermine consumer appeal. A more considered approach also reflected the Royal Bank's competitive position. Already having a branch network in England (the integration of which inevitably took strategic priority) the bank had no pressing incentive to pursue a cheap and quick solution, like the readily available viewdata-based option, particularly given that technological leadership *per se* seems to count for little in the banking industry.

In fact the impetus for the development of Royline did not come from immediate competitive pressures but from another quarter. This was top management's interest in corporate cash management systems of the sort developed in the USA by Merrill Lynch. As one senior Group Manager put it, Royline was envisaged early on as 'a sophisticated product aimed at the largish corporate end'. Corporate clients are usually multi-banked, and cash management involves pooling information about a company's financial activities. So Royal Bank needed to provide a service complementary to that on offer from other banks or risk being the missing link in the chain and losing corporate customers. The decision was taken to go for a powerful personal computer-based system that would provide a high quality of customer service, and to target the corporate and small-business market. This approach was specifically contrasted to the remote banking systems developed by the other banks: 'We didn't think people would want to look at their overdrafts by the fireside on Saturday night.'

Such a technology was to represent a major addition to the Royal Bank's portfolio of delivery systems, fulfilling a number of potential strategic roles. Royline was an innovative product, not just a delivery system, and was expected to create entirely new markets for banking services. It might also lock Royline users into Royal Bank services (a number of complementary services and system features were developed after the main system came on stream—a high-interest deposit account for small-business users in March 1990, and an on-line payroll facility and unit-trust information package for Royline itself). And Royline enabled the bank to position itself in a technology predicted to have a major impact on the industry. It might well have appeared prudent to establish such a technical platform, with market visibility and progression up the technological learning curve as long-term objectives.

Development of Royline

Senior level interest in corporate cash management was expressed in general terms, with a top-level group being set up to investigate the concept and some preliminary market research carried out. But the Systems Development department played a major role in initiating the project, and it was left up to them to work up a detailed specification.

Systems Development to a certain extent challenged the market-led emphasis. They were aware of the development of cash management in the USA and that, in a competitive market, UK banks would need to move in this direction. But the US situation differed, they stressed, in that it was stimulated by regulations against inter-state banking. Moreover, an operational impetus had in fact already existed in the form of day-to-day business pressure from clients who were demanding better interfaces with the bank. The bank had been developing new facilities which brought increased phone calls to branches and demands for automated payments. Large customers might phone into branches, to obtain information available on teller terminals, hundreds of times per day.

In this situation, Systems Development perceived a crucial space for themselves to define the system: 'The whole basis of corporate cash management came from the US, and it was being hyped up so much we had to address it. But many of our customers who were asking for cash management did not know what it was.' The department stressed that their input involved 'passing potentials up the line' so that Royline as a technical concept came from them, or as they put it, 'a technical solution to a business problem'.

Royline was a high-profile project involving a major commitment of development time. For Systems Development this priority meant a good deal of pressure. The level of sophistication was described by the Projects Manager in charge of Royline as 'the jagged edge of technology; we were doing things which had not been done before'. However, he also stressed that they met few problems of a strictly technical nature. The major challenges were more to do with the combinations of problems and co-ordination of the development groups. Royline's systems had to be integrated with existing systems involving state-of-the-art on-line technology:

One major new technical task was in automatic dialling and automatic downloading of data. The purpose was to eliminate any manual intervention and this involved new software packages. This was new to us and we did encounter some problems we didn't expect—particularly with encrypted data being switched to a PC. In a sense, all the separate system components were known to us but their combination was new.

Existing expertise did not need to be supplemented, however, and the problems were not of a scale to require changes in the standard approach to project management.

The functionality of Royline allowed the business client to obtain account information, while top-end versions provided direct connections for customers needing international currency payments, trustee work, share registration, and CHAPS payments. Direct CPU-to-CPU linkage was also possible for customers with mainframes. A development team continued to work on Royline to provide additional features. Systems Development was extremely enthusiastic and stressed the detailed requirements analysis they had conducted with clients and that Royline was the best type of system on the market, giving the bank a major competitive advantage:

We had an information system already in existence, so we inspected its relevance and made it available to certain customers on a direct link on a pilot basis. We took inputs from the rest of the bank and added to that our own corporate knowledge. We could see trends in the increasing use of PCs by customers in their own offices and we sought a technical solution which would stand the test of time and would integrate with the customer's own systems and procedures—and not merely as a stand-alone. We have been servicing these for a long time and know what customers want.

Implementation problems were confined to the on-site control of the Royline system. It was located in business offices and needed to be guarded against environmental hazards, which put the onus on the robustness and durability of the system.

Systems Development made a strong claim to high professional skills. The development of Royline was facilitated by a powerful and flexible programming language developed in-house (a Cobol-Plus language), and by a database structure and information systems which eased the impact of Royline on existing core applications. The claim to high professional standards was also reflected in a number of customer-oriented features. Whereas business analysts might have taken the line of giving customers what they want, Systems Development claimed to know customer requirements better than customers themselves. They took the demand for better interfaces a stage further. A requirements analysis, based on interviews with potential and existing customers, was carried out. Also an existing information system was made available to selected customers to pilot test the direct line. This information was married with Systems Development's own knowledge of trends towards increased PC usage by customers. As the Project Manager put it. 'We had to get right into the business requirements of the product.'

Similarly, in the case of data security, this was not particularly demanded by customers. Their main concern was that security codes should not be so strict as to impair usage. But Systems Development regarded security as an absolute priority given the bank's concern to protect customer information for business clients. Systems of encrypted data and storage were developed unique to each PC. But authentication devices separate from the PC were adapted which were highly customer-oriented; they were 'transparent' to users and did not interfere with usage.

CASE 3: CLYDESDALE BANK AND THE TELEBANK SYSTEM OF HOME BANKING

This case study is about the development of the Clydesdale's home and office banking system, Telebank; and in particular its processing system, called sp/ARCHITECT. The latter was developed on contract by an outside agency, and itself has a number of interesting features. In addition, the whole development happened against a background of reorganization and acquisition at the bank. The complex political relationship between Clydesdale and its previous owners formed a central historical context to the development. The case also illustrates the salience of niche markets for a bank like Clydesdale; Telebanking offered an opportunity for this essentially regional bank to expand its market. And, finally, these organizational features were deeply embedded in the technical design of the system and in the division of labour for its production.

Strategic Context

In 1987 Clydesdale was acquired from its previous owners, the Midland Bank, by the National Australia Bank (NAB). While Clydesdale had enjoyed considerable autonomy during their seventeen years of ownership by Midland, those freedoms had lately evaporated largely because of the constraints all the big banks felt in the wake of the overseas debt crisis in the early 1980s. During the last few years under Midland, the Clydesdale's autonomy had been eroded by the need to constrain costs. The acquisition by NAB therefore marked a turnaround in the fortunes of the bank, in so far as the Midland had treated them as their Scottish outlet and had restricted any independent attempts to change their customer or product base. NAB in contrast sought to use Clydesdale as their entry point into the UK market as a whole and were keen to promote new strategies.

Clydesdale was the smallest of the three Scottish clearing banks. The head office was in Glasgow and it had about 380 branches in Scotland. At the time of the study, Clydesdale's main business base was in agriculture, the traditional engineering industries around Glasgow, and in its sizeable share of the oil accounts around Aberdeen. While managers in these areas have considerable knowledge of customers and market openings, under the Midland they were restricted in the loans they could authorize. This made it difficult to expand products and services and to find new customers. The 'new Clydesdale' will be more decentralized, with branch managers having greater authority.

However, hitherto very little strategic planning had been accomplished. Only a couple of areas (entry into the mortgage market and student loans) started with any fleshed-out strategic philosophy. Otherwise the planning process had been curtailed by Midland directives to 'cut costs and then stop'. In this context, all major functional areas were being reviewed and top management was expecting over a dozen internal reports by April 1988. These were expected to form the basis of a strategic plan.

In the IT division they were beginning to recruit after a long period of stagnation. Partly this was because Midland used to cover certain activities for them, and partly it reflected the expansionist climate following the NAB acquisition. Within the division NAB were regarded as 'kinder masters': they wanted the bank to operate autonomously, which Midland clearly did not, and there was growth on the business front which was also very important for IT. The division had a new director who was an IT professional, someone who would fight their corner, and they felt much more in control of the direction of technological change.

Telebank: Strategic and Operational Aspects

Telebank was explicitly described as 'a strategic front runner' for the bank. It was seen as particularly important in supporting their business in England. It was claimed that technological advances were a distinctive feature of Scottish banks and very attractive to English customers. When Telebank was coupled with an ATM card, a full banking service could be supplied without a bricks-and-mortar branch network. Other delivery systems would be added on to the service (a key feature of the software, as we will see), and in July 1988 the Telebank telephone service was launched.

About five years before, the bank had independently begun a programme of branch automation which had been rejected by Midland. Permission to go ahead with Telebank was, it seems, something of a consolation prize. It was clear, however, that losing out competitively to Bank of Scotland's first-in-the-field Home-and-Office Banking System (HOBS) system had been the prime mover behind the Telebank development. The fact that Clydesdale was losing business customers to HOBS accounted for the strict time-scales that were set on the project, and for the decision to contract out large chunks of the development work. There was a widely perceived need to get a system in place quickly, and for the system to work well. This was one reason why the bank sought to use an external supplier.

From inside Clydesdale the development of Telebank was seen in a some-what more complex light as a logical extension of a broader technology strategy. During the 1970s their system of branch networking was linked with an ATM card to provide funds transfer. Then in 1982 they launched an EFTPOS card in selected petrol stations. They also claimed a corporate cash management system addressing the needs of larger business users. Thus Telebank came in at 'the middle sector: small-to-medium-sized business clients, and picking up what it could from personal customers'.

Clydesdale's management, then, were firm in their own belief that the system was wanted. They were keen to promote it to demonstrate their capacity to respond to new services being launched by other banks competing for their market. Telebank was thus important both as a symbol of the bank's independence from its parent and as a basis for future developments. As the manager of Systems Development put it:

It is not highly important in terms of our systems. Though remember it was extremely important at the time. Politically. It was immensely important politically. It was incredibly important that people here could see that we had done something outwith the Midland. Because beyond that point we were able to persuade Midland that we should project manage the group developments in home-and-office banking.

Underscoring this view of events the Systems Development Manager con-ceded that he was sticking his neck out when he signed the contract with Software Partnership because at that stage the Midland still had to be fully convinced. Here he is describing how the game was played out.

There were two major issues involved. One was that our Business Development Manager at that time wanted Telebank in as a defensive measure and was prepared to support it. And the other thing was that I knew Software Partnership well because I'd been on the Midland's working party with them. So I approached SP one night and we got together and we got the spec. and the contract and everything signed off within six weeks. . . . That was a very dodgy situation. I don't think I had outright support from my Managers at the time who were a wee bit afraid to baulk the Group. It was a fairly dangerous period for me.

Perceptions of the decision process differed, however. One senior business analyst suggested something of a dog in the manger attitude on the part of Midland; they could never have developed an out-of-branch system on their scale of operations, and they did not like to think that a mere subsidiary could bring one to the market. The Systems Manager saw things a little more charitably: they were unable to get a decision out of Midland because Telebank 'was never seen as a vote winner'. It was not seen as a high priority by the English-based Midland because they found it hard to appreciate the Scottish bank's needs. Indeed, Clydesdale themselves, at the time, did not see Telebank as a great income-provider, but as the basis of future developments; it would give them useful expertise and a profile with which to compete with Bank of Scotland. But at the time it was seen 'almost as a loss leader'.

Interestingly, Software Partnership's version of events, from a vantage-point outside, was even more 'rational'. The director of the agency pointed out that both banks were working on a common system, but their time-scales did not match. 'Clydesdale were much more anxious to launch a system ahead of Midland because of competition from HOBS. And as a result they (Clydesdale) decided to go their own way, without any friction between them and Midland Group. Midland were very well aware of what Clydesdale were doing.'

The reasons for contracting out most of the work on Telebank were more than the expected ones of time-scales and shortage of skills in writing front-end software. The decision also reflected the bank's interest in finding what solutions might be technically available, unconstrained by approaches established within the bank. As the Business Analyst indicated:

We wanted a completely new development and we knew exactly what we wanted. But there can be a danger sometimes in doing it in-house. You miss the proper understanding of the market, of all that's happening, of the options and technology, because you tend to tailor your cloth to suit your purse too much perhaps. And you end up with a product that supplies the business with the functionality it requires, but no more.

The implication here was not only that outside suppliers such as Software Partnership possessed specific skills for developing these new types of delivery system, but that they also had technical and market know-how not readily available in the bank. Indeed, this was to become a formal bank policy for systems development. After Telebank, Clydesdale decided that it was 'strategically correct' to opt in principle for outsiders whenever they were considering taking on 'market sensitive developments'.

Choosing the Software Partnership

The process of choosing the agency to develop Telebank looked different from different sides of the relationship. According to the bank, they took the initiative in opting for Software Partnership because 'they were the only ones who didn't flinch at what was a rather difficult shopping list to meet'. Another factor was that they were familiar with Tandem computers, on which the system would be based.

The choice was made through the occupational grapevine. The Systems Development Manager, who made the initial moves, knew the agency people well from earlier days under the Midland Bank when they had all worked together. The contract was not put out to tender, and the original understanding between the two was described as a 'gentleman's agreement' by the bank's Project Manager. The agency remarked that they had 'barely the design of a product' at the time the contract was signed. Clydesdale was visibly trusting the agency to come up with the technical capability they claimed to possess in home banking.

From the viewpoint of the software house, however, their own role was a rather more active one. They stressed their close involvement with the financial sector, and that they knew what is 'really important' to the banks. As the director of the company put it: 'So that puts us in a position that is very much apart from the standard provider of a package, which is not necessarily providing banking functions. We know in any package, including our own, what it is that's attractive to the bank and what is irrelevant.' Thus part of the added value they brought to the bank with the promise of a customized package lay in 'matching what they wanted to achieve with what was actually required'.

Both the bank and software house stressed the long-term relationship between them, which amounted to more than a one-off provision of a package. The bank's Business Manager referred to the agency as 'almost a subsidiary' of the bank. Indeed, it was in the nature of the software that they would keep going back to the software house for add-on delivery systems. For his part, the director of the agency thought the bank was a very sympathetic organization to have a satellite relationship with; the bank had some reputation as innovators and for trading with small start-up companies.

They have dealt with people in the past where they have been among the first purchasers of products that are perhaps not 100 per cent mature at that stage. . . . So choosing us wasn't so unusual for them, and that fitted very nicely with us. And we got on very well with the individuals involved which I think is very important. I think that decision they made about us is borne out by the fact that we've continued doing work for Clydesdale. And I believe—I like to think—that we have become a strategic supplier to them in this area.

Technology Choices and the Development Relationship

The agreement between the bank and Software Partnership had some interesting features. A system called sp/ARCHITECT was developed. This was a front-end processor, representing an 'extra' system between the mainframe and end-user devices. It was run on Clydesdale's fault-tolerant Tandem computers and was highly flexible in terms of driving a range of remote delivery systems. These could be built on readily as compared with the more conventional (videotex-based) approach which would have required new mainframe linkages. sp/ARCHITECT was designed on a modular basis to facilitate the installation of systems ranging from simple home banking to complex corporate cash management. In practice, the mainframe downloaded files after overnight processing, and all customer records were held on the Tandem front-end which then supports the branch network.

Generally expressed, sp/ARCHITECT had the virtue of being flexible without the necessity of overhauling major systems. It acted as a gateway to front-end delivery systems and Clydesdale's internal databases. This compartmentalization of systems permitted the division of labour and responsibilities between the software agency and the bank in the development process. As the agency director put it, the system has 'a low entry point but with the capability to expand'. With a number of modules linking through it was 'not the most elegant system', but it was claimed that sp/ARCHITECT would be developed to be 'much more straightforward or elegant in the way the technology hangs together'.

Clydesdale saved considerably on costs by allowing the agency to market the product independently under an agreement which provided royalties to the bank. Both sides accepted that the benefits were shared. Software Partnership was able to develop a family of products based on sp/ARCHITECT, which they successfully promoted. And the bank got a very good system because the agency was establishing itself and was 'intent on showing how good they were'.

The development process itself was handled by Software Partnership working more or less autonomously, with control from Clydesdale only at the project-management level. Systems staff were very happy with the agency's programming standards and made no attempts to set down methodologies. Their good practice and professionalism was emphasized, and it was to their advantage to have the bank sign off developments at an early stage. Nor were there any problems about splitting the work between agency and in-house developers. Software Partnership did all the front-end programming, which was clearly divided from the programs developed to access internal files.

Close involvement with the client was emphasized rather than very formalized project control. There also appeared to be a tolerant attitude towards time-scales. Clydesdale was under considerable pressure, with Bank of Scotland so active in the field, but recognized that the main thing was to get the quality right. These were high-visibility systems which 'carry enormous embarrassment potential' if they went down. But this flexibility seemed to have had no adverse effect overall; it was claimed that the whole development took just nine months to completion.

CASE 4: MUTUAL LIFE AND THE CUSTOMER CARE PROJECT

This study concerns a system of management of client information, Customer Care, developed by the life insurance firm, Mutual Life. Customer Care was envisaged as a large-scale system, the aim of which was to integrate existing departmental databases into a client-centred database, served by a central customer record.

The case study covers the early stages of the decision to adopt the new system. While it does not extend to the operational solutions that define processes of technological change, it does explore the problems of initiating change. Indeed, as the case will show, the initiation of technical change can itself be highly complex, and more than just a stage in a process. The type of change considered here had implications organization-wide and, moreover, occurred within the kind of decentralized, almost federal organization structure common in the industry. As a result, technological change was problematic. IT became a marginal part of the system, the main emphasis shifting to structural procedures. An organizational innovation (the Customer department) acted as gatekeeper for information and for users to gain access to customer data.

Strategic Context

The life insurance industry in the UK is dominated by a few very large companies. Their historic size, the long-term nature of their products, and their levels of overseas business give them power to shape the markets they operate in. Mutual Life is one of these giants. The company employed around 6,000 staff in 1989 with around 5,000 in the UK. This had more than doubled since 1987. More than half the total were based in the head office, reflecting a heavy degree of centralization. ML's overseas business formed around 20 per cent of total premiums, and only about 15 per cent of business came from Scotland itself.

What made Mutual Life and other Scottish companies different from their English counterparts was their mutual structure (protecting them from take-over or merger) and their use of intermediaries rather than direct sales agents. Despite its size, Mutual Life employed only about 500 sales people. They sold products directly to building societies, estate agents, accountants, solicitors, brokers, etc. Like other life offices, the core of their business was selling individual pensions and life policies through a diversified product range.

Savings products more visibly belong to Mutual than, say, endowment products which were sold through building society agents as part of an overall house-purchase package. Investments were either indexed (e.g. through unit trusts) or on a profit-sharing basis (e.g. endowment mortgages). But as with others who sell through intermediaries, Mutual avoided offering first mortgages, as this would make them competitors of the building societies who are their main agents.

Organization Structure

At Mutual's head office were based the main functional divisions of Actuarial, Marketing, Investment, Operations (including IT), and the largest clerical division, Administration, which contained the main product groups like Pensions and Life. No single department or specialist function had yet established a claim to map out the future of the organization, nor had any dominant alliance emerged. As we will see, the lack of an overall hegemonic rationale within the hierarchy affected the evolution of the Customer Care project.

Although all product departments had dealings with the functional control areas, each product area tended to operate independently as a complex but discrete sub-business. Strong cultural divisions mapped on to this structure; one respondent spoke of 'a kind of folklore attached to departments' that resulted in historical hostilities. With product departments run almost as independent fiefdoms, there was strong evidence of a bureaucratic and fragmented structure—or as our respondent put it, instead of being 'one big blob, Mutual Life is bits of blobs'. Inevitably cases got lost between the cracks, providing the incentive to change. We heard how the poor widow had to wait ages for her life bond money, or how Pensions were very nearly rude to the man who was big business to Life. Even between departments where contact was regular inconsistencies arose: 'As long as everything conforms to expected behaviour patterns, we cope with things very well and very efficiently. But any exceptions cause a fantastic and very disproportionate amount of expense and trouble to sort out.'

The Administration Division employed around 1,800 staff, with 600 each in the big departments of Pensions, Life, and Financial Administration. A fourth subdivision, Administration Development, employed around 50 and in practice was acting as the 'customer department' which was anticipated when the first reports on Customer Care were prepared. The company was anxious to minimize any organization restructuring, notwithstanding the revolutionary Customer Care retraining programme. Instead, the proposed Customer Department was to manage technological change. Once the client-centred databases were in place, the intention was for the Customer Department to 'own' client records and information on behalf of the rest of the organization. In this way ML hoped to avoid dramatic disturbances in the structure and in departmental cultures. The only proviso was that user departments would need to elaborate their own rules on how to routinely 'go through the client funnel'.

The Customer Care Project

The idea behind Customer Care was that of changing an account-based manner of holding information to a customer-based one. Previously Mutual's departmental record systems all held basic customer information. The planned technical change was to introduce client records holding three relational sets of information which could be captured by any department: information about the client; about his/her role with ML, such as 'holds pension with us' or 'her husband holds a life policy'; and the third set was about the specific business connection, such as policy type.

These technical changes were to occur in the context of retraining staff to 'sell' services to 'customers'. As the chief consultant to the project explained, Customer Care 'has more to do with attitudes than it has to do with technology'. Attempts to change the company culture were being introduced independently of any database restructuring. The package of proposals included training in telephone manner, a poster campaign around offices that proclaimed, 'The Customer is King' and exhorted staff not to leave their telephone for more than 30 seconds, a campaign to get staff to employ 'caring' language, and a wide range of 'communication education' in company broadsheets. Quality circles were also being used to punch home the message.

'Being nice' of course is part of the business. The fact that life offices all offered similar generic products meant that one of the few areas where it was possible to differentiate was around the level of service. In addition, there were recent changes in ways of doing business. One of the conditions set by the Financial Services Act 1986 was that life offices must produce disclaimers on staff who speak to the public.

The impetus for introducing Customer Care could be traced to several sources. The Sales and Marketing General Manager brought the idea back from the United States, and presented the benefits in terms of familiar arguments of ensuring customer loyalty, cross-selling, direct marketing, and the like. However, a number of financial institutions had been picking up on the theme of customer service, while senior managers in ML were enthusiastic for efficiency as well as for marketing reasons.

Getting Customer Care under Way

Undoubtedly the reception of the idea for Customer Care was very positive. However, early change champions who had a stake in getting the project under way may have overestimated its acceptability. One of the systems consultants for Customer Care assumed at first that powerful departments would take the lead, and direct other departments to make necessary changes in their operations.

We're having a little bit of difficulty getting people started. Getting people to take in the scope of this thing. It's sometimes a fact that people emerge in senior positions in the Admin divisions or in Finance . . . the set of those people and the set of people with imagination is sometimes mutually exclusive . . . I'm hoping it will be the Sales and Marketing people who will take the driving seat for this project.

An interdepartmental steering group had been established which reflected the fact that design overlapped quite extensively the work of different departments, as well as that of other corporate IT projects then being carried out. But it was a sign of Customer Care's early problems that analysts on the project were unclear about the role of the group, who gave the go-ahead on resourcing, and which managers were the main decision-takers. There seemed to be few processes—particularly the critical informal processes—whereby senior management could discover how specifications were translating into a model for change.

Since no one group was clamouring to be allowed to control the project, IBM was called in in a management consultancy role. They advised that a project sponsor be drawn from the user community. Branch Administration was duly appointed as guardian of the first phase of the project, on the grounds that they were the most regular users of customer information, and that they would stand to gain most by being in control of the cleaning up and recording of how customer information was held. Branch Administration, however, was also the most rule-based of user areas and the Deputy General Manager, informed that 'he had got the plum', had no special interest in the job of project sponsor. He believed that he would carry the project for the first year or two, but then 'naturally hand it on' to the Marketing Division.

IBM, seeing indifference as the main obstacle to getting Customer Care started, immediately suggested that staff be sent on an IBM-run Applications Transfer Training course. The ATT course was a six-week, full-time formalized version of brainstorming. In Mutual Life's case it was aimed at supervisory level staff and junior and middle management in Branch Administration, along with project analysts. The explicit aims of the ATT course were to enlist the commitment and support of staff, so that they would hold themselves accountable for a project's success.

By his own admission the senior systems consultant had not been able to bring the interface Customer department into existence. However, those in management sponsoring the project believed that the function had actually been quietly and uncontroversially created, and was already working steadily. The new section was part of Administration Development, called Customer Administration and Support Services (CASS). It was small, about ten people mainly women clerks, tucked away as 'an extra service' offered by Administration Development to the product departments. The section was headed by a woman whose role was 'helping people with queries on customers when they get stuck'; and its first mundane task was the semi-manual cleaning up of data on the policy-holder index.

CASS was set to become a full-blown Customer department, but still from within the softly-softly approach to handling the organizational response to new technical systems. The Deputy General Manager and project sponsor for Customer Care thought that the new department would be 'sort of on a par with' the product departments of Life, Finance, and Pensions, but that they would still handle the bulk of work. He spoke of 'encouraging dialogue' and that 'if nobody else is the right person to update some client information, we will update it'. This pragmatic version of the expanded role of Administration Development saw CASS and user representatives having to sell their ideas to each other 'so that they come up with something that will work'.

Operational Input

The actual development work on the client databases was being carried out by a small project team within Information Systems, the Customer Management group. They were developing the preliminary data models, and they liaised with CASS and another small project team building a corporate model. While Customer Management was part of the overall customer strategy, they in effect served to separate out the technical aspects. Given the massive organizational implications of the project, this enabled the company to go slow on the more problematic features.

The Computing Operations Division had been enlarged and upgraded, growing from 130 people in 1985 to over 400 in 1988. The status of the head of the division, as a General Manager, reflected both the increased importance of computing activities and the expansion of the division from a merely technical 'systems department' to a type of techno-business operations function. The agreed working brief of the new-look division was to 'look beyond machines into company operations and relate what the company wanted to do to systems possibilities'. However, renaming the division and taking in business areas like O&M, had not necessarily improved IS's capacity to articulate corporate goals, especially in relation to the big product departments. Speaking about how Computing Operations could affect change, the Divisional General Manager concluded that IS still did not have the authority 'to take a whole function by the scruff of its neck and change it. . . . Now, I've asked that question internally and yet I haven't got the answer or even a debate on it. What we're talking about here is changing corporate processes, and as you know we don't have much of a corporate stand-alone structure.'

Computing Operations was divided into three subdivisions: Information Systems, IS Operations, and Facilities. The first two were the normal systems development and computer operations departments. However, Facilities was a part of the division that had been reorganized on a quasi-market basis. It consisted of a set of internal 'boutique' services (which included Microfilming, Filing, Commissionnaires, O&M, Management Services, Premises, Space Planning and Purchasing) which were intended to give the user more direct control and responsibility over system prioritization and costs. The boutiques provided specialized expertise to be solicited and consumed by other IS staff, and some were directly on call to business users.

Customer Care was originally set up as a novel type of 'internal consultancy' based on one of these specialist boutiques. The consultancy role was supposed to act as a buffer between senior management and systems development staff, so as to produce a strategic view of the organization. In practice, however, without a power base inside the organization's working practices, the experts met significant problems in defining and legitimating their input into the product divisions. The Senior Consultant in the group explained that his supposed 'expertise' had marginalized him from the rest of IS, and his 'thinking work' set him up as a deviant case in the can-do culture of systems developers.

The consultancy group hasn't worked out as well as intended largely because nobody had a very clear idea of what it should be used for. . . . Certainly I have a couple of guys working for me who are very experienced and very knowledgeable technical men. But they are, in development terms, space cadets. . . . The frustrating thing about the consultancy area was that I didn't have any staff, so if I wanted investigations done it entailed getting the resources to actually get the stuff out. I had to do a lot of the stuff myself.

Within a year this means of implementing IT strategy had been virtually abandoned. The group subsequently became a development support team. They retained their consultancy role, but also took on the job of monitoring programming standards. This efficiency-related function helped to restore the group's credibility. It provided a real service to hard-pressed project managers and gave the power to impose working practices. But there were doubts about how the strategic view of technology could be slipped in amidst the pragmatics of policing standards, and doubts too about the continuing significance of the 'consultancy' role in driving Customer Care.

Mutual Life's Technical Systems

ML's existing systems had been built incrementally as virtual 'islands of technology', matching the discrete operations of the product areas. This meant there was duplicated information held on various departmental files, and only in the last two or three years had they begun to build semi-integrated networks. Perhaps making a virtue of necessity, the Customer Care sponsor, himself a senior user manager, argued that they actively chose to keep their databases discrete throughout the 1970s.

We chose to do it the way we did, rather than go for a mighty database when we felt the computer power and all the technology generally couldn't support it. At the time we were proved right as others tried to build a mammoth database and lost about five years, and then followed on after us, so that we were well ahead through the seventies, and we were making the necessary linkages as we went. . . . We developed as islands, a database for this and a database for that. But that did not stop our development transactions. As long as the information is on the machine we can get it at any time. It is having it there that is important, not having it all together.

This view was echoed by the systems consultant on Customer Care, who suggested that ML did not especially want shared data as this depended on buying leading-edge DB2 and network technologies. Nevertheless, it was at variance with the received wisdom about data integration and would pose a dilemma for the Customer Care project, which was based on the idea of eventually providing access to corporate databases tended by the Customer group.

Much of ML's effort in IT had gone on improvements in the efficiency of routine processing and on compulsory developments to meet legislative requirements. Non-compulsory projects like Customer Care were held up and the technical components of the project lagged well behind the retraining and marketing components. In fact, Customer Care was described as being barely into the planning stage and showed signs of a classic software crisis. While Mutual's use of their older databases may have been deliberately 'old fashioned, piecemeal and not flash', this undoubtedly had contributed to the development problems.

ML's manual records might well have held all the information the planned Customer Records would hold. However, even where they did have manually-held information, some of it may have been out of date, since the life span of products was so long, and manual records did not update information not directly concerned with the contract the client holds. ML did not, therefore, plan to reverse-engineer their files. Instead, they would first change how they held information on new customers, and then gradually replace 'certain key files by more customer-oriented files'. However, even here there were problems in generating a broader view of future corporate needs. The Systems Consultant lamented that the Policy Holder Index File 'should by rights be the core of future customer care but isn't' because systems designers did not challenge the users' specifications. Thus information on potential clients would not be recorded on the index. 'The user took a very narrow view of what a "policy" was. If somebody came along who was a potential client, that didn't get on the index because he wasn't a policy-holder. So as a result, the index is a fraction of the use it should be to us.' Data of this sort, on customers whose enquiries had not resulted in the conclusion of a policy, was of little value for internal administration but potentially extremely valuable for marketing purposes. We see here early evidence of groups (particularly IS) tending to act only within narrow functional roles.

The Customer Care project group had also debated the issue of whether to buy in a package or build a system, and had decided to build in-house. The issues were familiar ones. As the Senior Consultant put it, building systems from scratch is 'too messy' these days if it can be avoided, but the danger with a package 'is that it does 3,000 things you don't want and it doesn't do the dozen things that you really need'. Most of the respondents involved in the decision about the development thought that, though it was better to buy rather than make where possible, the buying option carried its own costs: 'You can't really go back to your users and say, "You really can't do that because the package doesn't like it and we can't fix the package", because that wouldn't carry any weight.' The conclusion was that, in the end, the cost of writing the interface would be almost as high as in-house development.

The Design Work

Systems design, though in its early stages, already seemed unusually organized. The internal consultant's job, located within IS Development, was newly created to handle planning for Customer Care, and for the first six months he and two other business analysts worked on an outline of the new information structures. Interestingly, for a project which referred to the whole organization, Customer Care was the first job of that type in the company for both the consultant and the analysts. Unlike many design staff who transferred internally into IS Development and the IS boutiques, and are familiar with user divisions, these staff came on to the project with little firm-specific knowledge.

Both the consultant and the analysts stressed the advantages of 'the fresh view'. True, they relied heavily on the potted histories of functions and jobs within ML provided by Administration Development. But the consultant argued the case for 'pure' expertise; he had hired the analysts for their systems experience and preferred those without organizational knowledge:

If you computerize what somebody currently does, you are computerizing something which they do in the absence of the technology. Given the technology, they might want to do it in a different way. We do need somebody to dream up an idea. That's why it's gold-dust to us to get people in direct from university, because they know very little about the company's habits. (Senior Systems Consultant)

The Senior Consultant initially devised the basic concept—that of holding three sets of related information—without conferring much with other managers or clerical staff. He stressed that the consultant's role was to 'dream up' solutions virtually intuitively. Taking this basic idea, the analysts worked with the formal technique of entity modelling. While this relied on the formal documentation of ML's procedures by Administration Development, it was an explicitly theory-driven method.

From my point of view it would be a mammoth task to try and understand six businesses in six months. I suppose that the scope of the study had to be fairly superficial in data terms, otherwise we would never have got this far. Basically we were looking at areas of the business that involved details about the customer or about his or her role with the company. We weren't looking in too great detail on policy-servicing aspects. (Customer Care Analyst)

The initial information structures were to be used as the basis of some future feasibility study, rather than a detailed design of the system. The analysts stressed any future design would 'have to set out very clearly the business problems, document the actual business procedures. But of course to go along with this we have to develop a future schema for dealing with business which could mean changes in organizational manning levels. It could mean an awful lot.' Thus the main design issues could lie in developing the interfaces between the new structures and existing systems, and would become increasingly difficult for systems designers to deal with. The internal consultant and the analysts emphasized how everything would be gradual and how the new data structures would be 'discussed clearly and in great length with the user community'.

CASE 5: HOME AND AUTO'S MANAGEMENT INFORMATION SYSTEM

This case study focuses on the development of the management information system (MIS) at the insurance giant, Home and Auto. MISs are typical of modern systems that are highly user-interactive, and require a high degree of user involvement in their development. We see in the case how 'champions' of particular methodologies can influence the development process. We also see the considerable problems of managing the tacit knowledge that user inputs frequently generate, and how these problems modified an intendedly strategic approach to IT.

Strategic Context

The Home and Auto Group, headquartered in central Scotland, was among Britain's largest general insurers. In common with other big general insurance companies, H&A derived much of its business from outside the UK domestic market. The group had major overseas holdings, particularly in the United States and Canada, deriving about one-third of its premium income from its UK activities, one-third from the United States, and one-third from other overseas operations. About 80 per cent of its business came from general insurance, primarily the household and motor sectors, together with commercial and personal accident. In 1990 premium income world-wide reached £3.5

billion. The UK operation as a whole employed 10,000 people, with 2,500 employed in Scotland. In the period under investigation, H&A was emerging from a strategically passive stage to engage in a limited diversification activity. This took the form of buying up a number of estate-agency chains around the UK, and the acquisition of overseas insurance holdings.

The Management Information System

The project examined was the development of the first corporate-wide management information system in Home and Auto. Designed for use at the head office, the MIS project had no direct relationship to broader strategic moves but reflected the longer standing strategy of commitment to core insurance activities in UK markets. Such long-term company-wide projects not infrequently incur implementation problems as the time-scale and scope create areas of conflict and vulnerability, and this particular case illustrated nicely the way in which original grand designs came to be replaced by more pragmatic solutions.

Staff from the Information Systems department and the Statistical Services department were involved in the MIS development and worked closely with Product Information Officers (PIOs) and relevant managers from user departments. Statistical Services in particular, and the PIOs to a lesser extent, provided examples relatively rare in commercial computing of users with a high degree of computer sophistication.

Looking at the actors involved, the Statistical Services department occupied a pivotal position in the company somewhat similar to that of actuaries in life insurance. The need for statistical-analysis skills reflected a distinctive feature of general insurance—though the level of statistical skills is nowhere near as complex as actuarial skills, and statisticians do not dominate the career structure as actuaries do in life insurance. (In fact, the contrast between statisticians and actuaries reflects precisely the distinction between general insurance and the relatively high-skill life insurance industries.) Statistical Services developed models and projections to evaluate claims experience and premium rates for policies. While being a major user department they had a dual role in systems development and acted as 'expert witness' helping to define the requirements of product managers.

The Product Information Officers originated two or three years prior to the research period, to some extent hand in hand with the adoption of RAMIS. This was a menu-driven end-user reporting language and the basic tool for data extraction throughout H&A. The PIOs worked within the user departments, producing the reports that formed the basis of management information, and performed the day-to-day work of data extraction, though their role was not classed as technical. They worked alongside Statistical Services, relying on them to check methodology, and they had until then been recruited from Statistical Services. Although most PIO moves out of Statistical Services were sideways, they were attracted by the less limiting career chances within product management positions.

Origins of the MIS

In the early 1980s, H&A top management received a nasty jolt when adverse market conditions conspired with an ill-timed increase in motor rates to produce a sharp drop in business. (H&A's competitors had taken note of the poor market conditions and held off their increases.) Top management was also aware of other political and technical pressures on premium rates. The computerization of rate books by third-party agents allowed the targeting of cheap and unprofitable rates, and there were pressures to deregulate cartel agreements for certain products. All of this led to demands from senior levels for improved management information in order to avoid such a situation arising in the future.

This impetus from the top coincided with motives operating lower down. The realization that management information was deficient and that the company was losing out on important sectors of the market had become widespread. But there was a particularly strong motive from within Statistical Services. The department had overall responsibility for management information but were unhappy with their dependence on the main processing systems. They were the 'management information hole within H&A' and badly wanted their own system.

The diagnosis coming from this quarter was that all the problems lay with the processing systems. Only skeletal information for renewals had been provided on documentation to Head Office, where it was keyed in. A distributed system had been developed, which meant branch staff keying in directly. But the data was still of poor quality because of poor staff inputting. 'If you got the premium in and the address of the individual, you were doing quite well.' Inconsistency was also a problem. Different reports used different definitions and data sources. As one Statistical Services Superintendent put it: 'Processing systems do not produce good MI. We realized that we needed something more strategic with management information. We needed an MI database and a project that actually concentrated on MI and not on processing.'

Statistical Services took up the gauntlet in 1983 and set up a Working Party to develop 'an overall plan to meet the corporation's requirements for management information support'. They defined the main types of report that reflected the information needs of Product Managers, and the levels of detail and frequency needed by different groups. Following the Working Party report, Statistical Services undertook the the first phase of systems development, but this foundered some eighteen months later. All sides acknowledged that this stage had ended in failure, although accounts tended to differ. Those in Statistical Services argued that their mistake had been in not defining management information in terms of the needs of senior levels of management, while the IS people pointed to Statistical Services' lack of computing expertise. 'They hadn't considered all the technical issues and it ended up being a bit of a disaster. It took two days to run a programme that was supposed to be done overnight.'

The 'Strategy Project' and IS Involvement

At this point Information Systems joined the fray. Sections within the IS department championed IBM's Business Systems Planning. BSP is a methodology for deriving the data needed to build systems. It is a descriptive framework for requirements definition, which models flows of information mapped on to organization charts and promotes a 'strategic' approach to management information. These influences within IS management culminated in the so-called strategy project.

A development team for the strategy project was brought together in October 1985. It consisted of an analyst and senior analyst from Information Systems and a superintendent from Statistical Services, and was charged with producing a strategy for a support system covering all classes of business. The project was controlled by a steering committee with representatives from the main business departments and chaired by the IS Manager. The project team went back to basics, using interviews and questionnaires to determine management responsibilities and information requirements in all the business departments. (It had been a criticism of the early demands coming from senior levels that there had been little reference to management's actual information needs.)

In April 1986 the strategy project team produced a detailed requirements definition, which consolidated the 1983 study along with the data from the interview survey. They updated the Reports Register and went to great lengths to establish rules for good data management and documentation. They also identified key problems like the inadequacies of existing reports and inconsistencies in databases and processing systems. On the basis of this, the project team moved on to the technical evaluation stage, and during 1986 investigated two database management packages: Supra and System 204. Neither package was seen as capable of satisfying user reporting requirements or the efficiency needs of bulk batch reporting. Once again, very large CPU times were the root problem. The evaluation exercise noted that RAMIS to all intents and purposes would not have been capable of dealing with the necessary processing volumes. In November 1986, in the technical evaluation report, the project team recommended deferring a decision on software pending further investigation.

Enter Pragmatism

The strategy project itself was now starting to run into the sand. This ambitious scheme had envisaged using base data rather than summarized data from the processing systems. In part this reflected a strong assumption in the Statistical Services department that the MIS would use base data. Statistical Services had always seen the MIS project in terms of creating its own database, independent of the main processing systems. However, the accessing of base data on millions of policies created huge volume problems. It was the assumed use of base data which led to the discovery of incredibly large CPU times, the constraints on RAMIS, and the earlier rejection of the two packages.

The 'strategic' approach gave rise to many more practical difficulties. BSP (along with other complex requirements definition frameworks) has been criticized for having little to say about the practical side of obtaining complete information, and the project team were finding out the problems of trying to fit real-life decision structures to a formalized model. The programmers and analysts involved spoke of trying to hit a moving target; there were constant dilemmas over whether parallel changes should be incorporated or left for a later stage. There were also difficulties in getting information out of user departments; the brief was to cover all classes of business but the departments were obviously only interested in and knowledgeable about their own information needs. The 'strategic' approach made it impossible to satisfy anyone until the whole system was completed.

Moreover, political pressures were mounting. The apparent lack of progress on the MIS project—the fact that the business departments were not seeing any new systems coming along for their use after nearly three years of development effort—was creating a major credibility problem for IS.

At the end of 1986 there was a turnaround in thinking. A more pragmatic, staged approach began to gain favour, reflected in the decision to focus on the particular needs of the Home department and to put strategic issues on the back burner. Other events had also overtaken the project. The IS Manager who had championed the BSP methodology departed and was replaced by new people who were of like mind in strongly favouring a step-by-step approach. The new IS Manager became increasingly involved with the MIS project and instigated a fresh round of software evaluation, while his deputy suggested looking at the DB2 package. This had originally been rejected because it did not have sufficient volume-handling capability. (Supra and Model 204 had been selected for trials on these grounds, though even they had resulted in very large CPU times.) However, the decision was taken to run the MIS database separate from the operational data of the processing systems, and to extract summarized data. In mid-1987 the report on these trials recommended DB2 as being the most cost-effective and as having superior end-user reporting interfaces.

The (Partial) Recovery of Strategy

The next stage was to implement the MIS. There were some eighteen departments for different classes of business in H&A, but the Home and Motor insurance accounts were by far the largest and had high priority for management information. Home was chosen for the practical reasons of having the most complete historical data needed to build up the MIS databases, and better support from their managers who were both ex-Statistical Services. When the system was being implemented in the Home department, the approach was tailored to fit. The PIOs in Home put together a detailed specification of the types of management reports they wanted, and as the programs were being written there was ongoing consultation to adjust output to current requirements. A follow-up reconciliation exercise then compared the new systems reports with existing manual data, and also with Home's own experience, so they could have confidence in the data. This exercise continued while the new reports were beginning to be used.

Interestingly, when the project moved on to the Motor department (and immediate political pressures had subsided because the business departments were seeing systems coming through) the strategic approach revived somewhat. There were attempts to build a generic system that could be applied to overall systems planning. As the Senior Analyst from IS put it:

With Home the strategy wasn't that detailed that we could immediately develop a Home system. I suppose we had a framework, but what we developed was really based on what Home department needed. Now that we are doing Motor we want to go back to the strategy to get an overall picture. . . . Home was developed to show ourselves that we could do it. But we really need to stand back now and get a system that will fit all classes of business.

However, there was no wholesale 'return to strategy'. The new approach was a pragmatic response to the potential problems of creating a massive overhead in maintaining different systems in all the departments. Also, the possibility of a generic system itself was viewed sceptically by some. Senior analysts and people from Statistical Services were most positive about the need for a company-wide system. But closer to the workface the programmer/analysts thought that while 'commonalities' could be found, a great deal of preparation in the departments would still be needed.

CASE 6: PREMIER FINANCIAL SERVICES' INDEX PACKAGES

INDEX was a packaged accounting system for running a credit-card operation. It was purchased by Premier Financial Services Ltd, a subsidiary of one of the main Scottish clearing banks. This case study covers the purchase of the package from the supplying agency, and the process of modification by them for running on the bank's mainframe. The focus of attention is the decision-making process—the stakeholders taking part, how their interests interacted, the importance of historical context, and how outcomes reflected political process. Also interesting was the contrast between two different organizational cultures, the parent company's 'banking culture' and the 'marketing culture' of the subsidiary.

Strategic Context

Premier Financial Services originated as an in-store credit card for a medium-sized retail chain based in Glasgow and Edinburgh. It was an extension of their standard credit facility, but was developed as a separate venture and during the mid-1980s was sold to the bank. Only the credit-card business was purchased, so new arrangements had to be made for Premier's data processing which previously had been handled by the retail chain. The commercial objective of the purchase was that Premier should extend their charge card from its regional base into a nation-wide operation. The bank then intended to sell the Premier card to its customers as a new financial product. The attraction of the card was that it was an established product with considerable potential for growth; it was also distinctive in the sense of being a 'working-class' credit card selling in a market, 'C1 and C2 sliding into the Ds', that banks had traditionally ignored.

For the bank, the purchase of the computer package, INDEX, represented an unusual and to some extent risky process of decision-making. Against all normal practice, the bank's own systems development staff were not involved in project management, and instead the supplier was asked to handle the implementation. The purchase also has to be set in the context of the acquisition of Premier, which itself occurred in the context of a reorganization within the bank that brought in a group structure. Against this backcloth, the purchase of INDEX became, in certain respects, a pawn in a much larger game that reflected the new role of Group Services within the bank.

Group Services was set up with a brief which included integrating the computer systems of the bank with its most important new subsidiaries. This gave Group Services authority to ensure optimal deployment of the central computing resource. However, the nominal authority to migrate skills around the group clearly had the potential for creating conflict. In the present case, the politics of decision-making centred on the decision that Systems Development, a pivotal department within the bank's Management Services Division, should not be involved in the purchase and conversion of the package. Throughout the implementation, Systems Development was the 'ghost at the bargaining table'.

Developments in the Decision-Making Process

The normal approach from the bank's point of view would have been for Systems Development to develop a system in-house or to identify and purchase a package and then handle the conversion. However, Systems Development managers, as well as other sources, confirmed that they had too much work to take the job on. A senior manager in the department claimed that though they would normally provide the interface between external suppliers and users, they had 'no concerns' about the product being supported by the supplier. INDEX was a one-off and a self-contained system; should it require integration with other systems in the future, Systems Development would expect to be in control of that. Admittedly, being 'too busy' raises questions about priorities in workload. But unlike most bank projects, the need to provide Premier with a computer facility presented the bank with a new user, and a fixed deadline (one that Systems Development had no control over), since the original owners of Premier would cease to provide the computing service on an agreed date after the purchase. Systems Development may have been willing to concede their involvement in the context of this deadline.

Other points of view, however, would be hard to reconcile with the gloss that Systems Development placed on the situation. Managers in Group Services certainly saw the political significance of the precedent that was being set. One Group Services Manager stressed their own winning role in the game:

I think what we're really talking about here is power. We're talking about a historical environment where nothing, but nothing, would happen in a computer development unless it was done either directly or under the control of Management Services Division. Now the implications of a user getting a system in and running without ever going anywhere near MSD ... if you were in MSD in a senior position, you would say, 'Wait a minute!'

Premier management put the matter slightly differently again: 'With the advent of Group Services, one of their briefs was to utilize resources and expertise group-wide, and they started pushing hard that the work should go outside MSD.'

The choice of INDEX came from the General Manager of Premier Financial Services. The existing software was old and had been heavily modified from an original charge accounting system, and was unsuited to the credit-card business. INDEX was intended to start the new venture off on the right foot with a system that reflected the business they had and wanted to develop. The features of the package that recommended INDEX to Premier management were, first, that it provided a basic system for managing a credit-card operation and for handling transactions (recording credit payments, purchases, etc.). In addition, INDEX was client-based, rather than account-based, and enabled Premier to credit-rate individual clients; no matter how many different types of credit a client had, these could be integrated and compared, and an overall credit line allocated to individuals.

The Premier management had a marketing background, and they were extremely enthusiastic about INDEX as a marketing tool. If you can credit score a person, and see whether they are not using all their credit, you can promote other products. There were great advantages in cross-selling and in the range of products that INDEX could deal with. Currently, they were marketing loans and claimed '8 to 9 per cent response rates, which is unbelievable'. Premier management stressed that INDEX provided no marketing information as such; it was quite clearly a card-management system not a promotional system. However, the package could be used as the basis of a market information system with the addition of customized software. They stressed the absolute necessity of having an extensive database on clients in their type of business. Thus quotations were being obtained from software companies for such a system which they hoped to implement shortly after the main package went live.

Formal control of the investment decision still lay with Group Services in the bank. Normally this would have caused no problem as Group Services management was reasonably happy to let Premier make their own business decisions. However, from the Group Services' point of view choosing the supplier, Computer Planning and Management (CPM), was the critical decision. The bank had had a previous and, according to them, disastrous experience of this particular agency when they had made 'a complete mess' of a project. In the early stages CPM caused 'a lot of nervousness' to Group Services; they stressed the 'deep historical factor' which gave the bank an aversion to using outside suppliers, and this one in particular. Systems Development constituted a strong lobby in the bank 'which says if we want a system we write a system'. Thus Group Services' endorsement of using CPM underlined the significance of the precedent being invoked, the attendant risks they were taking, and their nervousness at using an agency that had a poor reputation with them.

This point should not be exaggerated. Premier, after all, was a separate company and INDEX was not as yet integrated with the bank's systems. Still, INDEX was the only production system that the bank was not responsible for running and if problems had occurred, Group Services would certainly have been vulnerable.

Implementing the Package

Deciding where the computing capacity was to be located and where the software was to run was, in certain respects, quite separate from the purchase of the package. Premier was originally strongly in favour of a bureau service; a bureau would have been under their control and Premier management had had a long previous experience of using computer bureau services. Group Services management, on the other hand, regarded the clearing bank as the 'obvious place'. Given their huge data-processing operation, running INDEX on the bank's computers would give them no capacity problems, and there was also the question of interfacing INDEX with ATMs and other delivery systems at some future date. In the event, the decision was taken to run on the bank's mainframe. A senior Group Services manager said he suspected Premier would still have liked their own operation, though interestingly Premier management themselves claimed the opposite. They had, they said, come round to the view that the advantages of being relieved of all the data-processing headaches outweighed the control advantages to be obtained from using their own bureau. For them the important issue had been obtaining INDEX.

We can see that the adopted option had something for everyone. Premier had obtained the package they wanted, and Group Services had obtained the running location which best met their organizational interests; INDEX was being run within the bank so that an element of control could be retained, but it was outside the domain of the Systems Development department.

Although Group Services were initially worried about employing CPM, all the respondents emphasized how in the event they carried out the conversion work well. Because CPM's reputation had suffered from the previous 'mess' they had been involved in, they were extremely careful to avoid any repetition of past problems. CPM's professionalism in implementing INDEX naturally produced a sigh of relief from both Group Services and Premier. At the time the case study was being researched, they were some six months to completion and had so far 'hit every date'; all parties in the bank and Premier were very happy with progress.

The final piece of the jigsaw involved the future maintenance and on-line fault-finding for INDEX. Group Services decided that CPM should provide this service. Again, this was unusual; maintenance and trouble-shooting for packages, as for other systems, would normally be dealt with in-house. But this course of action followed from the decision to have CPM implement the package. One advantage was that with CPM responsible for maintenance, this took the pressure off the bank to monitor the development work closely. As one Group Services Manager indicated:

As to how they should do that [the conversion] we're not fussy. I should qualify that; the reason we're not too fussy is that in the short term we don't see the clearing bank taking over responsibility for this software. If, in a more normal scenario, the Bank's Systems Development people were going to do the maintenance we would look at the whole thing in a very different perspective. But with CPM responsible for maintaining it in the future, we're not too concerned with the methodologies they use.

One might question such an attitude towards control over outsourcing. Certainly a major disadvantage was cost. A maintenance service that provides a very fast response to faults, necessary for an on-line system, would be very expensive. And this arrangement might have to be reviewed in the longer term when the effects of maintenance costs become apparent. If the running costs of the package turned out to be too high it might be necessary to ask Systems Development to take it over—which highlighted another area of risk in the Group Services' strategy.

Project Management

One interesting consequence of the absence of Systems Development was that it left the project without its natural project managers. This void was filled in the end by a number of different groups, each contributing a part of Systems Development's normal role.

CPM was responsible for the conversion programming, the major part of the development work. But because they obviously were unfamiliar with the bank's systems there had to be some internal contact from the Management Services Division. In the event, the Computer Operations department was brought in by Group Services to take over the hardware side of project management when it became clear that Systems Development would have no role. This was another unique aspect of the project. Normally Computer Operations would never have even approached this level of responsibility; they would have had their job control language and all ancillary systems handed to them by Systems Development.

So this was very much a breakthrough for Computer Operations. And they made a great effort, in terms of the resources and the quality of staff assigned to the project, to see that things went well. They indicated their hopes for attracting more of this type of work. Moreover, the motivation of the Computer Operations staff was almost certainly heightened by long-standing friction between them and Systems Development. Other observers noted that Systems Development had a very low opinion of Computer Operations—'arrogant is the only word for it'—while the hostility was returned from the other side. So there was 'a little bit of politics bubbling away in the background' of this aspect of the implementation process, as well.

Interestingly, the Computer Operations department adopted a very strong orientation towards the bank's own systems. Having, as they saw it, taken over the mantle of responsibility in project meetings, they stressed the importance of getting the package 'modified in order to get it right for how we want it run on our mainframe'. For their part, Premier management had no complaints about the commitment of the Computer Operations staff but did have some reservations about 'culture': 'Their view is that they are the computer department of the bank. They do things a certain way and that's it. I tend to get a straight, no, it's not bank policy, whereas I'm looking for a bureau's answer, yes, of course we can do it.'

CASE 7: BANK OF SCOTLAND VISA CENTRE

This case study describes strategic decision-making around the commissioning and operation of Bank of Scotland's VISA Centre. The Centre was based in Dunfermline, some twenty miles from Edinburgh, and dealt with credit-card processing. By 1988 it was handling one million of its own cards and a number of others processed on a bureau basis. The case is therefore about one particular aspect of the modern information technology scene: the running of a high-volume processing operation. The other focus of interest is the buying-in of a processing package. This was one of the few cases in our study in which a large-scale package was smoothly and successfully implemented. The key to understanding this success was the fact that the package had been honed on other user sites before VISA purchased it, and also that VISA Centre was a newly created and functionally distinct unit in the bank. VISA managers therefore did not have to contend with mapping the package on to an existing structure and array of expertise. The benefits of buying even an organizationally complex package far outweighed the costs of customizing one for use.

Strategic Context

Between 1966 and 1972, Barclaycard was the only British credit card. This was the UK franchised name (later changed to VISA) of Bank Americard. By 1972 the Joint Credit Card Company, owned by the other three English clearers, had launched Access, the UK version of Mastercard, and from this point the take-up of credit cards and the number on offer began to grow quickly. Barclays was at this stage offering third-party processing facilities to others on a bureau basis.

Bank of Scotland (which was 30 per cent owned by Barclays until the mid-l980s) continued to pass on requests for cards directly to Barclaycard and to use Barclays to issue and run their credit card. However, 'at Barclays insistance . . . that's too strong a word; at Barclays suggestion, we decided to issue our own in 1982' (Assistant General Manager, VISA Centre). Bank of Scotland, therefore, became a card issuer and paid for their third-party processing to be done by Barclays. In 1982 they were issuing about 300,000 cards per year and were beginning to experience some service difficulties with the Barclaycard operation.

However, having entered this new product area at Barclays' prompting, Bank of Scotland was quick to see the advantages. Only licensed deposit-takers can sell credit cards, and in 1984 the bank struck an innovative deal with the Automobile Association in England to produce a VISA card exclusively for AA members. Through this the bank sought to extend their client base south of the border. The strategy worked sufficiently well for them to gain most of their new card customers from England—although in the process they came into direct competition with Barclaycard itself.

Barclays, meanwhile, decided in 1985 to ease out of offering its processing facilities on a bureau basis. This decision to get out of third-party processing left Bank of Scotland needing to look for another third-party deal or to chance setting up independently. The VISA Centre Planning Manager put it this way:

I think it was a discussion that began to take place between Barclays and Bank of Scotland and others. Did we consider it would be right to set up on our own? The volumes that we would be handling were over the break-even point. It was felt, yes, let's go. And not only that; let's look at what has happened in the States. What certainly is likely to happen here. And let's build.

Setting up the VISA Centre

The Assistant General Manager (AGM), who had worked previously as a senior systems development manager in the bank, was given the 'one man band' job of setting up the VISA Centre—'talking to Barclays, looking at what was involved in disengaging our business, looking at what we required in terms of premises, people, and a processing system'. After briefly considering sites in England, he opted for a greenfield site in Dunfermline's business park. This meant that the new business would be close to head offices in Edinburgh, while in addition Fife Region and Dunfermline District Council were willing to provide some of the set-up costs.

However, the main reason for choosing Dunfermline was demographic. Census and population returns for the area indicated a large supply of 'married ladies who are really excellent workers'. The VISA Centre could be staffed by this high quality but non-career female labour force. Much of the work available would be on a part-time basis, which could be arranged to suit the women's domestic arrangements. There was also a strong belief among managers that this expedient would solve many of the potential health problems of working with terminals. As the operations manager put it, working in a concentrated manner at a terminal for eight hours was asking rather a lot of most people; part-time work was 'more humane really'.

The decision to locate in Dunfermline was made by the AGM conferring with senior managers in the bank's Management Services Division (MSD) and his own General Manager, who was accountable to the bank board for the division in which VISA was to be included. From that point the work proceeded quickly. Barclays had asked for the disengagement in early 1985, discussions with Fife Region began in May 1985, and by July construction of the new site had begun.

One Senior Manager jokingly recounted that he and another Senior Manager had 'designed the organization chart over a pint at the Queen's Head'. This account of a face-to-face, informal decision process could well be true. Early in 1985 these two Senior Managers and the AGM were the only three people appointed. And the AGM—the only appointment during the earliest months—had certainly had a cleaner slate than most managers in his position in deciding the kind of organization he wanted.

From the outset the Assistant General Manager and MSD had intended to buy a credit-card processing package, rather than attempt to develop a system in-house. Partly this was because the bank was relatively new to the credit-card business—the AGM and most of the other managers he recruited later had to learn about credit cards as they went along. As he put it, 'none of us in those early days really appreciated just how complex and how complicated the credit card business is. It bears no relationship to granting overdrafts or personal loans.' So they did not want to risk building such a specialized system themselves. More importantly, however, Barclays had stipulated a disengagement time of only eighteen months to transfer all operations from their processing centre to the new centre(s). So getting a system quickly in place, which included software, hardware, working procedures, 'and the organization that would be required to support the process', was essential. Buying in this 'working system' happened in two main spurts: first, choosing the main processing package, and then buying the other systems and equipment with the package in mind.

The FDR Package

The package-buying decisions were made by the Centre AGM and a small number of managers from Systems Development in MSD who had expertise in this area. It was difficult to get any sense of any choice having been exercised, as both the AGM and others in MSD indicated that 'there was really only one package at that time'. Indeed, all the MSD people 'knew more or less from the outset that the software trail was just a verification trip'. However, technology in this business moves on very quickly. The AGM spoke of a 'leap-frogging effect' in this kind of operation. When they set up, he was in little doubt that they had the most modern system of any card operation in the UK. But he doubted that they were still in that position, since others had set up since using more recent equipment.

The package itself was supplied by First Data Resources (FDR), Nebraska. Earlier versions had been bought by other UK banks, and at the time of Bank of Scotland's purchase FDR was still actively selling the system in Britain and offering to customize it for the UK market. However, the bank opted to undertake their own conversion, a decision that subsequently seems to have been wise. In 1987 FDR set up their own UK bureau and went into direct competition with card-processing centres for third-party contracts, so they no longer marketed the package except on a sold-as-seen basis. They would not modify or maintain it, and any purchasers were very definitely on their own. The only regular maintenance contact that Bank of Scotland was to have with FDR was through a users' newsletter from which they can request enhancements. However, as the Centre AGM explained:

the longer we go the more difficult that becomes because some of these enhancements depend on having previous enhancements. And if you haven't got that fixed in, you're not in a position to get the new thing. Plus the fact that we did so much modification of the package in the early stages that it bears very little resemblance to what was actually sold to us.

The work MSD's newly formed VISA team did on the new package was indeed significant. Before design could begin, they had to buy the network management system from IBM to run the package. With no experience in this area themselves, and the deadline looming fast, they had to hire in programmers with this experience and train them very quickly in the bank's systems and standards. The package was finally purchased and delivered in February 1986, and all the modifications had to be completed, tested and working by September that year. The senior manager of the VISA development team stressed the work pressure this created. There was no leeway on the 1st September deadline, so he had to 'pour money and resource at it', working overtime and weekends throughout the preceding four months.

The modification work included tailoring the credit scoring system to meet UK credit criteria and consumer credit legislation, and automatic referencing of applications to credit agencies and county court judgments on debtors. This basic redesign work applied to all parties who use the VISA Centre facilities. However, further 'exclusive' score-card design work was needed to enable VISA Centre to use score-cards, both as a marketing tool and as the means to put in rule-form the finely tuned decisions about customers—to ensure that, in the words of the Planning and Development Manager, 'we are not cutting off too late and ending up with a lot of bad debts, or too soon and finding that we're rejecting that lovely band in the middle where most of your profit comes from'. Such information could only be owned and used by the bank. MSD's design work, therefore, had to allow for any third parties using the Centre's facilities to have score-cards uniquely tailored for them.

Technical Systems and Centre Functions

Following the choice of FDR, a range of complementary hardware and software was acquired during 1986 and 1987. This round of decision-making on 'what VISA needs' was perhaps more difficult and drawn out than the initial decision to buy the processing package. In the first place there were difficulties in knowing what a credit centre needs in terms of skills and organization structure. Secondly, there were difficulties in deciding which parts of the operation should be located in the VISA Centre and which hived off to other sites in the bank. Finally, as we will see, these difficulties presented themselves in a technological form—that of choosing from a range of possible processing systems.

One of the first tasks was for the managers to make an extensive tour of credit-card sites in the UK and Ireland to find out what work went on within them and what shopping list of equipment VISA Centre would need. Interestingly, although these were direct competitors, this did not seem to affect the co-operation that individual site managers were willing to give to others wishing to set up. VISA Centre managers spent a lot of time at this stage in operations such as Barclaycard, Trustcard, Amex and VISA International, obtaining information on configurations of equipment and the efficient running of systems. From Bank of Scotland's point of view, however, this combination of fact-finding and the drawing up of an inventory of equipment was unusual. Normal practice would have been for MSD to evaluate and select technical equipment without direct user involvement. But, as both the Centre Operations Manager and Systems Support Manager pointed out, the coming deadline and the fact that many of the VISA Centre managers were recently ex-MSD, made them as competent as MSD to choose equipment. So this somewhat hectic, 'make it up as you go along' approach was deemed acceptable.

MSD and the small number of VISA managers in place in 1985 opted not to have a Centre mainframe but to use the (fairly) new technology of megastreams to link VISA Centre with MSD's mainframe. This solved a problem for VISA in that they did not have to attract skilled operations staff to work in the splendid isolation of Dunfermline's business park. For security reasons they also decided not to build a new plastic embossing unit in the Centre, but to expand the MSD unit instead. (As an interesting aside, they went to some trouble to make the Centre secure so as to deter burglars who might assume that the plastic embossing unit was located there.) With these functions gone, the Dunfermline site was clearly taking shape as an operation predominantly made up of semi-skilled part-time local women overseen by a nucleus of managers.

The White-Collar Factory

Work organization at the Centre resembled a computer-based assembly line. Several hundred dumb terminals were linked to the mainframe for the entry of customer data and answering customer queries through the FDR package. The majority of staff worked on the terminals in a large open-plan space, subdivided at intervals by screens to separate off different functional areas. Except for the handful of women who directly supervised the labour process, all the work was screen-based; and all the pressures of cost and volume characteristic of highly intensive work systems were very much in evidence.

When you pay £50,000 per machine—you know, it cost us between half and three-quarters of a million to put that system in place. Then if a girl's away yattering or away wandering around the building, then we are not using the machines. So we do make sure that we have a reasonable throughput. (Operations Manager)

Efficiency reflected the operators' speed in putting through work as applications handlers and payment clearers. For example, the Centre management opted for a local telephone exchange system and a payments processing system, both of which made the women's work easier to monitor. The telephone exchange system, an IBM 1750, enabled calls to be distributed automatically and re-routed through the operators. The system alerts the supervisor if the woman taking the incoming call is longer than 30 seconds on the line. By then she should have either passed the call on to the correct area, or finished checking and answering the requested account details via her own terminal.

Customer payments processing was also run from the VISA Centre, although there was quite a debate within the bank before this decision was made. As with the argument for not establishing plastic embossing in Dunfermline, the Clearing department mounted a strong claim for this work, based on the automatic remittance facility it had in place for processing Giro and cheque payments. But VISA Centre management succeeded in getting the entire payments system located in Dunfermline: 'the decision was really to do with speed of response and trying to avoid confusing the customer. We didn't want one address for the customer to deal with for queries and another one to send their payments to' (Assistant General Manager).

Similarly, in the choice of technical systems the same emphasis on the efficiency of the woman-machine interface appeared. One of the Operations Manager's first jobs was to find a card payments system which could handle the industry standard. He set up a team of people from the bank's Clearing department and Standards department (O&M) and invited proposals 'from everyone I knew that produced paper handling equipment'. Detailed specifications were set out on the systems required, cost and time-scale; and the team of managers visited sites separately, 'so that we wouldn't get into the situation of just colluding with each other'.

Attention to the detailed nature of the work was considerable. The Operations Manager stressed how the Giro process especially needed redesigning because the poor readability of OCR (optical character recognition—as against the 'low tech' MICR) slowed down the women's speeds. They installed several remittance machines which, apart from needing the operator to key in the original data, have automated most of cheque clearance.

It MICR's the document, it captures the information, it puts a reference number on the back of the cheque and account slip, or the credit slip if it's come from the Clearing Department. It films the documents, back and front, and sorts them into buckets for whatever bank you want to clear them to. And it does all that in one operation at a speed of about 2,000 transactions an hour for the Giro credits and somewhere like 800 an hour for documents that involve keying in. (Operations Manager)

Developing the Work of VISA Centre

We have seen that the VISA labour force was polarized between a large number of part-time women doing unskilled jobs and a small number of permanent managers holding the 'career jobs' of planning and overseeing the work. When the Centre opened in late 1986, 180 people were employed to handle the 300,000 to 400,000 Bank of Scotland cards coming through. The Centre, however, was built with a capacity of over 1.5 million cards, so from the outset there were moves to develop further Bank of Scotland cards, to sell more cards, and to sell the Centre as a bureau facility.

By mid-1988 they had launched a new company charge card and were in the process of establishing their own Access/Mastercard, and they subsequently increased the sales of Bank of Scotland cards with innovations such as a 'charity card' which links each card sold to a charitable donation. Also, as Barclays were clearing out their third-party clients, Bank of Scotland was able to pick up Marks & Spencer and the Halifax fairly quickly. In 1987 they lost Marks & Spencer, but acquired a major new customer in Chase Manhattan, whose own cards came close to the half-million break-even point.

The VISA Centre now handled over a million cards, and once it launched its new Access card it would probably change its name to the Card Services Division, which would signal its being run as a profit centre. Strictly speaking, this was the case at the time of the study, although until recently the success of the Centre was not judged in terms of profit. As the Operations Manager put it, 'our role here is just another financial service for the bank. The fact that we can do some third-party processing and make some money as well is a bonus point really.' The definition of success had only very recently shifted from the number of accounts the Centre ran to the level of profit being made.

Organizational Links

The Systems Development department within the VISA organization was of special significance as the main route for VISA's contact with MSD. All changes to the systems manuals were routed through the Systems Development Manager. The reason for centralizing MSD's contact through one person was because the VISA Centre had its own user testing located in Dunfermline. On-site user testing made VISA unique in the bank. To separate user testing from programming and systems testing (which were done in MSD) was cumbersome and involved duplication of effort, but this arrangement reflected special aspects of the credit-card business.

Everyone else relies on MSD saying, 'Yes, it's OK', and being what they are, they'll have missed out in some way. Maybe got a cross-reference inside the program wrong. And we have user testing here because ours is a unique system. And maybe also possibly because we asked for it. (Systems Development Manager)

MSD and the bank's auditors had been happy to release user testing to VISA since credit-card processing worked on single-entry bookkeeping, unlike every other bank system which was double-entry. As the Systems Development manager explained, if user testing were to remain in MSD (who did not have experience of single-entry systems), we would have to either not user test at all or user test on the live system and have dummy accounts, which would make our auditors somewhat nervous—having accounts on the live system with transactions, with balances and so on, which would affect the bank's balance sheet. And if we wanted to test message-sending, it would affect Barclaycard or Trustcard, or VISA International in Omaha. So there were severe risks in not having a separate test system.

MSD's relationship with VISA was probably closer than with any other bank division. The VISA Centre was set up, as we have seen, with the choice of its technical systems and control of the woman-machine interface as priorities. From the earliest stages MSD managers were involved in weekly planning meetings with VISA managers and the two groups continued to meet regularly. VISA, an almost wholly automated facility, could not proceed with any plans for new products or new bureau clients unless it enlisted MSD's support in terms of development and maintenance time. This applied to current plans to launch new cards, and at a routine level all the terminal-based work in the Centre faltered if MSD accidentally disrupted the live system. It was not surprising, then, that MSD should think of VISA as 'better organized than any other area of the bank'. To MSD, VISA represented the nearest thing to a department conceived around their model of 'the good user'.

PART I
STRATEGY

The nature of organization strategy has long been of practical and analytical concern. Strategy is often seen as the top management function determining the direction the organization takes—what business activities are pursued, which markets are served, and which innovations and technologies are taken up. Strategy connects the firm to its environment, and through its formation and implementation ultimate success or failure is determined. Strategy is thus the chief means by which organizations seek to overcome uncertainties.

But, as we saw in Chapter 1, beyond these general observations there is little consensus. Rationalistic models have been widely criticized and, indeed, many managers themselves are all too aware of the problems of implementing grand plans due to friction in the organizational structure or resistance from groups. This has stimulated models in which initial plans are seen as 'attenuated' by negotiations down the hierarchy, before strategy is implemented. Other models move even further from rationalist assumptions to conceive of strategy as an 'emergent' phenomenon, while at the extreme some suggest that politics dominate so that strategy becomes a purely symbolic process, accompanying a more basic power play.

With regard to innovation, the unequal distribution of expertise in some ways simplifies and in other ways complicates these problems of analysis. Groups with key knowledge may be remote from the central commercial activities of the firm. And typically senior management may be relatively ignorant of the technical domain. Thus the innovative nature of IT suggests that top-down models will not serve in any case. On the other hand, new groups of experts like IS specialists present problems not only with the supply of expertise, but also with the definition of what constitutes expertise. Since IS is a strategic domain of knowledge, many groups will have an interest in controlling the area, which becomes contested terrain.

In this part these issues of strategy are related to the nature of IS expertise. The chapters examine how the knowledge deployed in innovation connects with durable organizational relationships and, beyond, with a firm's position in the sector. The themes explored highlight the links between the sector, the structures of expertise, and the strategic management of IT. We see how the social construction of knowledge connects economic pressures with the politics and structures of the organization. In the 1980s the emergence of a deregulated (and newly regulated) financial services industry was accompanied by erosion of pre-existing recipes and the dissolution of long-established networks. But such disruptive trends also made it possible for expert groups to renegotiate their positions. Innovation projects formed the terrain on which IS functions in particular sought to assert control over material or symbolic resources and strengthen their organizational role, as well as the means by which firms negotiated uncertainty.

In Chapter 4, we look at the relationship between firm and sector. We examine the role of the social construction of knowledge in connecting organizational action and environmental change. And we examine how our case firms interpreted and mediated sectoral uncertainty. While research has tended to rely on single firm studies, we explore how firms *negotiate the sector*—how they position their products in the market, and how the collective outcomes of action shape the sector itself. We note that the same market and same broad recipes for success can present very different problems to firms with apparently similar technologies. Negotiating the sector thus means combining market control with the sectoral interpretations available to the firm through its knowledge networks.

Firms are also characterized by unique configurations of competences and human resources. Relationships of co-operation and control persist between different kinds of specialist expertise. This *structure of expertise*—the theme explored in Chapter 5—allocates organizational roles to different expert groups (as in the management of innovation projects), as well as providing the framework for top-level decision-making.

We explore here how sectoral uncertainty produces tensions in established structures of expertise. The efficacy of the knowledge claims that IS groups are able to mobilize is built around technical expertise. But the competing knowledge claims exerted by more established groups of financial experts (bankers, accountants, actuaries) can act as a constraint on their success. Nevertheless, successful IS knowledge claims should reflect on the resources and influence that IS experts command, and should see their interpretation of sectoral positioning become a reference point for future policy. We describe instances in which technological innovation created space for the IS group to make claims to strategic knowledge and renegotiate the status of its expertise.

This emergent 'problem-space', and attempts to fill it, are further explored in Chapter 6. Here we view the innovation process as a site for defining the power, knowledge claims, and identity of the IS group. We consider how this may reinforce the dependence of the organization on the products and skills of IS workers. We also consider how IS groups may use innovative projects to strengthen their grip on the means of representation, that is, the symbolic practices through which organizations monitor and interpret their activities and knowledge.

A particularly important element in forms of managerial representation is the discourse of strategy. As a type of rationality, strategy is a means of organizing and monitoring cause-and-effect relationships, and secures institutional legitimation for managerial actions. As we discuss in Chapter 6, where IS functions deploy a *strategic rationale* as a way of coping with the uncertainties of innovation, this discourse acts as a vehicle for advancing their knowledge claims within the management structure. However, as the case studies show, whatever success these strategic claims enjoyed owed less to rhetorical fervour than to the IS group's ability to substantiate their claims through the implementation of innovative systems. The ability to manage strategic innovation depends ultimately on the shifting position of IS management in the structure of expertise, and on the ability of IS workers to deal with the contingencies of projects.

4

The Negotiation of the Sector

During the period of research, financial services was undergoing sweeping legal and regulatory changes which were challenging institutional demarcations. As barriers between banks, building societies, and insurance companies were lowered, new products, market segments, and organizational relationships became possible. In addition, IT systems had important effects on the interface between the organization and its customers. Some of the systems in our case firms we saw were prompted by competitor initiatives, and all depended to some degree on supplier networks and occupational links which traversed the sector. Thus an analysis of the firm's relationship to the sector has an important bearing on understanding strategic innovation.

One of the main problems of analysis, however, lies in the attempt to synthesize different frameworks. An emphasis on the inner dynamics of the firm tends to underestimate the contribution of external groups and networks, while precedence given to the market plays down the role of organizational forces in stimulating and shaping innovation. An emphasis on studying the firm in its sector was explicitly developed to surmount problems of the 'artificiality of absolutes like sector determinism versus unconstrained volition, or objectivity versus subjectivity' (Child and Smith 1987: 371). This attempts to overcome an epistemology based on the 'focal' organization which has tended to attach to strategy. Here material changes are seen as occurring in a market or environment, to which constructs of ideas (strategies) are developed in response. In contrast to this, firm-in-sector theorists have stressed that constructs also come from the environment. Particularly if externalities are recast as structured industrial sectors (rather than abstracted 'markets' or 'environments'), inputs in the form of recipes for action can be much better conceptualized. These develop at the sectoral level and are interpreted in the particular organization.

Still, the firm-in-sector approach was developed through a small number of longitudinal case studies of single firms and, as we noted in Chapter 1, may have shortcomings in examining the relationship between the organization and the broader sectoral context. Our own research based on case companies and projects encountered a range of inter-firm networks, including those involved in the supply of technology, occupational networks of technical and other specialists, and networks for information exchange between firms. This allowed us to chart how actors from interlocking organizations participated in the social construction of the sector and mediated the forces shaping it. In particular, we show how the expertise resources of groups combine in the formulation and implementation of strategic choices. Different expert groups were constantly striving to make sense of the firm's position in its sector, and rivalry between their interpretations was an important influence on the timing and scope of innovation.

SECTORAL STRUCTURE AND COMPETENCIES

To understand the basis on which firms negotiate their sector, we need to examine long-term interaction between the key competencies in firms and the emergence of major structures of the sector. Studies of sectoral evolution like Abernathy (1978) and Whipp and Clark (1986) argue for a convergence in the relationship between firm-level competences and structural features of the sector. This happens over time through processes of competitive evolution and organizational learning. As competition intensifies, the range of organizational choice is increasingly limited and firms engage in 'active learning' from rivals (Child and Smith 1987), reinforcing the tendency for a particular model to become dominant. Up until the 1980s this pattern was evident in the different components of the financial services sector. In particular, firm competences had become closely intertwined with structural features.

In Chapter 2, for example, we stressed how retail financial services evolved in tandem with the development of specialized competences. Trust in financial dealings, and its links with an industry culture of prudence and conservatism, are important for all financial service workers. Less obvious to the retail customer but equally important is the intermediary function. The delivery of services we saw was only one task; other parts of the intermediary chain may assume greater significance. The investment function, the securing of commissions on policies, the gap between premium returns and claims—all can be critically important for profitability. The industry can also be highly secretive about the details of financial intermediation if these sources are being concealed from the customer, so that an element of mystique is another facet of industry competencies.

Intermediary functions, however, still rely on banking and underwriting skills which continue to dominate. These have inhibited the emergence of general management expertise, including marketing and corporate planning. At the same time, the emergence of IS management reflects the increasingly information-based nature of financial services. The structure and skills of IS functions continue to be shaped by the processing needs of branch networks and policy databases.

Competition and Co-operation

Structural features and competencies constituted significant barriers to entry for the sector as a whole, as well as to intra-sectoral movement. External barriers were reflected in the difficulties institutions faced in penetrating national and regional markets. Barriers included the political and regulatory factors noted above and the competitive importance of infrastructures.

All the Scottish banks had made strenuous efforts to enter the relatively massive English market which represented their major growth route. But this traditionally had depended on a branch network, and of the three Scottish clearers only the Royal Bank has been a big enough player to go down that path. The 'technology route', or substituting for bricks and mortar with card-based delivery systems, we have seen represented a very significant part of the other bank's strategies. But while they remained enthusiastic and have ploughed much investment into these systems, some ambiguity still hangs over their success. To see this as a defensive response is certainly a possible interpretation.

The continued existence of intra-sectoral barriers to change reflected the tendency for growth to occur through acquisition of established businesses, rather than the organic expansion of business. As we saw in the case studies, Bank of Scotland had actually been quite successful in its preference for organic growth, though this was partly a question of making a virtue of necessity. It reflected the bank's competitors having made some less than successful acquisitions, which had not left Bank of Scotland trailing in market share. In contrast to this pattern, insurance was less dependent on branch networks, and both our case firms operated world-wide activities from their Scottish base. Insurance seemed less constrained by these entry barriers, and showed a pattern of organic and acquisition growth. In contrast again, the credit-card business was perhaps an interesting hybrid. Large-scale card operations tend to require the backing of a clearing bank and may come under some of the banks' market constraints—though in Premier's case they were in the process of expanding organically into a UK operation.

The implications of constraints on competition in the sector are equally important. At the level of product marketing, the intermediary and money transmission functions of service providers create a distinctive context for the customer interface. Though some products (travel insurance, for example) are readily purchased as commodities, the importance of trust, product complexity, and reciprocal information flows (the protocols of standing orders and direct debits for current accounts, for instance), tend to limit customer mobility and generate long-term customer loyalty. Local distribution networks, especially in banking, have also encouraged the kind of regional market found in Scotland. Localized distribution together with customer loyalty (and/or inertia) mean that, over the shortrun at least, financial institutions are not competing in a homogeneous market-place but are servicing distinctive market niches. At the same time, the non-material character of financial services constrains the marketing of products. For example, although competition in the current-account area has lead to market segmentation, attempts at competitive differentiation through product branding have had a limited effect.

Competition is frequently tempered by co-operation between firms in the sector. Indeed, an understanding of what was competitive action and what collaborative was itself an important sector-level construct. The VISA Centre case study was a good example here in so far as the case focused on the Centre being set up, a period when competitor/collaborator knowledge was to the fore. The manager with responsibility for getting the equipment in place indicated the different levels on which new knowledge was adapted. He reported that he 'spent half (his) life with Barclaycard and half running about talking to other people finding out what they did'. His contacts included Trustcard, Amex, and Diners in the UK and Ireland, as well as VISA International in the United States. The former sites were all competitors for credit-card business, but this did not affect the co-operation site managers gave to others wishing to set up. There seemed to be a version of normal practice which held for all card operations and referred to universal issues like the cost, availability, and efficiency of systems. As one example, the equipment manager said he learnt what average hourly keying-in rates to be expected from VDU operators.

In addition, bank and building society infrastructures are both linked into the nexus of the clearing system. Clearing-house structures like CHAPS have been opened up to a greater number of players, but a minimum level of co-operation continues to be a requirement for organizations engaged in money transmission. In the past this has constrained individualistic competition especially on the part of the banks. There are significant economies to be gained from co-operatively-based services that enhance customer benefits while spreading the costs between a number of participants. The imitability of certain product innovations means that competitive products can quickly become standardized commodities, subject to the economies of co-operation (Steiner and Teixeira 1990).

These factors tend to blunt the competitive impact of IT-based innovations as far as specific products are concerned. A classic example was the introduction of Automatic Teller Machines (ATMs). ATM programmes were initiated by some banks as a competitive innovation aimed at market share and market size. The favourable customer reaction did not lead to significant competitive advantage, however. Other service providers were able to draw quickly on their knowledge networks and links with technology suppliers to respond imitatively to the ATM innovation. In the case of a network technology like ATMs, there were strong incentives to allow customers to use their cards in other banks' machines. As a result, there has been standardization of card formats (e.g. magnetic data storage) and operating procedures (e.g. the use of Personal Identification Numbers), to provide technical compatibility and to simplify the use of equipment for the customer. Thus there has been a shift away from competitive service provision towards collaboration in the maintenance of a common delivery infrastructure. Indeed, in other areas—notably automated cheque clearing—this combination of economies of scale and network compatibility has promoted technical harmonization between banks.

Given already high levels of product uniformity, the importance of infrastructures and co-operation were an added incentive to uniform pricing and cartel formation. Co-operative behaviour and defensive strategies are reflected in concerted moves such as the major banks' entry into the house mortgage and 'high net worth' segments, the provision of interest-bearing current accounts, the development of common pricing strategies, and alliances with co-operative groups such as Visa and Mastercard (Howcroft and Lavis 1987).

An Emergent Sectoral Paradigm?

The above structural features and associated competences were dominant up to the 1980s, but since then the pace of change and levels of uncertainty in the sector have increased. Hitherto the sector had developed around recipes for action institutionalized in the operations of generic organizational and product forms. This had given rise to the clearing bank based on the current account, the life office based on life and endowment policies, and the building society based on the mortgage. The 1980s produced no obvious replacement for these dominant recipes; but there arose widely accepted though rather diffuse paradigms, in particular the idea of customer service coupled with explorations of the potential of IT. We saw a move from an administrative type of paradigm, in which IT was used mainly to process standardized data, towards a more active engagement with the customer and market. Firms across the sector began to develop extensive customer databases and other customer-oriented applications of IT. A number of banks and building societies also exploited the automation of clerical work in the branches by moving towards open-plan layout and the branch as a 'selling shop'.

In our own cases, in Bank of Scotland, CABINET was the technical basis for a move from a processing orientation to a market orientation. The highly enthusiastic shift towards a new 'marketing culture' was promoted by the business analysts, planners, and some project staff in the Management Services Division. We saw a similar enthusiasm in Premier Financial Services, though this was a case of marketeers entering the parent bank's structure via an acquisition and to some extent conflicting with bank culture.

But there was of course ambiguity here. It remains a matter of interpretation whether we see these changes as a full-blown paradigm or as something more embryonic or transitional. While the scope of IT applications grew, they were generally being employed in support of an existing architecture of service production and delivery. There was little sense of applications as elements of a concerted recipe which would displace established practices. In Mutual Life, for example, the Customer Care initiative had been refocused on human relations-type goals, while the technical systems for the project were slow getting off the ground. The company's massive databases, built around the federal divisional structure, formed islands of automation that acted as a brake on development, and we saw management justifying a much more piecemeal approach. Indeed, in both Mutual Life and Bank of Scotland/ CABINET, integrated database technologies had been eschewed. Thus existing IT systems could also constrain change—the familiar tale of having to rewrite 'ten million lines of COBOL code'—though in this sense the smaller Scottish institutions were frequently said to be quicker on their feet than their English counterparts.

Indeed, even if it were possible to be certain about a new paradigm of customer service emerging, the paradigm itself seems to contain inherent ambiguities. The old professional links between banks and their customers, based on discretion and trust, contained many certainties for managers. But having dissolved this, market relationships become fiercely competitive rather than based on agreed rules. When branches become selling shops, and a new quality of service to customers is a marketing opportunity, the line between service and salesmanship becomes increasingly obscured for managers.

At any rate, only a few relatively small-scale innovations in this period—notably remote banking which we take up below—gave any inkling of what a radically new sectoral recipe might look like. But if the absence of a dominant recipe created uncertainty, this was tempered by the degree of market control exercised by major firms. Their investment in branch infrastructures and related competencies allowed them to dominate certain market niches, making it difficult for competitors to emerge. This helps to explain the tendency for firms to continue to specialize around their traditional core areas. This was especially marked in relation to the building societies, some of whom found it difficult to compete in areas like short-term and unsecured lending given their lack of specialist expertise, while others found it difficult to penetrate technology-dependent product areas such as cheque processing because of high entry costs.

SOCIAL NETWORKS AND KNOWLEDGE EXCHANGE

The uncertainty of an emergent sectoral recipe placed even greater emphasis on the role of occupational and inter-organizational networks in transmitting ideas between firms. In this context, Shearman and Burrell (1987) have focused on the evolution of networks linking organizations with customers, suppliers, and even rivals, and stressed how management becomes 'part of a social network in which common perceptions, attitudes and behaviours are shaped and moulded' (p. 328). Such networks are a basis for exchanging information between organizations and for the exemplary role of significant others like major competitors.

Networks though are not static. Shearman and Burrell suggest they evolve with the sectoral life cycle, exhibiting different characteristics at ideal-typical stages: the community, the informal network, the formal network, and the club. Similarly, Child and Smith (1987) note that the increasing intensity of sectoral competition may alter collaborative networks as secrecy between companies prevails. In the confectionery industry this resulted in the increasing importance of equipment suppliers as sources of information on competitor production strategies. Such networks are particularly important in the development of technological innovations. Clark and Staunton (1989: 158), for example, stress the benefits of borrowing knowledge from other organizations. The strategic unit for technologies they argue is frequently a network of connected or competing firms, sometimes from different sectors.

The fields of knowledge that make up the financial services sector reflect the competencies of financial intermediation and how these have been assembled from disciplinary and experiential backgrounds. However, as sectoral uncertainties began to expose weaknesses in institutional knowledge bases, the interpretations produced by the traditional professional expertise of the industry began to be challenged by other forms of expertise. An example was the conflicting interpretations produced by professional and marketing knowledges. The latter defined users of financial services as 'customers' rather than 'account-holders'. Bankers and actuaries, on the other hand, traditionally saw the sector in institutional terms, emphasizing relationships with account-holders rather than the delivery of products to customers or markets. Only when deregulation opened up a wider scope for market forces did a marketeers' interpretation begin to displace the assumptions of bankers.

A rider to this is that in finance firms the actual carriers of the marketing culture were rarely marketeers. Though established forms of expertise were sometimes able to hold off the challenge of groups such as marketeers by selectively cannibalizing their knowledge, marketing functions did not by and large become powerful players. Our cases show how the changing sectoral context gave additional leverage to supplier networks and specialist IS functions. Where professional knowledge was relatively insular, IS management was engaged in forging inter-sectoral linkages with hardware and software suppliers. Indeed, such suppliers were instrumental in shaping the supply of computing knowledge available to IS managers. We can cite, for example, the role of IBM in the Customer Care project at Mutual Life, or Software Partnership in the Telebank case, to get a sense of the range of services and expertise which suppliers provided. For a key supplier like IBM the sphere of influence extended beyond the act of purchase and included flows of professional personnel, with ex-IBM staff featuring in management positions in a number of our case firms.

Apart from the vertical supply chain, there were significant lateral flows of knowledge and information between IS managers in the same part of the sector. Such co-operative exchanges were qualified by competitive pressures, however, as one IT Manager acknowledged:

We will meet at various times, at various conferences. In DP, for example, there is a bi-annual meeting where we all exchange views on what we're doing in relation to technology. At that level, we may not exchange the various products we are working on or the details of those products. But certainly we don't mind saying, 'We've purchased a number of PCs which are going to do this.' Or 'we've purchased a mainframe computer and a network which is going to do this.'

Some networks deliver information on the sectoral context, but when it comes to strategic developments organizations exploit a range of networks to adapt new knowledges within their existing distributions of expertise. The example above of the development of the VISA Centre showed this happening at several distinct levels. There were flows of expert personnel as managers with appropriate expertise were recruited externally, or from the bank's own Management Services Division, and there were visits to software suppliers and horizontal networks formed with other credit-card companies and card processors.

Negotiating the Sector

Discussion of the role of sectoral networks qualifies the firm-in-sector approach in one important respect. Where the latter emphasizes the transmission of 'recipes' and their assimilation in organizations, we highlight what can be termed the negotiation of the sector. This way of conceptualizing the firm-sector relationship partly concerns the active role of managers and expert groups in constructing the sector. Rather than seeing strategic development as a periodic switch from one recipe to another, it is better viewed as a process in which powerful organizational groups interact with the sector and seek to shape and interpret it. In this sense, negotiating the sector is a skilful process as different parts of the sector are more negotiable than others and the flexibility available to organizations is limited.

There can be a tendency to abstract notions of the environment and to expect firms in a given market to respond in broadly similar ways. But seemingly small differences in the market that an organization faces, and in its resources and expertise, will give rise to divergent strategic responses. Similarly, the notion of competition itself tends to be a rationalizing idea; whereas firms that 'compete' might be expected to exhibit like behaviour, in reality firms look for market niches and ways of avoiding head-on competition. The positioning of products in a complex market suggests highly differentiated activity, much of which is negotiated lower down in organizations, emphasizing the extent to which expert groups make a difference in strategic choices. The IS functions in our case firms often responded in highly specific ways to their sectoral contexts in positioning new products.

Emphasis on negotiation also reflects distinctive features of financial services as compared with the manufacturing paradigm that has informed many other studies. In particular, localized distribution patterns and regional markets have created unique market niches for the major financial institutions. This gives management a degree of control over at least part of the sector. There are also opportunities for more extensive control provided by sectoral incentives for inter-firm collaboration and the resulting alliances. These have played an important part in absorbing market uncertainty. Some elements of the sector, of course, are not so malleable. For instance, though the industry was able to exert some influence on the final form of regulatory mechanisms during the upheavals of the 1980s, ultimately legal intervention proved to be a *fait accompli* to which they mostly had to adapt. Thus between the completely negotiable and the non-negotiable parts of the sector, there exists a middle ground where influence and interpretation hold sway.

Negotiating the sector is partly an exercise in the effective deployment of market power. But equally important is the careful adaptation of the firm's position. Here we confirmed that sectoral networks were an important source of ideas and interpretations for decision-making. Indeed, a senior executive at Bank of Scotland suggested that networks were deliberately constructed for the purpose of manipulating sectoral boundaries, rather than simply for business opportunities. He spoke about keeping his finger on the pulse by discussing commercial issues with many groups.

Like we would discuss them with IBM. We will discuss things with British Telecom. We will discuss things with the Halifax Building Society with which we have a joint credit-card company or the AA for joint business. Or Standard Life whose insurance policies we sell, or all sorts of different people. For example, we own 22 per cent of First Mortgage Securities Ltd. which is a competitor of the Mortgage Corporation of National Homeloans. Why did we go into that? Why do we own 22 per cent of it? Because it gives us another window in a different world. If you walk down Princes Street you will see on shops: 'VAT refunds for tourists.' We have an associated company, in which we own 50 per cent, called the Foreign Exchange Company which is the market leader in that business . . . We try and have as many windows in as many different parts of the business as we possibly can. And we will try experiments here, there, and everywhere.

The emphasis on such 'experiments' indicates the types of problem facing financial institutions. With no great sense of a dominant recipe, uncertainty reflected conflict rather than consensus, and different kinds of expertise and networks tended to compete to articulate the most compelling account of the changing environment. In several of our case firms, expert groups within management constructed competing understandings of the firm's position in the sector. In this sense conflicting views over what systems should be developed, and what they should look like, reflected the claims to knowledge of how the organization should be positioning itself. The credibility of differing views hinged partly on their concordance with whatever consensus did exist across the sector, and partly on the status and influence accorded to the expert group within the business. The latter depended on the access enjoyed by different experts to strategic decision-making, but high status did not itself insulate the construction of sectoral interpretations from internal organizational processes. Attempts to negotiate the sector were realized through internal processes of competition and negotiation involving a range of expert and generalist groups within management.

Explicit formulation of strategy tended to be a secondary influence on the development of strategic innovations. What often mattered was the relationship between the IS function and top management. Technological uncertainty was frequently used by IS management to highlight the importance of their role in harnessing IT and in responding to the competitive sectoral context. While certain areas of core computing had been so routinized they no longer caused senior management much anxiety, the implications of IT systems for product innovation were becoming a cause for concern. Thus, in some organizations, IS management was able to present a convincing interpretation of the need for IT, so boosting the IS function's part in attempts to negotiate the sector.

The Case of Remote Banking

In this context, the technology of remote banking provided a good illustration of the way in which sectoral and competitive relations could enhance the status of well-placed expert groups. Scottish-based banks had particular reasons for an interest in this technology. Here was a system which had the potential to compensate for the regional concentration of their branch networks and give them access to new customer segments. The Scottish banks' enthusiasm for these systems was an important element in their negotiation of sectoral uncertainties. We will compare three systems in operation at the time of the research: Bank of Scotland's HOBS, the Royal Bank's Royline, and Clydesdale's Telebank (the latter two being subjects of our case studies). We show how variations in this technical solution reflected the banks' attempts at positioning their products and negotiating the sector.

By the end of the 1980s, no less than 20 different financial institutions were offering a remote banking product (also termed 'home banking' or 'electronic banking') to their customers. This was despite the fact that demand was still relatively weak and the returns meagre. Beyond the broad concept of delivering banking services to the customer's home or workplace, no dominant recipe had emerged to define either the delivery system or the market segmentation for this offering. There were many permutations of infrastructure, delivery system, and end-user from which remote banking products were being assembled.

Despite the financial and technological risks, Scottish-based banks were well to the fore in the development of remote banking systems. Their boldness here seems to have been a consequence of their concern to overcome the constraints of a regional base, and of intense pressures for imitating their regional rivals. The major innovator, whose efforts provided a catalyst for others, was Bank of Scotland. The commitment to remote banking as a major element in the bank's negotiation of a changing sector seems to have been a product of three major factors. First, their existing market niche was restrictive. The branch network was heavily concentrated in an already over-branched Scottish market. England, especially the south-east, was much more attractive in terms of growth potential, and as the bank had few branches there it would not be competing with itself (one of the reasons for the cautious approach of the English clearing banks). Thus, the bank was already committed to an 'English strategy' of some sort.

What clinched the development of remote banking, however, were two other elements in the expertise equation. The first was the prospect of a low-risk entry into remote banking via a collaborative relationship. The Nottinghamshire Building Society had made significant progress in overcoming the technical problems of operating remote banking by the Prestel public viewdata system and was actively looking for a banking partner. As the two organizations were not direct competitors, there were few of the usual constraints on flows of information and expertise involved in the design and marketing of the collaborative 'Homelink' system. While the incursion of building societies into banking services was a destabilizing factor in the sector as a whole, in this instance Bank of Scotland was able to manage that uncertainty through the formation of a cross-sectoral alliance. Added to this collaborative link, the other crucial element was the role their Management Services Division (MSD) had come to play in the bank. Under a new General Manager, who had previously been responsible for strategic thinking about IT in the Automation Planning department, MSD had begun to exert a powerful influence on the long-term thinking of senior management. Its role and stature within the bank were an important factor in linking the English strategy to innovative uses of technology.

The launch of Homelink in 1982 was followed in 1985 by the Bank's development of its own Home-and-Office Banking System (HOBS). This Mark II version of remote banking reflected the expertise of MSD and of the bank at large. It was technically successful, reflecting MSD's technological expertise, though the cost and user difficulties associated with Prestel reduced its attractiveness to corporate customers.

We can contrast Bank of Scotland's attempts to negotiate the sector with those of its rival, the Royal Bank of Scotland. As we saw in the case, the Royal Bank was less constrained by its Scottish base, having acquired an English branch network through its merger with Williams and Glyn's Bank. Within Scotland it also had the strongest corporate customer base, an extremely valuable part of its business and the envy of the other Scottish clearers. Its client base was one the Royal Bank very much wanted to consolidate; and the remote banking service that was developed, Royline, was a cash management system targeted at these corporate clients. It was not designed to span different sectors (personal, small business, etc.) in order to spread its market; it was aimed exclusively at the large business end. The functionality of the system we saw was very powerful; it was based on high-level PC technology and made use of specialized telecoms links, again not the type of facility designed for home use nor for many small businesses.

The stimulus for innovation came partly from the top, in terms of senior management's awareness of corporate cash management in the United States, but also from systems developers in terms of the understanding they claimed to have of client needs. These strategic inputs stemmed from a client sector well able to demand a high level of service, and a powerful internal systems development function that saw advantages in articulating these needs.

At the same time as the Royal Bank was developing Royline, the third Scottish bank, the Clydesdale, had explored yet another way of acquiring a remote banking product. At this time, the IS division within the bank was mobilizing itself around the aim of achieving greater autonomy from Clydesdale's parent, Midland Bank, and remote banking offered an ideal opportunity for IS to assert itself. But Clydesdale lacked the range of resources and expertise needed to emulate the in-house developments at Bank of Scotland or the Royal Bank. However, as in the Homelink project this was an instance where a bank exploited its sectoral networks to construct an appropriate mix of expertise. IS management at Clydesdale used the occupational grapevine to identify an external sofware house with the skills to take on a major part of the project.

The end-product of the joint Telebank development was unique to Clydesdale. The front-end systems were developed as a platform on which a range of remote banking facilities could be installed (allowing access via viewdata and also by personal computers with modems and by voice operated systems across the telephone). Telebank may have been a less powerful and elegant system that either Royline or HOBS, but its modular structure meant it was highly flexible and so suited the needs of both partners to the development.

Conclusion

The remote banking example provides insight into the way in which Scottish-based banks negotiated their sector *vis-à-vis* each other. There were elements of firms responding to unique market niches, of technological change being stimulated by suppliers and competitors' actions, and of the role of occupational networks in navigating the emerging terrain of a deregulated sector. Equally, the comparison of developments across the three banks revealed the importance of an intra-management negotiating process in constructing the sector for each firm. These processes of negotiation help to explain the ways in which firms appropriated new technology. In this example each bank developed distinctively different interpretations of the remote banking concept.

The inception and design of IT-based innovations could not be accounted for in terms of the sectoral context alone, nor as the free play of management choice. Rather projects emerged from a process of negotiation between firm and sector which reflected the competition between different forms of expertise. The connections which the negotiation process creates between sectoral change and the organizational distribution of knowledge meant it was unnecessary to make an artificial distinction between 'internal' politics and responses to 'external' context, or to counterpoise the subjective perceptions of management and objective pressures of the market. Negotiating the sector is part and parcel of the processes of competition and co-operation between expert groups reflected in the political ordering of expertise.

However, variations in outcome as well as other generic technologies were not simply a product of negotiation. Longer term structural relationships also produced different distributions of expertise. Even the above account of the organizational role of the IS functions in the banks gave a clear indication that their aspirations and relationships with other management groups reflected the long-run evolution of the firm as much as the contingencies of a particular technology. During a firm's evolution, structural relations between different forms of expertise selectively internalized and legitimated the knowledges and competencies which furnished the 'rules of the game' for the sector. Rules were shaped by the development of the firm itself and by the relative success or failure of particular groups in influencing the pattern of development. In the next chapter, we explore these patterns of the structure of expertise.

5

Structural Position of the IS Function

In examining the managerial processes around expert groups it is clear that expertise is not available 'on tap' to be inserted into decision-making. Nor is it a matter of simply controlling and motivating expert groups. Expertise itself is part of the social construction of knowledge and helps in defining the range of options open to management in the first place.

In the last chapter, we saw the sector being internalized and negotiated through the actions of expert groups. This chapter extends the analysis from the firm-in-sector level to the structural relationships within which the negotiation takes place. These structures of expertise involve relations of dominance and subordination between different forms of expertise, and reflect societal biases favouring professionalism as a mode of deploying expertise. They have evolved to favour certain organizational competencies and specialist forms of knowledge. At the organizational level, the structure of expertise is expressed through political coalitions which keep various forms of expertise in states of tension or co-operation with each other.

But structural relations between expert groups are not only about the balance of power. The opacity of expert knowledge to non-experts creates problems of integration and communication; monitoring and the integration of expert activities may be difficult because the expert's work process is tacit and uncertain. There are of course certain advantages to the specialized language of the expert. An elaborate language can facilitate communication and enable the more precise expression of deep knowledge. However, these advantages apply mainly to the internal efficiency of expert groups. For non-experts, the 'insider' language of experts is likely to obscure communication. Specialized language may be used to mystify an expert group's activities and forestall external control.

Thus, while structure fosters particular forms of expertise, by defining task specialization and group formation, structural boundaries can also divide groups. In this sense, careful management of the tensions between specialist knowledges and their integration within an organizational framework is necessary. In our case studies the formal structure of organizations and a variety of linking mechanisms—steering committees, project teams—were important for integrating different knowledges and fostering commitment.

Managing expertise requires the specialist language of expert groups to be related to other knowledge groups and to broader processes of the social construction of knowledge. Structural relations between different forms of expertise need to be related to the levels on which knowledge is constructed and deployed. Here the competing claims advanced by different kinds of experts within the organizational arena, and their ability to influence their structural position defines how expertise informs managerial actions and their legitimating rationalities. In technological innovation, relations between groups are sustained by the projects which get selected and how their development is managed. By influencing structure, powerful expert groups are able to manipulate organizational context so that their own specialist knowledge becomes indispensable (R. E. Miles and Snow 1978).

ORGANIZATIONAL STRUCTURE OF EXPERTISE

The formal distribution of tasks and responsibilities reveals much about a company's characteristic forms of management. However, structuring tendencies that create and deploy knowledge, and define the distribution of tasks, operate outside the formal level. Beyond formal structuring the knowledge claims of different occupational groups and competition between them helps to define the broad 'jurisdictional boundaries' within which the organizational roles and responsibilities become established (Abbott 1988). Below the formal level, longitudinal studies have highlighted the long-term effect of deeply sedimented rules and repertoires which emerge from organizational learning and sectoral evolution. They underpin the basic competencies of the organization and institutionalize forms of tacit knowledge.

Different elements of the structure of knowledge—the surface representations of formal structure, the provisional and occupationally networked expertise of professional groups, the sedimented formations of organizational knowledge—interact in a variety of possible ways. For example, Kogut and Zander (1992) see the 'higher order organizing principles' of embedded organizational knowledge as being partially reified in formal structure. Such 'principles' interlock with the rules and incentives governing group relations to produce coherent organizational responses. Technological innovation is seen to run more or less smoothly on these interlocking tracks (Kogut and Zander 1992: 389). However, this analysis tends to privilege the functional needs of the organization over processes of conflict and contradiction.

A more critical view would highlight the tensions between different forms of expertise. Indeed in our case organizations, the deployment of IS expertise created a significant amount of friction with firms' institutional structures and repertoires. Nor was the tension between IS expertise and traditional forms the only source of conflict. Certain groups such as bankers, actuaries, and investment managers have been privileged within financial institutions, and the position of IS in this sectoral context remained an important structuring influence. But while IS expertise has traditionally been relatively subordinate, its assimilation into an institutional repertoire was less important than the developing competition and co-operation between IS workers and other

groups. The uncertainties of sectoral and technological change created possibilities for realignment, and the role of IS functions in managing strategic
innovation reflected their growing stature in relation to traditionally dominant
groups. In this chapter we explore the changing position of IS within these
broader structures of expertise.

IS Expertise and Occupational Control

The occupational formation of expertise and structural relations at corporate
level are often interpreted in terms of a clash between the business orientation
of management and the occupational (i.e. 'technical') orientation of the IS
worker. 'The inherent conflict between management and professionals results
basically from a clash of cultures: the corporate culture which captures the
commitment of managers, and the professional culture, which socializes
professionals' (Raelin 1991: 1). Such interpretations, however, sidestep the
question of the centrality or marginality of IS expertise in organizations.

An occupational orientation for IT careers is not buttressed by any significant professional organization. The British Computer Society, for instance,
has comparatively little professional control over entry to the occupation.
Apart from an increasing preference for graduate entry, none of our case
firms required professional or vocational IT qualifications; indeed, in one
case, a computer science degree was seen as a positive disqualification. This
conformed with earlier survey findings which suggest that tiny proportions
(usually less than 5 per cent) of British IS managers demand a computer
science degree from their graduate intake (see Friedman 1989: 312). Thus IS
workers are not 'professional' in the classic sense of occupational control
having been attained outside the arena of organizational or state employment.
Their professional ethos and occupational status have evolved within organizational employment, and they fall into the category of the 'organizational
professional' (Friedson 1986: 32). Or as Whitley puts it: 'These rely on the
appropriation of a distinctive cognitive base to justify their monopoly of
particular problems and some autonomy in the selection and use of problem
solving procedures but share control over task allocation and assessment with
employers' (1988: 7).

IS expertise reflects a broader occupational formation linked to changing
technological knowledges and labour markets, while the deployment of such
expertise is influenced by norms of task allocation and assessment determined
within organizations. This has important implications. IS experts have options
on both organizational and occupational (i.e. multi-organizational) careers.
But the 'occupational project' of IS workers located in large user firms is
mostly about gaining status and influence within organizations, not autonomy
from them. Unlike in the pre-industrial professions, IS expertise has no legal
or institutional guarantees or protection. The task domain of most IS workers
has to be secured through rivalry and accommodation with other organiza-

tional specialisms. It follows that organization structures for IS staff have a dual character: they enshrine broader societal preferences by institutionalizing the jurisdictional boundaries between specialist groups (Abbott 1988), and the deployment of IS expertise is constrained as much by organizationally determined rules as by the cognitive base of the occupation itself.

In our study, organizational attempts to rationalize the IS role (thereby making it more predictable) were balanced by attempts to exploit the possibilities of IT for business purposes. Though we found little evidence of computing staff moving into the user departments of financial service firms, there were significant reorganizations of the computing function in order to accommodate and promote a business orientation in IT development work.

Expert Knowledge and Sectoral Context

Sectoral conditions in financial services clearly favour the application of IT. The sector has no material products and financial transactions are essentially information manipulations, so the scope for IT use is practically unbounded. However, as we have stressed, the sector is founded on the skills of financial intermediation. Although IT crucially supports such skills, by automating administrative processes and delivering services, profitability is still driven by the revenues from financial intermediation, not service provision.

The sectoral shaping of finance organizations has important implications for structural relationships between different groups. It helps to shape the arena in which knowledge claims are negotiated and competence demonstrated. The primacy attached to financial intermediation, for example, tends to cast IS expertise in a supporting role. As one senior bank executive in our study put it: 'We are not selling technology; we make money from the margin between the cost of deposits and the interest rate on loans.'

The sectoral context also affects the distribution of IS expertise in other ways. In banking and building societies (though not in insurance), elaborate branch infrastructures provide the local presence needed for customer relationships, and also provide great scope for IT applications. IT infrastructures developed linking branches with headquarters and with central clearing institutions. But this massive investment in branch networks has tended to inhibit development of a product-market basis for organizational structure (Storey 1987). Financial services remain difficult to 'brand' and have developed around generic products: the current account, the endowment policy, the mortgage. Investment in elaborate delivery systems has encouraged their use as the primary marketing channel in order to achieve economies of scale.

These structural factors explain the highly centralized location of IS functions. This yields important advantages including the cross-utilization of technical staff, a secure environment for mainframe computers, reduced needs for local data centres, and economies in the cost of software licensing

Bank of Scotland

Within the (non-executive) Board of Directors, chartered accountants were the largest professional group: 4 CAs in the 16-person Board.

At Management Board level, 7 of the 8 General Managers were Fellows of the Institute of Bankers (Scotland).

Mutual Life

At Board of Director level, chartered accountants were the most numerous professional group: 5 CAs or FCAs in a total of 14.

Within the Executive, actuaries (FFAs) were predominant: 17 of 29.

Home and Auto

Board of Directors: 2 CAs and 2 members of the Chartered Insurance Institute.

Executive: 2 CAs, 2 members of the Chartered Insurance Institute, 2 members of the Institute of Chartered Secretaries and Administrators.

FIG. 5.1 *Composition of Executive and Non-Executive Boards* (*Source*: Company Annual Reports 1988 and 1989)

agreements. Whatever the physical location of the IS function, however, its position within organizational structures of expertise has been determined very largely by the dominance of the mainstream finance professions. Many decades and even centuries of authority in financial institutions have given groups such as accountants, bankers, and actuaries a great advantage over IS expertise with a mere 30 years in the sector. The banking profession goes back several centuries, during which time accredited banking skills were formed out of the amalgamation of key activities in deposit-taking and lending. These included elements of what we would nowadays call, marketing, namely an understanding of the financial and infrastructural foundations of the bank, and the kind of local knowledge helpful for ensuring the acceptability of banking institutions.

The influence of the traditional expert groups reflected their heavy representation in senior positions, and the significance of their particular qualifications for careers in financial institutions. The banking qualifications of the Chartered Institute of Bankers in Scotland and the statistical expertise of the actuary in the insurance sector are pertinent examples. Actuaries make up the greatest per centage of professionally qualified staff in UK life offices, while in Scotland life offices seem to recruit and train more actuaries than they actually need (Draper *et al.* 1988).

The penetration of such professional knowledge to the top of the managerial hierarchy is shown in Figure 5.1, which presents information from three of our case organizations—one each from banking, life insurance, and general insurance. The predominance of qualifications from accountancy and the mainstream finance professions needs to be interpreted with care. Formal qualifications can only convey a limited sense of the influence of different kinds of expertise. Although none of the senior executives or directors possessed accredited qualifications in computing, this did not mean that knowledge of IT or computing was non-existent at senior levels. In our own case studies at Bank of Scotland and the Royal Bank of Scotland, both chief executives at the time of our study had spent time working in the IT or computing field. In the Royal Bank this experience had been gained in the institution's own computing function; at Bank of Scotland the Treasurer and General Manager had previously worked in the computing industry itself.

Corporate Role of IS Expertise

But we also have to be careful not to attach too much significance to job experience. In each of these cases, computing experience had been only part of a varied roster of managerial jobs. Such career patterns are typical of top management, and reveal little about the status attaching to IS expertise or the disciplinary sympathies of individuals. Moreover, the kind of computing experience possessed by these chief executives—dating from the 1950s and 1960s—would be of little direct relevance to current trends and applications.

Comparing the managerial influence of IS expertise with more established disciplines is not easy. Neither formal qualifications nor experience are sufficient. However, some impression of how different kinds of expertise affect the corporate world-view was gleaned from our interviews with senior management. IS expertise still had ground to make up before matching the traditional specialisms in the counsels of top management. For example, despite his functional leadership of the IS group, the Director of the Operations Division at Mutual Life saw no particular expertise or orientation attaching to his job: 'I think of myself as a businessman who happens to be running systems.' Yet, reflecting on his training as an actuary, he was happy to concede that his professional identity transcended functional roles: 'You are either an actuary or you're not—I don't think you become an ex-actuary.'

Understanding the role of expert knowledge in corporate structures (and ultimately in strategy-making) involves taking a longer view of sectoral evolution. From this perspective, the ability of actuaries, bankers, and accountants to maintain dominant positions depends on overall patterns of growth and competition in the sector. The 1980s brought new challenges of scale and diversity of operations to most large financial institutions, which had knock-on effects for the dominant coalition in each institution.

The large increases in business volume affected the demand for IS services, and all IS groups in our sample grew significantly in this period. There was a rise in staff numbers of over 250 per cent in three years at Mutual Life and 200 per cent in four years at Clydesdale—matched by increases in capacity and investment in computing technology. Legislative changes in particular created powerful imperatives for the revision of existing systems and development of new ones. At Mutual Life the ramifications of the Financial Services and Social Security Acts absorbed around 50 person-years of IS labour in one year alone. The increasing utility of IT for handling new administrative problems was also important; staffing increases in the IS function generally exceeded the overall growth rate for companies. There were proportionate increases in the numbers of IS managers and more elaborate internal hierarchies developed.

Another aspect of change was the tendency for financial institutions to grow by acquisition or subsidiary formation, rather than internal means. Among our case studies, Home and Auto acquired a chain of estate agents, the Royal Bank acquired a credit-card company and travel agents, while Clydesdale Bank was itself acquired by the National Australia Bank. Only in the Bank of Scotland's VISA Centre did we see a major development by means of internal growth. This pattern of growth had various operating consequences. At the Royal Bank, for example, growth via merger led to problems in consolidating two or more different computer centres and quasi-autonomous IS functions.

The formation of new corporate structures to manage financial conglomerates represents a potential threat to IS functions. When financial institutions eschew the 'financial supermarket' model of operation (supplying the whole range of financial services from one outlet) in favour of acquisitions and a 'department store' approach, they effectively reinforce holding-company structures. Such structures can affect the ability of IS functions to influence strategic decision-making, as they tend to favour the expert groups—bankers, actuaries, and accountants—who promoted growth by acquisition in the first place. The growing importance of holding-company management structures—with responsibilities to oversee IS operations and migrate IS skills and investment around subsidiaries—may undermine IS groups whose role and expertise are grounded in the core business. Whether the utilization of IS as a group resource will prevail over older structures remains to be seen. New roles may emerge during the power struggles that are in the offing over these diversification strategies.

IS groups might adapt to changing structures. Rockart, for example, has championed a new systems architecture that effectively fits holding-company structures (Rockart 1988; Rockart and Hofman 1992). Here computer applications are devolved to business users and line managers (e.g. in subsidiary groups), while core database functions remain centralized. Such a division of labour need not undermine IS functions' control of technology and might even enhance it. The articulation of database and related network management activities as non-substitutable skills is becoming increasingly evident. Indeed, in some of our cases (at the Royal Bank, for example) we observed an adaptation to such new roles.

STRUCTURE OF THE IS FUNCTION

Sectoral change creates opportunities for IS (and others) to exploit uncertainty. However, the ability to translate functional expertise into knowledge claims at a strategic level depends on how groups relate to the work of the organization, and how they relate to other expert groups. Terming the former 'internal structure' and the latter 'external structure', we can explore the dynamics that enhance or restrict the strategic influence of IS expertise.

Internal Structure

Many aspects of the internal structure of IS (such as systems development methodologies, implementation, user involvement, the division of labour, and career progression) are discussed in detail in later chapters. Here we focus on aspects of internal structure which relate to control of IT developments.

The critical question in this respect is the extent to which the practical details of IS work can be monitored by non-expert groups or managers outside the function. If such control were feasible, the requirements for highly specialist IS expertise and any connection to broader occupational movements would be attenuated; IS workers would become interchangeable with other non-managerial support groups, and IS work would be automated or would lose its special status and become assimilated into other clerical tasks. (Indeed, this has already happened with routine elements of IS work, like data entry and computer operations.) Where such control is not feasible, the management of IS expertise requires the creation of a formal, more-or-less specialized organizational structure, capable of controlling and resourcing the IS function and also of translating its specialist language into the organizational lingua franca. Questions of power and control then tend to centre on management's ability to contain the knowledge claims of the specialist function and to make effective decisions on its resources.

The internal structure of IS has an important effect on its broader organizational role, especially the way in which IS work is controlled by management. As computing technology developed, and applications became more extensively distributed, the scope of the computing function widened, leading to the horizontal division of labour between operations, programming, and systems analysis. Interpretations of this evolving division of labour vary, and some argue it enshrines de-skilling and increased management control (Greenbaum 1976; Kraft 1977).

Our research suggested signs of routinization with respect to more predictable aspects of IS work, But most areas remained highly skilled, confirming Friedman's prognosis.

Technical progress ... which arises from the cumulation of individually minor improvements is also important today. What distinguishes computer systems development is the extent to which technical change of this . . . type occurs. This is, in turn, dependent upon the inherent creativity which still characterizes systems development. (1989: 360)

The proliferation of IT applications has constrained the incorporation of skills into embedded hardware and software, while the uncertainty generated by continued innovation inhibits the routinization of IS work. As applications have moved out of the computer room into the wider organization, so has the mediating scope of IS increased, and requires the incorporation of organizational as well as technical knowledges. Thus many projects are highly dependent on user contacts during implementation (see Chapters 9 and 10). This has encouraged the reintegration of analysis and programming, most often by means of project teams, though in our case firms a more flexible analyst-programmer role was favoured by some—such as the Royal Bank and Mutual Life—which aimed at overcoming the diseconomies of specialization, developing clear career paths, and facilitating user communications.

Project teams were a more common means of pooling knowledge and achieving the co-operation necessary to absorb technological uncertainty. In most of our case firms, systems development was organized around teams, some dedicated to particular user groups and others to specialized tasks. This 'mirror image' division of labour, with groups of analysts and programmers permanently assigned to specific business areas, is very common in systems development; it helped to develop user-specific knowledge and build relationships with external departments. User-dedicated teams were a useful mechanism for controlling how work was prioritized and by whom. This distinctive structure could mean autonomy to develop systems work with little direct control, since programming teams worked closely with users. But it was also mentioned as the means by which programming effort could be focused on managerially defined problems not programmers' own approach to problems.

Labour-market considerations, however, tended to restrict managerial control. For instance the lack of autonomy of the IS function in Clydesdale, while owned by the Midland Bank, restricted its ability to recruit and retain staff. Clydesdale's inability to pursue major projects like IMPACT limited its attractiveness for IS careerists. The cancellation of that particular project damaged IS morale in the short term, and sent a message about the role which the function was to play within the bank. As one Manager noted, staff felt 'the need to be regarded as IT professionals rather than slightly irregular bank staff'. Such a need became easier to fulfil when the bank was acquired by the National Australia Bank, which permitted more local autonomy.

The interplay of task uncertainty and labour-market scarcity has promoted strong internal labour markets for IS workers in financial services. The limited forms of hierarchy which have evolved in IS facilitate internal career paths, as well as providing mechanisms for supervisory control. Managerial cadres in IS tend to be 'player-managers', promoted from the rank-and-file workforce and possessing the knowledge to effect detailed supervision. The strength of the internal IS labour market varies with the ability of organizations to recruit externally and to use temporary and part-time staff.

However, the extensive use of contract staff (which we found to be typical) did not necessarily indicate a weak internal labour market or undermining of the organizational role of IS workers. On the contrary, there was general mistrust of relying too heavily on contract staff, except for highly routinized or specialized kinds of work. The former was not regarded as a threat, because, as one IS Manager put it, 'it allows our people to go and do the more interesting things.' Nor were highly specialized contractors regarded as threatening, as they would normally be contractually-bound to pass on their knowledge to permanent staff. The Senior Project Manager on the Clydesdale/Telebank system, for instance, stressed that for underlying skills (applications, project control) there was little difference between in-house and bought-in effort.

To me there is no difference, really. It's just the type of software you're actually writing. They had expertise in writing software which we didn't . . . But I would say now that it's not true any more. Through working with us, they now have a knowledge of the business side as well. And again, our programmers now have experience in the presentation side.

External Structure

Though formal organization structures take little account of sedimented knowledge, or the role of inter-occupational rivalry in establishing task jurisdictions, they symbolize some aspects of the relative power and status of different forms of expertise. Indeed, changes in the organizational role of IS functions seem to have reflected a shift in top-management expectations which was experienced across the board in UK industry. As Feeny, Earl, and Edwards point out, 'Historically IS has been seen as a specialist unit representing technical excellence; now it faces more challenging requirements and a more senior, demanding customer set' (1989: 15).

Within a pattern of relatively continuous growth, initial forays into computing technology were typically accommodated in accounting functions, followed by steady expansion to departmental and, in most cases, divisional status. Interpretations of the pattern of growth are more variable, however, and reflect uncertainties about the trajectory of IS expertise. This is clear with respect to infrastructural investments in banking. Initially, computer technology was used to automate branch accounting and transaction processing. As branches operated independently at the time, systems were built around the branch as the basic unit, and embodied branch banking protocols such as the definition of customers as account-holders. Later, such infrastructures became constraints on progress; customer databases, for example, involved restructuring data around individual customers rather than account-holders. Similarly,

Corporate Service: unified function reporting to corporate management; any distributed IT is under central IS control. Those interfacing from business units act as 'negotiators'.

Internal Bureau: as above, but run as a separate business unit and profit centre. Charges other units for its services. Businesses may or may not be constrained to use the bureau.

Business Venture: similar to above, but with explicit mission to obtain revenue externally.

Decentralized: each business unit has own IS capability or employs external bureaux. No central IS responsibility except for corporate HQ.

Federal: in addition to above, a central IS unit reporting to corporate management, which has responsibility for certain aspects of policy and architecture across the organization.

FIG. 5.2 *Structural arrangements for IS*

early systems were designed to service branches overnight and were not well adapted for real-time product innovations like ATMs. In contrast, building societies developed real-time systems from the outset because the regulatory framework of the 1970s prohibited overdrafts on building society accounts, necessitating the constant updating of passbooks.

The IS functions in our sample differed somewhat in the detail of their infrastructure and IT systems. There were hybrid forms of internal markets in Mutual Life's boutique system, and at Bank of Scotland moves towards detailed costing of IS activities were well in hand. Still, the cases all fell into the Corporate Service category indicated in Figure 5.2. This contrasted with a broader trend towards federal or de-centralized structures reported by Feeny, Earl and Edwards (1989) and may reflect sectoral pressures towards centralization and constraints on product-market organizations in Scotland. None the less, this may simply be a trend in large institutions; certainly the Scottish-based insurance giants were global players in every sense.

Of course, the 1980s' technological and sectoral uncertainty meant it was unlikely that IS structures could survive without change, and virtually all our sample had reappraised the organizational role of IS expertise. At Mutual Life, structural changes incorporated the Systems department and O&M into an integrated Operations Division with its own General Manager. These changes accompanied the overlay of a functional structure on to product divisions which appeared to result from a shift in senior managers' expectations of IS: the aim was 'to look beyond machines into company operations and relate what the company wanted to do to systems possibilities'.

Organizational changes also took place at Bank of Scotland, where amalgamation of the Management Services and Computer Services Divisions owed much to the conflict within the existing division of labour, particularly when addressing issues with strategic or marketing implications. The bank's management board needed solutions not options in areas of major technological choice like ATMs and customer-services automation. The temporary paralysis of top-level decision-making that the inability to agree a common line had caused pointed up the degree of strategic uncertainty that IS functions normally control.

For the most part, shifting expectations about IS resulted in the incorporation of a wider range of technical tasks, and a voice at senior levels of decision-making through the creation of Divisional General Manager positions. Only in the Clydesdale Bank did we find evidence of fragmentation of the IS function. There a reorganization saw an Electronic Business Division being separated from the existing IS function. But even there the change was less to do with curtailing growth in IS than with handling further growth; Electronic Business was to incorporate plastic card activities and related developments which had hitherto been the responsibility of Clydesdale's parent, the Midland Bank. The 'pure' IS function remained intact and responsible for IT infrastructures.

CONTROL OVER THE IS FUNCTION

Day-to-day deployments could also be managed more easily, and over these the IS function retained much discretion and autonomy. In our case studies IS generally resisted control by other groups, notably business users (see Chapter 10 for more detailed discussion of user relations). These constraints help to explain the elaboration of different control systems, ranging from weak bureaucratic control to financial and market-based arrangements.

Bureaucratic Control

The increasing scope of IT applications brought IS workers into closer contact with users. Users, however, often had limited control over such interactions due to the uncertainty of IS work and the opacity of IS expertise. These factors advantaged IS specialists, especially in the kinds of detailed discussion in steering committees and project meetings. But IS groups did not have everything their own way. Though an imbalance of technical expertise might exist, new applications increasingly demanded marketing and organizational knowledge which strengthened the user's role in the development process. Moreover, the organizationally-convoluted nature of such applications, concerned more with information provision or product delivery than clerical automation, required greater interdepartmental liaison and middle and senior management input. Decision-making about IS resources and priorities could no longer be handily centralized, since user departments had to specify their requirements for practical as well as political reasons.

This created tensions for IS functions, which our case firms managed in a variety of ways. The complete decentralization of IS might appear to be one possibility. But financial service firms have particular features which buttress the centralization of IS expertise; notably, technological evolution around centralized systems supporting branch networks, and inhibitions on product-market divisionalization. Firms thus had to find ways of retaining a centralized IS resource capable of supporting mainframe-based systems, while responding to a widening range of user and market requirements.

In most cases, some form of decentralized organization was mimicked, while the internal coherence of the IS function was maintained. All our case firms incorporated a strong user element in their systems-development teams. Such teams normally responded to the demands of the department they permanently supported, thus building up local knowledge of that department within the team. Some organizations went further in devolving decision-making to user departments. At the Royal Bank of Scotland, for instance, not only did project teams shadow other bank functions, but for each team there was a User Liaison Group in which user management and IS specialists would agree on IT provision for that area. This partial decentralization was often complemented by the use of bureaucratic forms of co-ordination. Such forms preserved a degree of centralized IS control over resources, but gave user groups more-or-less powerful levers over IS decision-making.

One fairly standard device was for some form of project prioritization jointly negotiated by user and IS managements. Project requests from user departments would be ranked according to a combination of IS and user judgements. In the first instance users would assign a priority to their request for an enhancement or new development, and IS staff would agree or reassign it upwards or downwards. In the latter, more usual, case IS would provide users with a detailed justification of why reprioritization was judged necessary. This could accommodate a variety of pressures. It could allow some rational ordering of projects, so that projects which were urgent, feasible, or immediately deliverable at low cost could be quickly sanctioned. On the other hand, it could facilitate political negotiation by allowing IS managers quietly to give precedence to more tractable requests, or more powerful user groups. As the Group Director at the Royal Bank of Scotland wryly commented, 'It's the greetin' wean [crying child] that gets fed.' Project prioritization could act as an insulating device, giving users the feeling that their requests were being considered, while privileging IS staff in decisions over which projects went to the front or back of the queue.

Such prioritization could not defuse all of the tensions between IS and users, however. In some organizations the volume of user demands created an inexhaustible 'wish list', so that resentment emerged against IS as the rationing authority. In Bank of Scotland users gradually became sensitized to technical and cost constraints with experience of the joint prioritization system, and ceased automatically placing all requests as 'urgent'. But in other instances we found IS managers trying alternatives to bureaucratic forms of prioritization. At Mutual Life the IS Manager sought to get user departments to ration themselves, by requiring them to provide staff support for any request for IS development: 'If they're prepared to finance it and commit the staff necessary to support a business development, then we will provide the IS support . . . IS won't be the constraint.' This policy worked in parallel with a market metaphor—if not a thoroughgoing market mechanism—and the boutique arrangement for accessing facilities resources. By treating users as customers, IS management in Mutual Life sought to avoid the problems of a welfarist form of prioritization. Even so, the need for centralized control could not be ignored, and the Operations Director admitted that IS retained resources for their own technical infrastructure, to 'keep our own standards up to date'.

Financial Control

IT poses particular problems for financial control. What Steiner and Teixeira (1990) call the 'tyranny of shared costs' reflects the difficulty of apportioning central IT costs to users because of the infrastructural nature of the technology. Most organizations have some formal mechanisms for apportioning costs, but their accuracy is qualified by the additional costs of monitoring IT work and by the need for flexible relationships between IS and user departments. The use of common delivery systems—the bank branch being the classic example—makes the allocation of costs to specific products even more problematic.

IS activities have proved more intractable to accounting controls than, for example, more visible and routine manufacturing activities (Armstrong 1987). A manager in the Bank of Scotland's accountancy function also acknowledged this difference.

You can look at an engineering factory and you can see the product being built and you can say well that should not have taken twice as long as that, except maybe there is a bit more stress or a bit more sophisticated welding in doing that. It's very difficult to do that with a development project when it is all done on a computer. . . . If you can record your man-hours on the project, you have still got this problem with processing capacity, it's difficult to isolate completely.

But these difficulties do not imply that controls are insignificant. While it is difficult for an accounting function to exercise direct control, accounting controls may still be effective by providing a common language and unifying frame of reference for managerial decisions—the very reason for their relative dominance in industry.

Cost-centre and budgetary controls have also been developed (Feeny and Knott 1988). Our case study firms had similarly developed cost-centre status and the charging-out of IS services to user departments. Recent progress had been made in linking IS projects to costs in some cases, such as Clydesdale Bank, where one IS Manager commented: 'Three years ago you didn't know if it would cost you £1/4 million or £10 million . . . we knew the basics of the technology, but it didn't necessarily translate into the bottom line of cost.'

The pervasiveness of the common accounting language has implications for expert groups such as IS. Although the function produces its own stratum of player-managers with a computing background, at senior Divisional Director or General Manager levels of IS, specialist IS skills often shaded into finance qualifications. We also found that senior managers actively promoted the application of more elaborate accounting controls as part of their definition of their jobs. At the Bank of Scotland, IS management was keen to develop more precise means for allocating IS costs to users. And at Mutual Life the Operations Director used financial means for functional control—the function was 'not heavily budget-driven but we do look at costing . . . we look at how these costs are shaping up'.

While financial controls enhanced IS management's knowledge of project costs, their adoption also helped to justify the function's activities in the rest of the organization. During periods of increasing competition, accurate cost-ings are extremely important to the IS function in its daily dealings with other groups for whom computing services are a cost in their budgets. One accountant at Bank of Scotland, for example, stressed the vulnerability of large divisions not perceived as revenue generators: 'In any organization the profit centres will attack the cost centres, and MSD is the biggest cost centre we have.' The move to profit-centre status is thus perhaps illustrative of a wider trend—from general overhead to cost centre to profit centre—emerging as typical for financial management of IS (Price Waterhouse 1991).

Market Control

Despite the scarcity of certain kinds of IS workers and the problems of substituting for an internal IS function, there remains no guarantee of sustaining in-house provision. If an internal labour market becomes too costly, out-sourcing of IS expertise may be encouraged. Indeed, such patterns have already occurred in other areas of specialist expertise, notably R&D functions in the UK (Whittington 1991). Such developments will depend on the extent to which the nature of IT systems in financial services demands in-house expertise, as well as the relative availability of staff and services in external labour and product markets. The advantages and disadvantages of subcontracting were concisely summed up by one manager: 'We have devel-oped a whole new technique for meeting project deadlines. We sue' (Price Waterhouse 1991).

None of our cases involved a major shift towards a market or quasi-market relationship between the IS function and the host institution. Particular components of several innovation projects were sourced externally, but this did not reflect the substitution of the in-house function. Out-sourcing was almost always prompted by in-house IS managers themselves. The only instances which led to a reduction in the in-house role were associated with patterns of change in the firm as a whole. For example, the piecemeal addition of subsidiaries with varying IS needs, and external sources of IS supply, potentially placed central IS functions in a more market-based relationship with clients. Where mergers had created a structure in which divisions still used external computer bureaux, this created tensions for in-house IS management. Inevitably, the possibility of using third-party suppliers affected the 'selling' of the central IS function. In some cases the tasks carried out by external bureaux were more or less routine. But when it came to strategic projects, the need for extensive local knowledge and user involvement demanded close in-house control.

THE MANAGERIAL CLAIMS OF IS

The structural position of IS thus affords scope for influencing strategy and making managerial claims. However, the computing occupations enjoy a somewhat ambiguous reputation with management generally. Although the upper echelons of IS have achieved senior managerial representation, there is a gap between such senior people and rank-and-file programming staff (Murray and Knights 1990). IS workers also have an ambiguous position in the class structure, like other technical groups (C. Smith 1987). In many respects their work depends heavily on anti-hierarchical collegiate relationships with peers, which affects their organizational deployment. On the one hand, IS work has involved extending management control over other groups (seen by some as central to the organizational aspirations of IS), while their involvement with product-market systems has brought contacts with a range of groups and knowledges, increasing the scope of their organizational role but also making it possible for their specialist knowledge to be cannibalized by others.

The relationship between IS expertise and general management is clearly, therefore, open to interpretation. IS careers have occupational and organizational dimensions spanning the technical and managerial domains. In this context, the ability of IS functions to develop and sustain knowledge claims that conscript resources and shape the decision-making processes of management is crucial. Such claims can be made in a variety of ways. The simplest is a kind of 'default option' whereby general management is unable to exercise control over a specialist group because it lacks the relevant expertise. Specialist management with sufficient technical expertise for effective control is then necessary. As an expert group's role expands and becomes more than a satellite to the main business, so its knowledge claims expand. An increasing dependence of investment, sales, and profitability on the efforts of a specialist group is a strong incentive for general management to incorporate elements of the group's knowledge in its decision-making. Knowledge claims can also be developed via a group's symbolic contribution to the organization. There are great rewards for expertise which is able to represent an organization's activities in common terms to its senior managers (Armstrong 1989), as archetypically exemplified by the lingua franca of accountancy.

The simple default option involves a cadre of player-managers whose careers have been structured by the acquisition of IS expertise. Most middle and many senior managers in IS fall into this category. This does not mean that players are promoted to managers on account of technical virtuosity; straightforwardly managerial virtues are usually more important. However, the fact that career paths require an incremental accumulation of specialized experience—rather than the diversity of roles typical of general management—suggests that technical expertise remains an important qualifier for IS management.

The wide distribution of player-managers at middle and senior IS management levels is some indication of the strength of the knowledge claims made by the function. Such appointments achieve several things: they ensure the expertise necessary to control a specialist work process, they acquire an interpreter of that domain for general management, and they consolidate an internal labour market for retaining valuable IS staff by forming a career ladder from technical to managerial positions. Nevertheless, IS remains a support rather than a mainstream function, with limited penetration into general management. While player-managers were necessary to control the detail work of the IS function, occupationally-based expertise appears to have been confined there.

This does not mean that knowledge claims are necessarily limited to the problems of controlling IS workers, but it reveals how organizations absorb such technical knowledge. They attempt to compartmentalize IS expertise, with the result that within the 'black box' of the function available career paths are markedly more truncated than mainstream routes. Because IS staff work in a service function appended on to the line hierarchy, it is difficult for them to transfer into the mainstream at the highest positions (Atkins and Galliers 1992).

Strategic Behaviour

Though purist occupational (i.e. 'technical') expertise may have been the basis for earlier knowledge claims, IS functions have progressively extended their claims through firm-specific knowledge and contributions. Figure 5.3 illustrates this by reference to changes in the managerial representation of IS in our banking cases. IS expanded from small groups of specialists in O&M or accountancy functions, into departments, and eventually into full-blown

Bank of Scotland
1961: IBM 1401 computer installed.
1970: General Manager of Computer Services appointed (though no Computer Services Division established).
1971: Establishment of Bank of Scotland Computer Services Ltd.
1975: Reabsorbed into Bank as Computer Services Division.
1976: Assistant General Manager appointed for Computer Services.
1982: Establishment of independent Automation Planning Deptartment.
1983: Automation Planning and the Computer Services and Management Services Divisions merged to form the Management Services Division under a Joint General Manager.

Royal Bank of Scotland
1969: Merger of Royal Bank and Williams and Glyns, followed by establishment of EDP Division under an Assistant General Manager.
1977: A General Manager appointed for EDP Division.
1980: General Manager and two AGMs.

Clydesdale Bank
1965: First phase of computerization under O&M department.
1971: General Manager's assistant (Automation and Research) appointed with Managers for Computer Centre and Development respectively.
1973: Assistant Managers appointed for Automation and Research, and Computer Operations.
1975: AGM appointed for Computer and Automation area.

FIG. 5.3 *Managerial representation of IS in Scottish banks*

divisions meriting managers of Divisional General Manager seniority or higher. The fact that some of these were not player-managers indicates the growing organizational stature and influence of the IS function, rather than any weakening of the salience of occupational expertise.

While this successful expansion reflected the material contribution of computing technology in financial services, skilful political strategies undoubtedly also played a part. Drawing on the Strategic Contingency Framework proposed by Hickson *et al.* (1971), we can analyse the work of particular groups in terms of such critical factors as 'coping with uncertainty', 'workflow centrality' (the 'pervasiveness' and 'immediacy' of the work done), and 'substitutability' (the extent to which a group's role can be readily duplicated).

IS has steadily expanded into areas of organizational and product-market uncertainty from a stage of back-office automation. This appears to fit the 'reverse product cycle' model, in which service skills (such as IS) evolve towards higher levels of innovation (and hence uncertainty) rather than innovation occurring earlier, as in conventional product cycles. Increasing workflow centrality is indicated by the development of elaborate transaction processing and on-line delivery systems, which directly interface with the consumer. Problems in such systems are both pervasive and immediate. This was well illustrated in the Premier Financial Services case study where one manager pointed out the comparative insignificance of failure in an off-line batch processing system for credit cards, compared with the cataclysmic effect of a breakdown in a clearing bank's on-line systems. Moreover, IS expertise is increasingly deployed to assist product innovation, which takes IS into the strategic arena where it comes into competition with a range of different knowledges, creating new areas of uncertainty and new possibilities for advancement.

There are costs, though, in the attainment of strategic influence. The current status of IS functions owes more to combinations of organizational and occupational knowledge than to the occupation itself. And there are already strong organizational pressures tending to pull IS functions apart, such as end-user programming, distributed computing, out-sourcing, and outright de-skilling (Kraft and Dubnoff 1986; Murray and Knights 1990). This might suggest that the status of IS expertise has already peaked, and its integrity and coherence are at risk.

Some evidence from our study suggested that IS workers are being decentralized or integrated into other functions. And certainly there was pressure to submit to greater user intervention. But our case studies mostly pointed to incremental change. We found little evidence of users or distributed computing having diluted IS control or challenged centralized IS departments. Trends rather were towards expansion and consolidation into distinct information divisions. In the single case in Clydesdale where business analysts had been moved out, this may in time usher in the devolvement of control over applications to the new Electronic Business Division; but none of our respondents saw the reorganization as a threat, and indeed in systems development were happy to be able to concentrate on core technologies.

Strategic Positioning

The continuing expansion of IS relates to changes in the sectoral context as well as technology. Suppliers' incentives to stabilize product offerings are constantly overwhelmed by the competitive advantages of innovation. Uncertainty is exacerbated by the service industries' problem of disentangling product delivery from the product itself. This means it is hardly feasible for product innovation to be segmented into technology-driven and market-driven functions. Existing mainframe-based delivery and transaction processing systems tend to constrain product innovation. At the least, new products mean extensive conversion work to provide an interface with core systems, while major innovations may necessitate extensive rewriting of existing systems. In most cases, intimate local knowledge of core systems is vital to the innovation process, so that innovation cannot be readily separated from the refinement and maintenance of existing systems.

IS knowledge, therefore, remains at the heart of financial service firms, though it might become differently distributed through the organization. It may become polarized, with more strategic components appropriated by management, and the remainder falling to standardization and partial automation. This assumes that IS knowledge can be stratified according to the functional requirements of the business or market. But the acquisition and deployment of expert knowledge is bound up with membership of wider occupational groups, tending to frustrate attempts at functional stratification. The kind of IT appreciation required by senior managements in future therefore probably remains in the realm of the expert rather than the relatively untutored chief executive. An IS Manager at Mutual Life, in describing top management's role in the Customer Care project, provided an insight into what this might mean for the conduct of particular projects.

They are all very capable and talented chaps, but they're heavily into politics. They know which way the markets move, but as to actually having information about something like how Customer Management would work . . . I think that might be kept away from the senior executives. I don't think they are likely to have enough information to be able to judge in absolute terms.

We saw similar references to the capacity of those at senior level to conceptualize projects at both the Royal Bank and at Bank of Scotland and, indeed, have made the point before that much of the uncertainty in IT strategy has to be contained by specialist knowledge.

Another possibility is the consolidation of more occupationally oriented formations of expertise. This would mean redrawing the boundaries between expert and non-expert, and buttressing dependency on the IS function. If IS careers remain bounded within IS departments, the continued integrity of such departments will reflect companies' commitment to IT as a resource and underpin the status and career hopes of specialist staff. IS experts may therefore see advantages in continuing to exhibit unique skills. The advantages of this approach in terms of guaranteed career paths and defensible expertise may be at the expense of broader ambitions. IS managers might be pigeon-holed as technical experts, and indeed the hierarchies of many firms are palpably uncomfortable with technical groups controlling knowledge that may have a bearing on strategic decisions. As Armstrong has suggested, they exhibit 'a peculiarly British view of management which regards it as something quite distinct from technical expertise: which, indeed, in its more virulent versions, actually regards technical expertise as a disqualification for managerial positions' (1992: 43).

Conclusion

Clearly there are a number of possibilities with regard to the future role of IS expertise. Different alternatives may be followed by parts of what is an extensive and loosely defined occupational group. However, our analysis suggests that the managerial claims made by IS functions in financial institutions formed the basis for the influence of IS on management, especially strategic management, and reflected the particular role that IS expertise played in the development of the organization. The IS function's claims to contribute to corporate strategy depended on IS workers' control of uncertainty at a practical level, and on the inability of other specialist groups to exercise external control over the function.

The readiness of top management to listen was less evident. Sectoral evolution has nurtured the basic competencies of financial institutions and underpinned the dominance of finance expertise. Management structures and the conventional means of representing financial transactions resisted the incursion of IS expertise, which became identified narrowly in terms of maintaining and developing systems. This view helps to explain what Armstrong (1989) termed a 'high discretion, low trust syndrome' in the relationship of IS with general management. None the less, uncertainty about the market and the increasing scope of IT has undermined the existing order and enhanced both top management and user expectations about the role of IS. Although some IS managers have attempted to deal with these changes by redefining the boundaries of their domain and withdrawing from a demanding discretionary role in the allocation of IS resources, others, in contrast, have sought to expand the scope of their contribution to the organization and their role in strategic decision-making.

6

Strategy and Innovation

This chapter examines the ways in which sectoral and technological change is negotiated within structures of expertise. At the same time, expertise (including IS expertise) itself influences the interpretation of strategic change through knowledge networks and coalitions of interest. In this sense, innovations provide a critical juncture for the negotiation and reconstruction of the sector, whereby preconceptions and alliances may be challenged, and new avenues of knowledge deployment and occupational mobility opened up. Innovation projects may involve attempts to renegotiate the position of the IS function within expertise structures.

We start from the idea that the construction of a strategic rationale for IS work is an indication of the onset, if not the success, of such attempts. A strategic rationale comprises assumptions about outcomes, benefits, and drawbacks, and is the basis for economic and technical justification. It reflects the mobilization of arguments about the significance and utility of special knowledge for the success of an organization as a whole—that is, the adoption of a discourse about strategy.

As we will see from the case studies discussed at some length in this chapter, project development and the rationales constructed to manage it were influenced by the uncertainties generated by particular projects. These were a function of project scope, and also how this interacted with existing structures of expertise in the organization. The problems posed by a project depended on how far it challenged, or could be made to challenge, existing inter-professional jurisdictions. Sometimes this reflected a mismatch between a project's scope and existing routines and practices. But in other cases, the IS function sought to make certain projects problematic so as to challenge the routines or jurisdiction of another expert group. In either case, however, a strategic rationale was developed to justify bringing the 'problem' under IS control.

PROJECT SCOPE

Reviewing the scope of our case projects suggests one important influence on their management was their respective product-market impacts. Both VISA and Premier Financial Services/INDEX, our two credit-card projects, conformed to what McFarlan and McKenney (1982) have termed 'factory IT'; that is, they have a large impact on the organization, but little impact on the existing market. In both these cases product and process were relatively separate, and the choice of technology was largely to do with the acquisition of standardized processing systems. Certainly, the IS view of these innovations was governed by concerns for efficiency and timeliness, rather than broader questions about changes in market share and structure. Thus the justification for INDEX and VISA showed little evidence of a strategic rationale. In other cases, such as CABINET and Home and Auto's management information system, the design of the technology affected the organization widely, and in CABINET's case had important marketing implications.

We will compare the above cases in order to explore the development, and also non-development, of strategic rationales, and the implications of both these situations for innovation.

Premier Financial Services and VISA Centre

In order to meet their time and efficiency criteria, both Premier Financial Services and VISA revolved around the purchase and installation of a standard card-processing package: INDEX for Premier Financial Services and FDR for VISA Centre. In the Premier case, considerations of cost and speed also exerted a significant influence on the arrangements for installing, maintaining, and running the INDEX package. It was on these grounds, for instance, that the parent bank overruled Premier management's desire for their own computer centre and decided to run the package on their own mainframe. 'To get Premier set up with another computer processing centre quick enough was going to be difficult and expensive; it wasn't really practical within our time-scales.' However, this did not mean that marketing considerations were entirely absent from the choice of INDEX. Although the package was designed to handle transactions swiftly and reliably, specific features of the software commended themselves to Premier management as having marketing benefits. In particular, the client-based structure of the package meant that various kinds of credit arrangement pertaining to an individual customer could be cross-tabulated and credit limits determined accordingly. There were other benefits too.

From a marketing point of view INDEX has the ability of being structured from a customer point of view, so we can write to people as customers as opposed to account-holders. . . . It can offer an option card product, a budget product, a credit system, and within that we have a lot of scope to tailor the method of operation of each particular product in terms of the particular features of the way it operates. (Premier Marketing Manager)

Nevertheless, the marketing benefits of the package were of a different order from those associated with, say, a branch automation system. This was partly because the customer relationship in credit cards is narrower than in banking. Also, marketing elements were mainly to do with improving the quality of marketing information rather than enhancing Premier's competitive differentiation in the market segments at which it was aimed.

The initial rationale for Bank of Scotland's VISA Centre was underpinned by an equal sense of urgency about establishing a card-processing capacity. But this was less an offensive move on the part of the bank than a reaction to policy changes at Barclaycard. As we saw in the case in Chapter 3, Barclays had encouraged Bank of Scotland to establish their own product, as they were withdrawing from third-party processing. Faced with the problem of handling both product and processing themselves, Bank of Scotland management looked at the opportunities associated with credit cards and at the costs of different processing options. As with INDEX, the marketing aspects of the product were largely independent of the location of the site for processing transactions. The bank eventually decided that establishment of their own centre was justified on efficiency grounds. The computer package chosen, FDR, was installed on the mainframe in the Management Services Division in Edinburgh, while the labour-intensive tasks of dealing with paper-based payments and telephone enquiries were located in a new site at Dunfermline, chosen for its supply of female part-time and temporary clerical labour.

The rationale reflected in these two innovations seemed markedly more operational and efficiency-oriented than those of other projects in our sample. This distinction is not hard and fast, but depends on the sectoral context and structures of expertise within the organizations. It is possible to interpret both projects as 'strategic' as the business could not be supported without them. What makes them less strategic is not the tasks they performed but the standardized nature of the technology; put simply, credit card processing lacked the kind of managerial uncertainty which would qualify it as strategic. Standardized or 'black-boxed' technologies do not generate high levels of technological or market uncertainty, as their application is relatively well understood. At the mature stage of technology development, sufficient packages are available to serve the market in roughly the same way. Consequently, such technologies can be incorporated into well-bounded decision-making processes, governed by efficiency criteria.

Indeed, one comment that caught our eye in the VISA case was a senior manager suggesting that he and a colleague had designed the organization over a pint of beer. While this might seem an informal, even frivolous approach to duties, what was being claimed was a highly rational decision process—one that could carry on outside the work situation, between colleagues, and with no need to involve outside parties. This suggested a collaborative managerial culture, based on a relatively certain task set, and was a representation of how managers saw the VISA development.

Bank of Scotland/CABINET and Home and Auto's Management Information System

The routineness of a technology is less a matter of the particular tasks it is performing than how it fits the technical standards in the sector and the corporate structures of expertise. On the first point, technologies which have an undeniable customer utility should eventually become so standardized amongst service providers that they become commodity products, whose competitive effect is to raise barriers to entry; ATMs are the classic example here. In the same way, the routineness of a technology depends in part on its correspondence with an organization's existing patterns of expertise. Where a project does not fall within pre-existing boundaries of expertise, it is more likely to elicit a strategic response. Bank of Scotland's CABINET project and Home and Auto's management information system created significant uncertainties for the IS functions involved. Both were long-term exercises, which traversed functional boundaries, and in neither case was hardware or the work organization standardized.

As we saw in the case study, CABINET arose out of the long-term development of customer-services automation in the early 1980s. A number of issues, objectives, and solutions were considered which, together with the development of related technologies like ATMs and home banking, informed the rationale for CABINET. This was manifest in three major themes: direct cost savings through improvements in managerial and staff productivity, improving customer service, and the introduction of new services and products.

The emphasis placed by Bank of Scotland management on CABINET's likely contribution to cost efficiency underscores how rationales which are 'merely' efficiency-oriented often complement those with an explicit strategic objective. The strategic rationale for the project seems to have derived from a number of elements. The sheer scale of the project and the time scale over which it was to be implemented required a strong planning input. Moreover, CABINET was seen as an infrastructural technology, enhancing the Bank's core delivery systems within the branch network and also providing a platform for new products and technologies.

In essence, CABINET, in its widest interpretation, is the medium through which the bank's electronic databases, computer software, hardware, and telecommunications networks are being restructured to create a flexible overall system which will ensure we are not constrained in capitalizing upon banking technology developments as they unfold. (Automation Planning Manager)

Such a large-scale and innovative project demonstrated that where both intention and implementation are complex and uncertain, it becomes difficult to specify precise objectives and benefits. Though broad objectives can be espoused, the technological and organizational uncertainties of CABINET demanded 'the widest interpretation' through the formation of a strategic rationale.

In many instances, the emergence of a rationale underpinning a large project is part of a drawn-out organizational process. And often, for reasons to do with the structure of expertise, the organizational location of the group expressing a particular rationale is as important as the rationale itself. The Home and Auto case displayed both these features. First, the impetus for the development of a corporate MIS was seen as a convergence of many factors. Internally, there were problems created by the multiplicity and inconsistency of existing sources of management information, and by the emergence of a number of possible solutions for the upgrading of processing systems. There were also market pressures caused by the elimination of cartel-like rate-setting arrangements, and the increasing spread of computerized quotations and premium rate comparisons.

The single most important stimulus for the project, however, can probably be attributed to a form of organizational learning. When H&A sharply increased its motor premium rates in 1982, there was an adverse market reaction and the company found itself losing market-share to competitors. Publicly the chairperson put a brave face on things: 'In the private car account . . . we have given a lead to the market in hardening rates. I believe we were right in doing this and we intend to persevere.' But internal concerns about 'leading the market' led to a review of the ways in which premium rates were adjusted. Significantly, the pressures for change came not from the IS function, but from product managers, top management, and the Statistical Services department. It was only when Statistical Services had tried and failed to develop a corporate MIS that the IS department picked up the gauntlet. They first sought to develop the project through a rigorous application of the BSP methodology which had been developed by IBM (the IS Manager was a former IBM employee), with the aim of establishing a complete audit of the information needs of an organization. The aim was to use the BSP study in the development of an information strategy for the entire company.

The adoption of this worked-out version of a strategic rationale seems to have been a reaction to the narrowness of view which had dogged Statistical Services' efforts. Their project had foundered ultimately on a failure to take account of the excessive run times which their proposed MIS reports were projected to take on the mainframe computer.

In the ensuing period the strategy project was reviewed in internal reports which documented the evaluation of various software packages. It was only in a technical evaluation in 1986, however, that a financial justification for the MIS was defined. The system, it was claimed, would lead to a 'decrease in claims ratio which in turn will be reflected as benefit on the underwriting profit/loss in a year'. The report noted that Statistical Services had estimated that a 1 per cent reduction in the ratio would lead to a £5 million benefit across all classes of business. However, while the report claimed that such a reduction was a conservative estimate of the impact of a corporate MIS, it did not attempt to substantiate the relationship between the MIS and the quality of rate-setting within the company. One of the report's authors noted of the 1 per cent estimate: 'There was no grounding for that really. It was just a figure that everyone accepted would be the case.'

POLITICAL INTERESTS

The Home and Auto and CABINET cases suggest how the uncertainty caused by a project's scope influenced the adoption of a strategic rationale. However, as other cases show, it is not only a project's scope which may make it problematic; in some cases uncertainty has more to do with organizational politics surrounding a particular project and the symbolic resources that groups mobilize in making strategic claims.

Perhaps our best example of a project being the vehicle of a group's aspirations was Clydesdale Bank's Telebank project. The problems the Clydesdale IS function encountered in developing their remote banking system were partly generated by competitive concerns, but partly also by the function's pursuit of greater autonomy within the parent Midland Bank group. In comparison with these factors, technological uncertainty was less problematic, as was evident from Clydesdale's decision to out-source key parts of the development work to a software supplier. The Premier case was another which illustrated that the emergence of a strategic rationale may depend on the aspirations of the IS group, and its relationship with the rest of the organization, as much as on the project itself. And we can reinforce this point counter-factually by citing two projects where a strategic approach did not emerge, despite the accompaniment of high-levels of product market or technological uncertainty. These were the Royal Bank/Royline and Mutual Life cases.

Clydesdale/Telebank

As we saw in Chapter 3, Telebank was a remote banking system launched in the period after the Bank of Scotland's HOBS had reached the market and just before the launch of the Royal Bank's Royline. Much of the rationale for Telebank was similar to that of HOBS, in particular the ability to support business in England. Telebank was in some ways an imitative and defensive response to the potential loss of business customers posed by HOBS: 'We felt if Bank of Scotland was doing it, there must be something there.'

However, while Clydesdale management shared an emphasis on strategic and innovative uses of technology—Telebank was described as a 'strategic front runner'—they also claimed to have learnt lessons from the HOBS experience. Market research had been commissioned to determine the demand for remote banking. Armed with this information, Telebank, unlike HOBS, was aimed from the start at the business market and was based on a different technological infrastructure. It was conceived as only one product in a range of remote banking products. The range was eventually to include corporate cash management for large businesses and telephone-based home banking for personal customers.

All the advantages accrued to us coming in second. More advanced technology, learning from their mistakes, and able to take a view that Videotext wasn't the sole answer. . . . And also to launch it from the start as office banking. . . . The thing we said was, let it look in every way like HOBS, only better. But don't let it be our only home banking service, let it come in as the first line. (Electronic Business Manager)

Telebank was seen as an important competitive response in a changing market-place. 'We had made greater sense of home-and-office banking; we'd taken it a lot further than anyone else had. We'd moved from being second to Bank of Scotland, and through the use of this telephone system which was innovative, we've moved ourselves to being market leaders in the UK.' It was also presented as a logical extension of Clydesdale's technological virtuosity, succeeding innovative systems that included an earlier branch network and the development of Britain's first EFTPOS system.

The rationale for Telebank's development, therefore, drew heavily on strategic and marketing precepts. However, alongside these competitive responses, the impetus to project Telebank as a strategic initiative was aimed at gaining recognition for Clydesdale's autonomy and technical expertise. Even one of Telebank's champions felt that, in retrospect, in terms of their own systems, it was less significant than as a political gambit. The Systems Development Manager stressed that, no matter how strategic Telebank had become, its first importance initially was political; it showed that systems development 'had something outwith the Midland' and were making a bid to be a serious player.

Finally, another interesting dimension of the strategic rationale at Clydesdale was the claim to have a 'safe to fail' culture. This was part and parcel of the nimbleness of the smaller Scottish banks. Also, perhaps because Clydesdale was the smallest of the Scottish clearers, this rationale came through there clearest. In the development of Telebank, the electronic Business Manager with responsibility for the project noted:

We are small enough to be able to test-bed things without too much consideration as to cost if it doesn't work. Now I'm not saying that we just go into it and say, oh tough, over the wall and try again. But none the less we can take a less serious view if that doesn't work out. . . . The way we designed this, we had the space to fail and move over to something else; so we felt pretty secure.

He was suggesting that on two distinct counts the uncertainties of the project were contained: because the bank in any case was small, and because the front-end processing design allowed for flexibility.

Premier Financial Services/INDEX

The importance of inter-group rivalries in stimulating the adoption of strategic rationality was also illustrated by the INDEX package. We have already noted that the technological component of this project evoked little uncertainty and was dominated by efficiency criteria. However, this is not to say

that the project was entirely unproblematic. The parent bank's group function—which labelled this a strategic project—saw the organizational arrangements that it enshrined as having crucial importance. By awarding prime
responsibility for development work to an outside contractor, and not to the
bank's in-house IS function, the INDEX project set a precedent for the
future. The very fact that the package was technologically routine made it a
more powerful precedent in defining the role of the in-house IS function,
and increased its strategic implications. As one Group Manager put it, 'what
we're really talking about here is power'; in an environment where very
little happened in computing terms that was outwith the control of the
Management Services Division, there were major ramifications of a system
being implemented 'without ever going anywhere near Management
Services.'

Royal Bank/Royline

In the Royline case, the IS group's conception of itself as a powerful player
was reflected in their approach to remote banking technology. Unlike Clydesdale's IS function, which saw the equivalent Telebank project as a vehicle
for securing greater autonomy, the IS division at the Royal Bank saw
remote banking as part of an incremental pattern; market-related certainly,
but not impinging on the basic relationship between IS and the rest of the
bank. IS management emphasized their role of serving the specified needs of
the bank and to satisfy user requirements. There was thus no need for the
IS division to develop a unique approach to innovations such as remote
banking. The development was seen as a response to customer demand.
This had been stimulated by the emergence of corporate cash management
in the USA—'many of our customers who were asking for cash management
did not know what it was'—and by pressures at branch level and the
mounting number of phone calls and automated payments associated with
business customers.

The design and functionality of Royline was defined by Systems Development, who sought to target the system at business customers throughout the
UK. They saw it eventually encompassing a range of delivery systems and an
expanding range of functions.

But while Systems Development designed the technology, the impetus
behind the project came from senior management. The stimulus to develop
Royline had come when senior management set up a working group to
investigate corporate cash management. Thus, the rationale underpinning
Royline was couched in marketing and business terms and was determined
very largely outside the IS area. Even the Head of Systems Development in
the IS Division did not see the emerging potential of the technology itself as a
factor: 'There are business requirements for which we are finding technological solutions . . . You can't utilize technology for its own sake.'

Mutual Life/Customer Care

Like the Royline project, the impetus for Mutual Life's Customer Care project came from outside the IS function; in the first instance, from the company's Sales Manager. He presented it as an innovation which would tidy up the whole customer interface, with knock-on financial and marketing benefits. 'The great thing about Customer Care is that it enables you to sort out your billing and collection systems. So there is only one set of money transactions for the whole organization. But again that's only another part of the picture. All of this fits into a whole complex of not messing people about.' Although 'not messing people about' would not normally rate as an advance in strategic thinking, for a life insurance company it raises many possibilities for organizational and technological change. It poses a threat to the traditional product-based structuring of the business by bringing the customer into the picture as someone who is not just the 'holder' of a policy but may have many different relationships with the company. Similarly, it presages a restructuring of the gathering and recording of customer data; a mammoth task given the number of life policies held and the time span over which they are held.

Despite the uncertainties associated with the project, the IS function did not have the structural centrality to develop a strategic rationale for Customer Care, nor a commitment to strategic thinking. The General Manager of the Operations department, for example, was unimpressed by the usual distinction between product-market factors and financial efficiency. His comment was simply, 'It's strategically important to be cheap.'

So while the CABINET case showed an IS division co-opting different user groups, in Customer Care the technological infrastructure for the project was regarded as only one component and control was vested mainly in user areas. The definition of one key element of the project—the Policy Holder Index File—was carried out by an existing user. As a result, there was reportedly adopted a 'narrow view of what a policy was', which greatly reduced the potential usefulness of the Index. In addition, key roles in the management of this project were determined by the adoption of an IBM project methodology which placed control in the hands of the user sponsor. Reports on the strategic way forward by an internal consultancy boutique appeared to be largely ignored by the IS function itself.

STRUCTURAL POSITIONING

This review of some of our cases has indicated no automatic relationship between the technical features of a project and the way it is managed. The problems and uncertainties of change, within which strategic thinking develops, are as much to do with the IS function's position in the organization as with the character of the project itself. We have highlighted symbolic and political factors, as well as the practical issues of handling projects, that may lead to a strategic rationale developing. But problems are also generated by tensions between disciplinary groupings. Different expert groups frequently seek to 'make something of a problem' by interpreting it in terms of their own problem-solution rationales. As Abbott notes, jurisdictional claims between professions are associated with a 'current construction of the problem' (1988: 40).

The ability of an expert group to secure control of work against competing groups depends, first, on imposing its own interpretation of the problem, and secondly, on providing an acceptable solution. This ability is tested both by inter-professional competition and by the extent to which abstract knowledge is translated into actual solutions through the group's conduct of its work. On the first point, we need to bear in mind that IS is not a highly organized profession. The operation of labour markets more than formal systems of professional control is the key influence on occupational formation. But this does not preclude IS workers themselves from exploiting professional jurisdictions. Indeed, as Abbott notes of the movement of IS workers from programming into planning, the less organized professions may actually be advantaged in workplace competition; 'because they lack a clear focus and perhaps a clearly established cognitive structure, they are free to move to available tasks' (1988: 83). This freedom was evident in the CABINET case as MSD colonized a 'marketing perspective' as a component of their technical domain.

IS and Accounting Regimes

More generally, we saw in a number of cases that IS workers came into conflict with accountancy jurisdiction. In this they were reflecting the experience of many others. Faced by problems of appraising major technology investments, many managers using payback techniques are prepared to admit to the use of unreliable and possibly spurious information (e.g. Senker 1984).

This type of problem was partly a symptom of the increasing financial burden imposed by the very large IT investments at the end of the 1980s. But the clash between IS and accounting criteria was exacerbated by the uncertainty that attached to innovation. Resulting problems of jurisdiction and diagnosis were a powerful stimulant to the adoption of a strategic approach. In some cases IS managers confessed to paying little more than lip-service to the rules on investment appraisal. In Home and Auto, for example, IS workers experienced some difficulty in determining the financial benefits of their MIS, and admitted that their documented estimate was more expedient than accurate.

Beyond simply bending the rules, however, IT innovators may find that the options available for dealing with accountancy regimes are limited. Sometimes, as Loveridge (1990) notes, accounting bench-marks may be used 'as political devices . . . in convincing politically important others and justifying their determination to innovate'. Nevertheless, with the possible exception of Bank of Scotland, which is documented below, we found no instances of any concerted challenge by the IS function to accountancy rules.

Organizational Learning and Project Implementation

While there was little movement at the jurisdictional boundary between IS and accounting, there was greater fluidity in other managerial tasks. The adoption of a strategic rationale by some IS functions appeared to symbolize their more extensive managerial claims. Complex interactions occurred at organizational level between the nature of projects and the self-conception and position of the IS function. In the following account of two of our cases, Bank of Scotland and Home and Auto, we illustrate how such interactions were worked out over time, through concrete processes of IT development and implementation.

CABINET and Home and Auto's MIS

The organizational position and aspirations of the IS function have already been discussed from a structural perspective in Chapter 5. But a longer view of Bank of Scotland shows the importance of organizational learning in defining the role of different functional groups, and in revealing new relationships between technology and organizational practices. New relationships eventually become institutionalized in structural arrangements and managerial rationales.

This depends, in the first instance, on the 'unlearning' of existing rationalities and assumptions (Whipp and Clark 1986). As we saw in the case, this happened at Bank of Scotland in the late 1970s when the existing arrangements for decision-making on IT were discredited by a competitive setback over the adoption of ATMs; IT responsibilities then being shared between two divisions. The initial outcome of the debate was the bank's rejection of ATMs on the grounds that their labour-saving benefits did not outweigh the costs. However, subsequently, the Royal Bank appeared to be achieving competitive advantage through an extensive deployment of ATM machines. The ATM Working Party in Bank of Scotland was quickly reconvened, and the threat of losing customers prompted it to 'find' that ATMs could, in fact, be financially justified (Scarbrough and Lannon 1988).

The ATM episode could be interpreted in a variety of ways. However, it was followed by further dissension between the divisions on the future of branch automation systems—the precursor of CABINET. Conflicting views led senior management to believe that thoroughgoing reorganization was needed. Computer Services and Management Services were amalgamated, and a new divisonal director appointed who had previously been head of the Automation Planning group. This small group (of four managers) had been briefed to stand outside the disputing divisions, and to 'keep abreast of all developments in technology that might affect the bank, and interpret these as opportunities both for the bank and for improving the customer interface'.

At the same time as the CABINET project was being defined, therefore, structural and managerial changes were providing the new IS Division with a strategic mandate in the management of technology. This was reinforced by the exigencies of CABINET itself. Once a working party had recommended the system, the immediate problem was that of justifying the large-scale investment needed for an intractably long-term, integrated, and infrastructural technology. It was clear that the kind of financial criteria applied to incremental technology investments would not do; for this type of strategic project 'the infrastructural costs would always be too high'. Management simply had to bite the bullet and 'take on a longer term marketing view'. Emboldened perhaps by the CABINET experience, some IS Managers were prepared to extend the argument to cover all technology. 'In the end you can't justify technology, since it's inherently non-justifiable. You need it to stay in front of the market or protect against potential loss of business. But that's impossible to measure.'

The overall goals for CABINET did encompass financial benefits, particularly improved productivity at branch level. But inherent technological uncertainties about the final shape of the system, and how productivity goals might be achieved, united with the (equally uncertain) marketing possibilities of customer-centred databases. The connection which MSD forged between infrastructural modernization and competitive advantage in the event created the strategic space for CABINET within routinized processes of managerial decision-making. This allowed the project to evade the influence of accounting controls applied to existing business. Even a management accountant in the bank was prepared to accept that CABINET was 'a strategic decision, and the cost of not doing it was more important than the cost of doing it'. Thus CABINET achieved the status of a strategic innovation: 'CABINET itself is not a product; CABINET is a strategy. It's a strategy to attack the marketplace in the nineties.'

CABINET was thus untouchable, and a strategic necessity not only because its final shape and effects could not be classified or evaluated, but also because it was successfully presented as intrinsic to the bank's future development. The Chief Executive recognized this, while also recognizing the dangers. 'The danger with CABINET is that you go down a blind alleyway from which you cannot escape. The danger of not doing it is that you go out of business.' Indeed, the size and innovativeness of the project encouraged demands from other groups, making implementation all the more difficult. And along with increasing expectations for CABINET went an appreciation of the strategic position of MSD itself. If the new system fell short of expectations, the perception of MSD was also likely to suffer. Expectations had to be carefully managed, as one Senior Business Analyst was well aware.

I think we began by taking far too big a view of what it was. That was one of our mistakes. Because there was a lack of strategic thinking going on elsewhere, CABINET tended to become the repository for those ideas. . . . Because when we were proposing CABINET we did discuss these more strategic issues.

The CABINET case demonstrates that the emergence of a strategic rationale depends on structural and political conditions creating a space in which a rationale can be constructed, as well as upon learning processes which can situate strategy within an organizational context. This contrasts with the Home and Auto case. Although the management information system at H&A had been initiated by the same kind of competitive setback which had catalysed change at Bank of Scotland, the structural and technological context was much less auspicious. As we saw, the IS function only took control of the MIS project after the failure of the powerful Statistical Services department. When IS management attempted to map a form of strategic rationality on to their practices through the adoption of the BSP methodology, they were constrained first by the implementation process for this kind of technology, and secondly, by the position of IS within the expertise structure.

CABINET was more complex in design, but had the advantage of a protracted conceptualization phase and of being relatively free, at least initially, from dependency on user groups. At H&A, however, the MIS implementation was dependent on localized user knowledge from its inception. Furthermore, the structural position of the IS developers within the hierarchy made it difficult to carry out an adequate diagnosis of organizational practices. As one noted: 'The top-most level [of management and also of the corporate headquarters] was banned from us, perhaps because we were pretty scruffy.' As a consequence, the project quickly ran into difficulties as IS developers tried to squeeze complex reality into a formalized model.

We produced organization charts but this was one of the more difficult tasks. In a complex business you may leave areas of responsibility slightly grey. Like the individual Product Managers formally had some responsibilities, but they varied in their approach to product pricing and left different decisions to their product managers. . . . That was the first big hole we fell down.

So while CABINET occupied the space created by MSD's mandate and by long-term uncertainty, the H&A project fell down the 'big hole' of existing practice. The complexity and time demands of the project were compounded by political pressures from impatient users. After several years of development work, 'people were turning against the information strategy idea', and there was a feeling abroad that IS had 'analysed it to death'. Without support from top management, and in danger of losing face within the organization, a change in IS management facilitated a switch to a more pragmatic approach; 'evolution not revolution' as the new IS Manager put it. With an emphasis on tailoring the MIS to departmental needs, the project eventually made good progress.

Creating Strategic Space

The CABINET and Home and Auto cases help to clarify our understanding of the conditions under which a strategic rationale may be effectively deployed by IS groups. In their different ways, each case highlights the importance of the structure of expertise in each organization, and the practices of IT development and implementation. Strategic rationality is not just a way of interpreting problems, or a 'way of seeing' (Knights and Morgan 1991: 253). If an expert group is to sustain claims to control an area of work, it must be able to substantiate its diagnosis of the problem with solutions which make sense to an audience of powerful groups within and outside the organization—solutions which, in some agreed sense, actually work.

The failure of the BSP method in the Home and Auto case showed that simply mapping formalized procedures on to IS practices is rarely effective in creating solutions. Attempts to 'fix' strategy in the form of procedures and detailed plans may only heighten the tension between formulation and implementation, by distributing strategic tasks bureaucratically (Brunsson 1982) and by locking strategy into a given plan or set of objectives (Lenz and Lyles 1985). Conversely, for a long-term project like CABINET, the IS group's control of uncertainty and its unique possession of the knowledges needed for development helped to make the function's deployment of strategic rationality more than a formal exercise. In the process of re-negotiating its position in the structure of expertise, the IS function came close to defining strategic problems for the entire bank.

Even so, we are reminded of the constraints on the claims an IS function can make. Some organizations, for example, were willing to make structural modifications in order to better accommodate technology developments. In Bank of Scotland, the Management Services Division itself was a consequence of the technology initiative over customer-services automation; and at Clydesdale another whole division for electronic business had been formed. On the other hand, some implementing organizations deliberately sought to retain the status quo in structural terms. In Mutual Life we saw a number of different strategies being adopted in order to avoid major restructuring.

In addition, computing work practices are themselves project-based, and projects are discrete events. Unless work practices can be sustained by a flow of long-term projects they will lack the the continuity and pervasiveness which have been defined as crucial elements of strategic rationality (e.g. Hoskin 1990). Within a single project, the CABINET case showed that a strategic rationale is more readily sustained in the initial, conceptual stages than in later stages of implementation, when other interests are being engaged. Some of the projects we examined were managed within a self-consciously strategic framework while others were not. This had as much to do with the IS group's position in the broader corporate structure of expertise, as with any innate features of the project. In short, some IS functions projected a strategic rationale for reasons of organizational or occupational politics as much as for practical exigencies. Their ability to do so, however, was constrained by project-based practices for fulfilling the problem-solving and symbolic potential of a strategic orientation.

PART II

TECHNOLOGY

This section explores the knowledge content of technologically-related expertise in financial services and outlines the ways in which these elements of expertise are deployed and combined to produce the innovations we have studied. This includes the evolution of technical systems themselves (hardware and software) and also the decision-making that occurs around IT as systems are designed and implemented. The section thus builds a picture of technical innovation starting with the major instrumentalities involved, examining the range of technical uncertainties that beset the practical implementation of systems, and finally focusing on the essentially social issues of decision-making around development processes.

The key mechanism of expertise deployment is the *user-led* process that has prevailed since the earliest days of commercial computing. This involves inputs from sector- (and sub-sector-) specific, non-technological sources of expertise—i.e. in financial services from groups such as bankers, accountants, actuaries, and underwriters, as well as operative groups like clerical workers. It also, of course, requires the mobilization of technologically-related forms of expertise derived from staff such as systems analysts, programmers, and software engineers. And there are sources of expertise external to user organizations from producer companies and a range of consultants and software suppliers. Moreover, as our case studies make clear, the distribution and availability of expertise changes radically across the industrial sector. Different professional groups tend to dominate in sub-sectors like banking, (life and general) insurance, and credit cards, so that the structure of expertise varies considerably.

The historic links between financial services and IT reveal very well the active role the sector has played as a source of innovation in commercial computing, via the user-led mechanism. Chapter 7 examines this relationship, together with the state of the art in IT and its applications in financial services, particularly among our case studies. Major artefactual instrumentalities in the sector, like customer-service automation and decision support, are surveyed.

In Chapter 8, we explore the main process of IT innovation, namely the area of knowledge which has become recognized as software engineering. Software engineering represents a specialized category of expertise centred on the development of software systems. Throughout its history, software has been beset by problems which have their roots in the difficulties of managing expertise. This chapter traces the emergence of software engineering, outlining its principles and procedures, and provides a survey of the techniques (the methodological instrumentalities) employed in financial services. Our case evidence on the limitations of these practices and the extent of their adoption is examined, as well as the ways in which organizations have tackled the problem of making software expertise more accountable and responsive to business needs.

The deployment of complex technologies as working systems in organizations is, however, much more than a technical process. It is a protracted form of *implementation* in which available instrumentalities are combined with elements of local knowledge (e.g. of banking procedure, risk estimation) and organization-specific requirements, to produce new systems. This can be highly uncertain—particularly where strategic or innovative systems are concerned—and goes beyond design and installation to involve power processes and organizational strategies. Implementation represents the meeting-point between the strategic objectives discussed in Part I and the technical capabilities outlined in the first two chapters of this part. In Chapter 9 we examine the nature of implementation; we break down the overall process in terms of the decision categories of time, organization, cost, and design of work. The chapter emphasizes the novelty embodied in systems as a measure of true innovation—creative outcomes may lead to wider applicability than anticipated just as uncertainty can lead to systems failures.

Chapter 10 closes the section with another view of the main theme of user-led innovation. Rather than looking at outcomes (i.e. types of innovation), the role that users play in decision-making around IT is stressed. While it has long been recognized that 'user involvement' is a problematic (and political) activity, the chapter further explores the complexity of the user concept—innovation may be user-led but not necessarily led by users; the 'user' may be better thought of as an interest or relation rather than as an identity. A composite typology of users is developed on the basis of dimensions of organizational power and the possession of systems skills, and our case materials are analysed in terms of these different user roles. Finally, the central point of the argument here is that many questions of the nature and role of user innovation reflect the issue of *user relations* within the broader organization and the crisis of integration of IS functions; this in turn reflects an occupational transition from service function to strategic role.

7

Information Technology and Financial Services

The objectives of this chapter are first to examine the relationship between the financial services sector and the IT industry. This shows that the sector has not only provided the industry with a growing market for its products, but has also made an important contribution to the development of technology. The second objective is to review the current state of IT and its major application areas within financial services, highlighting those that are of special relevance to the case studies and the issues they raise for development practices. Information technology is often used as a catch-all for the vast range of modern communication and computing devices. However, the term is more than just a convenient umbrella for a heterogeneous collection of technologies. IT highlights the impact of digital technologies in drawing once quite distinct systems of computing and communications on to a single developmental path. Within the financial sector, the implications of this convergence are far-reaching. Where once planning and investment in computing and communications was piecemeal, there is now the realization that IT services must be integrated with the business function. The sector's attempts to respond to this challenge are best understood in the light of the history of its use of IT and how this has led to the emergence of in-house IT expertise.

Members of the financial services sector depend almost entirely on their abilities to acquire, manage, and analyse information. Meeting the increasingly complex information-processing requirements of a large, dispersed organization such as a bank calls for sophisticated infrastructures. In addition to intra-organizational requirements, the banks must daily reconcile transfers of funds; customers want out-of-hours services to be as flexible as possible and independent of the point of use; retailer systems need to be integrated with bank and building society systems to clear transactions and so on.

By sector, financial services is the largest business user of IT, and IT expenditure makes up about 20 per cent of the sector's costs. Financial sector purchases of IT world-wide were worth more than $8 billion in 1988 and were expected to nearly double in value by 1994. The sector's sizeable presence in the market-place for IT products and services has given it a significant influence over technological developments and trends, and the priorities attached to application areas by the IT industry. More than this, the sector has funded research and development and been an active contributor to technical innovations. User-led innovation typically arises when the conven-

tional producer-user relation fails to deliver. It represents yet another aspect
of the 'expertise problem', namely the difficulties that technology producers
face in gaining access to the user expertise necessary to anticipate needs and
make generic products meet organizational requirements. Owing to the highly
developed division of labour between users and producers, producers are
denied an intimate knowledge of users' needs (Lundvall 1988). Yet knowledge
of users' needs is as important as knowledge about the technological possibilities. The knowledge gap becomes an even more important issue as IT
applications become strategic in nature, since the uncertainty about requirements often implicit in these applications means that they can only be
properly determined at the point of use (J. Fleck 1988).

There is a discernible pattern in the changing boundaries of the producer-
user relationship, the line between what producers can provide (the 'core')
and what user organizations must themselves contribute to make the technology work in their specific context (predominantly software). As time goes by,
producers adopt and 'black-box' (i.e. standardize) user innovations and offer
them as part of the core. Rather than fixing the new boundary once and for
all, however, this triggers off a new cycle of user-led innovation and subsequent producer adoption and commodification.

When computers first appeared on the commercial scene, user companies
found themselves with no option but to recruit technical skills to fill the
gap—caused by the lack of applications software—between the basic capabilities of the hardware and their requirements. As late as the 1970s, the majority
of applications software in the financial sector was written in-house (Barras
and Swann 1983). Subsequently, though, the role of in-house IS departments
has gradually changed as the industry began to offer standardized software
packages for commercial applications such as payroll and ledger. Today the
range of packages continues to grow—as our case studies confirm. They also
demonstrate that the gap between products and requirements remains, and
necessitates the retention of in-house IT skills by organizations. Requirements
may be so user-specific that generic packages must be individually customized,
a role often assumed by in-house IS departments. Many applications have
become so organizationally convoluted that only the user organization can
properly assemble and maintain the component parts as a functional system.

In the following section, we trace the development of financial sector IT
and consider the impact on the types of expertise organizations have had to
deploy in order to make applications viable.

EVOLUTION OF IT IN THE SECTOR

IT's new role is emerging against a background of well-entrenched practices.
White-collar work has been undergoing a cumulative process of automation
for more than 70 years, and developments in business IT have their roots in

the office technologies of an earlier, pre-computer era. Machines have been developed to bring capabilities into line with common business accounting practice.

The implications of the new office technologies for user organizations, and the need for specially trained staff, were minimal up to the 1930s and 1940s. The strategy adopted by producers was to match product development with commercial accounting practice. This meant that user requirements could be satisfied from a range of standard machines, and usually the new technology was relatively painlessly absorbed within the main business departments such as accounting. The trend for separate data-processing departments came later as a response to the demands for increasingly specialized expertise which followed the introduction of electronic technologies.

The Growth of Commercial Computing

Computer manufacturers responded quickly to the demand for hardware, but failed initially to appreciate users' software requirements. Commercial users, in particular, were concerned to obtain the maximum utilization of what was a very expensive investment; they wanted some means of managing the hardware resources and the execution of programs—what is known today as an operating system—efficiently and with the minimum of human intervention. The lack of an industry product forced user organizations to devise their own solution to this problem (Fisher, Mancke, and McKie 1983). In what was to become a distinctive pattern of user-led innovation, once their value was realized, operating systems were quickly adopted by the computer industry and incorporated into its products. Also during this same period, the first high-level programming languages emerged out of joint work by computer manufacturers and large user organizations.

Business investment in computing increased rapidly in the 1950s (Campbell-Kelly 1989). The financial services sector, with its well-established data-processing requirements, and resources to invest, was in the vanguard of the change-over to the new technology. The sector accounted for the largest installed base by value, outside of the computer manufacturing and engineering sectors (Stoneman 1976). During this period, the concept of general-purpose programmable business machines became established, high-level, problem-oriented programming languages came into widespread use, and data processing began to emerge as a distinct function within business, with its own brands of expertise. With little or nothing in the way of application software on the market, user organizations had to rely on software produced in-house, and data-processing departments formed around the emerging skills and expertise associated with software design, programming, and implementation.

In the initial phase of financial sector computerization, the main emphasis lay in replacing human effort in the performance of routine clerical tasks. The classic example of this was the transaction-processing system, typically involving operations such as payroll and accounts. The typical financial sector computer installation consisted of a central mainframe, providing a batch service for handling customer accounts and other clerical procedures. A process of administrative centralization followed, since hitherto accounts had been handled by branches (Rajan 1984), and this in turn stimulated the development of technologies to handle the large volumes of data and requests for information. By the late 1950s, the increasing complexity and volume of financial transactions had made the sector's need for more efficient data management increasingly urgent. Conventional computer filing systems were not designed to meet such a stringent set of requirements, and this prompted the development of a number of specialist software tools which became known collectively as a Database Management System, or DBMS.

A database is a generalized, structured, and integrated body of data. The principal role of the DBMS is to manage the transactions performed on the database—the reading and updating of data—in a controlled, efficient, and reliable way. Guaranteeing safe transaction processing while maintaining a high throughput requires technology of power and sophistication. In applications where near 100 per cent reliability is an operational necessity, a high degree of fault tolerance—the capacity to survive failures within the system—is also required. As a major database user, the financial sector was influential in setting database development priorities and that of a host of related technologies, including mass storage devices, communications networks, and system architectures.

With the development of increasingly large and complex database applications came the need to formalize design, which in turn led to the introduction of the *data model*, a set of conceptual and operational tools for describing the database contents, its logical structure, and basic properties. The Codasyl (Committee on Data System Languages) data model was the first for which an industry-wide standard was defined. Most first-generation, commercial DBMS packages were based on this or similar standards. The emergence of databases brought a need for user organizations to add database designers, programmers, and administrators to their in-house expertise, although in many respects these roles were specialized versions of more common software tasks.

The early 1970s saw the first introduction of on-line facilities in bank branches, through communications links to central mainframe databases. These were used to support the handling of various 'back-office' services, i.e. all transactions which involve vouchers of one form or another (Rajan 1984). The introduction of the minicomputer made it economical to put processing power directly into branches, first to enhance back-office services still further and later to provide computer support for 'front-office' teller services (Barras and Swann 1983). In the UK, Clydesdale Bank set the pace in branch services when it networked all its branches in the 1970s. Every teller and cashier position was provided with access to the bank's on-line transaction-processing services. In this period, management also began to use IT directly with the introduction of management information systems (MISs), which harnessed the information collation and processing capabilities of transaction systems to provide regular reports and summaries of business activity. For management, the chief gains accrued from the scope for increased monitoring, controlling, and planning of operational procedures. By increasing the quality and timeliness of information, MISs improved line management productivity, though without fundamentally changing the nature of its activities. Developments in the 1970s marked the stage at which IT applications ceased to be discrete and became organizationally diffuse. With the emphasis shifting from data processing to communications, organizations found themselves having to recruit yet more forms of IT expertise, not least specialists in network management and implementation.

The 1980s saw two major technical developments. The first was the introduction of personal computers (PCs) in clerical and managerial roles. PCs were a flexible way of providing and enhancing computing resources for a wide range of applications, and the rapid availability of packaged software meant that user organizations needed to be less reliant on in-house resources in the general application area. The second development was the advent of digital communications technologies and networks like ISDN (Integrated Services Digital Network) with the performance and reliability required for the organization-wide integration of data resources. The financial sector invested heavily in systems integration during the 1980s, but progress—as we see from the case studies—has been uneven. Overall, progress has been fastest within banking and slowest within the building societies and insurance. This undoubtedly reflects the traditional head office–branch relationship patterns of the different sector members. In insurance, this relationship is much looser than banking, with the role of branch office generally being undertaken by independent agents. The drive to integrate procedures has therefore been correspondingly weaker and only now are there signs of change.

Large users, such as the clearing banks, have established their own intra-organizational networks. These networks now exist for services such as CHAPS (Clearing House Automated Payments System) and SWIFT (Society for Worldwide Inter-bank Financial Telecommunications), and moves towards integration are already evident in ATM and EFTPOS networks. Building societies and insurance companies, with their common business interests, are seeking to establish intra-organizational networks in order to exploit the cost advantages of EDI (Electronic Data Interchange).

The clear picture that emerges from even this brief history is of sector organizations building a sizeable and increasingly variegated range of in-house IT expertise. System managers, analysts, and programmers; general applications programmers; programmers with specialist language expertise in niche areas like fault-tolerant and real-time systems; database administrators, analysts, and programmers; network managers and programmers; specialists in systems auditing and security; and general operations personnel: this list is a representative selection of the kinds of IT expertise to be found in the typical financial sector organization today. Few, if any, of the developments in technologies and applications have led to a net reduction in the sector's need for in-house IT expertise and, as we will see, there is little sign from trends in technologies and applications of this pattern being reversed in the future.

CURRENT TRENDS IN TECHNOLOGIES

The financial sector's IT infrastructure has grown enormously in composition and complexity over the forty-year period since the introduction of computers. Core technologies are those which facilitate data management—the storage, maintenance, and access of data. Of these, the database represents the key to all internal operations and services. In charting a course for future technical change, organizations must give special consideration to the impact of new services and applications on the core. New services and applications may demand the collection of new data, new uses of existing data by current users, or by new groups of users within an organization. What is clear is that patterns of data use and of access within the sector are becoming much more variable and organizationally much wider than before. For organizations, this raises fundamental questions as to how data should be structured, and how higher levels of integration might be best achieved.

The financial sector's use of databases has been predominantly to keep track of customers' balances and transaction histories. Only gradually has the sector come to realize that this information has great commercial value. Marketing departments, for example, can use it to identify customers who might be interested in a specific product or service. In this way, marketing tools, such as direct mail, can be targeted more precisely and more efficiently, with the confidence that response rates will be increased. Unlocking this latent resource, however, has proved difficult and expensive. The sector is handicapped by ageing and inflexible database systems. Often data is inefficiently structured for applications not anticipated when the databases were first designed, and their piecemeal uptake means that organizationally the data is seldom well integrated. Costly reorganization is often the only effective answer. Customer information provides a typical illustration of the problems. Following traditional practice, the financial sector's databases have been structured around bank accounts or insurance policies, rather than the marketing concept of the customer. As a result, information about any single customer may be scattered across several different accounts, databases, and even physical systems. Apart from the dangers of inconsistencies arising amongst data common to the different databases, lack of integration makes the collation of client data impractical, or even impossible. From a marketing viewpoint, it is clear that account-oriented databases are poorly suited to building up profiles of current customers. Worse still, they are of little use for keeping track of potential customers; by definition, account-centred databases may only contain information about existing account-holders.

In Mutual Life, for example, customer data was dispersed between different departments, and consequently it was difficult to access and analyse and build an accurate picture of the full customer relationship. A Senior Consultant in systems development recounted some of the problems this had caused.

We send premium reminder letters which are produced by the computer to people who are in correspondence with our Actuarial department waiting for quotations on new premiums. We send a letter saying 'You haven't paid this premium. We are going to lapse the policy.' And the guy writes back and says, 'Look, I don't know what the premium is yet!' If we had the systems more integrated, more co-ordinated, we could have people better informed and the right letters sent to the right people only.

Most of our case study firms were acutely aware of such problems and had made plans to change to customer-centred databases. Three of the projects on-going at the time of the study—Bank of Scotland's CABINET, Mutual Life's Customer Care, and Home and Auto's management information system—had major database integration and reorganization components.

The transformation of the database into a tool capable of actively supporting strategic business goals, requires more than a reorganization of existing data, however. It needs higher performance hardware to meet the increased transaction loads and the growing demand for real-time, on-line transaction processing and improved levels of system integration to link databases and users together. But most importantly it needs more sophisticated tools for database design and management to ensure a fit with organizational needs. The use of IT in the support of progressively higher-level business functions is practicable only to the extent that technologies, tools and, methodologies for system design and development (see Chapter 8 for a discussion of the latter) acknowledge these concerns.

Database Management Systems

Recent developments in commercial DBMSs show the traditional technology-centred issues of machine efficiency and data storage (though still important) are no longer the exclusive focus of attention. Instead, emphasis is on the provision of tools to facilitate the design, implementation, and use of databases in a business environment. Database design begins with the identification of the basic kinds of data relevant to the business and the relationships between them. The ease with which this *logical* design is subsequently translated into a *physical* design is important and may depend on the type of DBMS chosen for the implementation and the tools which it provides. The most important of these tools is the data model.

The *relational* database represents the new generation of DBMSs. In the relational model, the data model is represented as a collection of tables, known as relations (Korth and Silberschatz 1986). This has the advantage for end-users of being relatively simple and intuitive to understand. Equally important, the relational data model enjoys the support of formally-based design techniques to a far greater extent than is the case for earlier types of data models. The relational DBMS is also less closely tied to the underlying implementation details than its predecessors. It allows the designer to consider the logical structure of the database independent of its physical structure (i.e. how the data is stored) so making it easier to ensure a match between the implementation and business requirements. As an example, consider the generic customer–account database and the all-important customer–account relationship. In general, a customer may own one or more accounts, and an account may have one or more owners, i.e. the customer–account relationship is potentially *many-to-many*. Older types of DBMS, such as the *hierarchical* model, could not directly capture this form of relationship without resorting to the wasteful replication of data, with attendant dangers of inconsistency. For the relational DBMS, however, there are no such problems; the many-to-many relationship can be represented in a natural and straightforward way.

In principle, therefore, with relational database technology, database design can now be driven by the requirements of the business and need no longer be compromised by technical issues. The reality, however, is less clear cut. One cost of the relational DBMS's improved support for business is poorer transaction-processing performance. As we see later, for some types of applications these performance penalties can still be a decisive factor when choosing a system.

Relational database products are now available from major IT companies such as IBM and their use is becoming increasingly widespread within the financial sector. So it would be surprising not to find the relational DBMS figuring prominently in our case study projects. In fact, both Mutual Life's Customer Care system and Home and Auto's MIS were being implemented using relational DBMSs. The Customer Care project mainly involved the creation of a new database, integrating previously separate databases into one to provide the basis for management analysis and services such as direct marketing. This new database was built around three fundamental sets of data. The first two identified the basic types of data within the database—customers and policies—and the third defined the customer–policy relationships. IBM's DB2 relational DBMS was chosen for the implementation.

Subsequent to Home and Auto's decision to adopt a relational DBMS for its management information system project, major performance problems were encountered—it took two days to process transactions that were supposed to be done overnight. In this case, as described later, these problems were resolved without sacrificing the business advantages of the relational DBMS.

At the heart of Bank of Scotland's CABINET project was a corporate customer-centred database to which all services, including ATMs, HOBS, and teller and management information systems, were eventually to be linked. Rather than choose a relational DBMS, however, the CABINET database team chose an older but more transaction-efficient type of DBMS, as they judged that a relational DBMS would not have been able to handle the anticipated transaction volumes. The central database was implemented using IBM's IMS, a hierarchical DBMS offering good transaction-processing performance, but arguably—given the earlier discussion—less atuned to business needs.

The case studies presented clear evidence, therefore, that despite rhetoric about 'IT supporting the business', any assumption that the more traditional technically-oriented issues such as performance have been eclipsed is incorrect. Where business and performance issues are in conflict, the latter may still dominate. Whilst it is services and applications which are generally nominated as strategic, their viability may often depend on the performance of the core, leaving system designers and implementers with difficult choices to make; the core is therefore by no means completely black-boxed and unproblematic.

Systems Integration

Cost trends that increasingly favour the use of small computers, rather than one large, central, time-sharing mainframe, mean that businesses can choose from a number of hardware options to meet their processing needs. However, taking advantage of cheap computing carries with it the danger of fragmenting the IT infrastructure. Banks, with their highly devolved structures, have been particularly vulnerable. Progress in back-office automation has come about largely through investment in minicomputers and PCs, but poor integration has meant that data captured on branch systems has often had to be re-keyed for subsequent transfer to head-office mainframes. Systems integration—the creation of a unified IT infrastructure—is vital for the elimination of such operational inefficiencies and for the effective, organization-wide utilization of data and resources; it is the other key issue in the targeting of IT at the support of new products and services. In this way, the benefits of PCs (flexibility, ease of use, low cost) can be retained without sacrificing the advantages of mainframe processing (ease of sharing information, performance). The processing load can be split between a 'front-end' (PC) and a 'back-end' (mainframe), the former providing a user-friendly interface and the latter the volume-processing capability. Systems integration can improve fault-tolerance, since failure of individual parts need not be fatal for the whole system. Customer information can be reorganized, and its accessibility improved, without the need to relocate or duplicate data physically. Account-based databases can be restructured to provide customer-centred access and integration of departmental data achieved without the creation of mammoth, centralized databases.

Not surprisingly, therefore, systems integration in some form figured in a number of our case projects. It was the major strategic objective of the CABINET project, the means by which Bank of Scotland's databases, software, hardware, and communications networks were being reorganized to create a more flexible infrastructure with the capacity to capitalize on future developments in banking technology. Branch support was provided by Philips P9000 series minicomputers. With their built-in capability for local and wide area communications networking, these machines were key to the integration strategy. Existing branch systems and services were linked together to create branch-wide data storage and communications and these in turn inter-connected to provide links between branches and to central database services.

Until recently, progress towards the achievement of systems integration on the scale of CABINET has been impeded by incompatibilities in hardware, software, and data, but this situation is now changing. The availability of low-cost/high-performance digital communications networks like ISDN, and industry support for non-proprietary system standards, have removed many of the technical obstacles. Lack of progress cannot be explained solely by historic technical factors, however. Problems of fragmentation can also arise through intentional divisions of labour and roles, as the Mutual Life case study illustrated. With its boutique-like internal structure, the company's database systems had evolved to match the discrete operations of each department and were described as 'islands of technology' by one staff member. The process of integrating its departmental databases had to surmount interdepartmental conflicts over standardization and ownership of the data. The solution was to create a new department—the Customer department—with the specific responsibility of owning client records on behalf of the rest of the company. The impact of systems integration on administrative procedures and data handling may be similarly far-reaching, and further fuels the long debate over whether IT encourages decentralization or centralization (Kling 1980; J. L. King 1983). For banks, systems integration enables the devolvement of data capture and input to the branch level, and extends branch-level data access to the whole organization. It also means that branch data is no longer immune from day-to-day scrutiny by head office. The CABINET project raised precisely these issues, and it was evident from interviews with branch managers that there was some disquiet about the loss of their prized autonomy.

Systems integration also highlights the importance of industry standards for the successful development and marketing of new technologies. Standards define the extent to which different producers' products can work together. Without agreed hardware, software, and data interfaces, systems integration would remain a paper concept. The planned creation of standards has often been complemented by informal market mechanisms—the domination by one particular manufacturer or overwhelming market preference. As the largest supplier to the financial sector, IBM has long had a privileged position; many of its products have over time become *de facto* standards. It is becoming increasingly clear, however, that the corporate IT market is no longer prepared to allow standards to be imposed by a single manufacturer, no matter how large and powerful. Increasingly, the favoured alternative seems to be the open systems philosophy, which is being championed by a coalition of large-scale user and producer organizations. In principle, the adoption of open systems will permit users to choose freely from any compliant hardware and software, secure in the knowledge that compatibility with existing and future systems is assured. One result is likely to be that the decline in IBM's domination of the financial sector will continue. Other manufacturers have already occupied niche markets; Tandem's range of fault-tolerant machines, used by Clydesdale and many other banks for high-availability on-line services is one example.

CURRENT TRENDS IN APPLICATIONS

At the applications level, the projects highlighted in our case studies reflect three principal areas. Not all of them could be described as strategic in the sense of conferring an immediate competitive advantage, but even those that lacked an apparent strategic dimension had been promoted with future strategic benefits in mind. Application areas and project scope did not necessarily correspond. The scale of the CABINET project, for example, meant that it crossed conventional application boundaries; and small-scale projects generally carried implications for applications beyond their nominal focus.

Office Automation

New applications of IT in financial services are indicative of the shift of concern away from back-office systems and operational efficiency, to improvements in management performance, particularly in the handling of non-routine problems and decision-making, and better front-office services to help the customer. This does not mean, however, that back-office systems will cease to play an important role. Indeed, the first two phases of CABINET were intended to address precisely these areas. Phase One dealt with the installation of basic account query services in the branches. Phase Two concentrated on providing branches with support for administrative work such as standing-order updates, calculating loan repayments, and analysing customer balance sheets. Complementing trends within application areas reflected the ever-growing demands for a whole raft of office systems such as word processing and electronic mail. The building societies and life assurance companies were actively engaged in projects to improve levels of office automation and to establish better communications between branches and with business partners. A case in point was an 'intermediary automation' project at Mutual Life. The company had been delivering quotations electronically for some time, but was now looking at ways of cutting out some of the participants in the supply chain—banks to life offices to intermediaries to customers. They were aiming to develop 'solution packs' that intermediaries (e.g. building societies, insurance brokers, and consultants) could purchase.

As Premier Financial Services and Bank of Scotland VISA case studies illustrated, back-office systems (in this case in the form of credit-card processing services) are still important components of more strategic applications. The information they capture is the foundation of management information systems and decision support systems (DSSs) such as credit-scoring and marketing services. This has led to a renewed interest in back-office systems, as it is now realized that data quality control begins at the point of data entry. In the past, the cost of badly designed back-office systems and monotonous input procedures has often been poor quality data. There was evidence in both the Home and Auto and Mutual Life case studies of this problem.

Premier's processing system included on-line authorization and on-line access to debt collection agency data. A separate system was being developed to exploit the marketing potential of customer credit data, while future integration of the credit-card system with other bank services like EFTPOS and ATMs was anticipated. Amongst Bank of Scotland's future plans for its VISA processing system was the use of credit data in the marketing of other bank products and services. Concern over credit-card fraud had prompted the bank to enhance the VISA system with a means to detect multiple card applications, essentially by checking the details of new applications against those of existing cards.

Management Information and Decision Support Systems

In the financial sector, as elsewhere, IT is becoming increasingly focused on supporting management decision-making. It has been the financial sector in particular, however, which has long been regarded as an ideal area for the exploitation of leading edge DSS technologies. As an example, the sector is playing a major role in the development of expert system applications—i.e. the embodiment in software of human expertise. A 1988 survey indicated that almost 50 per cent of insurance companies were using expert systems, and over half of the banks were either using them or planning to do so (Berber 1988).

Expert systems provide evidence of the continuing importance of user-led innovation within the sector. Much application development is being done in-house, since, by their very nature, it is the expertise of the user organization which is required to transform expert system technology into viable, functioning applications. Expert system development can be very costly, however. Finding out how experts in a particular field actually make decisions is not easy and has become one of the bottle-necks in implementation. Much of the expertise employed may be too deep or tacit, or too contingent on local factors to be generalized and transported into other decision-making contexts.

Amongst our case study companies, only Mutual Life confirmed they were using expert system technology. The comment of the Systems Development Manager in Royal Bank that 'five lines of COBOL' could do as much as any expert system he had ever seen was perhaps more typical. Rather, projects such as Bank of Scotland's CABINET and Home and Auto's MIS emphasized the need to create a viable IT infrastructure to provide the foundations for future MIS and DSS tools. In the case of CABINET, future phases were targeted at providing branch managers with DSS tools for applications like financial analysis.

Certain niche DSS applications, such as credit scoring, featured in both the Premier Financial Services project and Bank of Scotland's VISA project. Credit scoring is a way of calculating a person's creditworthiness and profit potential. A typical credit-scoring system is based on a statistical profile of profitable customers' financial behaviour and personal circumstances. Applicants' details are compared with the 'score card' as part of the approval process. Similar profiling techniques are used in marketing to select likely customers for new products and services. As noted earlier, these examples of DSSs are increasingly being integrated with the conventional transaction processing systems on whose data they depend.

Management information systems provide another example of the increased processing demands of new applications and the continuing tension between application goals and system performance (Steiner and Teixeira 1990). Home and Auto decided at the outset that its new MIS would be based on a relational DBMS, because this offered most flexibility when seeking to combine data from separate files. Evaluation of various relational DBMS revealed insurmountable performance problems, however, which were eventually identified with an earlier decision to use base policy information (with its enormous volume of data), rather than summarized data available from the processing systems. The development team decided to reverse this decision, rather than abandon the perceived benefits of the relational database; and IBM's DB2 DBMS was eventually selected. The cost involved was the MIS no longer having access to richer base policy information.

Customer-Services Automation

Increasingly, IT is being used within the sector to deliver services directly to the customer. ATMs (Automated Teller Machines) were the first of a now growing range of customer-operated services. The success of ATMs took the sector by surprise; their original role was merely to provide a cash service out of normal branch hours (Scarbrough and Lannon 1988). To capitalize on their popularity, new functions have subsequently been added. These include account balance querying, statements, and cheque book requests. Eventually,

ATM services will achieve the convenience of the telephone—a global network, accessible from virtually any location. EFTPOS (Electronic Funds Transfer at Point-of-Sale) is a card-based, automated retail payments system. Customer accounts may be debited immediately on authorization, or overnight as payment instructions are forwarded from the retailer's system to the banks.

Home-and-office banking provides direct customer manipulation of accounts through a personal customer 'interface', linked to bank systems via the telephone network. This is the ultimate in self-service, out-of-hours banking and is now beginning to make an impact. Costs have been lowered, and ease of use improved, by the development of telephone-based interfaces which utilize the keypad, or even voice, to select services. Bank of Scotland's Prestel-based home-and-office banking system (HOBS) was first in the field (Scarbrough and Lannon 1988). Royal Bank of Scotland's Royline service is a cash management service targeted at the corporate customer. The complete package includes the usual payments facilities and software for analysing business performance. A range of additional services is envisaged, including international currency payments, trustee and share services, and CHAPS.

The benefits of these developments lie in the way that IT can change the delivery and form of financial services. IT provides the opportunity to compete in new markets at low cost. Home banking systems, for example, enable building societies to move into banking and Scottish banks to gain a stronger customer base in England, without having to invest heavily in the traditional, costly branch infrastructure. IT also provides the key to competing in existing markets with new services.

Clydesdale Bank's Telebank service is more typical of the current generation. Unlike Bank of Scotland HOBS (which was designed around a videotex user interface), Telebank was modularized so that the functionality was separated from the underlying user access mechanisms. Software Partnership's sp/ARCHITECT package had been designed to enable a variety of customer interfaces—ranging from keyboard and screen, to telephone keypad and voice—to be added when appropriate. The advantage was that Telebank's customers would be able to choose the style of interface which they felt was easiest to use and best suited to their needs. For maximum service availability, the package had been developed for Tandem 'NonStop' computers, which have become a virtual standard in the financial sector for high-reliability applications.

These changes in service delivery mean that customers have become users of financial services IT. This customer interface is set to grow in scale and complexity as new customer-operated services appear, such as cash management facilities, and in scope as customers become increasingly concerned with maximizing their financial resources. Good user interface design for this category of user is very difficult to achieve. Amongst this group, age, education, and experience may differ widely. Employees may at least be trained in the use of new technologies, and they have colleagues around who can help them. For ATM or home-banking users, however, training is not a viable option. Banks have found it necessary to provide help desks and round-the-clock support staff for home-banking systems, which can be an expensive way of dealing with the problems of poor user interface design. Also, if a customer needs to call the help desk, the damage to customer confidence may well be permanent, even though the immediate problem may be dealt with successfully. For high-visibility systems, it is extremely important for service providers to minimize customer problems and failures.

Clydesdale Bank's approach to home-banking systems design and development reflected the growing awareness of the importance of the customer interface. The realization that they did not have the necessary user interface design expertise in-house was one of the reasons behind the Telebank team's decision to contract out this aspect of the project to an independent software house. As we saw in the case study, the risks the bank ran in outsourcing modules to the Software Partnership matched the savings on development costs—but real gains lay with the implicit skills being imported, 'the proper understanding of the market', and the technologies that would serve it. Telebank therefore provided an interesting illustration of the process whereby innovations (in this case Bank of Scotland's pioneering HOBS) become transformed into virtual generic application packages.

CONCLUSION: APPLICATIONS AND IMPLEMENTATION

Though IT's new roles have led to a shift in technical priorities, the pressure for improved system performance continues unabated. At Mutual Life, for example, demand for processing power had increased by a factor of 24 in just six years. A side-effect of the introduction of ATMs has been to increase the banks' need for real-time, on-line transaction processing of their main customer databases. The effective elimination of the daily 'close of business' period by 24-hour, automated customer services has wiped out the logic and convenience of off-line transaction processing. Moreover, opportunities for misuse and fraud will increase as the number and use of automated customer services grow. To counter this, out-of-hours banking requires basic information such as account balances to be kept constantly up-to-date.

Many of the business and organizationally-oriented developments in IT incur significant new performance costs. Sometimes, as we saw in the CABINET project, performance problems have led to the rejection of new business-oriented technologies in favour of older, but more transaction-efficient ones. The long-term solution to performance problems lies in the development of technologies more suited to new kinds of application. It is clear, therefore, that system performance is still a crucial factor in determining the limits of application viability in financial services. Rather than being eclipsed by strategic concerns, it is these very same concerns which will ensure that technical issues in the form of improved hardware, systems architectures, and software will remain high on the list of priorities.

Also, regardless of the paper benefits of new technologies and systems, poor implementation may exacerbate an organization's problems. The viability of almost all new services and applications currently appearing in the financial sector relies to a significant extent on the databases and the data gathering and processing services that maintain them. Much depends on the success of projects to restructure and integrate individual databases to provide access to the full range of customer information. The scale and complexity of such undertakings are typically large and their underestimation has been a recurrent problem. In many respects, this is hardly surprising, as such projects often conceal a high degree of uncertainty behind an apparently straightforward brief. Several of our case studies illustrated this point very well.

In the CABINET project, for example, development targets were rescheduled as the enormity of the task of analysing all the bank's databases and restructuring two million accounts became apparent. CABINET's developers also found it difficult to contain the expectations of end-users and retain the degree of control over the timing of the project's phases which they felt necessary. Home and Auto's ambitious MIS project quickly ran into problems which led to a significant downgrading of its objectives. One of the development team observed that 'originally there were optimistic expectations that an MIS could be introduced and implemented with the minimum of fuss. However, experience has taught us that it is not that simple.' Yet the success of even this more pragmatic project remained open to question. H&A's system was judged by many of its users to at best simply tidy up existing information sources and at worst to produce much irrelevant data.

The operational characteristics of the insurance business and, in particular, the long-lived nature of the company–customer relationship enabled Mutual Life to take a more pragmatic and incremental approach to database restructuring in its Customer Care project. The customer-oriented database was to be applied initially to new customers only, and the integration of the existing Policy Holder Index File would follow only after this data had been cleaned up, i.e. checked for consistency, duplication, errors, etc. This alone was estimated to require 250 man-months of effort.

Where the increasing availability of software packages has diminished the contribution of in-house IS departments to software development, this has often been balanced by a corresponding need to customize these generic products. For the more routine applications such as back-office systems, the degree of customization is relatively limited and may even be done by the package supplier, as in the Premier Financial Services case. In contrast, databases exemplify how important customization may be. As a packaged solution to data-management requirements, the database is only as good as the customization inherent in the design and organization of the data. In the case of systems which are organizationally-convoluted, the customization process grows in complexity and bears all the hallmarks of the more conventional software development project, with its attendant risks and uncertainties. These crucial implementation issues are taken further in Chapter 9.

There is also a need for tools which are easy to learn, easy to use, yet possess the power to assist in the solution of complex problems. Experience shows that systems with poor user interfaces will be used inefficiently at best, and at worst ignored. Now that virtually every employee—and indeed many customers—are users of financial sector IT, a user-friendly interface is crucial for this wider and less computer literate community. Meeting this challenge calls for different kinds of expertise on the part of systems developers and greater participation in the design and development of systems. The nature of user participation is highly problematic, however, in that it challenges the prevailing perceptions of roles within the design process. User participation in systems design and development is discussed in depth in Chapter 10.

Thus as the range of IT applications in financial services grows ever wider, they are becoming steadily more complex and the expertise necessary for their design and implementation increases in variety. The demands this places on in-house IT expertise is partly offset by a continuing process of commodification in which innovations become available as packaged software. Even here, however, in-house IT expertise remains important for the almost inevitable task of customization. Our cases studies provided examples of the 'buy' option being exercised in innovative circumstances and we shall return to examine this issue in depth in Chapter 13. There we see that although software acquisition is often characterized as a choice between 'make or buy', a range of forms of joint development between supplier and user was typical of our cases. It remains true though that the viable option for most strategic projects involved some 'make', and that in any case project management remained a key issue even with outsourcing. To understand more about the problems of software development and how they are tackled, in the following chapter we examine the principles of software engineering and the management of systems development.

8

Software Development Practices

In common with other major business users of IT, the financial sector has relied heavily on user organizations being able to apply skills in-house, especially in the area of software development. In-house computing expertise has emerged to fill a critical gap in functionality that lies between the generic products of the IT industry and the requirements of user organizations. This gap remains, despite the widening range of commercial software packages, and in-house development is still the largest single source of business software in the UK. A 1989 survey revealed that up to 50 per cent of all applications software is produced in-house (Brady 1989). Out of the estimated 300,000 IT professionals in the UK, 60 per cent work within user organizations (Quintas 1991).

The complexity of the software development process, and the often arcane nature of the expertise involved, has presented new problems of management. Over the past thirty years, a series of crises over the quality, costs, and timeliness of software projects has led to the emergence of 'software engineering'—a specialized category of expertise centred around the development of IT—with strictly defined procedures covering every aspect of the software-development process. Problems have not been confined to issues internal to the management of software expertise, however. The relationship of software expertise with its host organization has become of increasing significance as the scale and importance of business IT applications have changed. In his account of computerization in the business sector, Friedman (1989) identifies user relations as being the latest in a succession of developmental bottle-necks. The expanding range of potential applications requires intensified user involvement in establishing system requirements and specifications; but the prevailing organizational culture, with its established arrangements of techni-cal and non-technical expertise, makes this difficult to achieve.

This chapter traces the emergence of software engineering, outlining its principles and procedures, and relating it to specific problems within the software-development process that it is designed to address. It examines the evidence from our case studies of the extent of adoption of software-engineer-ing methodologies in financial services, and of how these organizations have tackled the problem of making software expertise more responsive to business needs. The size of the financial sector and its member firms, its history of involvement in IT innovation, and the often organizationally complex nature of projects undertaken suggest it is precisely the kind of environment to encourage the adoption of software-engineering techniques. Whether or not this is actually the case will shed light on whether software engineering is able to meet the managerial challenges the sector faces.

THE MANAGEMENT OF SOFTWARE EXPERTISE

Regularly throughout its existence the IT industry has found itself in crisis over its competence to design and deliver products that match client expectations. Since the 1960s, software in particular has come to epitomize this failure. In response, the industry has pursued a number of initiatives aimed at improving methodologies and tools for software development. Software engineering has been the cumulative result (Pressman 1992). Yet as each step in the codification of software practices has succeeded in alleviating one set of problems, new ones have emerged.

Whilst the apparent nature of the software problem has changed, its roots may be ascribed to recurring difficulties in the management of expertise, albeit of different kinds. The software crisis was first articulated in terms of project cost and time overruns. The solution adopted was the use of structured, standardized programming techniques. From the perspective of managing expertise these had the advantage of reducing—or at least codifying—technical expertise, making it easier for project managers to supervise and control the development process (Kraft 1977). At the same time, a battery of techniques for estimating resource requirements, productivity, and quality have been developed.

As the nature of business IT applications changed, the focus shifted from cost to user satisfaction. Ensuring that software matched the needs of users, and could be revised and extended when necessary, became the focus of attention. Structured analysis and design techniques and the software life cycle were introduced to locate the writing of programs within a larger process that included requirements analysis and installation and use. From the perspective of expertise, this addressed the question of user expertise (i.e. knowledge of tasks and organizational procedures), and when and how to make this expertise accessible to the project team so that it could be incorporated into design. Changes in the organizational role of business IT are the cause of yet more problems for software development. Success is now seen to depend on business priorities driving IT applications. In this guise, the software problem is fundamentally a question of how to ensure that it is business—rather than technical—expertise which drives decision-making about IT.

Software engineering provides a recipe for blending the forms of expertise necessary for successful software development. It attempts to define the ranges of expertise required on the part of technical staff, and how expertise should be managed, whilst satisfying the concerns of professionals for interesting work and career development. It also seeks to distinguish the categories of expertise held by clients, ranging from strategic decision makers to end-users, and to specify when and how their expertise should be input to the development process. At issue is how well such a formalized approach to the management of expertise can deal with the uncertainty implicit in innovation and the contingencies of organizational life.

THE EMERGENCE OF SOFTWARE ENGINEERING

The concept of software engineering emerged in the late 1960s and early 1970s, the period commonly associated with the first 'software crisis'. A growing discrepancy had become apparent between the dominant trends in hardware and software. The former was becoming progressively more powerful, more reliable, increasingly commodified and hence cheaper. Software, on the other hand, had become notorious for cost and time overruns, unreliability, and failure to meet clients' requirements when delivered. During this period, the IT industry's difficulties in satisfying the demand for more and better quality software were worsened by shortages of skilled programmers. Its response was to look to more traditional engineering disciplines for a solution. The title of the new discipline stressed the need for software development to imitate the theoretical and practical orientations traditional in established branches of engineering (Wallis 1979). Software engineering emphasized the importance of structuring the product itself and the process of its production. As Pressman (1982: 15) notes 'Software engineering is modelled on the time-proven techniques, methods, and controls associated with hardware development. Although fundamental differences do exist between hardware and software, the concepts associated with planning, development, review, and management control are similar.'

Structured Programming Methodologies

The introduction of the first high-level programming languages and compilers (FORTRAN for scientific applications and COBOL for commercial work) improved programmer productivity through being more problem-oriented, and by isolating the programmer and source code from the details of the underlying hardware. By the same token, this also meant that source code became more portable, i.e. it could be moved from one type of machine to another with the minimum of changes. By themselves, however, high-level languages failed to address issues such as the variability in programming style, which made it difficult for programmers to understand one another's code. This became increasingly important as the scale of software projects grew, necessitating the use of larger and larger programming teams.

Structured programming began as a set of stylistic conventions whose technical rationale was the facilitation of 'good' programming style as exemplified by the ideal of 'lucid code'. One of its earliest advocates, Edgsar Dijkstra, wrote a now famous paper condemning the use of programming practices which made the logic of the program hard to understand (Dijkstra 1968). Dijkstra and others went on to define a set of simple constructs which were complete in the sense that any program could be written using these alone. These constructs form the conceptual and practical foundations of structured programming. Subsequently, new programming languages embodying them were developed, and older languages like COBOL revised to accommodate them. With the establishment of methodological standards, the variability of source-code quality could be controlled, making it simpler for people other than the author to understand. Not least of the benefits was that it became easier for project managers to switch programmers from task to task.

Structured Teams

However, from the point of view of the software-development process, the most important idea in structured programming is modularization. This made it possible to establish libraries of pre-written modules which could be used off-the-shelf. Another major benefit of modularization for programmer productivity was that it provided the means for project managers to black-box each team member's work and implement a horizontal division of labour (Parnas 1972). Large-scale projects could now be cleanly broken up into component parts small enough to be tackled independently by individual team members. According to Brooks (1982), who had been a senior project manager for the IBM 360 series operating system (at that time one of the largest software projects ever undertaken), this approach to team organization was inefficient, however. In his view, there were two key problems in a large-scale software project: (1) maintaining its conceptual integrity and (2) minimizing the communications overheads of team work. To address these problems, Brooks advocated a strict division of labour between design and coding: 'In effect, a widespread horizontal division of labour has been sharply reduced by a vertical division of labor, and the result is a radically simplified communications and improved conceptual integrity' (1982: 50).

Brooks did not view structured software teams as a means of routinizing and de-skilling software production, however. He saw that too much control imposed on expert labour brought its own problems. Team members might become bored and restless if the rigid allocation of roles compromised their opportunities to develop new skills and further their careers, and there was value in maintaining role flexibility.

Each man must be assigned to jobs that broaden him, so that the whole force is technically flexible. On a large project the manager needs to keep two or three top programmers as a technical cavalry that can gallop to the rescue wherever the battle is thickest. Management structures also need to be changed as the system changes. This means that the boss must give a great deal of attention to keeping his managers and his technical people as interchangeable as their talents allow. (Brooks 1982: 118–19)

Structured Analysis and Design Methodologies

The software design process became the next focus of attention for dissection and formalization. It had been evident from an early stage that errors at this stage in the process would be more expensive to correct than errors in the actual programing, since they would involve the recoding of part, or all, of the system. Structured methodologies were devised to make the nature of each design task and its relationship with other tasks explicit. At the beginning, these methodologies simply addressed the tasks of logical system design, i.e. the definition of individual system modules and the derivation of a specification from which programmers could work. Over time, however, their scope was extended to activities preceding design, namely system specification—the process of defining precisely what role the system is to fill—and requirements analysis—the process of gaining an understanding of current circumstances and of user needs.

As requirements analysis and specification became increasingly formalized and distinct tasks, whose practice required knowledge of one or more methodologies, a new category of software personnel emerged with its own specialist forms of expertise, leading to a further increase in the vertical division of software labour. This is generically referred to by the name of systems analyst, though there are a number of aliases in common use, including system engineer and programmer/analyst (Pressman 1992). The systems analyst studies existing systems and procedures and, through a series of interview and review sessions, attempts to establish users' views on the role and function of the new system. One of the systems analyst's main skills lies in an ability to communicate effectively with users, to understand issues and problems as users see them, and to describe possible solutions in their terms. More recently another related occupation has begun to be noted in the software-engineering literature, that of business analyst. In so far as it marks a genuine distinction from the expertise associated with the systems analyst, the business analyst lays claim to more organizational and commercial knowledge. In this respect, the business analyst closely resembles the so-called hybrid manager—one who possesses technical and business expertise in more or less equal measure (Earl 1989; Palmer 1990; Skyrme and Earl 1990).

There are numerous examples of structured analysis and design methodologies, each prescribing its own techniques and notations for capturing specification information: e.g. entity-relationship diagrams, dataflow diagrams, flow charts (Pressman 1992). Methodologies in current use include Jackson Structured Design (JSD), Structured Analysis and Design Technique (SADT), Warnier-Orr (also known as Data Structured Systems Development (DSSD)) and Structured Systems Analysis and Design Method (SSADM). Though they differ in the details of their approach, and sometimes the range of activities supported, an examination of one methodology will be sufficient to illustrate the basic principles.

The first phase is **information systems planning**. Its objective is to provide a general analysis of IT system needs within the organization, and recommendations for specific projects and their relative priorities. The main goal is to place systems development under the control of senior business management and align it with strategic goals.

Project initiation is concerned with defining project terms of reference, team members, etc. SSADM supports this phase with detailed guidelines. The scope of the project is determined and the effort required estimated. The project team is selected and tasks allocated. Representatives of client department managers and end-users are also recruited.

The **feasibility study** phase addresses the technical and organizational issues raised by the project, in order to establish that the fundamental conditions for success can be met.

The **systems analysis** phase generates detailed requirements of the system. It begins with an analysis of the current system (if one exists), which is used to isolate the functionality. The requirements of the new system are then determined. This involves talking with members of the client department. Detailed procedures vary depending on, for example, whether a system currently exists which is to be replaced, or the requirement is entirely new.

The objective of the **business study** phase is to select the best of numerous technical solutions to the requirements generated in preceding phases. A detailed logical design is produced to show the new system's relationship with the rest of the business.

The **physical design** phase converts the logical design into hardware and software system components. It is the last phase which is part of SSADM proper. The output of this phase is passed to programmers for coding.

FIG. 8.1 *The major phases in SSADM*

SSADM is currently the mandatory methodology for UK Government software projects and ranks close to being a virtual standard within the commercial software industry (Ashworth and Goodland 1990). SSADM is composed of a number of phases; the major ones are outlined in Figure 8.1. SSADM is a data-driven method in that it attempts to define in the abstract the underlying structures of the business data, inputs and outputs, and how data flows through the system and is processed by it. The specification of the software and its logical design is then derived from this analysis. In common with other methodologies, the procedures the analyst should follow are documented in considerable detail. Each of the SSADM stages has defined inputs and outputs, which determine the order in which they are performed. Each stage is provided with its own guidelines and notations for capturing and describing the information it requires, and the information it must generate for use by subsequent stages.

It should be stressed that SSADM is still evolving. The number and content of the individual phases remain the subject of change. For example, variants or 'templates' of SSADM now exist to satisfy common software development stereotypes, e.g. application packages, and PC-based systems. So-called 'fast path' templates are also available for use when speed of development is paramount (Ashworth and Goodland 1990). There is, therefore, an acknowledgement of the inappropriateness of attempting to force software projects to follow a single developmental recipe, irrespective of circumstances.

The Software Life Cycle

The software life cycle, an ordered sequence of activities from inception to use, ties the whole software-development process together. After the work of the systems analysts is complete, the logical design must be coded, tested, and bugs eliminated. The working system is then installed and becomes operational. The inclusion of this final phase in the life cycle is an acknowledgement that the responsibilities of the project team do not end here; revisions may be required during its working life to accommodate changes in the hardware environment and to maintain operational effectiveness. Such tasks, though often prompted by widely varying patterns of events, are usually subsumed under the general title of system maintenance.

The guiding principle of software engineering is that the system should progress in an orderly way through a series of transformations, starting with clients' requirements and ending in a fully operational system. The need for flexibility in the application of software engineering was recognized at an early stage—there might be circumstances where the overlapping, or even iteration, of phases would be inevitable. Brooks, for example, cautioned against the belief that software can always be designed and implemented correctly the first time around: 'Where a new system concept or new technology is used, one has to build a system to throw away, for even the best planning is not so omniscient as to get it right first time' (1982: 116). However, economic factors have meant that this advice tends to be ignored in practice. It is reckoned to cost between five and ten times more to correct mistakes discovered in testing, and between ten and 100 times more in the operational phase, than to correct them during design. It is for this reason that the emphasis has shifted decisively from programming—to specification and design, and subsequently to requirements analysis—and that procedures for carrying out these tasks have become detailed and exhaustive. The overriding goal has been to ensure that mistakes are caught early, certainly before they reappear as problems in the operational phase.

Several variants of the life-cycle model have been proposed in recent years,

Requirements analysis
System specification
Logical design
Programming
Testing and debugging
Installation, operation and
maintenance

FIG. 8.2 *The waterfall Life Cycle*

but the so-called waterfall life cycle shown in Figure 8.2 is the most developed form (Pressman 1992). The scope of a typical design methodology like SSADM is confined to the first three phases of the life cycle.

Summarizing then, the response of software engineering to changes in the nature of the software problem has been to devise formalized solutions for the management and application of software and user expertise, and to place progressively greater emphasis on the early stages of the overall process. The result has been an increasing specialization of expertise, reflected in an extensive vertical division of labour. The expertise claimed by the software professional has become closely identified with techniques, tools, and systems, ranging from particular analysis and design methodologies, to specific programming languages, and even computer systems.

Computer-Aided Software Engineering

A growing range of computer-based tools is now available to support the analyst and programmer. These tools are referred to collectively as Computer-Aided Software Engineering (CASE). The market for software-engineering tools is divided into three broad categories (Case 1985). The first aims to provide software managers with general tools for project control—for example, planning, budgeting, and resource estimation. The second (sometimes referred to as Upper CASE) is intended to support the business or systems analyst in requirements analysis, system specification, logical design, and data modelling, and to help reduce errors in the early phases of the life cycle. Typically, this support comes in the form of tools that are matched to the types of documentation required by a particular methodology, e.g. data flow diagram editors. More sophisticated examples use embedded rules to semi-automate the validation and checking of data for completeness and consistency. To some degree, therefore, Upper CASE tools instrumentalize a particular software-engineering methodology. Some form of tool support for software engineering is now essential to cope with the vastly increased amount of project documentation and attendant administrative problems. Indeed, there is evidence that the take-up of structured methodologies is correlated with the availability of CASE tools (Maille 1990). As we shall see,

one of the reasons why Bank of Scotland switched methodologies wa
because the old one lacked computer support.

The final category of CASE tools (Lower CASE) is targeted on later phase
of the life cycle and, in particular, at making conventional programminj
obsolete. Fourth-generation languages (4GLs) represent a continuation of th
trend within programming languages to describe software at higher, mor
problem-oriented levels of abstraction. As a means to eliminate the codinj
stage from software development, 4GLs belong to the Lower CASE category
In practice, however, they have often been most strongly identified with 'end
user programming', i.e. tools to enable end-users to generate their ow
applications without the aid of specialist expertise. Apart from 4GLs, man}
application packages support end-user programming in some form, and on
of the most common and important examples of these is the spreadshee
(Nardi and Miller 1990).

The full implications of CASE tools for software expertise remains unclear
but thus far their impact has failed to match the early predictions of th
automation of program coding and elimination of IT departments by end
user programming. A recent survey of applications development revealed
however, that 10 per cent are now produced by end-users (Bray 1992).

The Critique of Software Engineering

We have seen that the rationale for software engineering has been that o
improving the quality of the product and lowering costs. Wallis, for example
reveals a typical technicist view of the nature of programming labour, anc
(perhaps unwittingly) gives the clue to other motives. 'Our work product:
must have structure so that we can measure their quality, modify them, anc
control their complexity. Techniques must have structure to aid creative, bu
limited, minds and to permit the effective management of work' (1979: 9)
More explicitly, others have stressed the degradation of programming by a
variety of high-level techniques. Kraft in particular has argued that software
engineering's true role is

not to facilitate good programming, but to make it easier to manage programmers . .
to make the social relations of programming like those of the machine shop, secretaria
pool . . . to transform a highly idiosyncratic, artisan-like occupation into one whicl
more closely resembles conventional industrial work. (1977: 38) . . . [it] transform:
work made up of separate but highly interdependent tasks into a larger number o
simpler, routine, and unrelated tasks. (1977: 52)

Kraft's analysis of software engineering was informed by labour-process
theory, with its emphasis on the employment contract and managemen
strategies for its enforcement. He argued that by standardizing the procedure:
of software development, software engineering would contribute to the
'industrialization' of this hitherto craft-like occupation.

Studies of software development since Kraft have generally failed to provide convincing evidence of his predictions of de-skilling. Friedman (1989), for example, distinguished between *direct control* regimes, where work is subject to close monitoring and strict rules governing its performance, and *responsible autonomy* which relies on the exercise of discretion and self-regulation by employees. Whilst management tends to prefer the former strategy, it may be constrained in its application by factors such as labour shortages and low substitutability of skills. Friedman reports a mixture of direct control and reponsible autonomy management strategies in contemporary software development. He attributes this to a number of influences, of which one of the most important is the changing nature of IT applications. As these have become more complex, expertise requirements as a whole have increased rather than decreased. The changing nature of IT applications also provides the basis of another criticism of software engineering, namely that the success of these techniques has been achieved at the cost of exacerbating what are now, in the new phase of organizational IT, more fundamental problems. The software crisis therefore continues.

The virtues of structured team organization, structured design, and the life cycle can be matched almost in a one-to-one fashion with those of structured programming—the use of clear control structures, and modular decomposition, to conceal design decisions and minimize communication. The whole process of software development has in effect been modelled around the concept of structure. The original concept of structured programming, which in the narrowest sense addressed only the goal of writing programs with reasonably explicit control structures, has been expanded to form the foundation for all aspects of the software process (Wallis 1979: 1). It is not surprising, therefore, that a major criticism of software engineering has been that it is too structured to accommodate the contingencies of real life. Weinberg (1982), for example, attributed failures of the structured approach to team management to 'trying to manage people as if they were computers'. Studies of programming team structure provide some evidence to substantiate this criticism; whereas hierarchical team structures work well for routine problems, and are good for meeting deadlines, egalitarian structures produce better solutions, especially for complex problems and where uncertainty about the nature of the solution exists (Mantei 1981; Constantine 1993).

In isolation, debates over whether software engineering is too structured explain little of the current problems within software. When put in the context of the changing nature of IT applications the assumptions on which software engineering is based become increasingly open to question. Applications in the past have been typified by:

1. a main objective of improving organizational efficiency,
2. requirements defined in terms of current procedures, and
3. a stable environment.

Thus the waterfall life cycle dictates that development proceeds through a succession of orderly phases, each increasing the detail and formality of description until the system is complete. The assumption is that all the important features of the system can be determined in advance (the output of requirements analysis, for example, is taken as an authoritative statement of what the system is required to do). In capturing such data, software engineering stresses abstract representations of the task and its environment—such as data structures and flows—and blames any lack of success on the failure to gather this information rigorously.

In financial services and other business arenas, however, applications of IT rarely fit the model. More often than not they are characterized by:

1. innovation, new products and services, not automation of existing ones,
2. absence of current procedures to provide a basis for requirements, and
3. change as an environmental feature.

Thus the criticism of conventional software engineering is that, where innovation is a key objective, the greater risk is that software will fail to meet requirements because of the inherent uncertainty over what they should be. In such cases users typically have only an incomplete idea of their needs, there is no existing system to serve as a starting-point, and paper-based specifications cannot give potential users a feel for how the real system will behave, even assuming that users understand them. Requirements analysis is performed, but with no verification that the decisions made are correct until the system is built, at which time the cost of fixing mistakes is greatest. Even worse, much of the effort expended following the detailed procedures of the methodology may prove to have been wasted (Dennis, Burns, and Gallupe 1987). Conventional software engineering leaves little scope for learning, with the result that the very problems it was intended to eliminate return in magnified form.

One solution is to introduce prototyping as a means of short circuiting the long feedback loop between requirements analysis and use. In the throw-it-away approach this typically involves building rudimentary systems quickly, as soon as a preliminary requirements analysis has been performed. Here the role of the prototype is to make design errors and misconceptions self-evident and to help users achieve a concrete understanding of the possibilities. Boehm (1986) has proposed the 'spiral' life-cycle model in which prototyping is combined with the waterfall approach. Development proceeds through a series of prototyping stages, with each one being evaluated before the next is begun. In essence, the four stages of conventional software engineering—analysis, design, coding, and testing—are combined into one phase which is then iterated several times.

The principle enshrined in prototyping-based approaches is that software engineering must acknowledge the reality that systems are often evolved rather than designed (Gilb 1988). The so-called evolutionary view emphasizes intensive user involvement, iteration, and the experimental—rather than formal—nature of design. It asserts that many important aspects of the process cannot be formalized and that major decisions cannot be strictly ordered. Whereas conventional software engineering places the highest value on formal knowledge, and an abstract conception of the system as pure data flows, the evolutionary approach emphasizes the importance of informal, contingent, and tacit knowledge held by users, and of situating design in the context of use. Most important of all, it argues that software engineers must learn to live with change as a fact of the environment and its implications for modification and reshaping throughout the life cycle. This implies a need for a wider range of skills, more flexibility, a less hierarchical organization of team members, and diverse patterns of communication within the project team and between it and users (Gronbaek, Kyng, and Morgensen 1993; Walz, Elam, and Curtis 1993).

Methodologies based on prototyping have become an established tool in the more specialized area of user interface design, but have yet to make a broader impact on systems development. Changing entrenched practices is naturally difficult, and given the shift of emphasis in the evolutionary approach from project management to the management of change, there are doubts as to how controllable such a methodology would be in practice, and misgivings about its potentially high costs (Pressman 1992). Indeed, it is becoming evident that the challenges of managing software expertise and the software-development process cannot be met through the application of a universal recipe for software engineering. On the contrary, methodologies are proliferating in recognition of the variable nature and circumstances of software projects, and that methodlogies must be chosen to suit.

DEVELOPMENT PRACTICES AND THE CASE MATERIAL

We turn now to our case studies for evidence of software-engineering practices in retail financial services and the light this may shed on the issues raised in the preceding discussion.

Work Management

First, our case studies do not provide convincing examples of the de-skilling thesis. Take-up of the full range of conventional software-engineering practices was patchy, and the case firms revealed a mixture of management strategies for software-development work. On the surface that of Bank of Scotland's Management Services Division, with its tight division of labour within and between project teams, approximated most closely to Kraft's description. The programmers there expressed dislike of rigid work schedules and management monitoring: 'every program you get you are told initially what the completion date is, and then the monitoring every week or two, how you are progressing, and how much work you can do, whether you are going to go past schedule dates and all this sort of stuff.' But these and other instruments of direct control, such as a policy that programmers must sign their work, had proved difficult to enforce in practice. Whilst all staff were expected to fill out time-sheets, the feeling was that they were a chore of little value and few apparently made serious attempts to keep an accurate record. Perhaps what management gained through 'worker visibility' meant losing the ethos whereby being trusted to do the job was part of the appeal of the team.

According to its project managers, Royal Bank of Scotland did not differentiate between analysts and programmers. Junior programmers initially did just coding, but as they became more experienced, they were expected to take on the responsibility for writing program specifications as well. Progression to more responsible tasks was considered essential to maintain staff motivation: 'With three or four years programming to full specs, you'd get fairly brassed off.' However, the exact form of career structure turned out to be a sensitive matter. In the past, the bank had used different job titles, but these had been dropped to avoid a 'them and us' situation. Here, as elsewhere in our case studies, specialization was perceived as a barrier to team work and successful systems development: 'Programmers think analysts don't know what they are talking about, and analysts say, "right the business requirements are this, I don't care how you do it".'

At Clydesdale Bank, there was no strict division between programmers and analysts, but structured design methodologies were clearly preferred and had been introduced to counter a 'very cloistered, very parochial' environment, dominated by what the Systems Development Manager described as the 'hippie programmer' culture. This phrase is typically used to denote a host of 'bad' practices, but chiefly idiosyncratic programming styles and a lack of attention to program documentation.

I wouldn't like to knock the Clydesdale organization, but the computing culture I inherited stemmed from the '60s and early '70s. . . . Some people hadn't even heard of structured techniques. . . . You always had this (resistance) problem. Because what you are saying to them is 'Your experience is no use. You have to learn this new structured technique.' (Systems Development Manager)

The particular programming methodology in use here was Jackson Structured Programming (JSP), a component of Jackson System Development (JSD). JSP lays down in considerable detail how programs are derived from the logical design of the system. To aid the management of programming work, the bank had a project-control system which broke projects down into tasks and allocated them to individual programmers. Programmers had to fill in time sheets and this information was used to compare progress with completion times as work progressed. According to management, however, estimates of completion times were generally provided by the programmers themselves rather than imposed.

At Mutual Life, programming teams were organized as semi-permanent fixtures and in a way which mirrored the company's functional divisions.

This came about as a way of preventing technical staff from setting project priorities, which had been the case in the past when a team could have found itself working for different departments at the same time. Dedicated teams were also seen as a way of building long-term relationships with user communities. Only one team was not tied to a particular department, and this had been given the Customer Care project. The division of labour between teams was very marked, but within teams rigid distinctions over job titles and responsibilities were generally avoided. Senior project management claimed that 'we do not put people into tight compartments. We allow them to show how much scope they have'. This was contradicted, however, by the fact that management's also expressed belief in the value of psychometric interviewing tests and their capacity to indicate 'very distinct differences between the analyst types and the programmer types'. It was the conditions of employment—particularly of contract staff—at Mutual Life which came closest to fulfilling predictions of de-skilling and routinization.

The practices of Software Partnership, the one independent software company amongst the case studies, made for an interesting comparison with those of the in-house IT departments. While we obtained only the view from the top, this did accord with a general picture of the software agencies and consultancies that natural divisions of labour have not been transformed. Software Partnership's organizational structure was described by one of the founding partners as being 'egalitarian' in nature, with work organized around the project and roles within it, rather than a formal company hierarchy of job titles. This 'matrix' structure was claimed to provide for good communications between staff, which the company believed was vital to the success of projects. Plans to expand from their present size of 35 to 50 were recognized as posing a potential threat to the company's wish to remain 'organic'.

On occasions where it was impossible to meet expertise requirements in-house, project managers in our case study firms sought other solutions. Clydesdale Bank's decision to contract out the development of Telebank's user interface software to Software Partnership was influenced by the bank's lack of experience and expertise in this area. Mutual Life's choice of a relational DBMS for Customer Care led them to bring in an outside expert on relational database design. In both cases, the fact that pure expertise was offset by a lack of firm-specific experience was portrayed as encouraging the all-important 'fresh view'. At Mutual Life, however, the reality appeared to be somewhat at odds with this claim, in that the expert actually relied heavily on formal documentation of the company's working procedures to establish system requirements.

Bank of Scotland had some of the most comprehensive house programming standards of all the case studies—'We have standards for absolutely everything'—which a senior training manager described explicitly as a control device to prevent programmers from holding them over a barrel. According to their own accounts, however, experienced programmers did not like the 'idea of being policed', nor did project managers like to see their role as enforcing standards. Their attitude towards working practices was often more relaxed and pragmatic than official guidelines would imply.

I think that most people accept the need for standards inasmuch as it makes it easier for someone else to read your code. But whoever writes the program is going to be different from someone else, so the feeling is that the standards are to that extent a waste of time. . . . It is a good idea for trainees, because it puts them into working the way the bank wants you to. But then what happens when you rub people up the wrong way when they have been coding for years and then somebody comes along and says 'Well you have put this in the wrong column' or something like that.

Tools

The majority of software in all the case studies was written in the traditional business programming language, COBOL, and other languages were used only where this was unavoidable. An example was the software for the Telebank project's Tandem fault-tolerant computers which had to be written in their own special-purpose language. And Bank of Scotland had to bring in Philips programmers for the P9000 series minicomputers, as software for these had to be written in the programming language C, which was not used elsewhere in the bank. Not surprisingly, the need for different languages was viewed as a problem by project management. Flexibility in the deployment of programming staff was reduced when demand for special language skills could not be met in-house.

Only at Bank of Scotland and the Royal Bank of Scotland was there substantial use of CASE tools. Bank of Scotland was using a proprietary tool for project documentation and program source-code version control, which also combined several project-team management features such as on-line time sheets. Royal Bank of Scotland had developed its own programming support tool, SCEPTRE, described as a 'high-level specification language' and used extensively in the development of Royline. We found little evidence of 4GLs as end-user programming tools. Interestingly, but perhaps not surprising given the threat of programming automation, technical staff expressed a general mistrust of 4GLs and of end-user programming, though this was often couched in terms of concern for system performance. As a Senior Project Manager at Mutual Life put it:

There isn't a 4GL ever invented which doesn't need strict control because as soon as you allow people to access data, they will keep jobs running for hours and they'll knock everybody else out. . . . The user programming thing still has a long way to go, and it could become a real pain in the neck.

It was also claimed that code generated by these tools was generally 'too big'. In other words, the view of more technically-oriented IT personnel was that 4GLs were too inefficient for serious use, which mirrors attitudes expressed in an earlier survey of 4GL usage (Hamilton 1986). Business analysts, in contrast, regarded 4GLs as extremely useful for requirements investigation, and we also found them in use as prototyping tools in the user interface design of CABINET. As one Business Analyst remarked, 'we found that we could generate screens quickly and connect them together to show users how it would look and we found that quite useful.' Here, at least, 4GLs had made their mark chiefly as Upper CASE tools, helping business analysts to investigate system requirements more thoroughly by giving users a better idea of what the system would look like.

Many of our case study organizations were using proprietary methodologies provided by their major system suppliers, reflecting the fact that CASE tools—and the methodologies they support—have become part of the IT industry's product range. With methodologies identified as part of the 'problem', IT vendors have recognized the advantages of being able to offer clients methodologies and tools as part of their 'solution'. Having also discovered that training is one of the main barriers to the take-up of methodologies and tools (Quintas 1991), the proprietary IT 'package' typically now includes training programmes. Alternatively, vendors will provide customers with assistance on a consultancy basis, hiring out experts to lead in-house staff through the basic steps. For example, when IBM realized that indifference was the main obstacle to Mutual Life's Customer Care project, senior management were offered the 'opportunity' to send some of their staff on an IBM-run Applications Transfer Training Course, whose principal aim was to neutralize opposition and generate committment.

Methodologies

Software-engineering methodologies were a major issue in the case studies. Bank of Scotland was in the process of piloting the introduction of a new methodology, Learmouth and Burchett Management Systems System Development Method (LSDM), having previously used parts of SSADM. LSDM is a variant of SSADM designed specifically to meet the needs of the commercial user. Like SSADM, it has three major stages—analysis, logical design, and physical design—and each stage is itself broken down into a series of steps. The decision to take on a complete methodology was influenced by the CABINET project and the conviction that its size made some form of structured approach essential. LSDM was eventually chosen from a short list of four, including SSADM, largely because LSDM was considered to be more pragmatic and less restrictive. Other factors in its favour included widely available training, the vendor's capacity to act as a consultant when required, and the promise of computer-based tool support for all stages. Senior project managers at the bank clearly found it difficult, however, to be certain of the benefits. Confidence in improved project management and quality of documentation was offset by concern for the overheads of training staff and misgivings that methodologies could also be a strait-jacket.

Whereas you can sometimes cut corners and do things when you would prefer to do them, if you are using a methodology you are much more forced down a more disciplined route, but more disciplined sometimes means less flexible.

Indeed, a Business Analyst expressed the view that experience was still the most valuable asset in his role and that methodologies should be used only as a framework. 'I don't think you can rely too heavily on a methodology. It provides you with a structure but that's not everything. There is always a danger with methodologies that we on the technical side concentrate too hard on things like data. We lose sight of the business problems.' Problems of uncertainty over the requirements for CABINET were being addressed by staging its development, which permitted organizational learning to take place.

Home and Auto had introduced IBM's Business Systems Planning (BSP) methodology at the time of the initiation of its MIS project. BSP is a framework for establishing requirements which models flows of information on organization charts, and is a development of Study Organization Plan (SOP), an earlier IBM methodology. However, this approach to requirements analysis has been heavily criticized for unrealistically assuming that the organization chart is how organizations really operate, and for imposing requirements on users rather than eliciting requirements in users' own terms (Friedman 1989: 263). Criticisms like these were borne out by the H&A project team, who found that the model was unable to cope in the 'grey areas' of the business where individual Product Managers varied in their approach; nor did the model help much in setting the priority for parallel changes. Eventually there was a change of heart in the systems department (along with a change of personnel at the top), BSP was abandoned and a more pragmatic, department-by-department approach adopted.

At Mutual Life problems with methodologies were also evident. The company had been using yet another IBM analysis and design methodology for the Customer Care project. This was described by company analysts as a tool for documenting the business as procedural steps in the form of standard diagrams, down to a low level of detail. The database design consultant commented that he would prefer a more data-oriented methodology such as SSADM, since the current methodology 'seems to give priority to business procedures more than data procedures'. Subsequently, it was decided to drop this methodology and a working practices committee was charged with selecting a replacement. Amongst those being evaluated at the time of our study were LSDM and Structured Design Methodology (SDM, also from IBM).

The difficulties created by the need to innovate were described by a Business Analyst at Bank of Scotland as follows.

The problem that the business analyst has to face is that they have to be innovators. They are often faced with an ill-defined problem, or a problem where there's a great deal of background of history which is perhaps confusing. They also have to face the fact that the user may have a vague idea of the problem, or indeed the wrong idea of the problem. They may have pre-judged the solution. All these things make it often difficult to get to grips with what needs to be done and why it needs to be done.

In this context, conventional software-engineering practice forces a commitment to important design decisions at a time when there may still be considerable uncertainty about very basic requirements. As Podolsky (1977) notes, 'The problem with the classical development cycle is that it assumes things will only be built once and that is in conflict with the real world.' In all our cases, senior analysts and project managers acknowledged this problem. As one Analyst put it, 'It's only when [users] get the thing and can work with it, that you begin to see the potential problems coming out of the woodwork.' In such circumstances, sticking to a conventional methodology can lead to software which, though technically excellent, fails because it has little bearing on real needs. Furthermore, as users become aware of the constraints of development, their response may make the problem worse. The CABINET case study provided an illustration of this potentially pathological process at work. As the project wore on, there was an escalation of user demands and aspirations which threatened to make the specification unwieldy and overwhelm the project. Eventually, Systems Development was forced to back-pedal on CABINET's capabilities. Deflating users' expectations was the only way in which they could stabilize the situation and re-establish control.

Software Engineering and Business Needs

In all the case firms, concern was demonstrated for increased corporate involvement in the software-development process. With the exception of the Royal Bank of Scotland, which tended to rely on IT staff's accumulated knowledge of user needs, the business analyst represented the strategy chosen to achieve this goal. The role of the business analyst was to identify business needs, undertake responsibility for requirements analysis and project specification, and pass the results on to systems designers and their programming teams. The emergence of the occupation was often accompanied by organizational restructuring, but there were important differences in the details of reorganization. Bank of Scotland opted to keep its business analysts within the IT Division, but split it into two parts. A pilot study had been run to determine precisely at what point within the LSDM methodology SIV would hand over to SIM. Its outcome confounded expectations and emphasized the need to adapt methodologies to organizational circumstances.

You have to overlap the methodology with our structure, with our organization. . . . Obviously the methodology is for the average company. But who is an average company? Everyone is different. . . . We thought that the obvious place to change from

SIV to SIM is at the end of stage A. However, one of the lessons from running the pilot study was that the break-off point was more appropriate after one of the specs within stage A.

At Clydesdale Bank business analysts had been unable to bring about a significant change in IT decision-making and the initiative for projects mostly still came from within the IS Division. One Senior Manager put this down to lack of IT expertise in the bank at large:

It's the wrong way but we've always been the ones to take the initiative. The business side are a bit slow in coming forward. The bank as a whole should be telling IT what we need from technology, not technology telling the bank. It gets difficult at times. The number of times we've written specifications and we've waited and we've waited for the OK and they don't really know themselves what they want.

As a consequence, a restructuring was planned. Following the Telebank project, the business analysts within the IT Division were to be reorganized into a separate Electronic Business Division. The aim was to prevent business analysts from getting drawn into technical issues and improve communications between the Bank and the IS Division.

You ended up in a situation in which IT could be accused of driving the business, and the business just couldn't make itself understood to IT. IT must never be made to feel that they're being driven, just as they're not allowed to drive. And the business must be able to feel that it can describe itself in its own terms rather than always having to relate those back to terms which IT understands. (Clydesdale, Electronic Business Manager)

In Mutual Life, the IT department had been renamed and enlarged to include responsibility for relating technology to business strategy. In effect, this meant the new Operations department subsuming business areas such as O&M. The success of this reorganization was questioned by the General Manager of Operations, who commented that neither IT nor O&M had the authority to 'take a whole function by the scruff of the neck and change it'. In a move in keeping with the IT Division's general boutique-like structure, an Internal Consultancy Group had been set up with the responsibility of acting as a buffer between senior business management and Operations, and carrying out strategic planning. Like Bank of Scotland, however, the consultants had problems defining and legitimizing the boundaries of their jobs to Operations staff. The consultants' role was to establish a direction for projects, but a Senior Consultant complained that Operations staff nevertheless expected detailed specifications.

I have to fight off people who think I'm doing something more. I walk into endless walls when I go to speak to the database people. And they say, 'Yes, but you must produce a completely finalized data model before we can discuss these things.' And I say, 'Well, I have no intention of producing any such thing.'

Mutual Life's fragmented organizational structure had made the establishment of a corporate IT strategy difficult. The Internal Consultancy Group proved ineffective, or as a Senior Consultant remarked, they 'seemed to be existing in a parallel universe'. In practice, its role was assumed by the Operations department, as the only group that could reasonably arbitrate between the business divisions.

Creation of the business-analyst role represented one way of trying to achieve strategic input within the software-development process. In both Bank of Scotland and Mutual Life, however, when a new speciality entered the organizational arena its claim to special knowledge stood as an accusation that others were either incompetent or ignorant in the 'expert' area. The staff of SIV saw it as part of their role to act as a buffer between SIM and users and, if necessary, defend the latter's interests; but there was evidence that this role was contested.

We are the in-betweenies, we have to fight for the users' requirements against what systems really think is best from a technical viewpoint. I think some of the (SIM) analysts feel 'why do we need these people, they are superfluous, why can't we just get on with the job'. I disagree with that. If we ever have any difficulties liaising with programming teams . . . it would be tenfold if the user had to liaise directly. We are there to create the interface between the two.

Finally, in the case of end-users, we found examples of their involvement in user interface design, but little evidence of a consistent and coherent policy for user involvement on a wider scale. In CABINET, for example, branch staff had been given the opportunity to use and comment upon prototype screen layouts. But the prevailing attitude amongst IT staff was that the final decisions should be theirs. 'We want to develop systems in a logical manner, they want to develop it in terms of the facilities they want. We like to think that they decide what the priorities are, but under our guidance.' User involvement in project management was generally realized through the project working party. Where working parties had been used they had been only a qualified success, however. The problem seemed to be that, in practice, working-party members were unsure whether it was intended as a forum for representing and incorporating everyone's views—a consensual, democratic device—or to police the systems builders—a conflictual, vetoing device.

CONCLUSION

The case studies provided no convincing evidence of the de-skilling of software expertise of the kind predicted by Kraft. They suggested the reason this has not come about reflected in large part the lack of 'social application' (Friedman 1989). True, de-skilling dynamics were present. There were managerial views reflecting programmers' 'limited minds' and plentiful evidence of direct-control techniques like time-sheets and project monitoring. But managers typically applied these only half-heartedly. Whilst project teams were typically organized around vertical divisions of labour, they were flexibly applied and staff encouraged to take on new roles. The de-skilling of specific programming tasks had been compensated by the emergence of new roles and new forms of expertise. Overall, skill requirements were becoming broader rather than narrower, and seemed less a product of de-skilling than of specialization; the emergence of the business analyst was a prime example. We also saw that moves towards increased specialization may be contested by more traditional forms of IT skills, though in this discussion we focused on the practical and organizational elements of the business-analyst role. In Chapter 10 social and political aspects, and the construction of these hybrid skills, will be explored further.

There was evidently a consensus that improved corporate involvement in IT decision-making, systems design, and project management was the key to making the IT function more responsive to business needs. The methodologies in use, however, typically attempted to address this issue by simply formalizing user involvement as a stage at the beginning of the traditional software life cycle. The problem is that by retaining a conventional software-engineering approach, user involvement of all kinds and at all levels of the business may be ineffective. Notably, it was business analysts who seemed most aware of the potential advantages of a more evolutionary approach, rather than other more technically-minded IT staff. In innovative high-risk projects, development tended to be staged (and those stages often extended by practical circumstances) in order to permit organizational learning to take place. In practice, therefore, the textbook methodology was being set aside for a strategy resembling that of an evolutionary approach, rather than the simplified image of the waterfall model.

User involvement in systems development may stimulate internal conflict or meet with resistance, as we also explore further in Chapter 10. The varied proposals for addressing these problems include changes in human resource management philosophy that empower users (Byham 1988); while at the most detailed level of specification, proposals for participative design themselves become virtual recipes for systems development (McDermid 1990). But, in general, software engineering has tended to neglect non-technical issues and the organizational dimension and, as we found in our case studies, this has led to its frequently failing to achieve objectives.

9

Implementation and Innovation

Implementation is the crucial phase of development in which technical capabilities and strategic objectives combine to produce economically effective systems in particular organizations. Implementation is the meeting point between the structural issues discussed in Chapters 5 and 6 and the technological issues in Chapters 7 and 8. In particular, where strategic systems are involved, sufficient novelty may be embodied for the resulting systems to be recognized as genuine innovations. Interaction between decisions made by managements in user organizations and the expertise contributed by technical personnel (internal and external) can thus result in creative outcomes with far wider applicability—a distinctive pattern of user-led innovation.

Computer developments in general have owed much to user innovation, and this has been particularly marked in the financial services sector. As well as exploring the major features of the implementation process in this chapter, we will examine the nature of the user-led innovation process in terms of the inputs of expertise involved. Of course, many different forms of specialist expertise can contribute, as was abundantly illustrated by our case studies, which involved programmer/analysts, business analysts, actuaries, statisticians, accountants, bankers, marketing specialists, and others. The manner in which internal and external forms of expertise are deployed is crucial, yet specialist expertise is not for senior managements to do with as they like. Issues of power and control and occupational affiliation enter, often underpinned by labour-market strengths and weaknesses.

THE NATURE OF IMPLEMENTATION

Some technologies are easily put to use. A television set, for instance, requires plugging into a suitable power source, several adjustments to tuning, and it is ready for use. Company-wide information systems, like those typically used in financial services lie at the opposite extreme. It takes great effort over substantial periods of time to bring such large-scale systems to the point where they can be used and, more importantly, to the point where they can secure some form of competitive advantage. This process of implementation, of getting complex technology to work and yield corporate benefits, has become recognized as a key aspect in the overall development of technology (Leonard-Barton and Kraus 1985; Rhodes and Wield 1985; and Voss 1988).

Implementation in this sense goes beyond technical development and installation *per se*. It involves the organization, its goals and strategies, and is the process through which technology is concretely deployed. As such, it is a crucial process as far as strategic innovations are concerned and is the prime locus in which decisions regarding technology take shape.

The difficulties in getting complex technologies to work effectively have been long recognized, though not widely acknowledged. Many of Bright's classic observations, for example, made originally with respect to the mechanical automation of the 1950s, are equally applicable to IT systems today (Bright 1958). The current round of IT investment has again brought these issues to the fore, and nowhere more than in financial services.

We may define implementation as the process through which technical, organizational, and financial resources are configured to provide an efficiently operating system. This definition is broader in scope than the use of the term in software engineering often denotes. In the context of the system development life cycle, implementation is frequently used to refer only to the final stages of putting a system into productive operation (McDermid 1990). This restricted sense more accurately equates to the installation stage of the cycle. Even the information-technology literature, however, recognizes the broader scope and importance of the implementation process (e.g. Swanson 1988). In research on the introduction of technology in general (rather than software or IT in particular), the importance of the broader conception is now well established (Rhodes and Wield 1985).

In financial services in particular, the complexity and importance of the implementation process is definitively demonstrated at the sharp end of activity by the emergence of departments dedicated to carrying out implementation activities. In Bank of Scotland, for instance, one department was explicitly titled Systems Implementation. Moreover, the emergence of this department followed a previous strategic setback with technology, namely automated teller machines (ATMs), which had demonstrated to the bank the need for a more systematic institutional approach to the deployment of technology (Scarbrough and Lannon 1988).

In the financial services sector in general, implementation represents the key process through which new strategic technologies are socially constructed. In terms of the overall argument of this book, it is where disparate strands of available expertise are brought together to produce new technologies. Rather than technology being unproblematically available from technical suppliers outside the sector, sector-specific technological innovations are being created within the sector, albeit in close (and varying) co-operation with external generic technology suppliers. As we saw in several of the cases, even where external suppliers were involved there were still thorny implementation problems to be accommodated before systems could be realized. So involved were these, and such was the nature of the resulting long-term relationship, that a supplier could become 'almost a subsidiary' of the purchasing organization. Through their involvement in these specialist activities, we found clear examples of niche financial software suppliers within the sector.

This highlights the crucial role of different groups within the financial services sector and helps to explain some of the peculiar features of the user-supplier relationships. It also points up the strategic scope and creative opportunity available at this stage of technology development. The resulting picture is far more enlightening and promising than the more conventional view, which stresses the mere application of IT techniques to organizational objectives. Rather, what we are saying is that, jointly with financial service firms, new large-scale information systems are being created. This is not a particularly recent development, as is clear from our previous chapter on the historical emergence of computer technology. The financial services sector has always played an important, if not fully recognized, creative role through the medium of evolutionary user-led innovations (or innofusion—J. Fleck 1988).

In this chapter we examine in detail the nature of the implementation process. This is first explored in terms of its major common features: *uncertainty, time, organization, cost,* and *work.* These broad, interrelated features define the arena in which technological elements and management issues combine to produce actual working systems. The *uncertainty* of technology development, compounded by other forms of uncertainty, is of central importance. Considerations bearing on the *time* dimension—because implementation is a process and exhibits varying characteristics over time—are a major source of problems for the practical management of implementation. Management decisions are always expressed through a determinate *organization*; IT, amongst all technologies, is peculiarly influenced by organizational structures given its characteristic penetration across a company's divisions, or even across companies themselves—as with the bank clearing systems and cash-dispenser networks. Management decisions are also concerned with the *costs* (or perhaps more accurately, the economic rationales) of technology introduction. Decisions over how the technology will be operated and controlled and what skills and training are required—i.e. decisions over *work*—constitute another area of concern as regards the eventual efficient running of the installation.

Following this, we examine the contribution of expertise to implementation, especially as regards the potential for innovation, and identify the mechanism through which user-led innovation is realized. This pulls together underlying themes on expertise, which involve the relative importance (or, indeed, unimportance) of the systems-design input and the nature of the implementation process as an arena for expertise struggles.

Uncertainty

Uncertainty is endemic in the implementation of new technology, and the newer the technology the greater the uncertainty. It is most brutally indicated by the failures that dog many attempts at exploiting high technology. Levels of failure as are identified probably underestimate the actual levels, due to a reluctance to report failure. This is perhaps truer of financial services, given the importance of prudence and trust in the industry and the volumes of other people's money handled. When one considers that estimates range from 80 per cent failure for complex company-wide systems such as computer-integrated manufacture (CIM), to 50 per cent for more or less standard stock control systems, the real existence of uncertainty is amply demonstrated (J. Fleck 1984; Bessant 1985).

In our own case studies, set-backs or delays were mentioned, rather than outright failures. Home banking, for instance, appeared to be an example of an innovation accepted as slow in yielding anticipated benefits. Despite an overall expenditure of some US$600 million, only 100,000 customers had been secured in the United States for various home-and-office banking schemes. In contrast, systems running on the state-sponsored Minitel network in France had enjoyed considerable success. In the UK, Bank of Scotland had pioneered developments, winning a considerable reputation as technological innovators. But initial response to their Prestel-linked home-and-office banking system (HOBS) seems to have been disappointing. Nevertheless, they had demonstrated that some sort of market existed, and their example was followed by other organizations, among them two of our case studies, Royal Bank of Scotland's Royline and Clydesdale's Telebank. Both of these organizations sought to circumscribe the uncertainties involved by employing rather different technical delivery systems from HOBS, and in the Royal's case by targeting the corporate user. In each case, the approach adopted reflected the distinctive expertise resources available to each organization—Royline being internally developed and Telebank developed in close partnership with an external supplier.

Of course, given the typically long time periods required for many large-scale strategic IT projects, such apparent euphemisms as 'set-backs' or 'delays' may in fact be fair descriptions. Success and failure are not unambiguously identifiable outcomes, but relative interpretations the appropriate application of which is negotiated or even explicitly socially constructed. What is frequently going on is an organizational learning process, in which recognized set-backs or mistakes are responded to, and recovered from, with later developments. Bank of Scotland's experience with ATMs, which persuaded them that they required a more systematic approach to technology, is a pertinent example. Another was the decision by Clydesdale Bank to 'come in second' with Telebank.

Strategic technologies of a very long-term nature tend to be prey to this kind of corporate game-playing. Firms with the strongest resource base, or highly articulated strategic rationale, may be willing to take the lead with technological innovations—to adopt an offensive strategy in Freeman's (1982) terms. But many firms will prefer a defensive strategy and learn all they can from problems flushed out by the leaders. As the home-and-office banking case illustrated, uncertainty arises for many different reasons; different types of delivery system interact with market structures in uncertain ways, offering ample scope for strategic positioning. A variety of specific sorts of uncertainty, each relating to a particular form of expertise can be identified as contributing to this compounded uncertainty.

Basic technological uncertainty is one of these forms. What is at issue is whether available technology can in principle be deployed in a real system. This type of uncertainty is usually minimized in commercial applications by the use of proven technology, for which there are well-developed occupational and service infrastructures and a base of available expertise. Even then uncertainty sometimes becomes an issue. For instance, the crucial importance of speed of response in many transactions has continually forced the development of faster computing hardware, and led to the adoption of hot-standby machines in parallel as a form of insurance. The emergence of Tandem Computers as financial service specialists has been largely due to their taking on these real-time requirements.

Development uncertainty is a more widespread and important form. Here the issue is not whether a particular system can be developed in principle, but whether it can be developed in fact, under specific time and budgetary constraints. The prevalence of this form of uncertainty is amply attested by virtually any issue of the weekly computing press, and reports of major project time or cost overruns. In Chapter 8 we discussed this problem which has been endemic to software production since the earliest use of computers —the so-called software crisis. Our case studies were no different; almost universally, slippages, constant renegotiation, and time and budget overruns were in evidence. The use of development methodologies and project-management techniques for implementation therefore is far from established. The compounded uncertainties of the implementation process mean that no one group of experts commands complete credibility; professionals other than IS practitioners—accountants, marketing specialists, bankers, actuaries—all have interests in, and can claim to make relevant contributions to, the development of computing systems.

Other more general forms of uncertainty relating to the structure of the industry were also very much in evidence. One pertinent issue was the availability of appropriate expertise, and the sectoral distribution of technological expertise between the agencies involved in implementation. Relevant questions included: Do technology suppliers fully appreciate the nature of the users' activities and requirements? Do the users themselves appreciate the nature of their own activities and requirements? Are those requirements well defined? Are they subject to pressures arising from competition? Or from competitors' strategic actions?

Dynamic pressures arise from changing infrastructural conditions: new legislation, agreements over standards, and the emergence of technological developments. Such changes affect organizations across the sector, although they can impact on certain implementations more harshly than others. For instance, it was suggested that delays in the implementation plan for Mutual Life's Customer Care project resulted because of the huge demands from changed industry requirements.

The actual technology bit ... that has made less progress than it should have done because we've been hit by the Financial Services Act, we've been hit by LAUTRO, we've been hit by the new pensions legislation. So we had to make changes and react pretty quickly because if the government demand something you can't say, 'Sorry. We didn't make it.' So that interfered with the amount of work we did.

Negotiations over standards and infrastructure are notorious strategic battlegrounds, as is well exemplified by the rise of SWITCH and the associated demise of EFTPOS UK (Howells and Hine 1993). Various forms of structural uncertainty interact and, as a consequence, in a service industry like financial services a reverse product cycle of innovation results (Barras 1990). Essentially this posits a proliferation of specific customized products rather than the conventional cycle of decreasing customization and increasing standardization with market maturity.

Uncertainty is not an absolute across all organizations; it is relative to the knowledge base of the particular organization, and depends on whether it has the expertise to circumscribe, if not eliminate, uncertainty of particular types. Thus the different sorts of uncertainty—market, technological, developmental, and structural—are systematically related to specific deficits of expertise. Organizations will seek to minimize the uncertainty they face, at the same time seeking to minimize the cost of trying to cope with all eventualities, by buying in the knowledge resources they perceive they lack. Implementation is a real-time game played with limited resources, in order to win strategic advantage against protagonists similarily engaged. A number of different ways of coping with uncertainty are therefore feasible, and a range of competitive strategies for technological innovation has been identified by analysts such as Ansoff and Stewart (1967), Freeman (1982), and Porter (1985, 1987). Each of the above causes of uncertainty are likely to affect more extensively projects which are designated as strategic because of their innovative and/or long-term nature. The implementation processes involved are likely to be correspondingly more protracted, more complex, and more organizationally sensitive.

Time

In implementation, time always appears to be in short supply. It was certainly a scarce resource in most of our case firms, even for those projects which were stand-alone and less organizationally convoluted, such as the remote-banking and credit-card operations. Furthermore, it would appear that projects identified as strategic were frequently long term. Indeed, being long term was one of the characteristics that helped to distinguish a project as strategic in the first place.

A starting-point for understanding the time structure of the implementation process is via the systems-development life cycle as used in software engineering. Different authors present more or less similar analyses of this cycle. Typical examples are the waterfall model (McDermid 1990) and the spiral model (Boehm 1986), as discussed in Chapter 8. We are not concerned here with the detail of the various steps (see Chapter 8 for this), but rather with the broad character of the process and how it relates to sectoral and organizational environments. It is sufficient here to observe that the implementation process involves a number of more or less distinct stages (though many different partitionings are possible), each of which requires consideration at certain times in the overall development cycle (Voss 1988). Most importantly it should be noted that the process is not straightforwardly *linear*, but involves *feed-back* and iterative interaction, especially between the design and preliminary realization phases.

The non-linearity of development is of central importance and at the heart of the problem of managing time. Otherwise expressed it is the problem of a lack of stability in requirements, notorious for changing in the light of the provisional solutions entertained. Prototyping approaches are frequently advocated for helping to overcome this major difficulty, and almost as frequently criticized for not achieving what they promise. Although uncertainty over requirements is arguably the main bugbear of software engineering, it also represents an important opportunity for absorbing further suggestions and refinements—i.e. for innovation—and is therefore *de facto* of considerable significance. The time distribution of effort, and mutual dependencies between the different tasks and stages of implementation, can be approached by means of the project-management techniques already mentioned. However, while these may help to contain the difficulties, they rarely succeed in resolving them into a predetermined sequence of routine tasks. The attempts on the part of IS practitioners to promote such methodologies can be readily understood as their bid to claim expert dominion over the spheres of uncertainty which are proving to be of strategic importance. In general, no strong overall linearity can be identified across different projects; the situation is one in which each case has to be dealt with in terms of the contingencies of its context (cf. McDermid 1990: ch. 17).

Certainly in our studies, distinct phases of development were usually clearly identified, but in ways that were often highly individual. Phasing sometimes appeared to have been adopted in order to distinguish a change of direction from a less successful beginning—as notably with Home and Auto's management information system. Interestingly, also, time phasing sometimes appeared to be explicitly adopted in order to allow organizational learning to take place. This was evident in Bank of Scotland's CABINET system, where future phases were planned to incorporate evolutionary improvements that came to light during earlier phases. Also, in Mutual Life's Customer Care project, the early phase was explicitly seen as providing a platform for the future, in which more ambitious enhancements and opportunities for cross-selling and the like could be exploited.

While the time dimension is, perhaps, the most crucial parameter implicated in the strategic nature of projects, volume or scale is another. Very high volumes of data have long been a distinguishing characteristic of financial service IT applications. Of course, scale and time are not always easily disassociated, with trade-offs between them usually possible in practice. Nevertheless, scale demands in financial services, coupled with time constraints, have resulted in considerable innovative pressure on the technology. At the same time, the new information technologies have enabled ever-greater scale capabilities, and ever-faster response characteristics, in a ratchet of technology development. Present-day credit-card operations, for instance, with millions of distinct accounts rather than the thousands typical of bank branch operations, would not be possible in the absence of IT. These are products whose current forms are intertwined with the capabilities of the technology. Major losses and risks (fraud and theft) in such applications are extremely time-sensitive, and force the pace in further technological developments such as voice or fingerprint pattern recognition and encryption algorithms.

Organization

Organizational issues bear on implementation processes in three main ways. First, there is the existing organization within which the new system being implemented is located. How does its structure constrain, pattern, or frustrate the new developments? Secondly there are the arrangements for carrying out the implementation process and for overcoming such problems as stem from the existing structure. How should tasks be distributed to execute the implementation plan? Cutting across these two aspects is the issue of work organization, namely the distribution of work and the allocation of responsibility for achieving the organization's operating goals, and how these alter with the introduction of new systems.

Thirdly the downstream effects, or impacts on the organization, represent the changes resulting from the new technology being introduced. In investigations of the relation between technology and organization there have been tendencies to assume the independence of technological developments and to focus exclusively on such impacts. We would argue in contrast that existing organizational arrangements, particularly the existing knowledge base of the organization and the prevailing distribution of available expertise, have an important shaping effect on the development of technology itself (Edge 1987; J. Fleck, Webster, and Williams 1990). Later in this chapter we outline this mechanism (the fundamental implementation equation) underlying the implementation process.

Organizational Structure

The organizational structure within which new systems are implemented has been an important focus of research and debate, and the relation between technology and structure explored in many directions. Burns and Stalker's (1961) compelling distinction between organic and mechanistic organizational structures has been remarkably influential and is still used as a base for many analyses of organization and technology (e.g. A. Campbell and Warner 1988). Mechanistic structures are characterized by clearly defined, non-overlapping task allocations, a clear vertical pattern of communication and control, and authority identified with *position* in the hierarchy. They are best suited to stable environments. Organic structures, on the other hand, are characterized by overlapping task *assumptions* (rather than allocations), extensive horizontal patterns of interaction and communication, and authority attributed primarily by reputation and demonstrated knowledge or competence. These appear better able to deal with rapidly changing environments and are more facilitative of innovation.

Internal barriers to change which offer resistance to the flow of information and communication (the effects of mechanistic structure) are particularly problematic (Skinner 1974; Bessant 1985). Barriers can arise for a number of reasons, including differing disciplinary perspectives or conflicting departmental loyalties, underpinned by distinctive bodies of expertise, as well as a variety of political alignments. Perhaps our most trenchant example of competitive differences within an organizational structure occurred in the Mutual Life case study. One of the key objectives of their Customer Care project was precisely to overcome the diversity of sources of information on customers and the problems of things getting lost between departments. One senior consultant in the IS division commented: 'But there are departmental ... not exactly religious fervour but some kind of folk-lore attached to departments because they go back further than particular people. And there are hostilities between areas of the same company for strange reasons that nobody can remember.' Underpinning these divisions there were professional expertise affiliations, although actuaries were generally dominant in the organization.

We did not encounter extremes of outright counter-implementation—that is, the deliberate mobilizing of organizational forces to bring down a project—

such as have been discussed by Keen (1981). But we certainly received hints of a lack of enthusiasm (for example the reluctance of some Mutual Life departments to take on the role of sponsor for the Customer Care project). Political choices and alliances that affected direction and orientation were often evident, as for example in the selection of Software Partnership by Clydesdale for development of their remote banking system.

But rather than merely constituting a viscous medium slowing down the implementation of IT (the conventional implicit model for the technology-structure relationship), organization structure also patterns the evolution of systems. Management information systems, for instance, typically develop some form of shared database from which distinct departmental services can be provided. As we saw in Chapters 6 and 7, a common theme in financial services was the move from disaggregated accounts (a processing view) to unified customer profiles (a marketing orientation). The latter is seen as particularly strategic in that it facilitates future developments—for example life and pension and investment services in Mutual Life; motor and general in Home and Auto; and a rounded financial advisory service in the case of Bank of Scotland's CABINET system. The design of these systems requires specialist inputs from experts: actuaries, general insurance assessors, and financial consultants, respectively. Hence the differing corporate structures of expertise give rise to or shape the resulting systems.

Precisely because such large-scale systems are organizationally convoluted —i.e. because they link the disparate parts of often very large organizations— the requirements for negotiation, and the opportunities for political machinations between different departments involved, are greatly increased. Moreover, precisely because such systems constitute unique configurations adapted to the requirements of the particular organization, they require an extensive degree of user involvement for their development (J. Fleck 1993). The need for some form of user involvement was a recurrent theme in our case firms, though it varied considerably. For instance, in its implementation plan, Mutual Life indicated that about 50 per cent of total effort in terms of man-months were to be contributed by user departments. On the other hand, customer service-oriented systems (such as our credit-card and remote-banking case studies) were less convoluted and more nearly approximated stand-alone installations, with less need for extensive user involvement. Consequently, the option of buying rather than making became a real possibility. Even here, however, when a standard package is available it still usually requires substantial customization for Scottish conditions (most available financial service packages have been developed in the USA) and for organizational-specific preferences. Issues of availability of expertise, confidentiality, and intellectual-property rights (involving licensing arrangements) are raised and, depending on the specific contingencies, especially the expert judgements taken into consideration, a range of divergent actions can result. This was well illustrated by the quite different routes followed by Bank of Scotland and

Royal Bank of Scotland in the implementation of their credit-card operations. These issues are explored in more detail in later chapters.

Organizational Roles in Implementation

A variety of roles have been identified as important in the innovation/implementation process, in order to surmount functional divisions and navigate projects through the troubled waters of organizational politics. Schumpeter (1975) noted the crucial part played by the entrepreneur in bringing about changes which disrupted the existing economic equilibrium. Entrepreneurs had the vision to see new ways of doing, and were able to persuade capitalists and bankers to extend credit and to organize, perhaps via other managers, the physical means for achieving their vision. A similar entrepreneurial role within the organization has also been identified. Schon (1963) pioneered the concept of the product champion as someone who backed a particular product. (In the context of our study, a more appropriate term might be project champion.) The SAPPHO study (SPRU 1972) confirmed such a role and also identified the importance of others: technical innovator, business innovator, and chief executive.

As a business becomes larger and more complex, the champion role becomes too demanding for one person and differentiates into several roles. This reflects human limitations *vis-à-vis* large organizational structures (cf. Simon's (1965) notion of bounded rationality). It is not possible for one individual to command all the required knowledge and organizational power necessary to mobilize that knowledge. Maidique (1980) reviewed early case studies and identified a number of roles and functions (Figure 9.1) in what he terms entrepreneurial networks, namely the social networks that support successful innovations. He also provided a dynamic analysis of the growth of complexity of such networks, as companies develop through stages of organizational development.

In larger organizations, people committed to projects at various levels are needed, including ultimate support from the highest levels of management. Senior sponsors rarely concern themselves with project details, their role being to authorize appropriate resources and legitimate the project, particularly where it strays outside the conventional ways of doing. However, champions do not face merely passive disinterest or undifferentiated resistance. Frequently, they push projects in competition with other protagonists who are pursuing their own favoured projects. In competitive situations, champions who can mobilize the most effective network of affiliation and support will be at an advantage. In such situations too the competition can become extreme, with political infighting and dirty tricks. The term counter-implementation (Keen 1981; Greenhalgh 1984) has been used to describe such activities, and the role of 'project assassin' suggested as opposing that of champion. In such situations, power is always implicit and indeed may become explicit (Davis 1984; Shea 1988).

Technological entrepreneur: the organizer of a technological venture who exercises control (typically by owning a substantial percentage of the equity) and assumes the risks of the business. Usually he or she is the chief executive.

Product champion: a member of an organization who creates, defines, or adopts an idea for a technological innovation and who is willing to risk his or her position and prestige to make possible the innovation's successful implementation.

Executive champion: an executive in a technological firm who has direct or indirect influence over resource allocation and who uses this power to channel resources to a technological innovation, absorbing most, but usually not all, the risk of the project.

Technical definition: the basic performance requirements and associated specifications that characterize a proposal for a technological innovation.

Sponsorship: the actions by which executives channel resources to innovative projects that they have chosen to support.

Business definition: a description of the business within which a firm competes and of the administrative practices that the firm will follow.

FIG. 9.1 *Roles and Functions in Entrepreneurial Networks* (*Source*: Maidique 1980)

Elements of all of these roles were observed in our case studies, including some more heroic aspects. The importance of the project champion was evidenced by major changes on the departure of a dominant champion in the Home and Auto study. There we saw that the abandonment of the strategic BSP methodology coincided with growing proof of its unsuitability when its champion left; the new management group became identified with a pragmatic, phased approach. Similarly, in Mutual Life, the importance of the champion's role was evident in a negative sense in the difficulties experienced in getting the Customer Care project off the ground. There the process had been institutionalized to the extent of formally allocating the role of project sponsor.

The divisional status of IS in most of our case organizations frequently provided the role of executive champion, exemplified by the heads of these divisions. In Bank of Scotland, for instance, the Assistant General Manager of MSD came from a banking background yet had a strongly developed interest in technology. This delicate balance between the status of a senior career banker, and someone who will fight the corner of the IS interest, was a potent combination for MSD as a major division in the bank.

At an apparently less dramatic level than the champion's, other practical role requirements have to be filled. Large projects need day-to-day management as well as advocacy. Thus the role of project management was recognized as crucial to implementation success, and meant building project teams that reflected various interest groups and sources of expertise in the implementing organization. Usually we found that the internal systems development division or department would take on project management responsibilities. We did find one exception in the case of Premier Financial Service's credit-card processing system. There project management was shared between the Computer Operations department and the system suppliers. For the former this represented an opportunity to play a more prominent role than normal. The success of the project in keeping to deadlines was credited to the efforts of Computer Operations, together with the professional performance of the suppliers.

The development of entrepreneurial networks and project teams must match the prevailing organizational structure and provide the expertise resources for effectively prosecuting the project. Particularly where the organization does not already have appropriate expertise in-house, or where in-house experts have already been co-opted by competing projects, the make-up of the project team may include external personnel from technology suppliers or consultants. Indeed, such arrangements are probably the most effective for the transfer of local and generic knowledge into working systems—for example, Mutual Life's use of IBM consultants, or Bank of Scotland's use of Philips programming staff.

Users in the Implementation Process

The role of users in the introduction of technology receives detailed attention in the next chapter. Several points, however, relate specifically to implementation. In the successful prosecution of innovation, user involvement is mainly relevant to the design of process innovations and instrumental products intended for specialist users (von Hippel 1988). Given the nature of IT-based strategic innovations in our present study, therefore, users were of central importance.

A succinct overview of the evolving importance of the role of the user is provided by Rockart (1988). He argues that line management, broadly conceived as those with particular business responsibilities, have had to play an increasing part as IT systems themselves have evolved through four eras. In the first, the accounting era, tasks were sufficiently circumscribed for the IS department to design and install with the minimum interaction with users, beyond training them in operating skills. In the second, the operations era, systems became of such complexity that the involvement of line management was necessary to specify and achieve efficient working, as changes in local working practices were necessitated. In the third, the information era, starting in the late 1970s and early 1980s, decision-support facilities were provided by IS while the responsibility for end-user programming, and the use of the information resources, lay entirely with line management.

But in the fourth era, the wired society, complex systems are integrating sub-organizational units and geographically distinct independent organizations. In such cases specific business concepts, requirements, and functions comprise the burden of innovation but lie outside the immediate ken of IT specialists. The latters' role is, therefore, to provide the facilities, hardware platforms, and network capabilities through which business tasks are achieved. Only line management has the knowledge and power to bring about the changes in organizational structure, functional responsibilities, and working practices needed to achieve successful operation. Indeed, Rockart suggests that implementation is too weak a term in this context; the process is one of far-reaching transformation—again emphasizing the broader conception of implementation we are employing.

As successful configurations become proven, and understanding about the critical factors and parameters becomes consolidated, we can expect the emergence of new specialists, differentiated across the domains of application that turn out to provide the most successful lines of development. But, at present, traditional DP staff and IT professionals often find their organizational expertise inadequate, with the result that other functional specialists, with more of the local and contingent components at their command, are able to exert considerable influence. This does not rule out the possibility of perspicuous technical specialists broadening their generic knowledge base by acquiring more business knowledge. Decisions over the introduction of IT are becoming organizationally embedded, and involve many more groups with different levels of interest and differing capabilities of affecting outcomes through their power and/or knowledge. As we have also seen, outcomes are by no means simply arrived at, nor can they be read off the organizational chart.

Cost

Whatever the precise nature of decisions over technology, at some stage every decision process has to engage with the issue of cost. Organizations which lose control of the costs of technology are usually commercially unsuccessful, even if they are technically successful. But because of levels of uncertainty surrounding new systems, estimating costs and benefits can be extremely difficult, and there is scope for interpretation and negotiation over the appropriate aspects to be included. With organizationally convoluted systems which cut across the domains of activity of different expert groups, conflicting evaluations are likely to be generated. Freeman has put this most authoritatively.

The general uncertainty means that many different views may be held and the situation is typically one of advocacy and political debate in which project estimates are used by interest groups to buttress a particular point of view. Evaluation techniques and technological forecasting, like tribal war dances, play a very important part in mobilizing, energizing and organizing. (1982: 167)

Some form of Cost Benefit Analysis (CBA) is frequently recommended, making use of investment appraisal techniques such as discounted cash flow which can take into account the rate of inflation, the time value of money, and the opportunity costs of capital. However, CBA has been criticized as telling unduly against longer term, higher risk, and more uncertain projects—that is, precisely those which might be described as strategic (Hayes and Abernathy 1980; Hayes and Garvin 1982). Assessment of contributing costs, therefore, requires the ability to deal with the financial aspects of high-technology implementation. This distinctive form of expertise is now under rapid development due to the unprecedented character and business effects of IT. Traditional techniques and methods, evolved in a far more stable environment where technology installations were severely circumscribed, are being fiercely challenged. Even in manufacturing, which is arguably less affected by information technology, since the basic transformations of physical materials into goods are relatively unchanged, something of a revolution is underway in the expertise required (see e.g. Kaplan 1990). In financial services the transformations are concerned directly with information and the ramifications are more pervasive.

One issue is the difficulty of dealing with intangibles, such as the loss of customer goodwill. With strategic systems which change the way an organization conducts business, intangible factors can dominate the anticipated benefits side. With Mutual Life's Customer Care project, for example, a senior consultant commented:

Somebody can produce a figure that says the actual technical developments are going to cost *x* and we go to Marketing and say, 'that's the cost'; but then you have to try and cost out the value of customer service. It's for (them) to try and establish the benefit figures; what hassle-free business is worth to the company. A lot of it is little things. In the pensions market, if you upset an employer he can take a very large lump of business away in one go.

And again, later:

So much of this project is to do with intangibles. What's the financial value of upsetting somebody that you don't even know you are offending? Five years down the road how can anybody prove that we've lost money because somebody was rude or careless today?

Similarly, in Bank of Scotland, the role of accountants on the CABINET Working Party was to provide effective project control—provision of documentation for costs of development, costs to completion, and effective post-implementation review. But none thought that cost should drive the development process.

I don't like cash being the overriding concern in a strategic decision like the branch system, as long as there is an awareness of cost as part of the overall thing. . . . At the end of the day if it is an extra million pounds it is an extra million pounds, and you cannot put the rest at jeopardy for the sake of that.

Thus the justification of these large-scale projects was not strait-jacketed by evaluation techniques. Because they were seen as strategic, the long-term competitive advantages and the intangible benefits were appreciated. This was implicit in the phased approach we found in many cases, where early stages of development were seen as providing the infrastructure for future enhancements and opportunities (such as cross-selling). Attempts were generally made to cost out and justify projects when the lineaments of the final system became defined, and some stability in the market response to the new initiative achieved. This can be seen, for instance, in the changing base for credit-card operations now that they are firmly established; interest-free credit periods have been changed, conditions for retailers' charges legislatively altered, and many operators now charge customers an annual fee. In some cases of strategic technology implementation, there is little choice due to the cost factors involved. Bank of Scotland's VISA card operation, for instance, was necessitated by Barclays' withdrawal of their third-party facilities. Opting out of credit cards altogether was not considered a realistic option, in view of the large customer base involved.

In general, electronic means of accessing customers, as represented by our customer-service case studies, constituted a broad alternative to new, or extended, branch operations which would involve considerable investment in buildings and associated facilities. The £40,000 annual operating costs for an ATM compare very favourably with the £1 million or so required for a new branch, or even with the marginal costs incurred in running existing branches 24 hours of the day to provide the same level of service. Likewise the costs of the algorithm-based, mass-production approach to credit-card operations, despite the associated high levels of fraud and default, compare favourably with those of the traditional bank manager-mediated loans system, which can deal with, at most, thousands of transactions.

Work

The manner in which work and workplaces are designed to interface with technological innovations is a major part of implementation. On the one hand, there are the work inputs into the design and implementation process itself, and on the other, the consequences for existing structures of work and working practices that a given technological system may have.

Work inputs depend on the range of expertise deployed on projects, and hence on the structure of expertise obtaining within the implementing organization. Work inputs constitute a crucial route through which expertise gets built-in to new technology configurations and thereby becomes reified. In this respect our case studies provided an interesting set of varying conditions. The division of labour amongst computing staff is especially important in this respect. The extent of a division or otherwise between business analysts and computer analysts, and between computer programmers and analysts were aspects often remarked in our case studies. These are not merely internal concerns, however, but are influenced by external labour markets. Due to the high rates of growth typical of IT, there are ample opportunities for computing staff to move between organizations and even industries, so that market power modifies internal organization.

A number of consequences related to the impacts of IT on the structure of jobs were in evidence. The white-collar factory environment of the VISA credit-card processing facility was the most obvious manifestation. In other cases, de-skilling effects on certain jobs were acknowledged.

I was mortified once when I went into our Premium Collection section and saying to the girl, 'Well, what's your job here?', and she saying, 'I do CP11s', and I said, 'Well, what's a CP11?', and she said, 'Well it's this transaction. I put this number in this box here on this piece of paper.' And I said, 'Well, why are you doing that?' She didn't know. Not a clue. Because she had no need to know. The job had been reduced to the point where she didn't really need to know. Mind you, I don't think she enjoyed the job any more through not knowing. And I don't think she did it any better through not knowing.

Under such conditions, it is unlikely that operators will be able, even if willing, to contribute any form of user expertise involvement to improving the substance of processing, though they undoubtedly would have much to contribute with respect to improving the nature of the task and working conditions.

Another important variable for workplace design is layout. This is increasingly important in retail financial services. With the move towards open-plan easy-chair spaces in which to advise customers—a radical departure from the traditional front counter and back-office arrangements—new layouts are part of the market-led culture. The manager of one of Bank of Scotland's main city branches, for example, saw customer-services automation as part of the new retailing approach to banking. Banks were traditionally intimidating places which used their (very expensive) high-street square footage very poorly compared with modern department stores. Technologies like CABI-NET would release staff and enable them to spend more time with customers.

You are hopefully going to sell more things, not simply for the sake of selling them but because, having taken the time to spend five or ten minutes to speak to someone, you find that they have no life cover, or the house insurance is about to expire, and you can do the same insurance for ten pounds cheaper. Now you will never find that out by sitting pushing paper around all day.

THE EXPLOITATION OF EXPERTISE

The broad categories of expertise that are essential inputs to the implementation process can be summarized in the fundamental implementation equation:

successful implementation = generic technology + local practical knowledge

The generic element, sometimes provided in-house or by IT suppliers, consists of instrumentalities—hardware, software, and development methodologies—supported by other components of knowledge necessary for operating. The local element may be contributed by users at various levels, and consists primarily of firm-specific, non-formal, or contingent knowledge components. The specific division of labour and knowledge varies greatly; large financial institutions usually have systems-development groups which command much relevant software and methodological knowledge. Hardware is nowadays always supplied from outside specialists, and most formal methodologies are initially transferred in from outside, though this is not always successful, as witness Home and Auto's dealings with BSP.

The local element of innovation, with company-wide and even sector-wide configurations of technology, is acquired through various mechanisms. In successful cases of implementation, local knowledge tends to become progressively embodied in generic knowledge. Firm-specific knowledge becomes appropriated by suppliers who then are able to offer it on to other users. At the same time, generic technology becomes implemented in forms suitable for exploitation by the user. This two-way process of knowledge transfer lies at the root of negotiations over the make-or-buy decision, as we discuss in Chapter 13.

One major finding from our research involved the differential recognition, in different industrial sectors, of the value of the various elements of the above equation. In the financial services sector users dominate rather than suppliers (as tends to be the case in manufacturing). Royalty payments flow to the user involved in the original development. We observed this pattern most clearly in Clydesdale's development of Telebank, in conjunction with Software Partnership. It is interesting to ask why this should be so. Is it the higher value placed on information in financial services? Is it the degree of competition among suppliers? Or is it the richness of potential rewards in financial services compared with manufacturing?

As suppliers' experience accumulates over time and across a particular sector, the possibilities for sector-specific technologies become thoroughly explored and developed into artefacts. As this happens, the suppliers' understanding of requirements possibilities grows. Thus, we move away from a situation in which configurations primarily reflect local contingencies, to a situation in which requirements are so clear and stable—or black-boxed—that standard systems emerge. In these cases, development becomes more technically-oriented—often in terms of defined efficiency measures—and concentrated in the hands of suppliers.

With respect to our case studies, it would appear that credit-card operations have matured to such an extent that standard packages are now the practicable starting-point—as exemplified by the use of the INDEX package by Premier Financial Services, and VISA's FDR, for their credit-card operations. Remote banking systems, however, are still at an earlier stage of development, with many strategic approaches still testing out the nature of the market for such services—as exemplified by the rather different orientations exhibited by Royline, Telebank, and HOBS—each of which was developed from scratch. In contrast, our MIS cases—Bank of Scotland's CABINET system, Home and Auto's management information system, and Mutual Life's Customer Care programme—were organizationally convoluted and a long way from stand-ardization into packages. Such cases remained stubbornly configurational, necessitating considerable internal effort and commitment in order to define the capabilities required.

Progress towards standardization and domination by suppliers is not an inevitable outcome. The variety afforded by configurations which must incor-porate organizationally-specific bodies of knowledge and practice may always be a source of competitive positioning and differentiation. Extensive automa-tion has been more recent in financial services. Some trajectories of develop-ment appear to have emerged—namely the credit card processing centres—with similar consequences for the routinization of work as in manufacturing. But there remains a far greater variety of products, activities, and services. This variety seems almost guaranteed to increase, creating market turbulence and high levels of uncertainty in technological developments for the forseeable future. Only in a very few cases (again with credit-card operations) will it be possible to attain the degree of stability necessary for well-defined trajectories of development and standard packages to emerge. Only in a few cases, therefore, will black-boxing prove sustainable over the longer term, and the differentiation associated with reverse product cycle dynamics seems set to dominate.

In short, computerization where of a strategic nature is extensive and complex, and implementation remains a process of building large information structures which many groups—management, users, customers—may cogni-tively inhabit (c.f. Kling 1987). It is far removed from the conventional view of applying technology as a mere means to an end.

Provision by Markets and Hierarchies

The internal IT environment has changed over the last few decades from one in which a centralized information-systems department provides a full range of services, to the notion of an 'information economy' within a business. In the model developed by Boynton and Zmud (1987), the information economy approximates a free-market system in which organizational sub-units can satisfy their needs for IT services by acquiring resources from a variety of sources, including the organization's IS function, external suppliers, or through their own actions. Any market advantage held by the IS function depends on technical and/or managerial expertise and an established line of information products or services. However, the advantage held by the IS function shrinks as other sub-units become skilled in newer technologies such as microcomputers, external databases, electronic mail, office systems, decision support systems, and work-stations. Business professionals are able to apply IT resources and provide technical support, while external suppliers may be more available to the consumer and better able to recognize and respond to the consumer's need than the IS function.

This analysis reflected the situation in Mutual Life in particular. There a specialist IS group was constituted as an Internal Consultancy Group, organized on a boutique basis, offering services to internal customers. However, a lack of established links with users meant that this group tended to become marginalized from the strategic arena.

Others have argued, drawing on the analysis developed by Williamson (1975), that there has been a trend (difficult to document statistically but supported by case-study material) towards transactions mediated through *market relations* rather than through *internal organizational relations* (i.e. hierarchies in Williamson's terms). Child (1987) in particular notes that the move to external subcontracting has been encouraged by turbulent market and technology conditions, typified by demand, innovation, and inefficiency risks. While stressing that technology does not determine organization, the use of IT does provide an improved basis for co-ordinating and controlling market or quasi-market transactions with external parties (Child 1987: 35). Subcontracting, however, will always be limited by the company-specific balance of expertise and control required, especially the local knowledge and expertise necessary for successful operation. The sensitivity of the organization's operational efficiency to the subcontracted elements is an important strategic consideration (i.e. a traditional make-or-buy calculation; see our discussion in Chapter 13).

Some implementing organizations deliberately sought to retain the status quo in structural terms. In Mutual Life, for instance, we saw a number of different strategies being adopted in order to avoid any major restructuring. On the other hand, some organizations were more willing to make structural modifications in order to better accommodate technology developments. In Bank of Scotland the Management Services Division itself was a consequence of the technology intitiative over customer-services automation; and at Clydesdale another whole division for Electronic Business had been developed.

10

User Relations and IT Integration

One of the most important changes in the nature of systems development in recent years reflects the forms of user knowledge being brought within the development process. As we stressed in Chapters 8 and 9, systems expertise is increasingly differentiated and distributed. Bringing together this complex of knowledges—as in the fundamental implementation equation (Chapter 9) —and controlling the relations between user groups and IS departments, represent key aspects of the management of expertise. Indeed, as more and more groups take part in developing and using information systems, a bipolar model of users versus developers becomes too simple. We might ask why user participation in development should be singled out at all. Why not make the distribution of expertise itself the point of reference?

There are, however, good reasons for retaining a special focus on user participation. Most simply, the term is actively employed both in the literature and in organizations, and relations with user groups are still problematic for IS departments. The expertise possessed by users can still be subordinated to that of systems developers, and the expertise gap between users and developers can readily become a 'power gap', accidentally or by intention. In some cases conflicting orientations to IT which traditionally separated users and developers persist, adding to the problems of joint decision-making. All these factors, which are taken up in some detail in this chapter, point to user participation in systems development having important implications for power relationships.

In our own case studies users were not invariably involved in systems development. With the more organizationally-bounded and routinized types of system (like the packages bought by VISA and Premier Financial Services), computer specialists completed the main development work with fairly limited contact with the end-user. This type of system had much in common with the traditional, data-crunching administrative systems installed in financial services firms in the 1960s and 1970s—systems that presented programmers and analysts with well-structured problems and relatively clear technical solutions. Nor was it invariably true that systems deemed to be strategic always needed user involvement. The Royline cash management system seemed to have been developed without any input from its external users (i.e. accountants and managers in client firms). The Royal Bank's systems-development managers defined Royline as a product to be sold to customers, not a system to be jointly developed. They stressed their detailed knowledge of their clients' needs (and an implied lack of any need to consult them).

None the less, for more organizationally complex IT systems users did need to be closely involved in systems development, and in many of the cases we looked at users featured prominently in the development process. For example, Home and Auto's management information system was a typical development that simply could not have gone ahead without user involvement. Here the original manual information was frequently deficient and was manipulated by users in idiosyncratic ways. Data from different lists had to be combined and standardized, and if the new MIS was to be an improvement over the manual system all this had to be somehow incorporated on a single database. The feedback and reconciliation, which were necessary if business users were to have confidence in the data, were so detailed that they had to be conducted at the programmer level, which dictated a close integration between business users and system developers.

THE CHANGING ROLE OF USERS

As organizational relationships with users have moved to the centre of the systems-development process, however, the definition of 'user' has become increasingly ambiguous and an ever-widening variety of groups has been brought into this role. Internal IS departments, for example, can act both as developers and users. When an organization is being supplied with a system by an external hardware manufacturer or software house, the internal IS department would be regarded by the outside supplier as the user. If the IS department is mediating between the supplier and some organizational department that will operate the system, the IS people would see the other internal department as the user. When IS departments act as users, however, they are expert users. The term 'end-user' has been employed to distinguish these from non-IT skilled groups that work directly with systems. But increasingly, as the skills and knowledge necessary to build information systems extend across different groups, these simple distinctions have ceased to serve. It is better to regard the user as a function or role that different groups move in or out of, rather than a fixed identity of particular groups.

Types of User Relations

In attempting to develop classifications of users a number of different base variables have been suggested (see Friedman 1989: 183). One factor that has proved critical in distinguishing between groups is the extent of possession of IT skills. However, the line between expert and non-expert has become blurred; users have acquired levels of relevant skill short of becoming programmers or systems analysts. The level of computing knowledge can be employed to differentiate between relatively non-skilled users who remain clients of IT professionals, and users who can direct and participate in the systems-development process via their possession of relevant knowledge. In this vein, Rockart and Flannery (1983) suggest that different types of users can be placed on a scale, progressing from fairly low-level accessing of data, through the use of command languages to generate statistics and reports, to users who deploy procedural languages to develop their own applications, and finally to support personnel who work within functional areas and have the full range of programming skills.

A second critical variable reflects the possession of degrees of power and influence within organizations. Classifications based on the hierarchical position of the user have highlighted the increased usage of IT by higher levels of management, and the implications of this for how influential users (rather than groups such as data-entry staff or clerical workers) relate to systems. However, a ladder of hierarchical positions that reflect organization structure is perhaps too superficial a breakdown. Instead, there are good reasons for focusing on a broader conception of organizational power. This concept was developed by Child *et al.* (1984), and has a hierarchical component, but was primarily employed to refer to the use of IT by groupings based on function or occupation. It usefully stresses the institutional power base of IT in business functions. In our own research, we saw that the broad influence of IT professionals had been immeasurably boosted by the divisional status of IS. Similarly, business users were frequently defined as departments rather than individuals or managerial levels. This can be an important distinction given the influence that individual users can have if they are members of powerful departments.

We will not attempt a general typology, but instead put forward a classification of the major types of users found in our research settings. Strictly speaking this is not a ranking if two variables are being combined, but the classification is nevertheless comprehensive and helpful for understanding processes of user participation. The variables of organizational power and IT expertise help to distinguish five broad types of user groups.

1. *In-house IT specialists.* These are internal IS departments which are the clients of external IT suppliers. In the Clydesdale Bank the IS department played the role of internal IT users who commissioned a system from a software supplier. These were knowledgeable users, well placed to ensure the integration of the bought-in system into the bank's networks. Similarly, the systems staff in VISA Centre were clients of Bank of Scotland's Management Services Division, who were external to VISA management though still a division of the bank.

2. *Non-programming users.* These are employees who directly operate the information system. Clerical staff, computer operators, and data-entry staff are examples of this category of users. They are all generally found in banking and insurance, although they were not directly represented in our study. However, in the Premier Financial Services case, Computer Operations

from the parent bank formed part of the project management team in the conversion of the package. They provided an interesting example of a user with relatively low organizational authority and IT design skills playing a significant part in systems development and cutting across the organization's established power structure.

3. *Functional support personnel.* These types of interactors, who are computer-sophisticated and provide support for users from within their own functional areas, were rare in our sample. The only case, the Product Information Officers in Home and Auto, were few in number (one or two to each user department) but were important in channelling users' input into systems development.

4. *Computer-skilled business programmers.* Separate departments of users who have a high level of computer sophistication are another relatively small category in commercial computing (the skilled internal user is far more common in technical and scientific computing). Commercial computing does contain some such groups; accountants and actuaries are often IT-skilled. And our study contained one clear example of this type of user. The Statistical Services department in Home and Auto were internal business users comprised of occupations such as statisticians, economists, and computer specialists, and who developed models to evaluate claims and premium patterns. They played a significant role in systems development, helping to define the requirements of product managers in business departments.

5. *User organizational groups.* This category of internal business user has produced the really significant changes in user relations. A majority of our cases, including Home and Auto, Mutual Life, Bank of Scotland, and Clydesdale, revolved around the integration between IS departments and major business users. These were groups, unskilled in the design of computer systems, for whom technological change required more and more active forms of use and development knowledge. These groups were powerful in organizational terms and potentially able to enforce their needs. They provide key examples of user participation to which we will return.

This wide range of user groups has meant that in practice it can be difficult to generalize from or model decision-making around systems development. In attempting to develop models, therefore, writers more recently have emphasized the open-ended nature of organizational power. Models of decision-making around IT have sought to define the boundaries of social action around systems development and have stressed the network of actors involved. Types of broad interests stemming from three main sources, namely users, specialist developers, and the representation of strategic/corporate groups, are seen as comprising the key set of relations between players (Kling 1987, 1991). As Walsham (1993: 55) points out, these network or web models have shown the need to extend the boundaries of the focal activity of software development. The metaphor of a network of social action by its nature is extendible, to reflect the distributed nature of IT knowledge and the increasingly complex divisions of labour involved.

The Integration Problem

However, the social context in which development takes place is perhaps most critically defined by issues of integration. The technical question of systems integration (from Chapter 7) has a parallel in the social relations between IS and business users. Now that users frequently are powerful organizational groups, the issue of user relations more closely resembles that of the integration of IS into wider organizational structures. Indeed, a crisis of integration of the IS function into mainstream business functions frequently underlies many user relations problems. Early research had already pointed to a clash of values between computer specialists and the organizations in which they were employed (Mumford 1972; Pettigrew 1973). A strong ethos existed in computer departments that encouraged the treatment of users as 'factors rather than actors' in the development process. At the same time managers in other organizational functions often resented their dependence on IT, the technicalities of which they did not understand. In most large establishments the integration problem has been eased because the differentiation between IS staff and other members of the organization has been reduced. The sort of technocratic isolation that early research described, where IS staff had very distinctive values and work styles, has gradually changed.

Our cases provided interesting insights into this aspect of levels of integration. Attempts to integrate databases to produce multi-purpose information systems were becoming commonplace by the early 1980s. But the approach in large-scale schemes frequently shifted to more modest systems relying on separate databases. At the Bank of Scotland we saw that the early stages of 'strategic thinking', to initiate the CABINET system of branch automation, had led user groups in particular to have very high expectations. But later on Systems Development saw it as their job to make people 'think more realistically' about what CABINET could do, especially as the design and development process was producing something closer to 'just a branch terminal'. Similarly, at Home and Auto we saw that considerable resources had been put into an earlier, highly ambitious management information system, based on a corporate database methodology imported from IBM. But lack of progress precipitated a crisis of confidence in the information-systems department and brought in new management committed to a more pragmatic, phased strategy. This in effect meant a scaling down of the integration problem by approaching it one department at a time. Cases like these illustrate a nice irony: the era of integration between users and computer professionals has shown up the extent to which the problem has been underestimated. Here there was actually a reduction in the required level of integration in order to provide realistic chances of success.

Such an analysis puts into perspective some of the hype surrounding IT. As information technology becomes more all-embracing and strategic, significant constraints on the organizational power of the IS function arise. At the same time as becoming more strategic, IS departments are having to share control of systems development with powerful business actors: user involvement in IS means IS involvement in the business. This process was very evident in banks and insurance companies. These long-established and conservative institutions have highly articulated power structures, based around the major business departments and branch networks, as well as around the dominant rationales of industry specialisms (i.e. bankers and actuaries). The wider involvement of IS departments, and the penetration of IT into key business tasks, meant that IS started to come up against these established organizational power bases. Somewhat paradoxically, therefore, as the IS function becomes more strategic it swims in a bigger pool, and thereby becomes relatively a smaller fish.

INTEGRATION STRATEGIES AND USER PARTICIPATION

The task of integrating knowledge from both users and developers of systems is increasingly perceived as a central concern in the management of systems expertise. The problems of poor intercommunication and aligning IT with business needs have stimulated a range of integration strategies stressing the need for systems people who understand strategic goals, users who can become more proactively involved in systems development, and software-development methods which better allow for intervention.

However, there are important implications for the skills implicit in user roles. Behind the rise to prominence of user relations lie a number of potential competitive and technical factors. Changes in core technologies are frequently claimed to have shifted the locus of control over IT towards users and away from developers. New technologies such as personal computers, area networks, 4GLs, and database management systems, form a basis for distributing the functions of the computer core into user departments. But core technologies in the supply of information systems seem to have had a minimal impact on user relations to date. There is a considerable skills constraint on most forms of distributed computing. Core technologies require high levels of systems and programming expertise—in other words, real computing skills rather than the ability to use command-level languages. Hence many of these systems remain underutilized or are used as productivity tools only by IT professionals themselves.

In the case firms, the learning barrier appeared still to be too high for less sophisticated users to profit from core technologies. Personal computers tended to be used for less important project work; 4GLs were hardly in evidence, while database management systems and other on-line facilities were in any case controlled from the IS departments rather than being developed on users' own initiatives. Another strand of technical advance, namely the wave of new applications, is much more directly linked with management control and decision-making functions. These are computer systems which, while not being core technologies or requiring the use of procedural languages, allow for extensive enquiry and interrogation by the user, the generation of standard reports, and the like. Most of the automation and information systems that we studied fell into this category.

In addition, there has also been a recognition of the political nature of systems development, and the problems for integration strategies created by power relations. Some have contrasted a conventional rational perspective on organizations with the implicitly more realistic political one (Franz and Robey 1984). Similarly, in an early and influential article Keen (1981) stressed the tactical responsibilities of systems developers if they wanted to implement systems successfully. They could no longer conveniently assume that organizations are rational arenas; they had to be aware of the power context and the building of alliances with influential users as integral to the task of systems development. However, the 'expert power' possessed by IT professionals has also given cause for concern.

Hitherto user groups such as clerical and data input staff and computer operators have occupied positions of low organizational power and have been largely excluded from systems development. We saw something of this in the VISA case, where there was no attempt to consult the women who formed the large data-entry workforce, or to obtain their detailed knowledge of the work when designing the system. A perception of this fact—the exclusion from design and development of the very groups who spend their working lives with systems—has helped to stimulate an interest in user participation. In this context, a vision of good practice has been urged on systems developers which places the user at the centre of the development process. Models such as Lucas's (1974, 1981) creative systems design and Checkland's (1981) soft-systems approach put forward strategies for the improved efficiency of systems that also enhance users' experience of IT. User participation in all stages of the development cycle—analysis, design, installation—mean that users themselves become stakeholders in, not merely beneficiaries of, technical change.

Part of the stimulus for broader approaches towards participative design has come from the work redesign movement, which grew out of the Human Relations school and the socio-technical systems approach (Mumford 1972, 1983). The emphasis is on alternative techniques to conserve workers' skills and discretion, and to roll back the worst effects of Taylorist job design. Researchers here have been active in developing models of human-centred systems development, and have also recognized the knowledge and power constraints. Thus Kyng (1991) argues the need for new approaches to systems development given the severe constraints on users' ability to acquire technical skills, and also developers' commitment to business applications. Divisions

Strategic orientation	Strategy
1. Breaking down IT/user barrier; integration arenas	User involvement
2. Improving users' IT skills	End-user computing; information officers
3. Improving IT specialists' business skills	High-technique individuals: analyst/programmers; hybrid managers; business analysts

Fig. 10.1 *Strategies for Meeting User Needs*

between users and developers mean that co-operative design requires support in the forms of complex simulation techniques. Similarly, Kling (1991) has criticized the 'relentless social imagery' of much of this debate, questioning whether it is possible to overcome the power constraints inherent in capitalist enterprises. And Gronbaek, Kyng, and Morgensen (1993), while stressing the creative potential of users and the importance of involving them, also emphasize the problems in bridging the knowledge gap; a major commitment is required for co-operative design to become a reality.

These proposals, however, have to an extent been overtaken by events in the real world of commercial and industrial computing. The problems of integrating IT with the mainstream business are now seen to be the central IT management concern. The 1990–1 Price Waterhouse Computing Opinion Survey, for example, showed that the top problem for IT managers, up to about 1987, was that of meeting project deadlines. Technical problems and problems of managing the time dimension (discussed in Chapter 9) reflected the internal management of data-processing departments and the earlier software crisis. Since 1988, however, meeting deadlines has been progressively overtaken by the problem of integrating IT with corporate objectives; by 1990 this was being mentioned by around 40 per cent of IT managers. Thus the development effort has shifted from the time-related technical problems with which IT professionals have long been preoccupied, to the behavioural and socio-political ones of interaction with users. Strategies for managing user participation are now perceived as the key to the integration problem.

Types of Integration Strategy

With this in mind, a range of user strategies has been set out in Figure 10.1, which again concentrate on the strategies found in our case firms. While not claimed to be exhaustive, this is a comprehensive typology which includes key integration strategies. It covers the possibilities of joint relations between users and technical specialists, and of the two respective groups extending their mutual skills into each others domain.

Strategies are here categorized into three types: (1) those that create organizational intermediaries or set up structural arenas in which integration takes place; (2) strategies which permit the user to acquire skills with which to interact with IT staff and cross the user/IT interface; and (3) strategies where IT staff acquire business-relevant skills to achieve integration. Of course, these are not always alternatives; some strategies are usefully operated alongside or are dependent on others. They also overlap, since all aim at the same objective of integration, and in any case they are implemented in different ways at different installations. Nor are all these types of strategy first and foremost to do with participation in systems development; some are more to do with the effectiveness of using systems which have already been developed. However, in practice, any strategy for making users more effective as users will also enhance their ability to participate in systems development.

For one of these potential strategies there was little evidence of diffusion. End-user computing has often been seen as the ideal solution for users to communicate with developers on an equal footing. But the barriers to providing large numbers of users with IT skills, such as a working knowledge of 4GLs, are frequently too high. Weaker forms of end-user computing are much more in evidence, reflecting the spread of computer awareness and of specialist tools like report generators and database enquiry systems. But these represent only a partial solution of the integration problem. We observed only one stronger variant of end-user computing. Our single example of this was the Statistical Services Department in Home and Auto. They were referred to informally in the organization as 'senior users', and we saw in the case study that they had considerable influence in shaping the development of a management information system. However, encouraging such specialist users does not represent a general strategy for spreading computer literacy among large swathes of users. But the other two strategies in Figure 10.1 were more widespread.

User Involvement

Many of the means of integrating the effort of IS departments with that of organizational users represent some form of user involvement in systems design. However, the term itself has come to refer to the organizational procedures and structures that enable users to influence the development of systems for their areas. Other strategies like pushing users up the learning curve, distributing the computing core, or employing evolutionary design methods may be a critical part of user involvement, but represent longer term responses. Simply enabling users to define what their needs are, and setting up a structure of meetings in which participation can take place, are much more direct means of integration.

That user involvement is a differentiated process has long been observed. Several writers (e.g. Land 1982; Ives and Olson 1984) have identified different levels of participation. These vary from consultation with users, where decision-making power remains in the hands of IT staff, to users having an influence over design and development equal to that of IS. Implied here is that developers invariably attempt to enhance their control by retaining the weaker forms of user involvement. Mumford's (1983) notion of a 'hierarchy of participation' suggests that indirect, consultative forms of involvement tend to be confined to strategically important decisions, while users are only allowed significant influence over less important decisions. In practice this means IT staff taking early decisions on basic design and only involving users later, when operational decisions are required. Indeed, the notion of 'captive users' whose interests are manipulated by IT specialists has been widely reported (Ehn and Sandberg 1979; Kyng and Mathiassen 1982). The systems developer's role can be powerfully symbolic, consisting of a technical discourse which is seemingly rational yet conceals the pursuit of narrow interests on the part of developers (Robey and Markus 1984). Friedman (1989: 274) makes a similar distinction between levels of 'formal' and 'detailed' user involvement. Formal user involvement is largely symbolic, and includes things like users identifying opportunities for development and signing for specifications. While these procedures seem to place power in the hands of users, the real initiatives invariably come from the systems-development functions. In contrast, detailed user involvement requires users to play a role in the management and staffing of projects, or it can mean users assuming responsibility for the delivery of applications systems (Rockart and Hofman 1992).

Though formal involvement in project management dominated, Friedman (1989: 274) found that surveys conducted in 1972 and 1981 did show a modest increase in detailed user involvement. This suggests that mid-1980s surveys may be dated on this point, and that user relations may have become a more central concern. Our own study was not a survey and we cannot confirm rates of diffusion of these practices. Our case studies did suggest, nevertheless, that organizations are putting certain user-oriented procedures into place. In Bank of Scotland, Mutual Life, Home and Auto, and Premier Financial Services, there were well-developed arrangements for project management that embraced detailed participation by users.

In some case studies, we can point to examples of users playing the game to their own advantage, and cases which revealed the pressure that IS departments can come under if they fail to produce. At Home and Auto, pressure from users when their expectations were not met caused a shift to a safer, more pragmatic approach in order to complete developments. Only when the pressure was lifted was there a return to a more strategic (and risky) line. Indeed, in some organizations powerful and relatively independent business departments sought to adopt a tactic of resisting involvement in systems development. By keeping IS at arm's length, and refusing to play the game of 'commitment', they pressed IS to redesign anything they were unhappy with.

The way the problem of user involvement has been formulated therefore needs qualifying. 'Involvement' is a value-laden concept that urges egalitarian forms of participation (especially against a background of low-status users traditionally having been excluded from any real part in developing systems). However, elaborate models of user involvement can impede understanding of real organizational processes. What is not taken into account is that increasingly users are better able to take care of their own interests. Rational models of how users ought to be integrated into systems development cease to be appropriate when users themselves are powerful organizational actors. In short, user involvement in IT is political only in the sense that all decision-making is political. The capacity of users to resist control, as well as the increasingly complex divisions of labour around systems development, have underlined the open-ended nature of decision-making and stakeholder power. Certainly our own cases revealed a range of forms that user relations can take and the non-determined participation of interests like specialist developers, influential users and corporate management.

User Relations in CABINET

The Bank of Scotland development, for example, was a large undertaking and user relations were correspondingly complex. We saw that systems development had 'talked up' the project in its early stages in a form of symbolic control, and that they were also alert to other ways of manipulating users' commitment.

We've got to make sure we've got them in . . . because without that commitment it will become a Management Services project which nobody else actually believes in or is interested in. It would become 'our fault' if things go wrong. And I suppose part of that process is getting their input without letting that necessarily dominate everything.

Users' less favourable views tended to build up in later phases of the development, which reflected the classic pattern of their advancing up the learning curve and so becoming increasingly critical and demanding. From the development point of view this can occur too late for the system to be easily rewritten. Users from the branches saw the decision-making around CABINET as a political process in which stakeholders spoke from the position of their own interests.

Systems are always keen to remind us that they are only there to do what we decide they should do. But the reality in my opinion is that they can influence it an awful lot. . . . If the developer tells you that particular thing is going to take 500 hundred man-years to develop, it's difficult for a layman to say it's only going to take 300 years.

Similarly, branch managers in hindsight regretted they had played a too passive role on the Working Party groups, and favoured changing chairing responsibilities from MSD to the branches. As one argued, if the branches' interests had been represented by senior branch people, and their viewpoint 'put across more forcibly than perhaps it has, then maybe we would have had one or two of the phases that we still have not got'.

Still, users were not impotent in the power game. The network of project

management committees provided the 'integration arena' in which they participated and where the game could be played out; and users too had forms of
pressure they could apply. At one stage the credibility of the Management
Services Division became an issue; development on CABINET had 'stuttered
to a halt' because staff were taken off to work on EFTPOS, the 'next rising
star'. But from the branches' point of view CABINET was far more important
and they had been 'used to something useful coming along every so often'. If
the flow dried up, then the acceptability of the system was in jeopardy,
exposing the vulnerability of MSD as a very large cost centre. There was also
evidence of successful involvement on the part of users. Branches variously
reported that the CABINET systems teams were responsive to requests for
changes. Several of the branch respondents commented that CABINET was
an unusually good project because so much care was taken in the committees
to 'keep users advised and to consult with them'. As to the problem of MSD
being in the chair: 'In the event of any sort of conflict of interest it conjures
up in the mind of the person being consulted, well, they are not answerable to
anyone other than themselves. But in fairness we have always been asked.'

User Relations in the Customer Care Project

In Mutual Life in 1980s an elaborate formula for selecting projects for
development had emerged, which computing had been partly instrumental in
bringing about. The Computer Operations Divisional Manager professed to
adhere to a policy of picking organizational winners. He had ruled that the
division would not be a barrier to any system that any department wanted to
introduce.

What we have said to each division and to the company is that the IS department will
support any business objective that the divisions have, provided they can support it
both in terms of their manpower and their finance. . . . So anyone can get any
development they want up to their maximum ability to support it. If they cannot
provide the manpower they cannot get the development. They become the constraint.
Of course, that's not totally infinite in the sense that they have limited resources. I
raise this point because we don't need to do a balancing exercise. We don't have to
decide between Investment and Actuarial.

A number of outcomes emerged from this basic policy. First, departments
which already had the biggest budgets, largest staff numbers, and greatest
representation on user committees were most likely to succeed in getting the
applications they asked for. It would seem that IT was explicitly used to
reinforce existing relations of power. Secondly, this kind of rule multiplied
the number of sites for decision-making, and the attribution of responsibility
became correspondingly difficult. Applications often got nominated and designed without it being apparent where the initiative had come from. Over
the long term, it seemed probable for working practices to be cumulatively
altered by a process of 'computerization' which was experienced as innocuous,
neutral, and attributed to no one.

Thus, even if only successful protagonists got support, it remained unclear to the IS design staff which subset within the user community they were building for. This lack of clarity left considerable space for IS staff to negotiate which applications or systems actually did get built, regardless of any guarantee that all funded projects would be completed. Similarly, the rule that Computer Operations was officially subservient to users did not mean that the division could not initiate or prompt technical change in directions which they chose. Here is the Divisional Manager again: 'We obviously make users feel that they organize our priorities, but under that we will retain some resource that we may have to use to keep our own standards up to date. Things that he (the user) wouldn't be fussed about but that have to be done in his benefit.' Though the main business departments owned data and access to it, decisions on access were made with IS prompting in the background: 'the trick here is to make these people who are responsible listen to the prompts ... So we are servants but not servile!'

High-Technique Individuals

The creation of high-technique groups, combining certain IT skills with business skills, in order to mediate between IS and business functions is another key strategy for surmounting user relations problems. The required IT skills are those of analysis (such as the ability to produce initial project reports that form the basis of later detailed specifications) and project management. This approach has led to a number of proposals for producing individuals with interface skills. A number of strategies in Figure 10.1 are relevant here: analyst/programmers, the so-called hybrid managers, and business analysts.

Analyst/programmers

It has been suggested that the division of labour between programming and analysis, a marked feature of earlier stages of computer systems development, is now being reversed. We are seeing the reintegration of these two roles in order to enhance the work experience and career prospects of IS staff. Friedman (1989), for example, regards this as evidence of his claim that responsible strategies towards computer staff dominate the current stage of computer systems development. In our own case firms, it was more common for IS departments to continue demarcating programming and analysis, with user-contact being very much the province of systems analysts, though some operated alternative policies. In the Royal Bank, which probably had the most developed IS set-up, they claimed a strong policy of integrating the two roles, referring to all IS staff as 'systems developers'. In Home and Auto, the roles were divided, but in the case study it was noted how programmers were beginning to interact with users in developments like the management information system, and the role of analyst/programmer was coming into existence *de facto*.

However, we have to question the real extent of role integration. Friedman's evidence partly reflected the growth in smaller establishments where labour is naturally less divided. In large establishments the survey data may have been picking up systems managers' intentions and claims. The reality we found was that, while IS managers liked to stress that they made no rigid distinctions between the categories of programmer and analyst, and were anxious to provide programmers with creative and career-enhancing work, the familiar grade, career, and status differences between programming and analysis jobs remained in place. It was still normal practice to begin working as a programmer and move on to analysis as a mark of promotion or experience. In Mutual Life, for instance, psychometric interviewing tests had been introduced which showed 'very distinct differences between the analyst types and the programmer types', and for initial placements they bracketed people into jobs accordingly.

Hybrid Managers

The perception amongst IS managers that technical staff have poor communications and business skills and that IS departments tend towards an isolationist ethos has been widely reported (Couger and Zawacki 1980). Systems analysts have long filled the preferred role of the more generalist IT professional, and the move towards programmer/analysts, or programmers with some exposure to users, is an associated trend. However, the historic perception that IT staff need a broader range of skills has hardened up recently with the focus on user relations and the integration of IT into organizations.

The most recent solution to the problem has been the call for a new breed of 'hybrid' managers, a term pioneered by Earl (1989) to describe managers with both technical and strategic abilities: 'hybrids are people with technical skills able to work in user areas doing a line or functional job, but adept at developing and supplementing IT application ideas.' This envisages combining IS expertise with organizational and managerial knowledge at the individual level, rather than further specialization of the IS function. The thrust of the hybrid manager debate has mainly been at the level of training policy and professional development (British Computer Society 1990). But some difficulties of creating dual-skill staff have been conceded. For example, Earl notes that the career implications mean IT staff would need to become less occupationally oriented and more locally centred on their organizations (Skyrme and Earl 1990), yet such changes are clearly at variance with essential features of the IT occupations. Also, Simpson (1991) raises doubts about whether hybrid skills constitute 'solid knowledge' at all—and whether the half-way house of the hybrid manager is worth pursuing if it endangers the educational processes that currently produce general managers and computer scientists. In an industry, some areas of which are overrun by 'cowboys', hybrid forms run the risk of lacking credibility with general management and IS management alike.

The hybrid manager was a comparatively rare sighting in our case firms. The migration of IT-skilled staff into user areas was illustrated by the Product Information Officers (PIOs) at Home and Auto. The PIOs reflected a strategy of computing functions being supported within business areas. However, the PIOs saw their careers lying within user departments and had become increasingly assimilated. They only partially solved the skills problem in so far as they had become detached from a technical base and were renewing only a limited range of IT skills. In the Clydesdale Bank and Bank of Scotland, on the other hand, hybrid skills had formed the basis of an entire new occupational grouping. The business analysts there closely resembled the hybrid definition of specialists at 'the interface between business and information technology' (Simpson 1991). In Clydesdale's new Electronic Business Division the business analysts claimed to be 'genuine hybrids' and had been structurally separated from the IT Division. But in Bank of Scotland in particular we were able to explore in detail the implications of creating this category of high-technique intermediary.

Business Analysts and Hybrid Skills

As we have seen, at Bank of Scotland systems development was the chief responsibility of two departments: Systems Implementation (SIM) where analysis and programming was conducted, and the smaller Systems Investigation department (SIV) which housed the business analysts responsible for making the business case for a project. The business analysts in SIV had careers and skills that pointed them towards banking rather than computing. In part this reflected the smaller size of SIV, and the fact that there was little chance of the business analysts seeking promotion on the systems side. One business analyst we interviewed, for example, noted that she had some computing in her undergraduate degree, but she had come originally from the branches. She considered herself first and foremost a banker. Time spent in the Management Services Division (MSD) was good experience, and she would not want to go back into the branches; she hoped to pursue her career in the main head-office departments.

Business Analyst Role

SIV had a true hybrid role on the interface between systems development and users. They articulated this role quite effectively in terms of their usefulness as an intermediary; SIV talked the language of both sides and was able to make effective compromises. One member reflected on their key problems:

If there's no business process at the moment, then it's not just a matter of going in and analysing what somebody's doing in an office and writing that down in some formal or informal way. The most problematic areas for us are the areas where we don't do anything at the moment because the user doesn't have an existing system. . . . With the best will in the world what you have come up with is a product which needs to be tuned again and again. Gradually people would get a clearer idea of what was required to be done. Systems evolve, so the direction you push them in has to be the right evolutionary direction.

However, the key problem of non-experts communicating with experts was only partially resolved. SIV could not, for example, write up the Project Investigation Report (the initial specification of a system) by themselves. They involved SIM staff early on for information on feasibility and alternatives, and on time and manpower resources. On the other hand, it would be mistaken to assume that the business analysts missed having real computing skills. Several members of SIV had had programming skills in the past, but stressed that these were rarely called on in their work of project investigation.

The Business and Technical Relationship

The effectiveness of SIV as hybrid managers partly rested on where they stood in relation to users and developers. On this point there was clearly a potential for conflict between SIV and SIM. Banking skills were crucial in SIV and the business analysts looked to the bank for their careers. This level of differentiation between the bank and computing meant continued ambivalence over the boundary between Investigation (the bank side) and Implementation (the technical side). Undercurrents of antagonism directed at SIV's lack of computing skills perhaps reflected SIM's desire to protect their own knowledge base. Rather than being accepted as a rational response to uncertainty inherent in innovation, the need to iterate was viewed within SIM as a sign of lack of competence. A good business analyst was 'someone who defines the thing properly and gets the specification correct first time, and does not have to make lots of changes; someone who actually thinks ahead of anything that is going to impact on it' (SIM programmer). Consequent on the partial failure of these forms of expertise to mesh, a degree of tension existed between the two groups not unlike the programmer–analyst divide. 'A lot of SIV reports come to us in draft form. Some get hammered because they haven't asked the right questions. They don't know what the right questions are. So we're not a fan of SIV, I suppose' (SIM programmer).

However, the relationship was complex and other evidence pointed to SIV being allied with SIM rather than the users. Despite SIV's banking bias, the decisive factor was organizational structure and the placing of the two groups in the same division. Thus there was evidence of business analysts taking on typical computing priorities—the need for development schedules to be set several years ahead to prevent being 'swayed' by pressure from users, and clear ideas about who were good and bad users.

On project working parties and in their strategic influence over systems developments, the business analysts and systems developers had gained much from their alliance. A good deal of uncertainty existed about whether they were intended as a forum for representing everyone's views or to police the systems builders. Middle-level business managers, unused to being consulted in detail about technical change until CABINET, were often unsure what was expected of them. MSD, in the mean time, capitalized on this and filled the power vacuum with the clearest definition of the situation.

CONCLUSION

It has been stressed in this chapter that one of the most important changes in systems development in recent years has been in the role played by users in the development process. Rather than a simple situation of a developer (an IS department, say) building a system for a user, systems development frequently involves a range of organizational and occupational groups. Thus systems expertise no longer resides in the heads of IT professionals alone; increasingly knowledge is distributed and users are recognized as legitimate providers of systems expertise. As we saw in the last chapter, the combination of local and generic knowledges lie at the heart of implementation. In financial services IT is vital to the work of business departments, and these have the organizational power to ensure that meeting their needs is how success in systems development is defined.

The complex analysis and design problems of recent years also demand a far higher level of communication and co-operation between users and IS departments. User involvement in particular needs to be seen as part and parcel of decision-making and a naturally politicized process. In this vein, our case studies showed quite clearly how the relationship between users and developers hardly reflected a democratic urge to 'involve' users at all; often it was simply not possible, let alone desirable, for systems to be developed by computer specialists working in isolation. New applications have had a major impact in shifting the balance of power in favour of users. Certainly this type of strategic application constituted the direction of change in our case firms. Branch automation systems, client-centred databases, management information systems and cash management systems were all being implemented. These do not require users to deploy complex technical skills, but they deal with less well-defined information structures and key business tasks. This strategic aspect provides the basis for closer integration between users and developers and is changing the nature of user relations.

However, any simple notion of users becoming more powerful obscures other, more subtle changes. The more powerful organizational groups have long been users of IS services, but strategic applications are requiring more active forms of use and development knowledge from them. IT is becoming more relevant to their central tasks at the same time as the old divisions of labour that isolated knowledge in the IS department are breaking up. These changes are accompanied by the emergence of new market structures and new core technologies, but are not necessarily caused by them. The influence of occupational and organizational factors, especially associated changes in structures of expertise, need to be emphasized.

These changes in the nature of systems and of user relations have meant increasingly high levels of required integration. Indeed, the crisis of integration of IS functions within business institutions lies behind the renewed interest in high-technique individuals. A perception of this need has in turn led to more detailed prescriptions for combining business and technical skills—represented most recently in the notion of the 'hybrid' manager. In a sense, though, this initiative represents an attempt to circumvent some of the problems of the management of expertise. For if key interface skills can be integrated within the person of the hybrid, complex problems of relating business and technical orientations may be solved at a stroke. However, this chapter has suggested that unfortunately these solutions are more problematic. True, many new occupations in areas like networks, database management, client-server systems and applications, contain strong hybrid elements. But the extent to which a high level of systems skills can be sustained by groups cut off from their occupational base remained in doubt. The case material revealed the many cross-cutting loyalties and types of differentiation that exist between specialist and generalist skills, and a continuing crisis of integration of IS in these organizations.

PART III

EXPERTISE

The final part presents an account of expertise itself, and draws together the main themes of the book in an analysis of the management of expertise. We explore the central importance of skills management both in the strategies and practices of organizations and in the labour and product markets through which expertise is traded. The management of expertise encapsulates the *deployment* of expertise (how skills are organized) and the *formation* of expertise (the acquisition and development of skills).

In terms of the deployment of expertise, the skills content of the computing occupations has been under almost continual revision because of advances in technology, while managerial attempts to respond to new bundles of skills reflect the uncertainty involved in aligning technical expertise to business objectives. The focus on the formation of expertise highlights the different strategies available to the firm. These range from a grow-your-own approach, developing technical expertise in-house, to recruiting skills on the external labour market. Either may offer particular advantages or disadvantages to the firm, and may be appropriate to particular situations. As we shall see, developing expertise in-house may be the favoured route to fulfil requirements for local knowledge types, while external recruitment may be an effective means of acquiring knowledge of newer techniques and fostering alternative approaches to systems development.

We begin in Chapter 11 with a schema of the 'ingredients' of expertise which addresses its political and economic aspects, as well as knowledge content. We distinguish how knowledge is acquired, how it is distributed, and how it is valued. The tendency to identify expertise with formal knowledge is unhelpful; analysis must address different kinds of non-formal knowledge as well. The knowledge needed to solve problems is often fragmented between specialist areas, and in many cases boundaries between expert groups have become institutionalized. This complicates the process of reformulating knowledge and brings us to consider power—the efforts of groups to claim central status for their knowledge holdings, and the settings of unequal power within which rivalry occurs. Finally, in so far as knowledge is located outside a firm, the work of internal experts can be substituted by external experts, or by the supply of artefacts. Expertise is thus tradeable on labour and product markets, and rivalry between experts may take an economic form. We note the problems in establishing an appropriate price for technical labour and raise the problem of IT professionals and their relations with general management.

In Chapter 12 the issue of IT careers is examined through a detailed study of one case. The Bank of Scotland's Customer and Branch Automation Network (CABINET) was of a size and duration that provided an excellent illustration of the richness and complexity of expert technical labour. We examine how career trajectories reflected the strategies of different occupational groupings and reflected organizational policies for the recruitment, promotion, and development of staff. We chart the main segments of technical labour involved in the CABINET development, showing how in carrying out their roles they collaborated with a range of other groups. We stress the importance of collaborative networks and look at variations between the fluid networks of the user interface and the more narrowly focused links between technical specialists. And we explore the different strategies pursued by IT staff in articulating their claims to be expert and valuable. Finally, the chapter examines the contradictory relationship between the technical expert and management. Career trajectories across the Management Services Division reflected strategies to conserve technical and managerial skills and legitimate the relationship between managers and managed.

Chapter 13 analyses the choice that organizations face between incorporating expertise into the hierarchy and various forms of market acquisition. We show how choices between the use of consultants, subcontracting, and buying in software as packages cannot be reduced to an economic calculus. The use of external expertise may mean that knowledge requirements stretch beyond the skills base of internal staff, but equally may be pursued in order to increase the substitutability of internal expertise. IT users with a systems-development capacity have the choice between satisfying IT needs in-house or looking for products through the market. As we saw in Chapter 7, the financial sector has always been a leader in in-house development. But the boundaries between what has been produced in-house and what provided through the market have been continually redrawn, as innovations have become commodified or 'black-boxed'. Hardware and core software have long since become the preserve of the IT industry. Now, however, the 'make–buy' question is being asked of a range of applications software. Not least of the factors to be weighed is the so-called package paradox, namely the dangers for users of dependency on a sole supplier. In this uncertain setting, we found the role of previously under-researched 'relational' forms of contracting to be particularly significant.

11

The Dimensions of Expertise

Expertise involves substantial forms of knowledge, as well-organized patterns of identifying and applying appropriate knowledge. Intellectual skills include formal and non-formal knowledge of systems, while the structure of organizations represents the primary arena for establishing legitimacy and the forms of power. And external markets and occupational structures mediate the transfer of expertise between organizations, or the trading of knowledge. These divergent aspects suggest a framework for understanding the detailed nature of expertise (and subsequently the management of expertise). The three components reflect *knowledge* (the substantive component of expertise), *power* (realized through the institutional structures of the organization), and *tradeability* (the exchange of expertise through labour and product markets, and occupational networks).

A variety of schema have been advanced to explore skill and expert knowledge. Reflecting particular concerns or disciplinary backgrounds, these often give emphasis to particular dimensions. Labour economics, for example, views skill in terms of its market scarcity and would tend to sideline any social or political constructions in the definition of skill. Labour-process theories, on the other hand, emphasize the political dimension. Here Braverman (1974) stressed that skill distribution reflects managerial control strategies, particularly work degradation. Cockburn (1985) saw skilled status, and the construction of male and female work identities, reflecting gender-biased political processes. She stressed that work acquired a gendered identity particularly through the affinity between men and technology. Also Foucault, in other contexts, emphasized the interdependence and simultaneous construction of power and knowledge structures (Foucault 1980).

We would argue it is necessary to consider all three aspects in order to encapsulate expertise adequately. While it is possible to collapse the different aspects, this would be at a cost to the richness of explanation. We remain sceptical of accounts which reduce expertise to a single dynamic, whether of political process or economic logic. We therefore seek an integrated approach which remains open to these heterogeneous facets of expertise. This is not to imply that the economic, political, and knowledge aspects of expertise can be separated; but we find analytical merit in considering them separately, while noting the linkages between them.

Use of the term expertise highlights the importance of knowledge, while recognizing that knowledge is socially created and 'carried' by people. Expertise does not simply involve bodies of ideas, but ideas which are embodied in individuals and groups located in specific social, political, and economic contexts. The bearers of expertise may be differentiated according to the organizational and sectoral structures they work in, and the technologies they work with. They may pursue contradictory interests in these complex settings, characterized by (often unequal) relationships of power. Achieving the status of expert does not depend solely on the knowledge possessed by groups, but also on their ability to legitimate their status—through political processes within the organization and beyond—and to assert the value of their know-ledge—whether directly through markets or through indirect measures of the value of their knowledge for the organization. Thus expertise needs to be dynamically modelled, showing how it is situated, embodied, and negotiated in collectivities of people.

In this chapter then we examine why the 'management of expertise' is important, particularly in a context of the rapid deployment of IT. We consider the structure and character of expert knowledge, power and the politics of expertise, and its tradeability. Finally, we examine specific aspects of the management of expertise in the case studies.

Expertise and Technological Change

The application of new technologies and working systems invariably means changes in the *distribution of knowledge* in an organization. Sometimes the introduction of a new technology may *diffuse* knowledge across a wider band of people; knowledge embedded in the new system may be distributed across a branch network or extend new tasks to particular occupations. Conversely, the introduction of new technology may serve to *concentrate* particular kinds of knowledge. The users of new systems may be marginalized, while technical experts monopolize the role of change agent and become a technocratic élite.

Increasing levels of automation have also highlighted continuing problems in the availability of appropriate expertise. The 'skills problem' is endemic to new technologies. It cannot be solved by simple increases in the volume of formal training, in so far as the speed of development and diffusion of new technological systems outstrips the lead time for training. No matter how much formal training is provided it will perennially tend to be out of date.

One authoritative report (Buckroyd and Cornford 1988) has suggested the problem is not so much a skills crisis as a skills management crisis, which seriously affects the areas of manpower planning and personnel development. Though many managers already attempt to relate information about skills that exist in organizations to their understanding of future needs, such exercises are usually done in general occupational terms, rather than in terms of what specific sets of skills and knowledge are required. Indeed, it is a moot point whether management is able to forecast what these new bundles of knowledges and skills might be—especially given the turbulence in technologies and systems. Uncertainty may reflect whether a technology can be made to work in a particular situation, and whether technical personnel have the capabilities to make it work. Much current turbulence in financial services stems from changes in the sector's commercial environment, rather than the 'IT revolution' *per se*. As we discussed in Chapter 2, the financial services sector is changing in ways that have not always been evident to the players involved. These forms of uncertainty interact, causing distinct specialist groups, including computer-skilled people and other change agents, to revise the basis of their knowledge and their claims to expertise, in order to address changing demands as they perceive them.

The IT Occupations

Since its inception commercial computing has diversified into distinct occupational sub-specialisms. Development of the computing occupations, and the formation of IT expertise, have been closely related to the development and deployment of technologies, as computer hardware and software have been commercialized and diffused.

Over the forty-year period, the jobs of computer workers have reflected differences between the broad generations of systems, with the difficulties in operating hardware having greatest significance in the early stages. From around the mid-1960s, operating system software became a main focus for development (Peláez 1988). Some of the tasks hitherto carried out by applications programmers in user organizations were progressively automated and absorbed into the core of hardware and operating systems. Hardware manufacturers began to reclaim some of this territory into the machinery itself (and back into their own organizations) in order to sell more machines. A computing industry emerged (Howells 1987) to which career programmers flocked. However the convergence of IT skills within the supply sector remained partial (Brady, Tierney, and Williams 1992); with the widespread commercial application of computers, user firms continued to employ around half of all IT-skilled workers. In parallel with these developments came innovations in computing languages. The advent of high-level languages made it easier for programmers in user organizations to apply computing to business problems. COBOL, for instance, was designed for business use and became the dominant language for applications programmers.

In the current era, in which IT is central to an ever-growing range of organizational activities, the emphasis has shifted to better matching IT to user requirements. As discussed in detail in Chapter 10, new strategies and occupations have emerged to cope with uncertainty at the user interface. In several of our case firms we reported the emergence of organizational and technical specialists—like the PIOs in Home and Auto and the business analysts in Clydesdale and Bank of Scotland—who facilitated linkages between the business and IS.

As a result of such developments, the skills required by systems developers have changed. As components of computer systems have fragmented, and arrays of new tools, languages, and techniques provide new solutions, so the unified 'craft' of the programmer has dissolved into a range of splintered tasks and activities (Kraft 1977). This differentiation into sub-occupational specialities relates to a number of changes: a polarization in the *location* of computing workers between the computing industry and user firms spread across different sectors; the segmentation and elaboration of *technical compo-nents* (hardware, operating systems and languages, software applications), as well as changes in the *problematics* within which they are applied; and the sheer *growth* in the volume and range of computing work being undertaken (Anderson 1982; Connor and Pearson 1986; Buckroyd and Cornford 1988). However, the most direct influence over computing occupations may be attributed to *managerial strategies* for the organization and control of comput-ing work. From the 1960s onward, a remarkable level of manipulation of job titles, career structures, recruitment practices, departmental structures, and monitoring strategies operated to diversify computing work.

EXPERT KNOWLEDGE

In stressing the relation of expertise to power and tradeability, we do not imply (as some have) that expertise lacks substantive content. Nor would we argue from the opposite extreme that knowledge is distinct and autonomous, the possession of which automatically confers expertise—though again some theorists do so argue (e.g. Popper (1979) and his sphere of objective knowledge).

The account of expert knowledge here partly overlaps with the discussions in Chapters 1 and 4 of competence which reflected industry-specific abilities. In exploring further the substantive content of expertise, we can draw attention to certain general factors. It is important first to recognize that knowledge and information are immaterial goods, which makes it difficult to value them. Information, especially as processed in IT systems, has no intrinsic value; it requires interpretation within some context and translation into a potential for action. Meaning and significance have to be attributed in terms of existing knowledge about a particular situation. Consequently, the value of information and appreciation of its importance varies widely. To resolve the intransigent problems of copyright and patenting, the allocation of intellectual-property rights tends to focus on a concrete form, rather than intangible information or knowledge (see Peláez 1990, on the copyrighting of software). Indeed, the difficulty of valuing pure knowledge leads to a general characteristic of knowledge agencies, namely a tendency to transform their knowledge into a more appropriable form as tangible products. In such forms knowledge is more easily traded (as we see in the final chapter in this section).

Thus knowledge and information are relational and their significance depends on particular contexts and human agents. This contrasts with the economic notion of information trading which assumes that knowledge is a freely available, relatively frictionless entity to which any individual agent has access. In reality, knowledge in areas like science and technology is unevenly distributed across social groups. This state of affairs follows from the nature of knowledge and its generation, rooted as these are in the prevailing division of labour. Knowledge exists not in its own right but as *socio-cognitive* structures of varying complexity, in which substantive content is 'carried' by social groups, with a lesser or greater degree of commitment depending on the costs of acquiring and maintaining their knowledge investments. Given the necessary involvement of groups, social, organizational, and political factors are inextricably woven into the perception and expression of expertise. Such factors are not ancillary and cannot be separated out from knowledge or information content.

Scientific knowledge constitutes perhaps an extreme case, being strongly formalized and subject to impersonalized and 'objective' assessment. In science, the costs of knowledge acquisition and maintenance are high, and based around richly interconnected communities of more or less equal peers. Many studies have highlighted the social nature of knowledge structures in science—with scientific communities (Polanyi 1946, 1967) linked by paradigms (T. S. Kuhn 1962) or 'thought collectives' (L. Fleck 1979). Technological and other types of knowledge relevant to innovation, with which we are more concerned in the present study, bear important similarities with, as well as differences from, the scientific case.

The Nature of Expert Knowledge

Socio-cognitive structures can thus be conceptualized along two major dimensions: the differing *nature* of the knowledge involved, and the *distribution* of bundles of knowledge among the carriers. Taking the first of these, the economist Winter (1987), noting the lack of adequate terminology to describe the nature of bodies of knowledge at a detailed level, suggested a set of taxonomic dimensions: tacit/articulable; non-teachable/teachable; non-articulated/articulated; non-observable in use/observable in use; and complex/simple. We develop these to identify the key socio-cognitive features of knowledge involved in innovation.

First we highlight *formal knowledge* such as theories, formulae, etc., usually available in written form as textbooks and manuals. Expertise is often (but misleadingly) assumed to be synonymous with formal knowledge. In contrast, the importance of *informal knowledge* reflects a concern with rules of thumb and 'tricks of the trade' learnt on the job over a period of time. Sometimes informal knowledge may be partly available in written form (e.g. in working manuals for the documentation of software). It tends to be concentrated amongst people sharing common interests or a common work-place or trade.

While formal knowledge offers universal or generic solutions and methods for problem-solving, the importance of *contingent knowledge* includes distributed and apparently trivial information, highly specific to the particular environment (e.g. 'local knowledge'). Contingent knowledge tends to be extremely voluminous and is rarely concentrated in one person. Rather, it is widely distributed through an organization, including the lower levels of the hierarchy. Its importance is often overlooked or undervalued.

Another element associated with know-how, and important for mobilizing other forms of knowledge, is *tacit knowledge*. Tacit knowledge is rooted in practice and experience and is transmitted by apprenticeship and training, through 'watching and doing' forms of learning. It is not readily articulable and not easily communicable. It has been widely identified as a major constraint on the diffusion of technology (e.g. Basalla 1988).

Finally we point to general *cultural*, or *meta-knowledge*. This refers to background knowledge including general social and cultural assumptions, values (i.e. what is considered important), and prevalent beliefs. An example might be the conceptualization of technocratic rationality as objective, ungendered, and apolitical. This is usually taken-for-granted knowledge, only noted at times of dramatic change or in clashes between different groups.

These different elements are not mutually exclusive and their boundaries may be poorly defined. From the point of view of a technical specialist, knowledge of the user firm and industry is contingent; from the point of view of a banker or underwriter, technical knowledge may well be seen as contingent. In this sense, perceptions of skills can differ radically according to the vantage point. In Bank of Scotland, for example, we saw an accountant defining his role on the Working Parties as that of a 'layman', while a bank manager commented elsewhere that IT expertise was 'just a manual skill' in relation to professional banking expertise.

Nevertheless, these distinctive components of socio-cognitive structure provide a means of relating the knowledge content of expertise with its social embodiment—i.e. its associated expressions of power and opportunities for trading. The differing composition of bodies of knowledge reflect the various components, from formal through to meta-knowledge, and their distribution across social groups. All components are crucial for applying expertise effectively, but the informal, tacit, and contingent, are especially important given the bias that has existed towards considering only the formal knowledge level as important and the rest ancillary. Our research showed that greatest value in practice was attached to *experience* in computing expertise in almost every case. The importance of non-formal knowledge elements meant that few exceptions arose where managers sought to divorce a new project from local culture or practices. One example (discussed in more detail in Chapter 12) was the external recruitment of a specialized team of Philips programmers for the CABINET project who were not inculcated with IBM standards. Similarly, Mutual Life recruited an analyst with formal training and experience in entity modelling, but with little firm-specific (contingent) knowledge, to be independent of existing approaches in designing databases for their Customer Care project.

Finally, a wide range of *institutions* tends to be involved in technological innovation, and as a result socio-cognitive structures are highly differentiated. The institutions include user and supplier firms linked in complex webs of supply relationships, as well as independent experts and a range of promotional, advisory, and educational agencies. There is also a range of bodies formed to promote the interests of knowledge carriers, often based on protecting the skill and knowledge investments of those who have gained access to the particular area of expertise (e.g. the professional and certification bodies for bankers and actuaries).

The Distribution of Expert Knowledge

The distribution of socio-cognitive components varies according to the technical development under consideration. In the case of sp/ARCHITECT, for instance, it was possible for a relatively closely-knit systems group to develop the architecture of Clydesdale's telebanking development. In contrast, in extensive developments of branch automation, like the Customer Care project and CABINET, the participation of widely separated groups was necessary, involving co-operation between business departments, branches, and equipment suppliers over several years.

The nature of innovation also varies with the emergent divisions of labour, whereby distinct components of knowledge become the preserve of specialists. This contrasts with many areas of scientific activity, where there are very shallow organizational hierarchies approximating to the collegiate ideal of undifferentiated communities of equals (Polanyi 1967). Members of these overlapping neighbourhoods would share skills and knowledge that did not extend far beyond the neighbourhood. Thus scientific work has much in common with traditional craft activity (Ravetz 1971), but differs from many areas of modern technology where extensive divisions of labour involve staff specializing at different levels and in different technical components. IT is clearly one such area of modern technology with an elaborate division of labour.

These institutional and disciplinary structures effectively fragment the population of people involved in technical development, so that it becomes impossible to talk about 'the technological community' in the same way that we might talk about 'the scientific community', or even 'the banking community'. Instead of overlapping neighbourhoods, there is a mosaic of often quite separate interest groups. Specific application areas and technical functions become a focus for the emergence of specialization, and detailed strategies ensure the transfer and distribution of expertise between different groups. Of course, networks of informal communication and professional contacts still serve a function of integration, especially in the form of informal know-how trading (von Hippel 1988). In an industry like financial services, where the development and take-up of technologies tends to be extensive, initial design involves reconnaissance tours and site visits as an intrinsic part of 'defining the situation'. Nevertheless, relationships between groups are also mediated by such non-integratory practices as formal contracts, market exchange, and by the physical transfer of technology itself. The play of power relationships is rendered explicit and is marked by the emergence of specialist agencies focused on those concerns.

Fragmentation between specialist areas of IT expertise is also reflected within individual organizations. Often formalized, and sometimes confrontational, relations persist between different interest groups arrayed around technologies. Much work on technical change has documented such divisions, not just between workers and managers but also between distinct professional groupings such as engineers and accountants (Armstrong 1985; Richardson 1987). These are shaped by socio-cognitive structures (the bodies of knowledge associated with different groups of experts), and vary according to particular technical developments and the relationships between suppliers and users. Often political conflict and negotiation will be endemic; at times it will emerge in open hostility. In our cases we found expert factions adopting different positions, underpinned by their 'knowledge commitments'. Negotiations between them, sometimes through conflict-solving arenas, served to structure technical decisions and influenced the design outcome. Sometimes these processes also served to frustrate developments. This occurred, for example, in the stalemate over how to proceed with integrating the database for Mutual Life's Customer Care project, where no one group was able to assert their view. In the CABINET project, conversely, the potentially conflicting expectations of different groups were managed over the life cycle of the project—sometimes to promote radical expectations and later to stabilize the project.

Vertically and horizontally fragmented expertise, reinforced by underlying interest affiliations, creates formidable barriers to entry and expertise transfer. Once practitioners have made an investment in a particular area, they become *de facto* committed. It is perhaps only in a crisis that knowledge barriers can be dismantled and reconstructed in a non-incremental fashion. In the case firms, the pushing together of separate knowledge terrains, and linking certain types of expertise and types of authority, created space for the emergence of new knowledge domains. For example, in Clydesdale we were unable to study the outcome of the new Electronic Business Division, but the bank certainly regarded the alliance of all staff concerned with card services and business analysis as an important strategic step. In Bank of Scotland the systems implementation staff, proponents of technological development, and the business analysts forged the new strategic alliance in the Management Services Division which, as we saw in the case, laid claim to being a 'magnet for strategy'. Interestingly, too, this new knowledge area was influential enough to make a home for another expertise, namely the enthusiasm for marketing that attached to CABINET. The 'strategic awareness of the market' had been consciously added to the armoury of MSD's occupational skills.

POWER AND EXPERTISE

As we have seen, the knowledge and skills exercised in 'doing technical work' have become uncertain in the context of the commercialization and spread of computer-based technologies. Uncertainty represents the link between the knowledge and power aspects of expertise. Rearrangements of expertise are rarely to be explained in simple functional terms, as the result of changes in skill requirements neutrally dictated by technology. When uncertainty is high, the relative nature of knowledge and the provisional nature of claims to be expert are evident. Under such conditions, the exercise of power can appear most naked—with competing expertise claims revealed through open conflict. (We saw this, for example, in the VISA case, where the setting up of the new installation appeared remarkably conflict-free, but this had been preceded by an earlier stage of rivalry over where components of the operation were to be located. Also, in Bank of Scotland, at the outset of their customer-services automation project, the O&M Department and Computer Services had proposed conflicting approaches which set off far-reaching changes.) Conversely, when uncertainty is minimized, power may be concealed within the dominant knowledge. Indeed, the emergence into dominance of one particular form of knowledge or rationale is itself the outcome of the play of different sources of power.

Two connected themes on power and uncertainty are pertinent here. First, as labour process theorists emphasize, expertise must be managed precisely because it relates to power relationships between managements and workers —albeit skilled or knowledge workers. Knowledge does not arise in a vacuum, but is created, concentrated, diffused, and traded within elaborate structures of control. Exerting and resisting control is an intrinsically unstable process, constantly enacted and never finally achieved. Here conditions of uncertainty and the relationships of power amongst specialists and generalists will reflect different managerial strategies. These factors also determine whether work done by a person counts as 'skilled' in the first place; whether the possession of particular skills and knowledge is noted and recorded within and/or outwith the organization; whether the expert has access to information about other jobs or other accounts of 'what's happening' in the field—in short, whether managers and potential employers recognize the expert as expert.

A second theme, emphasized by political analysts, develops the connections between power, uncertainty, and expertise. Power is rarely exercised through coercion but usually achieved by consent—through hegemony rather than domination (Gramsci 1971). Rather than simply imposing narrowly conceived interests, dominant groups project a world-view which 'naturalizes' their role and cements alliances with others by relating their sectional interests to perceived overall interests. This framework highlights the double importance of experts in mapping out options and in creating and legitimating consent. It suggests that an important managerial strategy for coping with uncertainty in political arenas is to have recourse to experts and expertise as a legitimating device.

Theorists such as Habermas (1973) and Offe (1984), analysing how state rule is exercised, point to the emergence of 'technocratic' policy-making. This involves a continuous search for legitimation through seemingly neutral forms of knowledge and rationality, through the non-partisan advice of 'expert' knowledge workers. Foucault (1979) plays down the role of the state in his systemic view of social power; the state was central for sovereign power but less so in the disciplinary age. But Foucault nevertheless sees expertise as a key aspect of disciplinary power. Experts of all kinds exercise normalizing judgements of others, and construct the very categories of knowledge with which the behaviour of others is controlled. In each of these accounts, recourse to experts and to expertise provides the ideological means of conflating public and private interests, fudging conflict between them through technocratic interpretations, without eliminating the tensions which make legitimation necessary (see also Heyderbrand 1983; Fischer 1990).

There are, of course, limits in applying to the commercial sphere an analysis of expertise in public policy. In the former there is no need for actors to appear as equal citizens before a disinterested state. Having recourse to specialist staff to solve problems that affect profits makes straightforward sense for commercial firms. Nor are private organizations subject to a democratic prerogative, so that when people assent to the wage contract they also assent to the exercise of managerial power. Nevertheless, concepts from political theory can offer insights into managerial decision-making. Radical changes in the orientation of firms typically involve the construction of a hegemonic vision of the mission of the organization.

In analysis of the social construction and validation of expertise—especially technocratic expertise—the political perspective goes beyond the immediate labour process and examines broader social and political structures. Technical and other forms of expertise have acquired particular social status in the current era. This does not deny that knowledge and skill are real, but does query the idea that expert groups uniquely possess the knowledge needed to solve problems in their domains.

For instance, Habermas's notion of technocratic expertise challenges the idea of the 'rational' use of experts. In many cases it is not necessarily efficient or rational to have exclusive recourse to specialists officially designated as experts; other people may also possess the same or other knowledge that may be just as crucial. But because of the dominance of an expert élite, and the relationships of power obtaining in organizations, many see their know-how downgraded to the status of 'common sense'.

The VISA Centre was a telling example. A greenfield site in central Scotland was chosen precisely because of its ready supply of part-time, non-career women. These women were exclusively employed for their cheap, reliable, fast, yet 'non-expert' skills. Managers did not solicit them for information about how many documents could be processed per minute, or how long the average enquiry phone call took, even though they were clearly well placed to assess crucial contingent details. Instead, reflecting the power relationships within the Centre and beyond, which defined these women as non-expert, managers adopted a less direct way of finding out; they consulted technical and managerial experts in competing installations, and extrapolated to their own situation.

The Politics of Technical Expertise

This illustrates why managers may more readily have recourse to experts, given pervasive assumptions about experts' ability to provide apparently objective solutions for problems. Some of the contradictions involved in this privileging of technical expertise can be observed in the lack of fit between public and commercial policies for training, and employers' recruitment practices. To solve the 'IT skills crisis', the state responds by supplying yet more graduates with formal knowledge of computing. Though some organizations emphasize possession of certified knowledge in the IT domain, employers in financial services (as we see in Chapter 12) gave most weight to practical knowledge, and recruited those who possessed experience and reputation—including many who were not computer science or computer studies graduates.

Chapter 9 elaborated how systems development often involves an array of experts while, simultaneously, constraining the access of 'non-expert' users to decision-making processes. Thus recognized forms of specialist knowledge emanate from the structural changes in the organization of work that result from technological change. But arrays of expertise are linked with the power mechanisms, and experts themselves may be exploited in order to offset managerial problems of control and planning. The IT-skilled occupations, in this sense, sit on an uncomfortable fence, and technocratic ideologies highlight the disjunction between the relative power of 'technical' and 'non-technical' managements. As one report on systems analysts puts it:

Like a number of new specialist occupational groups, the designers are scientific 'elitists' who can have a professional contempt for managers who have no scientific training or culture and possess managerial authority by claims to 'experience' alone. As with many science specialists, the secular claim to both autonomy from managerial control and high status is implicitly legitimated by a quasi-religious belief that they alone hold the key to unlocking the answers. (Newman and Rosenberg 1985: 404)

However, this kind of account of the autonomous (i.e. 'non-managerial') occupational affiliations of technical experts is countered by other technocracy theorists. Writers such as Dickson (1974) and Fischer (1990) offer an alternative interpretation of the politics of expertise. They stress that technical specialists are employees in organizations and participants in capitalist labour markets, who act within the terms of an existing power base with which they collude.

Management, in short, defines the standards for technological development and has long-established connections to the kinds of expertise needed for the purpose.... Seldom has management given the technical experts who develop workplace technologies much say about how they will be used ... management has often employed technical experts more to legitimate and rationalize its own authority and control of the organization than to encourage technological advances *per se*. Technical expertise has thus long been controlled by management to serve its own interests. (Fischer 1990: 319).

Following such a formulation, IS departments control technology which has been pervasive and far-reaching in its application, and concerned with changing organization and business practice; computing expertise is in this sense subservient to capitalist and managerial interests. This view that the alignment of capital and expert is straightforward and durable may be questioned, however. Elsewhere we have explored forces that create tensions in this relationship and potentially 'degrade' the IT occupations. For example, the potential marginalization of IS specialists from top-management posts and strategic decision-making (see Chapter 12); also conflicts that may arise from repeated work reorganization aimed at cheapening and controlling expert labour (see Chapter 8).

Even where technocratic expertise is aligned with managerial or corporate interests, there remain problems in deploying experts who still possess their own occupational identity. The resort to experts, in turn, creates new difficulties for managing their activities particularly in legitimating managers' authority and competence in technical arenas. Managing expertise, then, is not an apolitical process. To understand the problems of managing technical change in financial services, it is necessary to analyse the realities of power which underlie the misfit between the sectoral and business knowledge of managers and the computing knowledge of technical staff.

THE TRADEABILITY OF EXPERTISE

Procedures for managing knowledge and expertise tend to be less routinized within any one organization's domain of control, given the external labour markets and professional affiliations that compete with company loyalty. The economic dimension of expertise is thus particularly relevant in managing the power/knowledge relationship in 'leaky' product and labour markets. The existence of an external market, through which knowledge or expertise can be traded, affects the extent to which managerial control can be exercised, and determines the relative scope of hierarchical structures of governance rather than markets (Williamson 1975). If skilled practitioners know they can sell their expertise to another organization, this gives them a power base within their immediate places of work.

The central issue, however, is that knowledge, because of its immaterial and relational nature, cannot readily be traded in normal market transactions. In the first place, it is difficult to value knowledge before any transaction has actually taken place; and once knowledge has been made available to a purchaser it cannot then be taken back. This creates risks for buyers and sellers of being exploited by opportunistic behaviour of the other party. The problem of 'information asymmetry' is a major one for knowledge providers in attempts to win a fair exchange for their offerings. As a result, providers and consumers may resort to indirect measures of the value of knowledge: purchasers may select a supplier on the basis of reputed ability; where the knowledge supplied takes the form of an artefact, the supplier may choose only to release parts of the product for evaluation (particularly in the case of software, with its near to zero reproduction costs); and where knowledge is provided as a customizing service, provision usually resorts to time-charging as the basis for exchange, rather than the value of the knowledge itself.

This difficulty of identifying the intrinsic value of knowledge work was well illustrated in the Mutual Life case. An internal consultant complained that his expertise in providing strategic advice to the IS Division was marginalized and virtually ignored. In the eyes of the busy IS managers, he was 'an oddball' who had been allocated the task of writing strategy reports precisely because the company was unsure what else to do with him. His aggrieved account of his treatment stood in contrast to the company's use of external IBM consultants who had organized (for a handsome fee) commitment-raising training sessions.

Time-charging leads to attempts to reify knowledge so it can be more readily tradeable for its full potential value. IBM's conversion of their brainstorming sessions for the life office into a structured course was a case in point. Reification can also be achieved by embedding the knowledge into some other form of physical product. We can see this in computer service companies, which tend to develop from offering a pure service to offering software products. A clear example of a proprietary product was Software Partnership's sp/ARCHITECT, the telebanking application for Clydesdale Bank, which was sold on to other banks.

In the absence of reification, or arrangements to account or charge for knowledge services, it becomes easy to undervalue the contribution of the knowledge producer. The structuring of programming and systems-analysis labour into development teams leaves the work of individuals virtually invisible (at least to everyone except the other team members) and highlights a dilemma for expert labour. Substitutability between experts assists the management of collective work (e.g. as a guide to deployment, recruitment, and promotion). Someone with unique skills may be hard to employ and some degree of commonality and comparability of skills is required. However, if taken too far, this may undercut the ability of individuals or groups to claim to be indispensable, or even valuable. In Chapter 12, we take this discussion further showing how experts address this dilemma in internal and external labour markets. Of course, as suggested above, expertise is not a monolithic entity. The different kinds of knowledge (formal, informal, contingent) have differing implications for knowledge acquisition, management, reproduction, and use. Appropriate forms of training and suitable arrangements for trading vary.

Trading Non-Formal Knowledge

Most readily tradeable via product markets is knowledge embodied in tools and instruments or specified techniques. D. de Solla Price (1984) describes these as instrumentalities, and points out the importance of such externalities as a link between science and technology, and the major element in technology transfer. With complex instrumentalities such as software packages, however, other elements of knowledge are needed to evaluate and use the instrument. These are often intangible and less easily dealt with. Where complex packages are bought in, companies have to make arrangements for staff to be trained in their use, and in some cases customization and maintenance, and the need for this type of knowledge input is usually underestimated (Webster and Williams 1993). Formal knowledge and knowledge readily made public (though not necessarily readily understandable) is also easy to trade and manage in concrete written form. Though often difficult to generate in the first place, it is easy to copy. Again, as with instruments such as software packages, trading has to be followed by training in order to make the knowledge content understandable and operational.

At the other extreme, tacit knowledge cannot readily be separated from the people who carry it; typically any exchange means moving people around. In the case of tacit technical knowledge, large 'transfer fees' are not unknown in industries like electronics (although the programmers and analysts in our case firms did not have the opportunity to emerge as visible stars in this sense). Tacit knowledge also lies at the heart of the design problem of getting users to make their requirements explicit. Two primary ways of encouraging tacit knowledge to come to the surface have emerged: the structural solution of the 'working party', and the methodological solution of using iterative approaches like prototyping (see Chapter 8 for full discussion).

Contingent knowledge is a particularly interesting, though under-appreciated and only indirectly valued, form of knowledge. It is not difficult to acquire—it only requires being in the right place at the right time. It comprises a wealth of seemingly trivial bits of information and a familiarity with particular situations and sets of agents. The women in the white-collar factory in the VISA case, and the IBM consultants in Mutual Life, each held their own sets of contingent knowledge. The VISA women, however, were less well equipped to claim value for their contingent knowledge. Knowledge of what to do in certain contingencies tends to be indirectly valued as 'experience'. The debate over the transferability of experience from one area or organization or industry to another reflects the contingent base for such knowledge as well as the uneven ability of some, over others, to claim their contingent knowledge as having labour-market value.

An important point about contingent and other non-formal knowledge is that it is, by its very nature, distributed across many agents—from shop-floor personnel such as branch staff, who are familiar with particular procedures or the idiosyncrasies of their operations, to sales people who have a well-grounded knowledge of their respective territories, to senior managers who are familiar with the political map. It is with contingent knowledge and tacit knowledge above all, that the strictures of bounded rationality apply.

Contingent knowledge is traded, then, in terms of employing people with requisite experience. Moreover, since contingent knowledge is often seen as trivial—at least in economic and commercial terms—it is relatively cheap to acquire, the main cost being the time spent in gathering it. Again, these issues were well reflected in our case studies of credit-card operations, where experience was stressed as being important, since it was quite different from banking activities. Those involved in setting up the VISA Centre found ready access to other credit-card operating sites, which suggested that trading in contingent knowledge trading was not highly competitive.

MANAGING EXPERTISE IN FINANCIAL SERVICE FIRMS

As well as IT specialists, many groups in the finance sector have their own domains of expertise, such as underwriting, actuarial knowledge, knowledge of the stock market, or of branch banking. The power and influence of such groups stem directly from perceptions of their command of requisite knowledge. Thus it was not merely technical expertise which required management. Given the divisions of labour and control, the generalized issue of how to manage expertise became acutely important. The traditional domains of many groups were threatened by deregulation and the accelerating rate of technological innovation, while new opportunities were also being opened up. For example, cheap computer power radically changed the activity of actuaries, traditionally one of the highest status professional groups. Also, in our credit-card case studies, credit-scoring techniques utilizing various data sources were routinely used to provide credit facilities. This differed markedly from the basis on which a local bank manager would grant an overdraft. Even the expertise of top management was at issue, because organizational boundaries and objectives were being transformed by deregulation and competition. The situation had become a fluid one in which multilateral negotiations and challenges to every base of expertise were more the rule than the exception.

An Overview

Our research identified key features of the management of expertise in financial services. First, we noted the many approaches explored by management to deal with the strategic implications of technologies. In some smaller companies, top management attempted to become sufficiently technically literate to understand and evaluate the implications themselves. Elsewhere, selected technical people were co-opted into senior positions so they could, in their own persons, unite the requisite technical and business policy elements in order to make evaluations. We found evidence for this at the VISA Centre, where all the senior managers of this technology-led division were drawn from Bank of Scotland's Management Services Division. Some decisions were devolved to the professional judgement of technical staff who, in exchange for a secure professional status, were relied on to provide appropriate information for top management to act on. In some organizations (usually new ones) technical people were beginning to compete with other groups to become, themselves, the senior strategic cadre.

The second aspect of managing expertise concerned the manner in which technical staff required for the actual development and operation of systems were functionally accommodated within (or indeed outside) organizations. Financial service organizations are major users of IT, and in all our case firms we found special arrangements for the accommodation of technical staff. These involved the establishment of fully-fledged IS divisions, often located out-of-town in a custom-built computer centre. As discussed in Chapter 5, the structural location of IS had varied, often starting out within an existing traditional department such as accounting, or operating as separate subsidiary companies. A range of factors were at play: the relative scarcity of IT skills, a tight labour market for certain kinds of IT work, as well as the security implications of financial service computing. Staff were frequently paid on a separate salary scale from managerial and clerical staff or differently located on the standard scales (at higher rates) and receiving bonuses and perks.

Where the labour market for IS staff was tight, where new systems were sporadic rather than continuous and/or the perceived risk was high, or where cost control over IT became a major issue, strong pressures favoured some form of contractual relationship. This was sometimes internal (as in Mutual Life's use of a boutique system to allocate development resources) or external (of which our cases included several examples). Contractual relationships raised the issue of whether to 'make or buy' technical developments, which is treated further in Chapter 13.

Finally, there were important trends in the location of technical expertise. External supply of technology and expertise appears to be under an effective monopoly of general computing suppliers—which reflects the importance of the finance sector for IT suppliers. This may not remain the case indefinitely. As the use of IT in the sector matures, we are beginning to see the emergence of a specialist financial IT supply and service infrastructure, relatively autonomous from the IT industry in general. This was already evident in the areas of software services and products, and networking technology. In our case studies, for instance, Tandem represented a specialist (though not exclusively) finance-oriented hardware supplier, and Software Partnership a niche specialist software supplier.

Within large financial service organizations we expected to see a 'leakage' of technical personnel into other functions. In our case studies, however, there was actually little evidence of this. Bank of Scotland's MSD managers moving to the VISA Card Centre was one possible example, but even that could only be called a relative leakage. More common was diffusion in the other direction, with qualified people from other areas—especially accountancy and management science—entering the IT specialist domain. The Systems Investigation subdivision of Bank of Scotland was made up almost exclusively in this way, and all of the senior IT management in Mutual Life were all trained actuaries. The emergence of user interface roles seems to involve the colonization of IT by the business more than the other way around. Given the relative scarcity of suitably qualified technical IT people, and the strategic importance of IT, we might expect some form of internal negotiation between existing groups to capture the emergent IT function for themselves. This indeed appeared to be the case, and our research suggested that the conditions determining the respective power of competing groups were more important than the substantive tasks involved.

Conclusion

In this chapter we have explored the complex and subtle nature of expertise. Expertise clearly has to do with substantive *knowledge*, coupled with a facility for deploying and exploiting that knowledge as an expressed 'skill' or competence. However, as this and other research, particularly in the sociology of scientific knowledge and labour-process studies, has demonstrated this is not the whole story. Depending on relationships of *power* within and between organizational groups, practitioners can claim rights over particular forms of expertise, and may even be able to impose their definition of what constitutes legitimate knowledge or expertise in some domain. The power of practitioners to 'define the situation' may flow from the exploitation of a traditionally recognized status or organizational position, or it may have explicitly economic roots. In a tight labour market, or where there is high demand for the outputs commanded by those holding expertise, the issue of negotiability in the market-place—i.e. the *economic tradeability* of expertise—becomes of crucial importance. This constitutes a third aspect of the effective management of expertise. Not only does expertise have a substantive content, it is also associated with negotiation over the value and legitimacy of content, as expressed in market exchanges.

We understand expertise, therefore, as a complex relationship between varying knowledges that different groups possess, coupled with their ability to claim special value for that knowledge based on their relative structural power in and between organizations. The mobilization and deployment of the resulting expertise can be seen clearly in the routes through which it is traded in labour and product markets. These issues are examined in detail in the next two chapters.

12

IT Careers: Organizational and Occupational Strategies

INTRODUCTION

In this chapter we explore the career and labour-market aspects of IT and related jobs. Through a case study of the development of a computer application in a bank, we examine how an organization acquires and deploys specialist labour, and the ways in which individuals and groups develop their skilled status. This involves the internal diversification of IT occupations, their occupational mobility and career development, their position in the external labour market, as well as the organizational power of these jobs and their position in managerial hierarchies. These concerns reflect two sorts of influence on the management of expertise: the managerial strategies pursued by organizations to form and deploy specialized technical expertise, and IT professionals' own career strategies in building and acquiring skills.

In selecting a single case for a detailed account of these issues, the chapter departs from our main methodology of constructing a sectoral account from a range of case studies. However, the development of expert careers is a process in which the interaction between organizational and occupational factors is condensed and cannot readily be encapsulated by large-scale survey methods. For technical experts, in particular, careers tend to be built through the acquisition and legitimation of skills. So while many studies have afforded snapshots of the organization of IT work, it is also necessary to examine the formation of expertise over time—the recruitment and development of IT specialists and their promotion into managerial roles. Career trajectories are thus critical for understanding the organization and control of IT labour.

One of our case studies in particular afforded this opportunity, namely the CABINET project in Bank of Scotland. The bank was typical of the financial organizations we studied in having a long-established body of in-house expertise. But the case was unusual in respect of its scale. CABINET was a full-blown programme of branch automation; it required its own division of labour in systems development, and lasted through distinct phases for several years. A study of the staff involved in CABINET allowed us to build up a picture of the career histories of a range of expert groups.

A detailed survey of CABINET staff was undertaken using interviews and self-completion questionnaires. It examined the roles of respondents, their duties within the project, the skills they employed, and the network of others to whom they related. It addressed previous career history, training, and professional attainments. The survey covered 25 individuals across the bank's Management Services Division, and included the majority of expert and managerial staff then working on CABINET. The information was supplemented by personnel data supplied by the bank. The chapter then highlights the formation and management of groups of IT labour, as well as the relationship between IT specialist and general managerial labour. Before addressing our findings, however, it will be useful to review existing analyses of these topics.

The Organization of Expert Groups

Labour-process analysis has argued that programming has been transformed from a craft into an 'industrialized' activity (Kraft 1977; Greenbaum 1979; Kraft and Dubnoff 1986). However, as we saw in Chapter 8, the weight of recent evidence suggests the evolution of computing skills is more complex. Despite efforts to automate programming, and end-users' hijacking parts of the development effort, IS departments contain few staff without specialist skills, and the dynamic nature of the industry has a capacity to contain seemingly paradoxical changes (S. Kuhn 1985). Indeed, the continued scarcity of technical specialists arguably inhibits employers from adopting techniques of job degradation and increases the ability of employees to resist them. There are considerable difficulties in achieving the continued appropriation of skills from labour, whether by technical or administrative means. Such tendencies may be countered by the accommodations between managers and managed, and are mediated through prevailing ideologies and cultures.

As we also saw in Chapter 5, Friedman (1989) placed the issue of de-skilling in a longer perspective and argued that direct-control strategies were employed for a period in response to the 'software crisis'. But while priority attached to the productivity and cost of software production favoured the rationalization of IT labour, even then the extent to which managements pursued these work degrading policies was limited. Today, in the 'user-relations' stage of computer systems development, the concern to match IT systems to user requirements overrides any simple tendency towards de-skilling.

In particular, requirements for IT specialists to be responsive to user needs conflicts with the application of a narrow techno-economic rationality to software production and results in systems designers being accountable both to managers and to the consumers of their products. Friedman's notion of responsible work strategies was well illustrated by one of the Bank of Scotland's business analysts who had moved into the role from general banking work. She stressed that computing was a 'totally different working

		Internal Labour Market	
		Undeveloped ILM	Developed ILM
External Labour Market	Positive Worker Power on ELM	A. Independent Mobile Professional	B. Company Professional
	Negative Worker Power on ELM	C. Insecure Contract Worker	D. Dependent Worker (1) Valuable to Firm (2) Obsolescent

FIG. 12.1 *Winstanley's Model of Labour Market Power*

environment' from the branches, where work was closely supervised and structured. In MSD you were 'on your own' and needed to be well organized. Similarly, one of the systems programmers in Home and Auto stressed the value placed on autonomy. There was little direct monitoring of their work and a good deal of negotiation between programmers and analysts. In his work he preferred to deal with analysts who gave more general program specifications to those who produced more detailed ones. So while internal diversification was taking place, this was a process not of fragmentation and routinization but specialization. Regarding such specialization, the literature has focused almost exclusively on systems analysts and programmers; our study addressed a broader range of IT specialist occupations.

Winstanley (1986) has developed a useful typology of specialist labour, which we can use to compare 'expert occupational' with 'expert organizational' jobs. She highlights the power technical workers derive from the external labour market and the extent to which an internal labour market protects skilled occupations and encourages an organizational component to expertise. She differentiates four types of technical specialist, in terms of their ability to exert power on internal and external labour markets (Figure 12.1).

This schema is valuable for indicating the diversity of settings in which holders of skilled jobs may find themselves, in terms of the level and kind of skills they claim, and their ability to translate skills into career opportunities. Staff who do not acquire an 'organizational' (i.e. contingent) component of expertise may be marginalized as C-type workers; they may be 'experts' but if their skills are readily available on the ELM they may find themselves dispensable. In contrast, those who fail to retain an 'occupational' component may become locked into their employer in variations of the D-type model. So long as they continue to be valuable to the firm, their position remains secure, but the employer's construction of the job may undermine their reputation as expert staff.

Successful members of skilled occupations may possess a sound occupational basis to their expertise, becoming A-type employees. But the trick for the most successful is to optimize their possession of both occupational and organizational skill bases, becoming B-types, and maximizing their opportunities on both the internal and external labour market. What the typology does not reveal is the trade-off between occupational and organizational skills. In so far as they are are mutually exclusive, the traditional conflict between 'professional' and 'company' orientation in employees would persist. This would also constrain the development of hybrid staff with IT and social skills. The B-type company professional probably never can attain the level of specialist skills of an A-type independent mobile professional, but the extent to which this balancing act can be achieved will dictate success at negotiating the career structure. These questions cannot be resolved a priori, but will be determined by the character of expertise involved and their social bases.

Technical Change and Managerial Labour

At the heart of our survey enquiry lies the apparent discontinuity between technical specialist and general managerial labour. This is partly reflected in the low levels of technical expertise amongst managers, particularly at senior level, and the perceived shortage of general managerial skills of IT specialists. Managerial or non-technical occupations will often fall within a single 'line' of authority—a career ladder which potentially stretches from the shop-floor to the corporate heights. There are difficulties in scaling the heights, of course, but in principle the route is a straight line, and the necessary capacities evolve gradually. In contrast, technical occupations contained in 'service' functions are appended on to the line hierarchy. Technical staff tend to have truncated career paths and may have to build career strategies around skills in complex and contradictory ways. To get to the top may involve 'moving across' into a more central career-development line. This has been acute for IT specialists who have typically been contained within specialized service departments. And while a function like IT is characterized by diversification and growth, it remains a service function and career paths have definite limits. As a result, perplexing choices may need to be faced. Expert groups may see the danger in becoming 'too technical' and closing off career chances, but it is still a daring expert who tries for a managerial career by repudiating his or her skills.

In such situations, strategies by which to navigate are needed. We are not referring solely to individual career strategies here. Individuals always need strategies for the simple reason that career success is difficult and competitive. But with expert occupations, and career paths that are often constrained and complex, the collective skills and career strategies of identifiable groups need to be examined. Nor should we expect the skill profile that a group presents to be a simple reflection of the necessities of the job. Skill profiles themselves are part of the collective strategies groups use to resolve the career dilemmas they face.

The growth in the size and strategic importance to firms of IT remains the backdrop to these issues. The notion that IT is central to competitive advantage seems well established. Less clear are the implications of this for the status of IT occupations, now that their functional role has grown beyond the technical provision of operational support for the firm. The common-sense, if rather uncritical, assumption is that as IS departments become more central to the organization there will be a growth of hybrid managers who combine technical and general managerial abilities. This could be fulfilled by generalists acquiring increasing familiarity with IT and some limited technical competencies; equally it could involve opening up general managerial careers to IT specialists. Several inside the IT community have anticipated new avenues of career growth. Owen (1986) sees IT managers on a 'steady ascent' towards the corporate superstructure. And Winkler (1986) speaks of them 'going on the initiative' and becoming more involved in business issues, adopting the role of change agent, and ceasing to be 'too technical' in their approach to problems.

The actual outcome may combine both elements in differing degrees and reflect a combination of circumstances. Though organizations may become more dependent on the 'information occupations', their influence is still mediated by extraneous social and political factors. One possibility is that IT managers and staff may not be able to exploit the opportunities arising from the wave of technological innovation. Technical people may be excluded from the role of information strategist on the grounds that they lack the managerial qualities required. At this extreme, M. Campbell (1983) gives a highly pessimistic view of an occupation under siege: 'there are few examples of data processing managers progressing to high management positions; still fewer to board level'. Less gloomy but still critical, Harvey (1987) points out that the 'new breed of managers' who occupy the crucial boundary-spanning roles need to understand the technology but do not need to be special-ists.

These views reveal some of the career dilemmas that IT people themselves perceive. The structural position of IS within an organization is rather ambiguous. As we argued in Chapter 4, the success of an IT élite in scaling the organizational hierarchy appears to depend more on their ability to develop a 'strategic rationale' for the role of IS as a whole in the organization, than upon their internal differentiation from rank and file IT workers. If we accept that the development of IT occupations has not been characterized by degradation and de-skilling, this is clearly good news for the bulk of IT careers. Nor would it appear necessarily bad for the prospects of an IT élite. The crucial empirical questions, we would argue, come down to the precise nature of the internal dynamics of IT occupations. Do these support a relatively static view of 'no de-skilling'? Or can we speak of collective mobility being based on a more dynamic version of occupational enhance-ment? Certainly the traditional boundaries between main IT functions which have defined career progression and departmental structures are blurring, and within this changing scenario occupational interests have to be explored. To do this we turn to our survey.

TABLE 12.1. *Management Services Division grading structure 1984–1988*

Description	Grade	1984	1985	1986	1987	1988	Increase 1984–8 (%)
Managerial grades		46	50	3	60	66	43
Top management	M5+	4	5	6	5	6	
	M5	6	4	1	3	2	
Senior Manager	M4	6	5	14	15	19	
	M3	8	13	8	10	9	
Manager	M2	8	6	5	12	14	
	M1	14	17	19	15	16	
Supervisory grade		177	195	218	254	279	58
Project Manager	S5				40	42	
Senior Analyst	S4	27	28	34			
Analyst/Programmer	S3	48	56	66	90	100	
Trainee Analyst/Prog.	S2	51	54	56	53	73	
	S1	51	57	62	71	64	
Clerical grades		160	181	189	252	273	71
Security		51	53	74	95	97	90
Punch room		64	89	96	37	35	−45
TOTAL STAFF		498	568	630	698	750	51

MSD AND THE CABINET PROJECT

The Management Services Division (MSD) in Bank of Scotland is a fine illustration of the richness and complexity of expert technical labour. As we saw in the initial case study, MSD was formed in 1981 when the bank board decided to merge the Computer Services Division (which had been run during the 1970s as an independent service) with the bank's Organization and Methods Department. This move was partly an attempt to resolve the differing views of CSD and O&M about the way forward for branch automation (which eventually led to CABINET). By bringing these groups together, the bank sought to combine their expertise in systems development and business analysis. The restructuring created a powerful alliance and single centre of IT expertise within the bank. MSD experienced continual growth during the period under study. The numbers employed in MSD rose steadily from just under 500 in 1984 to 750 in 1988, as part of the 1980s expansion throughout financial services.

TABLE 12.2. *Management Services Division male and female employment by grade 1988*

Description	Grade	Male	Female
Managerial grades			
Top management	M5 +	6	0
	M5	2	0
Senior Manager	M4	19	0
	M3	8	1
Manager	M2	13	1
	M1	15	1
Supervisory grades			
Project Manager	S5	35	7
Analyst/Programmer	S3	79	21
Trainee Analyst/Prog.	S2	51	22
	S1	45	19
Clerical grades			
mainly computer	C5	46	37
liaison and computer	C4	64	44
operations	C2	12	67
	C1	2	1
Security		46	51
Punch room Part-timers		23	12

Grading Structure

The grading structure of MSD, and numbers of staff employed across the grades and types of jobs in the period 1984–8, are shown in Table 12.1. Programmers and analysts were placed in the supervisory grades, reflecting the remuneration for skills and the professionalism of IT staff. The clerical grades were a minority in MSD and mainly employed in computer liaison and computer operations. This contrasted with the bank's branches where clerical grades have been the main point of entry of staff. Overall numbers increased by 50 per cent over the period. Growth was skewed towards the lower clerical and supervisory categories, notwithstanding a reduction in the number of part-time staff mainly employed on data entry in the Punch Room and who were displaced by the progressive shift to on-line data capture.

One notable change came in 1987 when the S4 grade of Senior Analyst was renamed Project Manager, and upgraded to S5. Before this move, as Table 12.1 shows, there was little scope for upward mobility from programmer/ analyst grades to managerial ones. The change in name and grade was intended to clarify the managerial status of this position, and its significance as a point of role transition. Though this upgrading clarified the opportunities

254

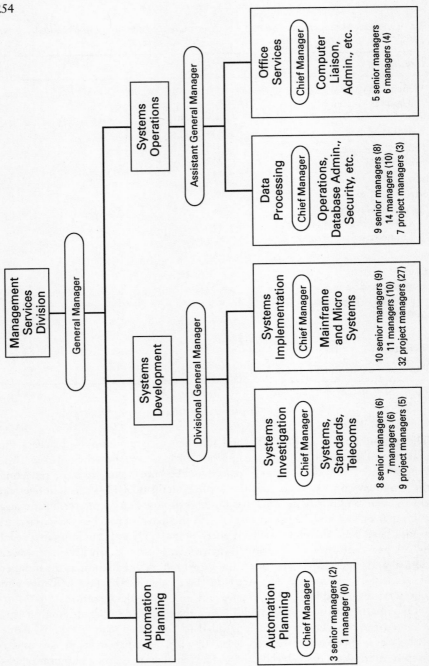

FIG. 12.2 *Managerial Structure of Management Services Division, showing the number of managers in departments at January 1990 [1988 figures in brackets]*

for advancement, it did nothing to remove the career obstacle. Promotion of specialist staff from the lower trainee grade (S2 to S3) was more or less automatic, and the senior analyst/project manager level (S4/5) represented the first career block. Many of the programmers and analysts were already in the upper gradings anyway, so the bottle-neck remained. Nevertheless, there has been a continued increase in the number of Project Managers. Advancement opportunities were enhanced by expansion in some of the managerial grades—in particular, at senior management level, M3/4, which doubled in numbers from 14 in 1984 to 28 in 1988. This disproportionate increase, combined with the departure of top management, created opportunities for advancement for staff who succeeded in entering management positions.

Overall we can see that, in a period of expansion of MSD, there have been opportunities for career development from technical to managerial roles. But, paradoxically, the staffing pyramid was becoming relatively broader at the base. Without further expansion in MSD the individual's chances of future promotion will have declined slightly. However, the overall pattern does not conform to the model of de-skilling of technical staff. Staff are congregating at the top of the different grading spines—which themselves were enhanced in 1987.

The sexual division of labour in MSD was extremely skewed (Table 12.2). Female staff predominated in the lower clerical grades; women were virtually absent from managerial grades (all chief and general managers were men). Between these two extremes, the proportion of female staff tailed off towards the higher grades. Women were relatively well represented in the intermediate grades—they made up over one-third of the programmers and analysts employed on grades S1 to S3—but only accounted for one-fifth of project managers.

Thus women were by no means excluded from the technical function and managerial grades. They tended to be concentrated, however, in particular positions, such as business and systems analyst, which were less exclusively concerned with technical competencies. These jobs emphasized communication and 'person skills', so it would seem that women had made an entry into the technical function through their possession of stereotypically feminine skills. Still, this need not signify that IT-skilled women occupied subordinate roles. The combination of interpersonal skills with technical ability was applicable throughout the division, and in many ways paralleled the expertise claimed by senior management.

Departmental Structure

The structure of MSD is shown in Figure 12.2. This also gives the managerial complement of the separate departments for 1990 and 1988. MSD had two functional subdivisions: Systems Operations and Systems Development, together with Automation Planning, a small team concerned with long-term and strategic planning of technological change in banking systems.

Systems Development, the larger division, represented an initiative in clustering two forms of 'competing' expertise: Systems Investigation (SIV) responsible for business analysis and systems evaluation, and Systems Implementation (SIM) which was concerned with the actual development of software. SIM's programmers and programmer/analysts were organized into project teams headed by a project manager, though staff on occasion were members of more than one team. Most SIM staff were engaged on mainframe systems development, an activity that continued to grow between 1988 and 1990. SIV's business analysts occupied equivalent grades to the systems analysts and programmers, and worked under the same project management form of organization. Most of the expansion in SIV happened in the largest group, concerned with software systems, although smaller groups responsible for standards and telecommunications saw some growth too.

Systems Operations, the smaller MSD division, comprised the Data Processing department, concerned with maintenance of the infrastructure (computer and network operations and systems security) and database administration, and the Office Services department responsible for administration and computer liaison (help desks) to users in the branches. Systems Operations had a range of small groups responsible for specific activities and had not in general adopted project-centred methods. This pattern, however, was beginning to change. The Systems Programming, Database Administration, and Operations Support groups all took on additional project managers. Other groups in Data Processing (production control, production support, network operations) did not exhibit significant changes in size and management structure, nor did the other department in the subdivision, Office Services.

So while significant growth had taken place in MSD during 1988–90, these changes were not distributed evenly. They reflect a change in structure and organization as well as the size of the division. Computing surveys have well established the idea that growth and diversification in the IT industry have expanded career paths, and that new opportunities have come in all areas, especially in the interface with IT users (Friedman 1989). Our detailed evidence broadly supports this finding, but also highlights the influence of technological change. As Figure 12.2 shows, the project-manager level was greatly strengthened. The thrust of expansion came in core occupations tied directly to the development of new software. At the same time, operational and administrative functions began to take on the features of work organization of these core groups, reflected in the adoption of work structures based on the model of project management.

The CABINET Staff

We can gain a better view of these changes by looking at CABINET itself. As we saw in the case study, the CABINET project provided an integrated solution to a wide range of information transactions and involved the redesign of many of the computer systems developed over the previous twenty years. CABINET was the largest computer project ever undertaken by the bank, and the repository of much of the bank's thinking about strategic and operational improvements. A project of this scope created many new opportunities. For example, a team of Philips personnel was contracted on a long-term basis, to oversee the work being done on their equipment, and to train a group of bank staff in the skills needed to interface bank systems with the Philips P9000 system. This constituted a significant skills transfer. Re-creating the P9000 skills in-house expanded the range and variety of development work, and meant wholly new career chances that will remain after the development of CABINET has been completed.

At the time of the study, almost every functional group in MSD was involved in different phases of the project. For CABINET to succeed, MSD had to manage an array of technical, managerial, and business specialisms in the division and across user departments. The project spread across many of the bank's activities and departments, and progress in the early specification and pilot stages had been slow and difficult. As a result, tight management had been adopted. Responsibility for short-term implementation was delegated to some sixteen user committees. A typical CABINET committee numbered four to six, with at least two MSD people—usually one 'technical' person from SIM and one 'bank' person from SIV—together with users. This diverse and extensive management structure opened up career horizons. Many of these jobs had considerable career potential involving technical staff in managerial-type work and wider contacts in the organization.

In the survey of project staff the main sources of information were self-completion questionnaires returned by twenty-one staff, and detailed interviews with six staff, one from SIV and five from SIM. There was some overlap, with four interviewees also returning the questionnaire, allowing us to cross-check its accuracy. Combining these sources gave twenty-five responses across the division: mainly from SIM (14) and SIV (7) in Systems Development, but also from the Data Processing department (4) in Systems Operations. The survey covered four senior managers, three managers, seven project managers, four SIV business analysts, two SIM systems analysts, and five SIM programmer/analysts.

The survey addressed:

1. the work role of respondents;
2. the network of people they were in contact with—those they reported to, those who reported to them, and others they dealt with in the course of their work;

3. the skills and knowledge they used in their jobs;
4. recent job movements and earlier employment history; and
5. respondents' educational attainments and professional qualification/memberships, together with a range of background data including age, sex, and time spent working in the bank, in their current job, and in IT-related work.

SURVEY FINDINGS

The survey findings revolve around two areas: the ways in which expertise was acquired and deployed, and the career development of technical staff into managerial grades and relationships between technical and managerial labour.

The Formation of Technical Expertise

The sources of expertise for the bank included recruitment of formally trained or experienced specialists, and the internal training of non-specialists. Comparing the relative importance of these different sources suggested that experience in IT jobs, rather than formal IT training, was the key qualification for recruitment and promotion of specialist staff. We also examined the detailed division of labour of the different groups involved in CABINET, relating their roles to the different types of expertise they claim. We were able to identify distinctive patterns for different groups of specialist labour, in terms of their knowledge base and their range of skills. These attributes depended on the tasks undertaken and the networks of interaction deployed in carrying them out through which expertise was renewed and demonstrated.

Education and Work Experience

There has been much discussion in recent years of the 'skills gap' in IT, not all of it providing consistent policies for the training of computer scientists. Exhortations to increase the number of graduates in IT have contrasted with suggestions that current provision for training in is unduly theoretical and narrow. And while industry has argued that IT graduates lack the combination of technical and 'people' skills they require, bodies like the British Computer Society have proposed that this might be resolved by the formal education of hybrid specialists (British Computer Society 1990). However, these debates have been conducted with little reference to the ways in which industry actually acquires and develops IT expertise.

Our survey yielded a detailed picture of the recruitment and skill-development practices in MSD. The majority of staff surveyed (72 per cent) came to MSD with prior experience of IT (these data are not shown in tabular form).

They had spent on average four years mainly as programmers or programmer/analysts. Interestingly, these staff were drawn in almost equal numbers from manufacturing, the public sector, and the financial sector. So there was no policy of recruiting exclusively from an industry sub-group of IT professions, nor was knowledge of finance applications a prerequisite. Thus, though the bank sought experienced staff, firm-specific knowledge remained important for career progress. Industrial IT experience was the most significant factor affecting the rate of promotion within the organization.

The background of project managers showed that some had worked for MSD in this key transitional post for over ten years, with only modest prior IT experience (average 1.5 years). The remainder had worked in MSD for a much shorter period (3 years on average) but had extensive IT experience outside the bank (average 12 years). From this we can infer that extensive industrial IT experience (internal or external) was a prerequisite for promotion into IT management. Experienced recruits, however, still went through a (relatively short) period in MSD technical grades prior to promotion. There was a trade-off between external and internal experience as preparation for promotion, though the strength of the internal labour market at MSD favoured the latter.

Those whose IT experience started when they came to the bank comprised staff who were taken on about twenty years ago and had now reached a senior position (3 respondents), also junior grades who had moved into programming after spending a number of years in routine computer operations jobs (2 respondents). Their career progress has been significantly slower than their peers. Two respondents were employed at Bank of Scotland before they became involved in IT. They were both business analysts who recently moved from supervisory positions in bank branches to undertake project evaluation (with a low requirement for technical specialism). This appears to be a relatively novel phenomenon. The bank is still willing to train suitable staff internally.

One-fifth of our respondents (a senior manager, a manager, two project managers, and a programmer) did not have a first degree or equivalent. The remainder, which included some staff with postgraduate qualifications up to Ph.D., were split equally between those whose degree was in or related to IT and those with a degree in an unrelated subject.

The lack of a degree was definitely associated with slower career progression. Managers without a degree had spent over three years longer in the bank and in IT work than their colleagues. The two project managers without first degrees had both spent twenty years working in IT—eight more years than their graduate counterparts. Amongst these older staff members, whose involvement in IT began when they joined the bank, we saw the vestiges of an earlier grow-your-own skills strategy, which prevailed in the 1960s when IT graduates and experienced staff both were in short supply.

Despite the importance of a degree, the kind of degree did not seem significant. Possession of a degree in or related to IT, made little difference to the grade achieved. A handful of respondents at various levels of the organization possessed professional qualifications (mainly from the British Computer Society). Their distribution would indicate that these qualifications were not a major factor in career progression though in some cases they may have represented an attempt to redress the lack of educational qualifications. Though formal credentials may carry some weight, MSD clearly did not operate anything like a 'graduate barrier', either for recruitment or promotion.

Given the greater weight attached in recruitment to industrial experience over formal computing education, the value of possessing a first degree (whether or not in IT) may be in showing that the holder possesses learning ability. In this respect, the debate about improving computing education may misread the problems. The lack of preferment of staff with prior IT experience in the finance sector indicates there is no distinctive industrial sub-group of the computing occupation. Taken together, these findings suggest that industrial experience affords general competencies relevant to IT work, but that this also requires firm-specific skills or combinations of skill—points confirmed in the following section.

Division of Expert Labour

A series of project groups were involved in the different phases of CABINET. At the time of the study, SIM programmer/analysts were mainly involved in Phase 2 applications (though some were maintaining Phase 1 applications software). The fifteen programmers directly involved were organized in three groups, each specializing in different parts of the software infrastructure, with occasional overlap between them: (1) The P9000 group responsible for software for the new Philips P9000 equipment, (2) the Batch Mainframe Processing (BMP) Systems group responsible for corporate databases updated overnight on a batch basis, and (3) the Corporate Database Access (CDA) group concerned with accessing databases for information for the P9000 equipment. These teams of programmers, and a further team of four systems analysts, each had a project manager. They reported to a manager and senior manager with primary responsibility for CABINET.

The SIM analysts were mainly concerned with Phase 2, producing specifications and plans for system implementation and testing. Analysts' responsibilities were organized around application areas, in contrast to the programmers who were differentiated according to their technical function and responsibility for particular domains of the IT system. The other SIM group with immediate involvement in CABINET was the Computer Systems Assurance Unit (CSAU), a specialized group responsible for the reliability of systems and integrated systems testing.

In SIV, a team of business analysts (one of the four such teams in SIV) was involved in the analysis of proposed Phase 3 CABINET applications. In the Data Processing department two groups of technical staff were involved: one provided technical support for the P9000 equipment, and the other maintained the database architecture and data models for the bank's systems.

Each of these groups commanded distinctive types and combinations of expertise. Taken in sum, they represent technical knowledge (of the bank's systems and of languages, tools, and techniques) and organizational and managerial knowledge (of banking operations together with evaluation, communication, and decision-making skills). We also found distinct patterns in the range of people these groups were in communication with. The tasks undertaken by specialist groups, their network of contacts, and the manner in which each group defined its own skills reflected the deployment of distinctive combinations of expertise. Figure 12.3 summarizes the different segments of expert labour involved in CABINET.

Strategies for Acquiring Expert Status

In analysing these different patterns of expertise, and their implications for the expertise claims of different groups, we can draw on Winstanley's (1986) analysis discussed earlier. Her framework is based on market dimensions which indicate how skills are verified, and represents a useful first step in analysing expertise. But there were major differences between our groups in terms of skills strategies and how expertise was generated. In order to explore this, a more complex schema is required.

The analysis can be extended by drawing a parallel with the articulation of generic (e.g. occupation-specific) and organization-specific knowledge. Generic expertise will tend to be based on formal knowledge, and be readily obtained and validated on the external labour market; organization-specific knowledge, which enhances the worker's value to the firm through its internal labour market, will include a stronger contribution of contingent and informal elements and tends to be acquired through experience. In this way we can characterize the groups of MSD staff in terms of the *range of skills* possessed (whether they specialized in one area or deployed a diversity of skills), and the *form of skills* (distinguishing formally acquired and validated technical skills from skills which tend to be acquired through experience and may be specific to the organization/application). This extended framework enables us to categorize the skills profiles of the seven project groups (Figure 12.4).

Thus the dichotomy between the BMP and P9000 groups highlights alternative strategies for claims to be expert through the possession of highly specialized skills. At one extreme, BMP's claim was based on the internal reputations of expertise acquired through experience. At the other extreme, P9000 expertise was based on the possession of externally validated knowledge. In Winstanley's terms the P9000 group represents Type A (Independent

1. P9000 Development Group

The P9000 team were the most technically oriented group of programmers. They were mainly new recruits, as existing staff would not want to become 'ghettoized' within MSD's internal labour market. The P9000 programmers equated their skills with competence in particular languages (COBOL and C), and in using IBM's proprietary IMS system and PTM (Philips Technology for Managers). Their claim to expertise rested on highly technical skills, and particularly on the sorts of skills which have value on the external IT labour market. The group's project manager was exceptional in being the only person in this position surveyed who did not mention managerial skills in his job, citing instead technical knowledge of software.

2. Batch Mainframe Processing (BMP) Systems

In contrast, the BMP group emphasized their experience of the bank's own systems. They worked on reconfiguring the logical relationships of the massive batch-processing systems, using primarily in-house techniques not available on the external labour market. It was striking that these staff did not articulate their expertise in terms of languages and techniques; instead they cited knowledge of CABINET, of the bank's working practices, and unspecified development methods and tools. Their claim to expertise was thus based on an internal reputation, namely their ability to develop novel approaches to dealing with large and complex databases. Though their expertise was not formalized around externally marketable skills, their managers identified them as having the highest level of technical skills; perhaps because of this they did not need to base their expertise claims on formal universal skills.

3. Corporate Database Access (CDA)

The third team of programmers, in CDA, pointed to their familiarity with a wide range of specific languages and tools, rather than their possession of in-depth knowledge of any. Their senior manager described them as a 'hybrid group' with the lowest level of technical specialism. Their jobs were concerned with information transfer between the bank's main databases, and involved interacting with many development teams.

4. Computer Systems Assurance Unit (CSAU)

The fourth technical team, CSAU, was a small group involved in planning and co-ordination system testing for Phase 2, using tools such as IMS and TPNS. In this work they drew heavily on their experience of the bank's systems, and referred to each other and to the project managers of SIM's three programming teams. The systems analyst for the group had a very different role from other SIM analysts; he referred primarily to project managers and highlighted his own technical knowledge. The CSAU manager similarly emphasized technical expertise, and was directly involved in CABINET assurance testing.

5. SIM Systems Analysts

The four systems analysts and their project manager each dealt with particular application areas: access control, on-line updating, managerial facilities, plastic card on-line updating, and account/service requests. The group dealt with a range of user and MSD departments. The prime skills cited were verbal and written communication, followed by knowledge of existing computer systems and business practices, and an ability to analyse problems from different perspectives. The analysts referred to numerous others—analysts, programmers, project managers, and people in other departments. Technical competence was required of SIM analysts, but it occupied a relatively minor role, and was overshadowed by their claim to communication and planning skills. Not only did the SIM analysts point to different skills from the programmers, they also referred to a much wider range of people in MSD and the rest of the bank.

6. SIV Business Analysts

The SIV team involved in the proposed Phase 3 of CABINET applications comprised four business analysts and a project manager, reporting via a manager to a senior manager. Their role included investigating business requirements, undertaking cost/benefit analyses of new facilities, and developing a strategy for customer information and marketing. The SIV business analysts—even more than the SIM systems analysts—referred to a diverse and loosely structured network of players, largely outside their department, and on a range of levels in the organization. Like the SIM analysts, they identified collaborators only in general terms (in contrast with the network of specific contacts identified by the programmers). The SIV business analysts highlighted their special access to management, and claimed the same types of expertise as them, such as interviewing, analysis, report writing, conducting meetings, and being aware of the bank's business objectives.

7. Data Processing

Finally, in the DP department there were two groups of programmers involved in CABINET: Systems Programming (technical support for P9000) and Database Administration (implementing database architectures from high-level data models). These DP sections differed markedly from the SIM groups in that middle and senior managers continued to emphasize the technical component of their role, and their possession of technical skills over managerial skills. In their work this group and their managers referred to staff from at least 20 teams and departments in MSD, as well as software suppliers.

FIG. 12.3 *Expert Groups Involved in Project Development*

Mobile Professionals). The strong position of the BMP group as Winstanley's Type D (Valued Dependent Workers) emphasizes the point that some technical skills are company specific. Other groups were less specialized but deployed a wide range of skills; they correspond to Type B (Company

Range of skills

		Narrow			Broad
Form of Expertise	Formal Knowledge	P9000			
				CDA	Systems
				CSAU	Analysts
				DP	Business
	Experience Based	BMP			Analysts

FIG. 12.4 *Form and Range of Skills Deployed by MSD Staff*

Professionals). By offering skills that matched the bank's requirements they retained their value to the organization and may also have kept open a potential to trade on the external labour market, at least within the banking sector. This applied to CDA and CSAU's articulation of a wide range of technical competencies, and the SIM Systems Analysts and SIV Business Analysts who possessed a range of organizational knowledges.

Thus IT staff attain expert status with a subtle variety of strategies. The P9000 group were foremost in stressing their formal technical skills. But the programmers' senior manager suggested these were less highly valued in MSD than experience of the bank's computer systems. The reluctance of existing MSD staff to join P9000 was to be expected in so far as other groups were closer to the model of the Company Professional. The P9000 group were relatively new recruits and faced the classic dilemma of the 'staff' employee—whether to pursue organization-specific skills or retain their attractiveness on the external labour market. The bank is an organization with a strong internal labour market and long tradition of in-house systems development; its employees generally pursue advancement internally. The rewards of the internal market might therefore encourage a group like P9000 to pursue organizational status. On the other hand, an 'occupational' strategy may remain attractive. Any tendency for organizations to acquire IT solutions externally through the market-place—particularly where these were based on radical technical innovations—would encourage the continuation of mobile professional status.

The example of the CDA group reminds us that the value of experts to the firm does not rest solely on their level of skills, but may also derive from particular combinations of skill—in this case fairly low level technical skills, combining both formal techniques and knowledge of specific technical practices and systems, that match the organization's requirements. The business and systems analysts also exemplified skill combinations. They possessed a range of knowledges—generic skills (in communication and evaluation) and contingent knowledge (of banking and of the bank's methods of operation). They also deployed some technical knowledge of the particular systems in the bank, as well as general principles of systems development. Such combinations of skills were crucial in the implementation process, and also included skills that could be generally applied in the management of change (like evaluation techniques and 'people handling' skills). The range and type of expertise articulated by these groups was very similar to that of MSD managers. In other words, the groups projected managerial rather than technical skills and so articulated expertise claims through their reputation as potential managers. By emphasizing their proximity to senior managers, and involvement in the bank's strategic concerns, the analysts were enhancing their position and indicating their preparedness to move into managerial posts.

One point of ambiguity with Winstanley's schema was reflected in the status of the BMP group. This rested on skills not available on the labour market and places this group in Type D.1—dependent workers valuable to the firm—which seems to conflict with their particularly high status as technical specialists. While the bank might radically revise its in-house systems, rendering these skills obsolete, alternatively the lack of such skills on the market reflects an exceptional scarcity (and a positive labour-market power) rather than lack of value. However, there is probably little point in trying to apply the schema too rigidly. The position of a group like BMP reminds us that knowledge workers do not necessarily articulate or seek to validate all their skill requisites, but favour those which give them advantage in a particular context. While the BMP group's status was assured they had little need to play up other skill possessions.

Networks and Specialization Strategies

The other main variable that accounted for how expertise was intensified and consolidated was the *networks of contacts* that existed between groups. Whether a job-holder's role is specialized or not is partly a consequence of whether his or her group interacts within a narrow or extensive network. It depends on the *tasks* undertaken (whether complex and poorly bounded or more readily delineated), and the character of *interactions* with others in conducting their job (which may be specialized or may reflect a diffuse knowledge network). The latter two variables are closely related; tightly bounded tasks indicate specialist and technical interactions, while more diffuse, poorly defined tasks are indicative of less specialist interactions. For practical purposes, the two variables can be collapsed, allowing us to distinguish the MSD groups in terms of a breadth of network variables and the degree of boundedness of interactions in undertaking tasks (Figure 12.5).

When the network of contacts and types of task are considered, the seven groups cluster into three broad categories: the business and systems analysts, the programmers, and a third group we describe as technical interface staff.

1. The business and systems analysts referred to an extensive range of people in MSD and beyond. Their collaborative networks were fluid, diffuse,

Breadth of Network	**Boundedness of Interaction**	
	Tightly-Bounded Tasks/ Specialist Interactions	Diffuse Tasks/ Less Specialist Interactions
Extensive Network	CSAU Data Processing	
		Business Analysts
		Systems Analysts
	CDA programmers	
	BMP programmers	
Narrow Network	P9000 programmers	

FIG. 12.5 *Network and Specialization Strategies*

loosely specified, and proved difficult for respondents to define. They exercised considerable autonomy in their work; their jobs had a low level of specialization and were highly individualized.

2. The SIM programmers reported very different patterns of networking. Their work was collaborative and focused on a narrow range of people in similar roles. We also found smaller, but notable, differences between the three groups of programmers. The highly technically oriented P9000 group had relatively weak links with the rest of the organization; most of their interactions were vertical within their own team or with the external supplier, Philips. The BMP and CDA programmers did liaise with people outside their team, though these interactions were still fairly localized, and the CDA team in particular had a quite tightly specified technical role.

3. The technical interface category referred to a variety of people responsible for maintaining the integrity of the IT infrastructure. In the survey they were exemplified by the Computer Systems Assurance Unit (CSAU) in SIM, and the Database Administration and Systems Operations groups in the Data Processing department. They reported an extensive range of contacts, based on tasks of software support and maintaining database structures, though their interactions were mainly with other technical staff in highly specialized functions and their roles were tightly defined.

The model of work organization of the technical interface staff marked them as a new category responsible for interfacing with the user (Friedman 1989). They were distinctive in their technical orientation, their interactions with a range of technical staff, and in the continued technical role of their middle management. They represented a narrower form of technical specialization than the programmers (whose technical focus was complemented by responsibility for the development of applications software directed to achieving organizational change), while their responsibility for maintaining the IT infrastructure involved them in contacts across MSD and with suppliers, though this was only indirectly related to the achievement of change in the bank.

The SIV and SIM analysts were like the technical interface staff in having extensive networks of contacts. The analysts were at the interface of the technical system and the bank's users, whilst the technical interface group liaised between different parts of the technical infrastructure (e.g. within the IT division, and between it and hardware suppliers). The technical interface staff and the programmers were alike in terms of the specialist nature of their work, but had contrasting patterns of specialization. And the programmers and analysts were unalike on both dimensions; they had different types of networks and task responsibilities.

This allows us to distinguish three approaches to the utilization of expertise:

1. *Extensive non-specialization*: analysts undertake fairly diffuse roles and operate in an extensive network of technical specialists and users.

2. *Intensive specialization*: programmers perform a broad range of tasks and relate to a narrow range of actors closely associated with a particular part of the IT system.

3. *Extensive specialization*: technical interface staff undertake tightly specified roles while relating to wide networks of technical specialists.

Intensive specialization is perhaps not surprising in that it conforms to the established view of specialism—a functional division of labour allows highly specified roles to be conducted within a narrow network of contacts. Similarly, its mirror opposite, extensive non-specialization, is also perhaps what we would expect of the business and systems analysts' jobs. Groups were spread along the diagonal between intensive specialization and extensive non-specialization, indicating possible trade-offs between specialism and generalism. However, the technical interface staff departed from the diagonal with the pattern of extensive specialization. The need and opportunity for extensive specialization arose with the elaboration of the IT infrastructure. The work of the technical interface staff revolved around tasks across the IT infrastructure, such as software standards and maintaining the network, and involved contacts with a wide array of people, albeit still confined within technical functions. Thus they had not always had to trade possession of specialist skills for a narrow role in the organization. Their networks reflected the increasingly extensive nature of the technology and the tasks needed to maintain its integrity.

The pattern of extensive non-specialization confirms the obstacles to imposing task fragmentation and routinization on staff who interface between users and the technical system (Friedman 1989). Extensive specialization, conversely, highlights the technical interdependence of elements of the IT system and the requirement for forms of technical labour to maintain system integrity. From a labour-process perspective, the technical interface staff might perhaps be seen as controlling and supervising the work of programmers. However, there is no indication that they recognized such a managerial role. They construed their work in technical terms, and those of system performance, and down-played any managerial role.

Lack of evidence of direct control of the work process should not surprise us. An information-based organization like a bank is heavily dependent on IT systems and must ensure their reliability and performance. The advantages of control and cost-saving measures must be set against the potentially enormous costs of system failure. Certainly Bank of Scotland attempted to ensure the levels of internal expertise necessary to maintain its systems. Overall, the findings pointed up the tensions between pursuing the specialization of functions (in order to intensify the formation and economize in the deployment of expertise) and the maintenance of broad roles and exchange of information between groups. The attempts to resolve this dilemma gave rise to diverse strategies and opportunities to segment functions and construct new systems architectures, particularly as IT systems diversify.

IT-SKILLED CAREERS

The skill profiles and patterns of interaction involved in the conduct of different roles bore on the ways in which staff developed their expertise, gained access to new types of social network, and sought to enhance their standing in the organization. This brings us to the question of career progression and, in particular, the paths into managerial levels. We have seen how technical experts exercise much more than exclusively 'occupational' specialisms; many have been able to colonize 'organizational' knowledge sets. We now explore how IT staff utilize these skills in attempting to capture that most valuable of organizational resources, the career.

Heimer (1984), for example, has stressed the importance of social networks in yielding information about potential new posts to employees, and information about the individual to the managers. Particularly for skilled technical labour, where task uncertainty is always high, networks are crucial for the acquisition of reputation and for skills to be legitimized. Other important features in constructing a career include being in an organization which structures jobs into a sequence, occupying jobs which enable workers to learn skills that lead to promotion, and opportunities to influence how information about the worker is made available to seniors in the hierarchy. As Heimer points out, key factors in the formation of expert careers are 'whether a person's abilities are developed, whether such development is noted and recorded, and whether the person has access to information about jobs and potential employers have access to information about him or her'.

In MSD, several of these elements were in place. Viable career sequencing in particular seemed well provided for, through the strong internal labour market and sequential grading structure. The clearer such structuring, the better, for it allows workers to plan their careers in the sense of knowing what experience they lack and need to acquire, or what skills and accomplishments carry most kudos. MSD offered an elaborate career structure. Though there were career bottle-necks, as we have seen, management had sought to remove at least one of them. In a period of long-term expansion there had been significant outlets into managerial grades. Thus the formal grading structure did offer relatively long and progressive career paths.

In this section we are particularly concerned with the boundary between specialist and managerial work, and how the career progression from technical specialist to manager was achieved. This raises questions about the means by which staff were able to acquire the skills needed to become managers, and the reputations or credentials needed for promotion. As we show below, the opportunities and mechanisms for demonstrating such competences were different for different types of specialist staff. This touches on the local culture and values (meta-knowledges) that prevailed in different parts of the division, on the different ways in which legitimation and control were achieved, and the relation between managers and managed for different kinds of specialist labour.

The Articulation of Managerial Skill

When groups are asked to describe their expertise, the skills they choose to highlight reflect their strategies for enhancing their position in the organization or labour market, as much as the tasks they actually perform. In other words, the way in which workers present their roles and expertise is of crucial importance. In assessing expertise claims, it is essential to enquire which skills and activities are valuable in the construction of claims on promotion.

This point was demonstrated by the systems analysts. Possession of high levels of technical skills is certainly one way for workers to enhance internal and external market power. But though the SIM systems analysts possessed high levels of formal skills, they played them down and instead stressed their close working relationships with senior managers, and their experience of organizational practices. We have already noted how the business and systems analysts reported types and ranges of expertise similar to MSD managers. Their work involved a range of tasks carried out within collaborative networks that were extensive (involving peers and senior staff) and loosely defined. In this respect their work organization strongly resembled that of their managers. These jobs would appear to be advantageous in pursuing promotion, as they offered myriad opportunities to obtain managerial-type skills, to gain information about jobs elsewhere in MSD and the bank, and to negotiate the construction of their reputations.

Conversely it should not be presumed that the technical specialization and focused knowledge networks of programmers prevented them from acquiring managerial skills. To the contrary, programmers gained direct person-management skills because, in contrast to the individualized work of the analysts, programming was a collective activity. There was a relatively informal division of labour within programming teams. Staff undertook a mixture of tasks—those with greater experience tended to be allocated investigative tasks and took on more responsibilities—in preparation for the promotional shift to project management. Skills were developed through experience more or less in the master–apprentice style of learning. More experienced staff took a degree of responsibility for the development of junior colleagues in allocating work, and also in staff appraisal. As a result senior programmers gained valuable experience in the managment of teams.

In pursuing the intensification of technical expertise MSD had developed, in effect, twin-track careers. We did not find the traditionally limited career hierarchy, whereby systems analysis was the sole route out of programming. The bank did not want to siphon off highly experienced programming staff, but instead sought to offer career progression for the different types of specialist labour, which ultimately took these workers into managerial functions. As one senior systems development manager put it, 'There is a role for a good programmer who has communications skills and personal skills.'

This type of skills-maintaining strategy helped to open up additional promotion paths and career chances, as well as resolving the classic career dilemma of specialist workers. The programmers did not have to 'move out to move up', but had a line of advance of their own. Thus while the analysts arguably had flexibility to move into a wider variety of jobs, it would be wrong to take at face value their own emphasis on diffuse managerial skills and assume this gave them greater career opportunities. The career histories of respondents show that programmers as well as analysts have been successful in moving into managerial grades.

In this context, project managers were an important intermediary in the transition from technical specialist to manager. This role had spread to most parts of MSD. They were recruited from amongst the programmers and analysts, and showed a similar orientation and skill profile as their respective expert groups. Given the organizational knowledge networks of the systems and business analysts, their project managers saw their jobs as primarily involving managerial and people skills. Programmers' project managers, in contrast, did not articulate their claims to seniority on the basis of managerial skills; they legitimated their right to manage in terms of possessing the same technical ability and experience as their staff. (In the extreme case, the P9000 project manager did not claim any managerial expertise at all.) These project managers also retained a hands-on involvement in programming, proving they were still 'part of the tribe' of technical specialists. All this reinforced the idea of dual career tracks, in that this group did not, perhaps, feel that articulating their technical skills would damage their chances of advancing into management.

The managers and senior managers, in both SIV and SIM, occupied generalist roles—in resource allocation, deploying labour, and interfacing with other groups. The skills that these more senior groups reported reflected activities like personnel management, problem-solving, communications, planning, and scheduling of activities. The possession of technical skills was occasionally cited, but these managers seemed broadly homogeneous. In contrast, the senior grades of managers of the technical interface groups emphasized their direct involvement in the tasks and problems of their areas. They claimed a range of technical skills and their interactions were frequently reported as being highly specialist.

Thus, even amongst managerial grades, we found a distinction between job-holders who saw themselves exercising a generalist role and the technical interface staff whose networks reflected their specialized functions in maintaining the IT infrastructure. This dichotomy points to differences not only in the ways that expertise was deployed in carrying out a particular role, but also between the cultures of departments. Some managerial staff prioritized their technical over their managerial skills as a consequence of the specialist knowledge networks they were involved in. Hence the borderline between specialist and managerial orientations occurred higher up the grading structure amongst these groups than it did for groups involved in new systems design.

Career Paths

Finally, we turn to the career paths of respondents as the means by which the transition into managerial grades was achieved. As part of our survey we asked respondents about their occupational history, which was supplemented by information on job changes during the period of study.

This revealed a steady pattern of career development, with staff by and large joining in junior technical roles and working up through the grades. Most staff had spent only a short period in their current jobs (on average 3 years). Because promotion was almost exclusively within the ranks of MSD, the length of employment in the bank was a good indicator of the grade achieved. Most programmers and analysts had been recruited straight into the job (perhaps after a short period as trainees) and had spent an average of 4 years there; project managers had 7 years prior experience in the bank (though, reflecting the fact that it is a new and expanding grade, they only had spent an average of 1 year as project manager); senior managers averaged around 13 years working for the Bank before getting their current position. This points to the strength of the internal labour market (though some had taken nearly three times as long to reach managerial grades as others).

Within this picture, a more detailed pattern of career trajectories emerged. Where we have data, career paths were mostly linear—by vertical promotion from programmer, to programmer/analyst or senior programmer, to project manager, and finally to manager and senior manager. However, the migration of staff between different groups in the division highlighted the ways in which expertise was developed cumulatively through careers. The career-development policies of the organization were as important as recruitment in shaping the type and combination of expertise deployed by staff.

Patterns of internal mobility differed between the lower-level technical staff and their managers and senior managers. We discuss each in turn. To simplify the account we adopt the following terminology. Staff changes may be:

vertical: promotion up the hierarchy within the same group or department;

diagonal: promotion involving a shift across the hierarchy to a new group or department; or

horizontal: shifts between departments or groups without moving to a higher position.

Horizontal moves are either:

rotations: between adjacent posts in the hierarchy (e.g. between groups in the same department), or

transfers: between non-adjacent positions (e.g. to different departments).

1. *Programmers and analysts*. Only a minority amongst the programmer and analyst grades had moved diagonally or horizontally between groups. These somewhat exceptional career moves appear to have been initiated by individuals as a result of particular career preferences. The dominant pattern of career development was vertical—from programmer to programmer/analyst to senior programmer or project manager—within the same group or department. Project managers were almost all recruited vertically from the staff they now managed, and when in due course they were promoted into managerial grades, they moved vertically within their groups.

These highly visible programming career routes testified to the strength of the internal labour market. If programming had a 'normal' career structure, it was less institutionalized in the newer specialisms in the division. Thus the transfer of general bank staff to business analyst posts, together with the recruitment of outsiders, indicated a more recent strategy for bringing in new types of expertise (experience of branch work, evaluation, and budgeting skills). These recruits necessarily lacked detailed experience of the bank's systems-development procedures. This less clear-cut route may have been a by-product of SIV's growth, but also pointed to a separate culture and set of orientations in SIV from the rest of MSD.

At the lower levels of the division, therefore, staff development strategy emphasized specialization, and reflected a policy of maintaining high levels of technical skill. Other things being equal, specialization is to be expected as an effective and economical method of developing an intensity of skills on the IT shop-floor.

2. *Managerial grades*. Career development among the managerial grades was more complex and is set out in Figure 12.6. Given the limited number of managers in our survey, we drew on personnel information about managerial promotions and transfers in the whole division in the period 1988–90.

In contrast to the pattern of promotion at lower levels, the main form of promotion between manager and senior manager grades was by diagonal promotion between functional groups within MSD (accounting for four of the recruits into this grade, compared with one vertical promotion), with a further two recruited from other parts of the bank. Diagonal moves also figured in staff promotions above this grade, though numbers were too small for reliable extrapolation. Another distinctive pattern of job change, more marked among lower tier senior managers, involved horizontal shifts. These were overwhelmingly *transfers* between different functional departments, rather than mere rotations between adjacent groups.

Taken together, we found three relatively distinct patterns of job change: vertical promotion for the programmer/analyst and lower-tier managerial grades, horizontal transfers for lower-tier senior managers, and diagonal promotion in senior grades. Thus, going up the hierarchy, there were increasing pressures to circulate between ever more disparate jobs, and clear indications of a strategy to broaden the experience of senior staff. As a SIM senior manager noted, 'When you are approaching senior manager positions, the bank wants to move you around to give you experience. Otherwise it is very difficult to develop different skills, to get you working with different people and in different environments.' The fact that this exchange of staff came into play at senior levels suggested the strategy was primarily about developing expertise on broader objectives and the nature of IT systems.

We also identified variations in the overall pattern that appeared directed towards promoting particular expertise profiles. Some departments, notably Production Control and Computer and Network Operations, had particularly high rates of change at senior management level. These were the most specialized of MSD's departments and had a strict pattern of vertical progression at technical levels. It seemed as if the bank were seeking to offset any tendency towards a sectional, technical orientation, by bringing senior managers more into line with generalist skills.

A similar end may be achieved via the pattern of career movement in SIV. Despite being a small department, SIV was an important channel for the horizontal and diagonal transfer of staff. The department itself was oriented towards organizational rather than technical issues, and SIV analysts had frequently had branch banking experience, and so could be placed elsewhere in the organization. The movement of staff into SIV, and their migration to other parts of MSD, therefore, indicated one method by which the new emphasis on IT as a strategic resource may have been diffused.

Collective Mobility and Occupational Change

This chapter has examined an organized body of IT-skilled labour and shown how 'expert segments' form within a network of computing occupations. Expertise, with its particular flavours, competencies, and statuses, accrues to

274

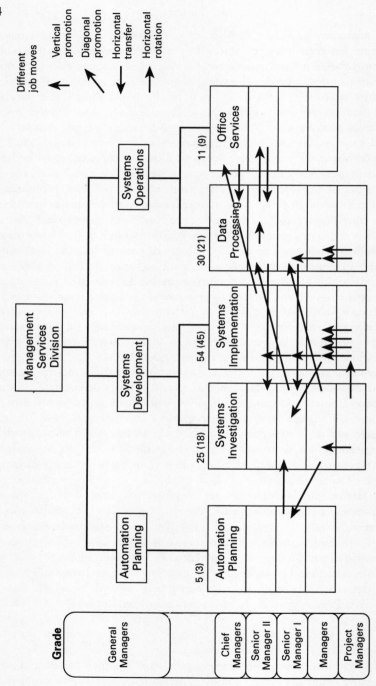

FIG. 12.6 *Promotion Pattern in MSD 1988–90, showing number of managers in departments at January 1990* [*1988 figures in brackets*]

groups as a consequence of the conditions within which work is organized, but cannot be reduced solely to the tasks required to create and maintain IT infrastructures. Also implicated are the managerial strategies to deploy expert labour and groups' own strategies for pursuing expert status. Expertise is not a measure of technique, pure and simple, but a product of the way that careers and knowledge networks operate in detail. Our findings can be summarized as follows.

First, a marked distinction existed between technical and analyst jobs. The former were specialized, operated within a localized set of contacts, and were closely scrutinized by peers and managers; the latter were less well bounded, and involved an extensive network of contacts. This broadly confirms the claim that roles emerging from the user relations needs of systems development enjoy a high degree of autonomy, as they are accountable to both user and system-design management (Friedman 1989). However, technical work was itself differentiated. It ranged from 'narrow but deep' to 'diverse but shallow' technical competencies, which encompassed both generic formal knowledge and technical skills that in their nature or combination were experience-based and organization-specific. Intensive specialism in particular areas was compensated by extensive forms of specialism amongst workers concerned with maintaining the integrity of the IT infrastructure. The latter involved narrowly focused tasks that were conducted though wide networks of collaboration and information exchange between expert groups.

Patterns of expertise were shaped by interaction between the strategies pursued by organizations, and the occupational strategies of particular groups of experts. Winstanley's analysis of labour-market factors was developed to highlight the links between 'organizational' and 'occupational' bases of expertise. Programming groups like BMP attained their technical status by displaying bank-specific skills, while the P9000 group emphasized their possession of skills valued on the labour market. Other groups based their claims to expertise on both internal and external labour markets. However, in a strong internal labour market like the bank, organizational opportunities for creating expertise were exceptionally well developed. The 'company professional' role represented perhaps the most viable strategy for achieving expert status. Even for the P9000 programming group, with a strong occupational component to their expertise, we speculated that internal rewards might encourage a shift towards organizational strategies and a company professional role.

In order to understand expert strategies fully, however, we needed to go beyond snapshots of labour-market power. The career negotiated over time is the chief means of acquiring competencies. We saw that a number of distinct career routes exist for programmers, analysts, technical interface staff, and managers. Vertical promotion through the programming grades served to intensify technical expertise, while horizontal and diagonal job changes higher up helped to create a cadre of technical managers with a wide expertise base and common approach.

The social construction of career was of crucial importance. There was often a critical 'gap' between the actual skills deployed and the skills a group chose to emphasize. The strategy for claiming expertise also varied over the course of a career in a complex process of engagement between lower and higher grades. At one extreme, groups like the systems analysts announced their proximity to management by emphasizing their organizational rather than technical skills. At the other, technical staff who possessed organization knowledge and person-management skills often did not list them as important competencies in their jobs. The managers (and even senior managers) of some specialist functions emphasized their proximity to their staff by highlighting their technical competence. This suggests that managerial authority involves a two-way process of accommodation and legitimation between lower and higher grades, within local cultures and value systems. It shows that groups exercise choice about which skills they highlight; and the pattern of reportage tells much about the strategies available to groups in pursuing status and promotion, given their role and position in the organization.

These findings are pertinent to broader notions of collective mobility. Murray and Knights (1990), comparing the success of professional groups like accountants, have reasoned that the failure of IT staff to create an occupational hierarchy has hampered their 'collective mobility project'. Only such internal divisions within their own occupation would enable an élite of IT managers controlling a set of clear administrative techniques to distinguish itself. However, Armstrong (1990) challenged this connection, arguing that occupational division and degradation may be one route to collective mobility, but 'possession of a technique for controlling labour may *not* be considered as a necessary condition for successful competition for positions of control' (p. 27). If this argument is sustained, we can distinguish two versions of the collective-mobility project: one for an élite of managers (the usual interpretation), and another for the bulk of the occupation. Clearly the two are related in so far as élite mobility opens up a total career avenue enabling middle-rankers to see through to the top. But there remains a distinction between élite mobility carried out under conditions of de-skilling, and a mobility project more truly collective which enhances careers and occupational circumstances more widely. Though we found that élite mobility for IT skilled staff had been restricted, this does not prevent organic growth of the occupation representing a broader expansion of career opportunities.

In short, because of a tendency to regard élite mobility narrowly, as the only form of collective-mobility project, broader and more dynamic forms of occupational enhancement may have been underestimated. As our findings indicate, enhancement of the IT occupations is occurring on a number of fronts. The strategic behaviour of IT people in socially constructing their skills suggests an embryonic ability to create the kind of strategic discourse necessary for élite mobility. Similarly, the survival of technical skills further up the hierarchy indicates that a 'language' resembling that of the specialists has increasing currency within higher reaches of management.

13

The Economy of IS Expertise

In earlier chapters we outlined the way in which expertise mediates the relationship between technology and organization. In so doing we highlighted various aspects of the management of expertise, and in particular factors which underpin a specialist group's claims to organizational competence. It could be argued, though, that such a focus overstates the power dimensions of expertise and insufficiently attends to the economic pressures shaping IS skills and technology.

The need to take account of the economy of IS expertise is underlined by our findings on strategic innovation. The relationship between sectoral product markets and the evolution of the IS function is such that the organizational role of IS needs to be set against an established tradition of in-house development. We found evidence of a recent shift towards greater utilization of external expertise in the case firms and projects. This followed a pattern of collaborative development as well as external supply. The contribution from external expertise ranged from training and consultancy, through the provision of software packages, to more extensive collaboration over a number of years.

We have already noted the close relationship between financial service firms, and IT suppliers in Chapter 7. In our case firms' projects that were deemed strategic and innovative were often dependent on outside suppliers—a finding which demanded attention to the influence of the supply sector on the deployment of expertise. This is not to discount the importance of internal forces of organizational and occupational politics. Indeed, some writers have analysed the use of external suppliers in terms of internal considerations of power and control. Friedman (1989), for example, argues that the use of market-based sources of technology and expertise gives management a more effective means of controlling the internal IS function, by increasing their substitutability and reducing their strategic power. Whittington (1990) makes a similar observation about the externalizing of research and development activities as a means of humbling in-house functions perceived by other parts of the organization to be 'ivory towers' or 'masonic lodges'. Thus market controls may help to delimit the influence of IS functions which, given their distinctive culture, competencies, and work traditions, may not fit well with the rest of the organization.

Nor is it necessary to externalize completely the sourcing of technical expertise in order to achieve a political impact. The mere possibility of outsourcing expertise creates implicit competition for the internal function. It may force it to justify its role in economic terms and 'sell' itself to user groups and subsidiary companies. Even where there is little possibility of direct competition between internal and external providers, the design of accounting systems and the language of 'internal markets', 'customers', and 'contracts' may be just as effective in applying pressure.

The penetration of this type of market-oriented thinking has many political and ideological ramifications for corporate bureaucracies and management functions. There were clear trends in the 1980s towards the decentralization and out-sourcing of technical expertise (Whalley 1986). Such trends resulted in a proliferation of supplier and consulting firms in the systems and engineering areas (Francis and Winstanley 1988), and an increasing level of extramural R&D (Whittington 1991).

The greater the scope to substitute for internal provision, and the greater the exposure to market forces, the more plausible becomes the argument that management of expertise is more strictly an economic matter rather than explicable within a framework of organizational politics. If the rules of the game are predominantly economic not political in nature, the internal deployment of IS expertise should be understood very largely in terms of its economic advantages over external provision—once of course the basic necessity to secure substantive expertise for the implementation of IT systems is allowed.

Williamson (1985) has advanced a theory to explain the dynamics of make–buy decisions. He argues that all forms of economic activity can be understood as 'transactions', and that variations in the institutional form under which transactions are governed reflect their relative efficiency in handling different types of transactions. Whichever form succeeds in regulating a transaction at the lowest cost will prevail. Given this framework, Williamson provides a comprehensive analysis of the conditions under which market or hierarchical control of expertise is more likely. Assuming that individuals are liable to cheat on contracts (opportunism) and are unable to fully anticipate or completely understand complex situations (bounded rationality), Williamson argues that the following features of a task or transaction make it more likely to require a hierarchical form of control.

1. *Technological inseparability*: where the task is closely interdependent with other tasks for purely technical or physical reasons. This demands integrated forms of planning, co-ordination, and control which market relations cannot provide.

2. *Asset-specific investments*: apart from physical or site specificity (due to specialist tools or economies of inventory and transport), the major form of asset-specificity relates to human assets. This arises through the 'learning by doing' processes which generate tacit and contingent forms of knowledge that are organizationally specific, and not easily transferable. The latter (as we saw in Chapter 11) can be contrasted with formal skills which are transferable

across a variety of contexts. Human-asset specificity—the formation and deployment of organization-specific skills—rests on the employment relationship and hierarchical control. Within a context of internal labour markets and career structures (as argued in Chapter 12) individuals have an incentive to develop the kind of organizationally specific skills not available on the external market. Equally, in-house deployment allows employers to develop highly specific or 'core' skills, and offers economies of scale in skill formation and application.

3. *The complexity and uncertainty of the task*: the extent to which the task can be pre-specified and satisfactory outcomes identified. Complex and uncertain tasks cannot be efficiently handled by market-based contracts because of the scope for opportunism. The employment contract, however, together with supervisory control and engagement through the employment relationship, provides a more adaptive environment in which blatant opportunism gives way to goal congruence.

Williamson's analysis of the organization of work from the sole perspective of transaction costs thus encompasses a variety of contexts in which expertise is deployed. We can use it to examine the patterns of market and in-house provision in our case findings and, in turn, to reflect on the usefulness of Williamson's own account. Before considering our empirical findings in detail though it will be helpful to discuss the broader processes involved in the commodification of IT.

BLACK-BOXING AND THE COMMODIFICATION OF IT

We refer here to 'black-boxing' as the tendency in technological development for elements of uncertainty and complexity to become compartmentalized and bounded, segmenting parts of the technological system from uncertainties and complexities elsewhere. This describes ways in which artefacts may be created, together with particular divisions of labour, through the simplification, standardization, and commodification of parts of the system. Strategies for black-boxing are promoted by users and suppliers of technology, and include:

—the *stabilization* of particular technological components (artefacts and the bundles of skills involved in their manipulation). For example, the creation of turnkey software packages; the emergence of industry standards such as we discuss in Chapter 8; standardization procedures for programming languages and communications protocols, and measures to simplify the external interface of black-boxed elements to allow their use on the basis of lower levels of expertise, e.g. menu-drive database enquiry applications;

—the increased *portability* of a system which enables it to be removed from one context and applied elsewhere with little modification. This can be done laterally, so that solutions can be generalized to other parts of the system, e.g. software libraries, or longitudinally to allow parts to continue to be applicable even though other parts of the system may change, e.g. operating systems;

—the *segmentation* of different phases of development. This takes at least two forms: the *modularization* of different components of a technical system, and the separation of technology into a set of different *levels*, of which the earliest example was perhaps the differentiation between 'hardware' and 'software'. Software is itself segmented (Grindley 1988) between systems and utilities (e.g. operating systems, programming languages, compilers), application tools (e.g. database management systems), and applications solutions. The last divide into a general function (e.g. accounting) and industry-specific types (e.g. banking, automated funds transfer). Segmentation marks a degree of autonomy between the development of different components of the technological system, such that the interaction between each set of components is restricted;

—and the *commodification* of IT (Swann and Lamaison 1988; Swann 1990; Brady, Tierney, and Williams 1992). This involves the standardization of technology so that increasingly large markets can be pursued and economies of scale achieved in production. The latter factor is highly attractive in software production because of the need to spread the high costs of labour-intensive development and because reproduction costs are low (Peláez 1990).

The segmentation of technology together with the market opportunities of standardization provide ample support for the Williamson analysis of expertise. Modularization and segmentation highlight the market advantages of technological separability, while the technology itself is based on generic rather than asset-specific knowledge and learning. Moreover, functionality and performance of the black box are visible, which fulfils the need for information about the transaction to be externalized to allow utility to be specified against price. This is facilitated by technical standards that provide a framework of technical knowledge within which systems can be developed and assessed.

At the same time analysis also defines the limits of the market-based exchange of software. This is primarily to do with the problems of knowledge and complexity. Technological change in financial services encompasses the generation of new knowledge in both the financial and IT supplier sector. As Teece (1988) has pointed out, the attractions for user firms of the black-boxing of technology are greater where innovation has mainly been conducted outside the user industry, and where new knowledge is difficult to copy. On the other hand, in so far as supplier firms rely on innovation to sustain or create markets, they have a competitive incentive to undo existing regimes of technology transfer through their own programmes of innovation.

TABLE 13.1. *In-house development of software*

	Projects involving in-house solutions (%)
Systems software	14.5
Utilities software	11.8
Application tools	18.6
Application solutions—general	53.6
Application solutions—industry specific	59.9

Source: Brady 1991.

Equally important in delimiting the scope of black-boxed solutions is the extent to which innovation projects involve not only the generation of new knowledge, but also the application of local, organizationally specific knowledge. E. von Hippel (1990) described such knowledge as 'sticky data', and argued that in such cases innovation processes need to remain close to the user applications domain. The evolution and elaboration of such systems over time creates complex, non-standard boundaries and demands the deployment of tacit and organizationally-specific forms of knowledge (J. Fleck 1988). The same applies where knowledge is deliberately withheld from the market-place for reasons of security or competitiveness.

Commodification and Financial Services

These considerations allow us to explain the uneven pattern of commodification of different parts of the IT infrastructure. Thus, hardware today is the archetypal black box, available as more or less standard, commodified solutions. The situation in relation to software is more uneven, as shown by a recent survey of software in computer-using organizations in the UK and Ireland. Brady (1991) found that around two-thirds of all installations used packages as items in their major development projects. He also showed that 20 per cent of software was developed wholly in-house, without recourse to packages. However, the most significant finding was the distribution of in-house versus packaged solutions between the different types of systems development (Table 13.1).

Thus in-house involvement prevails in relation to application solutions (for general applications such as payroll systems, and for industry-specific applications like finance-sector applications). Here local knowledge of the specific user context would be at a premium. In contrast, there was almost total reliance on packaged solutions in respect of 'lower levels' of software-operating systems, utilities, and application tools. These concern machine-related functions and standard facilities which potentially can be generalized to a wide range of functions. Where applications can be divorced from particular user contexts, they can be made available as black-boxed solutions, and the skills needed to create technologies can be concentrated in the supply sector (Brady, Tierney, and Williams 1992).

While some writers have predicted a wholesale shift towards commodification and packaged software (e.g. Grindley 1988), our analysis highlighted the uneven and contradictory nature of this process. The attractions of a package are that it offers time economy in the acquisition of complex computer systems. There is also an opportunity for the introduction of a new system, and for a company to make a fresh start in the development of its computer networks. But any decision to install a complete black-boxed package, without preparatory customizing to link it to in-house systems and organizational practices, usually creates serious problems. The black box of a software package necessarily makes fundamental assumptions about an organization's structure, operations, work processes, and market environment. Though broad functionality may be specified, many detailed aspects of the package and user requirements are often hard to specify in advance. The gulf between them may only become evident over time. In particular for the many American-derived systems, the US organizational environment assumed by the package may be impossible to imitate. Stable elements of the package may sit uneasily in the non-standard organizational dynamics of a firm with a UK-centred conception of itself and its market.

These points highlight the constraints on applying standard packages in a context of pre-existing systems and organizational practices. In a number of our cases, however, the use of packages was closely linked with the creation of new business areas. This greatly enhanced the applicability of standardized solutions, as organizational practices could be developed in tandem with the implementation of the software. A good example was provided by the experience of Bank of Scotland's VISA Centre.

The VISA Centre Development

As we saw in the case study, with no pre-existing knowledge or systems to build on, the time and cost advantages of a standard package were overwhelming. The importance of the former factor was particularly critical. Barclaycard had stipulated a disengagement time of only eighteen months to transfer all operations to the new centre. So getting a working system quickly in place, which included software, hardware, and the organizational practices required to support the system, was essential.

The package-buying decisions were made by the VISA Centre Manager and a small number of systems-development managers within the bank who had expertise in evaluating packages. At the time VISA Centre bought it, the American suppliers were still actively selling the package in the UK, and offering to customize it for the UK market. VISA Centre opted to undertake their own rewriting, however, and that decision in hindsight seemed to have been particularly inspired. In 1987 the suppliers set up their own UK bureau in direct competition with card-processing bureaux (including VISA) for third-party contracts, and they no longer modified or maintained the package. As the Centre Manager recognized, they were now on their own. They could still purchase updates, but

the longer we go the more difficult that becomes because some of these enhancements depend on having previous enhancements. And if you haven't got that fixed in, you're not in a position to get the new thing. Plus the fact that we did so much modification of the package in the early stages that it bears very little resemblance to what was actually sold to us.

The Package Paradox

Despite strong elements of a centrally planned operation at VISA Centre, then, this case well illustrated the problems of dependency that may arise in the acquisition of black-boxed solutions. The economic advantages of packaged software rest not only on their immediate utility, but also on the possibility of upgrading and customizing over time. The decision to purchase a package may lock the user into future dependency on the external supplier. This tension between the economic advantages of packages and the potential dependency built into their acquisition can be summarized as the 'package paradox'.

Once a package-based system has been installed, the user organization faces a choice about which direction to take in future development. There may be a tension between the supplier's technical development of the package, and the organization's requirements for changes to the package itself and the work practices surrounding it. Figure 13.1 indicates how these technical and organizational goals may come into conflict. Thus extensive customizing will be expensive and reduce the cost advantages of using the package. So many resources may be put into customizing that the user may just as well have developed in-house. It may, moreover, undermine the integrity of the package, leading to reduced reliability and problems in obtaining maintenance and updates from the supplier. User firms may be forced to develop an unwanted in-house capability in order to maintain an increasingly less useful package.

Thus where an application has clearly defined boundaries the use of a standard package is highly attractive, as the VISA case illustrated. However, the advantages may erode rapidly over time, as the system becomes increasingly configured to local technological and organizational requirements. And, given problems of dependency, there are important incentives for in-house involvement in the implementation and customization of packages.

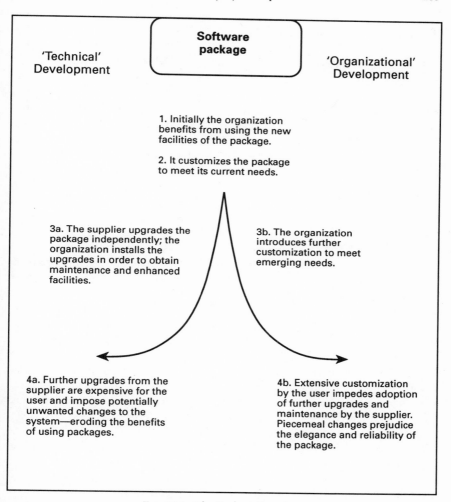

FIG. 13.1 *The Package Paradox*

COLLABORATIVE DEVELOPMENT IN THE CASE FIRMS

These limitations mean it was hardly surprising that our study revealed a pattern of packaged solutions limited very largely to low-level software functions, or to highly discrete applications. In the applications area the customizing of packages requires specific knowledge of the user organization and its context. User organizations clearly possess extensive knowledge of their own operations, far more than outsiders such as external suppliers could possess. But this does not preclude the allocation of high-level application tasks to external suppliers. As our case studies reveal, however, they make it more likely that such tasks will involve collaborative development. Close supplier-user links have been identified as playing a central role in the development of IT-based technologies (J. Fleck, Webster, and Williams 1990).

But, while collaborative development greatly extends the applicability of generic packages and skills, it creates its own distinctive problems. Unlike the acquisition of black-boxed solutions, which rests on a precise contractual relationship, collaborative development relies on a working arrangement between supplier and host organization. Such a division of labour needs to be based on formal contractual arrangements, yet also has to encompass the uncertainties and contingencies which development may throw up. This is easiest to achieve where technical tasks, though complex and uncertain, are nevertheless largely discrete, allowing the boundaries between in-house function and external supplier to be identified. This was clearly so in the Clydesdale Telebank project.

Clydesdale Telebank

The key feature of the Telebank case was the distinctive architecture proposed by the suppliers, Software Partnership (SP), whereby the remote transaction processing system would be separated from the bank's customer databases and from the interface used by the customer (e.g. voice recognition, videotex). This black-boxing of functions permitted a division of labour between external supplier and customer. But other aspects of external supply were more problematic. The development of a collaborative relationship showed how formal contracts may be superseded or supplemented by non-contractual forms of co-ordination and control. Moreover, the Telebank electronic banking system had strategic connotations which were none the less developed very largely by the outside supplier. In other cases we have described, uncertainty arose in customizing or interfacing a pre-determined package, whereas the development of Telebank involved a degree of innovation that created major uncertainties about the final shape of the system.

Far from following tightly written contracts, Clydesdale and SP engaged in a jointly regulated innovation process. The willingness of each side to accept the attendant uncertainties highlighted the significant gains they saw accruing from innovation. An important consideration was the potential for knowledge-trading. On one hand, SP was keen to establish a reputation for providing secure, public-access architectures in the finance-sector niche and needed to elicit knowledge about banking practices and systems. As the Director reflected:

Unavoidably we've picked up a lot of expertise and knowledge about what *really* matters to a bank. I would not for a moment suggest that we are the kind of organization that understands banking as a business to the same level of the people who are responsible in those areas. But what we do understand is what is *important*. We can make sensible judgements when we assess or incorporate technology. We can tell what really counts and what doesn't. And I think it's the 'what doesn't' which is the most important. So that puts us in a position that is very much apart from the standard provider of a package which is not necessarily providing banking functions. We know in any package, including our own, what it is that's attractive to the bank, and what is irrelevant.

For their part Clydesdale believed that through using this supplier they could gain access to information about what was happening in the sector in relation to out-of-branch banking, and thereby obtain a more 'competitive' solution than would have been developed in-house. As one manager put it, there could be a danger of missing 'the proper understanding of the market' by developing in-house. For the bank to gain additional knowledge of the sector was particularly important. Here is the Director of SP again:

From 1985 on, the whole subject of home banking was very much in the air in that everybody was publicly saying that there was no market but everybody was actually privately preparing for it. The whole approach of the banking market-place was that everyone wanted to be second. Nobody wanted to be first and nobody wanted to be last. They all wanted to be second.

While each side appeared willing to embark on open-ended innovation, how was that process to be managed? Given the degree of uncertainty and the potential for opportunism, we might have expected Clydesdale to develop elaborate monitoring arrangements. Instead, we found a much more relaxed approach; Clydesdale management was 'generally happy with' SP's programming standards. The decision to pursue a co-operative rather than a controlling relationship certainly had something to do with the social climate in which knowledge-trading took place. It reflected an awareness of mutual interests in a successful outcome. Put simply, the benefits of successful innovation—especially in relation to the costs of failure—were greater than could be achieved from attempting to cheat on the relationship.

SP had major reasons to be committed to project success. At the time Telebank was commissioned, the suppliers had acted as technical consultants to the banking community in the UK for a number of years and had used their fees to fund the design of their product, though not to build the product itself. The Telebank contract fortuitously gave them the chance to develop their front-end architecture into a saleable package. They made a deal with the bank that, in return for developing Telebank at a reduced cost and paying some royalties on future sales, they would retain the right to resell the software platform (though not the presentation software) as a generic package, i.e. as a new black box. SP's reputation with other banks would inevitably be enhanced by this high-profile project.

The IS people too had their own agenda; in the context of a recent acquisition they needed to establish themselves as a force in systems development against a legacy of this activity being run down under the previous owner. Managers enlisted an external supplier to ensure the rapid development of a telebanking system as a way of demonstrating their competence to the new parent. And the bank as a whole also benefited from joint development. By commissioning the software house to develop the front end they saved on development costs. Clydesdale had no interest in marketing their in-house systems and saw no competitive costs in SP doing this, as their proprietary interfaces were protected.

So, while it is easy to outline economic advantages in the abstract, what seems to have made it possible for each side to grasp these advantages was something which transcended the circumstances of the contract. This was the social and occupational linkages between the groups. Key figures in the deal had worked together on earlier projects and for earlier employers. Clydesdale management did not tender for suppliers to develop Telebank, but were themselves approached by SP management through the occupational grapevine. Indeed, the project went ahead on the basis of a fairly loose specification and relaxed monitoring, precisely because both parties were IT professionals who had a shared understanding of the problems and complexities of the innovation process.

Home and Auto

The Home and Auto case underlined in particular the importance of problem definition as a pre-condition of the acquisition of black-boxed solutions. The character of in-house expertise, as much as the functionality of the black box itself, defined the fit between package and function.

H&A had initially rejected packaged solutions to their information needs. It was felt that any management information system needed to operate with base data, and the packages available simply could not do this to acceptable processing times. This specification threshold was overturned, however, through a personnel change. A new managerial team brought about a new perception of the problem. When it was understood that an MIS could be developed on the basis of summary data, two standard packages, IBM's DBII and Supra, were re-examined and the former was favoured.

However, while H&A had resorted to a standard package, there was little evidence that the motivation was economic. Given the failure of an earlier 'strategic' approach to management information, the IS department was under considerable pressure to deliver some kind of system, even if this meant compromising their strategic intentions. Moreover, the cost of the package was financially justified in only the crudest terms, on the grounds that its cost was only a fraction of the overall IT expenditure. DBII is more or less an industry standard, with skills in its use widely available.

Premier Financial Services

In our final example, Premier Financial Services, an external supplier, CPM, played a dominant role in system development, and (untypically) went on to become the maintenance provider for the system. At one level this case seemed to show a logical, even linear, relationship between the nature of the task and eventual outsourcing of the development and maintenance.

The acquisition of Premier by one of the Scottish clearing banks provided a well-bounded space for the implementation of a packaged solution, CPM's INDEX. Card processing is a standardized technology and the new system would simply be a direct replacement for an earlier outdated and inadequate one. There was some early disquiet about the supplier; the bank had had a previous and, according to them, disastrous experience of using CPM on a project with a group subsidiary. But this was offset partly by the robust nature of the product, as the General Manager at Premier noted.

There was no real contention over which was the best package. Most of the contention was over the two organizations. CPM had an unfortunate experience with one of our subsidiaries. They completely messed the project up. But eventually we decided the product was so strong I wasn't going to budge easily.

Also, the uncertainty over the supplier's reputation, and any possible need to monitor their work, was moderated by the decision to award them the maintenance contract.

The broader context, however, revealed that the rationality of these decisions was contingent upon underlying organizational circumstances. A critical role had been played by the newly established Group Services function within the bank. Not only did they demand a more protracted period of package selection, they were instrumental in opting for supplier-led development instead of the in-house Systems Development department. Indeed, this decision helped to structure the remaining options on the package. The logic of linking development and maintenance was probably a function of intra-organizational demarcations; with Systems Development distanced, and with links already established with CPM, the normal practice of in-house maintenance might not have seemed prudent. Conversely, though CPM's role presented a precedent in development work, the package was not a critical system for the bank and did not carry the same risk as if the on-line systems had been involved.

At one level, then, this case provided a clear instance of black-boxing. The existing software at Premier was old and heavily modified from an original charge accounting system, and unsuited to card processing. INDEX was intended to start the new venture off on the right foot. It provided a system for managing a card operation and handling transactions. Moreover, it was client-based rather than account-based and enabled Premier to credit rate individual clients; no matter how many different types of credit a client had, these could be integrated and compared and an overall credit line allocated.

But while the functional and economic advantages of INDEX were clear, these had to be worked through organizational politics. The emerging relationship between Premier and its parent organization centred on the role of the newly created Group Services, and the degree of control it exerted over subsidiaries. This greatly complicated the process of package selection. Although Premier managers had indicated a preference for INDEX, Group Services insisted on a full evaluation which, after nine months, confirmed the choice of INDEX! There was also the question of the centrality of Systems Development at the bank, and the amount of influence it would exert over development work in subsidiary companies. This led to the decision to contract out the customizing and maintenance. As we saw, this was risky in both technical and political terms. There was the possibility that CPM might botch the job, and Group Services ran a further risk in their attempt to break Systems Development's monopoly on conversion and maintenance work. In the early stages, these factors caused much nervousness at Group Services.

PROVISION BY MARKETS AND HIERARCHIES

This account of black-boxing and the make–buy decision raises important questions about managing expertise. The view that patterns of expertise deployment are largely a product of an economic imperative to minimize transaction costs contrasts sharply with our analysis, which focused on the strategic claims made by particular groups within a managerial division of knowledge. Our case findings have tended to highlight constraints on the external supply of expertise and technology. Dependency and localized knowledge, we saw, placed limits on the role which external suppliers could play. The extensive use of suppliers for lower level tasks and collaborative work has to be set alongside the tendency for higher-level knowledge and control functions to be monopolized by in-house IS functions.

One important finding involved the diversity of motives which lay behind the use of external suppliers. Although external supply tended to be presented as a matter of expediency rather than policy, the factors which made it expedient were often a reflection of organizational concerns not economic pressures. This is not to say that economic factors were of no consequence. But these factors were often the last considerations in a lengthy process of decision-making. Economizing on time, not cost, was the key concern in many instances; and in several cases the use of an external supplier was strongly motivated by internal politics.

In contrast to Williamson's (1985) analysis of the use of expertise, which counterposes market against hierarchy in the allocation of transaction costs, our case materials highlight collaborative relationships in the evolution of institutional forms. The cases show that the internal and external supply of expertise are by no means mutually exclusive. Indeed, over time, the emergence of internal and external IT sectors reflect a symbiosis rather than substitution.

The occupational linkages noted in our cases play a particularly important role. They provide a basis for often informal mechanisms of co-ordination and control needed to manage joint development work and other forms of collaboration. They bridge the gap between the market and institutional forms of control. And, in the context of knowledge-based services, these networks provide a means for conveying indirect measures of a product, firm, or expert through, for example, reputation.

Information Markets and Organizational Power

Here we can pull together strands of argument from earlier chapters on the nature of the financial services sector and the internal power of IS functions. These types of decision take place in a wider sectoral and industrial setting which some suggest has important consequences for the organizational power of IS. In the information technology context, some have argued that the internal IT environment has changed from one in which a centralized IS department provided a full range of services, to the notion of an 'information economy' within a business. In the model developed by Boynton and Zmud (1987: 61), for example:

the information economy approximates a free market system in which organizational subunits can satisfy their needs for IT services by acquiring resources from a variety of sources, including the organization's IS function, external suppliers or through their own actions. Any market advantage held by the IS function in this information economy depends on technical and/or managerial expertise and an established line of information products or services. However, the advantage held by the IS function lessens as other subunits become skilled in newer technologies, such as microcomputers, external databases, electronic mail, office systems, decision support systems and CAD/CAM workstations. Business professionals are increasingly able to apply IT resources and provide the necessary technical support, Additionally, external suppliers of IT resources may be more available to the consumer and better able to recognize and respond to the consumer's need than the IS function.

Drawing on Williamson, the suggested trend is towards market transactions rather than internal organizational relations or hierarchies. Child (1987) in particular has noted that the move to external contracting has been encouraged by turbulent market and technology conditions typified by innovation and inefficiency risks. While stressing that technology does not determine organization, Child argues the use of IT does provide an improved basis for co-ordinating market or quasi-market transactions with external parties.

Behind this suggested rise of market relations in the supply of software lie competitive and technical changes in the IT sector itself. The growth of an independent software industry, and the enormous diversification of applications and techniques, have created a demand for specialist skills which large business organizations—the traditional site of programming effort —have been unable to meet. The slack has been taken up by independent software houses and consultancies, and the wider options available to business users have had knock-on effects inside firms. These give rise to make–buy considerations in the availability of computing expertise. The alternative sources for software supply enhance the profile of users in the development process relative to IS departments, which see their monopoly powers eroded.

That said, the question of a market element as a cause of change has been limited in practice. Friedman (1989: 229), for instance, noted that where users go outside firms for software products, in very few cases is this without the IS department ratifying the purchase or having the final say. Similarly, Child (1987) pointed out that subcontracting will always be limited by the company-specific balance of expertise and control, especially in terms of the local knowledge required for successful implementation. The sensitivity of the organization's operational efficiency to subcontracted elements is an important strategic consideration.

However, even this does not fully explain the nature of relations with suppliers. The idea that alternative sources of supply necessarily erode the power of internal systems departments is a static, zero-sum conception. It does not allow for the development of information technologies that enhance the influence of both IS functions and users, and it obscures the socially constructed and reciprocal relationships involved.

In the cases described above we saw IS departments involved in decisions to buy in skills and taking on the role of contractor. Clydesdale provided perhaps the clearest illustration of the deficiencies of a model of rational market power. There the IS department retained its patronage over systems development, and the emphasis was on trust as a means of overcoming considerable uncertainties in the new system. In the Premier Financial Services case transactions were closer to a market model. But the purchase and conversion of a package became part of a complex tussle between a newly-fledged corporate group and the influential Systems Development department. The resort to an external supplier did reduce the power of systems management in relation to a coalition of Operations and Group management. But we would have to question the outcome of any power struggle over a less routine, more strategic system.

These fundamental changes appear to be driven by changes in the nature of computing expertise and the distributed applications systems that that expertise is creating, rather than being market-led. Indeed, the idea of a rational market in systems supply is problematic in so far as the commodification of information systems produces nothing like a simple commodity. Even in cases like Premier and VISA, where the bought-in package was for routine data processing and did not require extensive customizing, conversion to run on the internal systems took several months of development work. The skills needed to oversee such a process inevitably created proprietary techniques and dependencies which favoured internal solutions. Thus market relations is too bland a metaphor. Nor is the choice for users of being able to go elsewhere for software much of a reality. The actors involved are not just alternative sources of supply, they form part of a knowledge community through which links of patronage extend. IS departments are able to mediate the organization and external occupational communities, and they enhance their network power inside their own organizations. Hence there is a dynamic relation between internal and external contracting, and if anything external markets in the supply of systems extend the influence of internal IS functions in their role as gatekeeper *vis à vis* the occupational community.

Knowledge and Control

The role of occupational knowledges and inter-sectoral linkages, then, have important implications in mediating the free play of economic forces. Further inferences can be drawn from what we described in Chapter 4 as the 'social constitution of the sector'. One is that polarization of the transactions between market and hierarchy is less likely than the emergence of what Butler and Carney (1983) term 'managed markets'. In these, certain hierarchical mechanisms are prevalent and serve to augment the operation of market forces. Such mechanisms include the development of procedures and standardized solutions, and mutual adjustment provided by meetings and negotiations. Given the importance of social and occupational linkages, managed markets are characterized by trust relationships and an ethos of partnership rather than *caveat emptor*.

Another inference concerns the basis of Williamson's distinction between market and hierarchy. These alternative forms of governance structure are predicated on the operation of a single economic imperative: the pursuit of transaction cost efficiency. This is open to a number of questions. For example, we may doubt that that economic pressures necessarily create governance structures that minimize transaction costs. There is also the presumed fallacy that, as one mode of governing transaction is found wanting, another is always ready to solve the problem.

The idea that wider forms of industrial organization, not just polar types of efficiency and power, are stable and represent distinctive areas has been widely suggested (Butler and Carney 1983). And the co-existence of different modes of control or governance poses an important challenge for Williamson, which at one point he does recognize. He briefly introduces an entirely new category of relationship, namely relational contracting. This 'develops for transactions of a recurring and non-standardized kind' (1985: 73). Relational contracting requires an alternative control structure, bilateral governance, in which the autonomy of both parties is maintained but 'removed from the market and organized within the firm subject to an authority relation'. Williamson takes the analysis no further, remarking that 'bilateral structures have only recently received the attention they deserve, and their operation is least well understood' (1985: 76). However, it is clear that the alternative category resembles the type of managed markets and the forms of joint development we have been exploring.

Williamson's account remains hinged on a direct relationship between the underlying presumed imperative and the resulting mode of governance or control. This emphasis on the mutual exclusivity of institutional forms contrasts with our findings of the blurring of institutional demarcations, and different institutional forms co-existing and overlapping. As we saw, this was reflected in collaborative development in the supply of IT—and conversely in the internalization of market relations within hierarchies. The latter we saw in the Mutual Life case where a specialist group became internal consultants, organized on a boutique basis, and offering services to business users. A lack of established links with users, however, meant this group tended to become marginalized, which suggested limits on the extent to which markets can be internalized.

In accounting for these observations two issues stand out. The first is the distinction touched on earlier between knowledge and information. Williamson views the control of transactions as depending on the most efficient fit between the informational needs of the transaction, and the information-processing features of different institutional forms. In contrast, our cases highlight the role of shared occupational knowledge in facilitating flows of information. To the extent that such knowledge is embedded in the trust-inducing context of an occupational group, it helps to explain the way in which transactions may span institutional forms. It also suggests that economic pressures need to be understood in terms of the evolving linkages between user and supply sectors, and the formation of occupational networks between them. These make possible the operation of economic pressures and encourage complementarity and co-operation rather than substitution between sectors.

The second point concerns the relationship between institutional forms and knowledge. Williamson argues that knowledge is harnessed by institutional forms in the pursuit of transaction cost efficiency. In contrast, we have suggested (in Chapter 12) that different groups articulate their knowledge possessions in relation to technology and organization, and seek to harness them to their own interests. The patterns of internal and external supply in our case studies, though influenced by economic and political factors, were also strongly influenced by the knowledges available to internal and external suppliers. External supply was most likely in situations of novel applications of new business development where there were few pre-existing knowledges or competencies in the implementing organization. Similarly, collaborative development, and the forms of collaboration adopted, reflected the distribution of knowledge between players, between the industry and organizational knowledge of the in-house function, and the generic knowledge of the supplier.

Nor are these constraints simply a matter of what Williamson terms, asset-specific investments. This notion would suggest that determination of the form of control for a particular set of skills or knowledges is separate from the emergence of such skills or knowledge. In the innovation projects we studied, questions of knowledge were intimately linked with questions of control—supporting Commons's (1970) view that transactions involve not only a material exchange but also a transfer of control. The so-called package paradox related less to the relative efficiency of in-house customizing versus enhancements from an external supplier, than to the problem of being dependent on a supplier for the future development of a system.

The relationship between knowledge and control is particularly strong in the context of innovation. Williamson himself saw transaction efficiency being achieved by a series of organizational innovations which secure more efficient means of controlling transactions. But innovation processes are not only difficult to control, but are instances where efficiency and competitiveness can only be determined by those whose knowledge shapes the innovation. In determining the future boundaries of business, innovators are also determining the knowledges around which it will be based—and excluding other skills or knowledges from positions of centrality. To put this into Williamson's terms, the asset-specificity of different skills or knowledges is not inherent in the transaction itself, but is defined by the emerging shape and structure of the organization. And that, as we have noted earlier, is a product of the unfolding competition between different knowledges and expressed through the emergence of strategy and the implementation of innovation.

This is not to say that economic pressures have no influence on the management of expertise. But it is important to differentiate between forms of expertise which are intertwined with and forms which are detached from emergent structures of control. The influence of economic pressures seems to be greatest for the latter, with considerations of efficiency emerging strongly beyond the point of indifference, where the locus of control of a particular task or function is seen as of no great consequence to the organization. In the former case, however, the influence of economic factors operates indirectly and is worked through the politics and the strategic evolution of the organization. The pursuit of a particular notion of economic efficiency may involve, as Willman (1983) notes, the strategic use of power in order to shift the locus of control.

As the case studies show, however, the relationship between expertise and control is fluid and influenced by perceptions of the substitutability (Hickson *et al.* 1971) of particular groups. While the locus of control for certain tasks may be influenced by the competition between different forms of expertise, this process is by no means insulated from considerations of transactional efficiency. The knowledge claims of expert groups must meet not only the *internal test* of the competing claims of other occupational and managerial groups, but also an *external test* of their relative efficiency, as defined by the claims of technology suppliers and consultants.

The impact of that external test is likely to be influenced by a group's success in claiming strategic knowledge. In this connection it seems highly significant that in the majority of our cases decisions on the internal or external supply of technology and expertise were taken within the IS function, with little or no involvement of senior management. This reflected the centrality and the monopoly of IT knowledge that IS functions enjoyed. On the other hand, instances where make–buy decisions were outside IS control were in precisely those organizations which, for reasons of strategic and structural change, had begun to challenge IS claims to strategic knowledge.

14

Conclusions

This study has examined the innovation process through a focus on the management of IS expertise. Expertise is both an important focus of theoretical debate and a practical problem which has become more pressing as organizational and technological change have called into question traditional management models. Perhaps ironically, organizations respond to this dynamism, and its attendant uncertainties, by employing new kinds of expertise and new means of deploying skilled resources. These range from attempts to integrate distributions of knowledge to more systematic efforts to redefine the underlying structures of knowledge around which products and development processes are based.

Such initiatives are highly visible in the IT field. In financial services new knowledge distributions have, for example, involved the reconceptualization of branch staff as having a sales as well as a service role, while more fundamental divisions of knowledge have seen back-office automation shifted to the support of managerial tasks and the delivery of services. Changing perceptions of the problem of applying IT—from first hardware and then software supply, towards the relationship between systems development and the user—have had profound implications for the nature of systems expertise itself. Managerial concerns for the expertise problem increasingly reflect measures such as the development of elaborate integration mechanisms, the creation of 'hybrid specialists' and joint development teams, and the external acquisition of expertise from consultants and software houses.

The Study of Expertise

Expertise itself raises questions about the relationship between knowledge and knowledge claims, and the social structures and processes by which knowledge is produced, communicated, and validated. Assumptions about that relationship are built into many theories of technological and industrial change. Some assume a one-way relationship, in that scientific and technological knowledge is seen as acting directly on social structure. These include 'linear' models of innovation, in which technologies emerge from initial research and development and diffuse as stable technological fixes; and also 'impact' models which see technologies having determinate effects on social relationships like employment levels, tasks, and jobs (Rothwell 1986).

There has been an extensive critique of the technological determinism of such approaches (Williams and Edge 1992). For example, the linear model of innovation neglects the complex and uncertain processes of interaction in innovation, and downplays the importance of user knowledge. As our study indicated, the IS functions of user firms are important innovators and producers of knowledge as well as the IT supply sector. And end-users, with their intimate knowledge of organizational activities, can make a vital contribution to applications solutions. Thus it is hard to maintain a rigid dichotomy between the initial production of knowledge and the context of its implementation and use (J. Fleck 1988). The focus on expertise also makes an important contribution to debates around the 'social shaping' or 'social construction' of technology (Callon 1980). Some social constructionist accounts of the microprocesses of technological change have, arguably, neglected the influence of broader institutions that help to determine the composition of the groups of actors involved. The expertise focus, by addressing the particular kinds of knowledge which groups mobilize in the innovation process, and the role of occupational and inter-firm linkages in the transfer and validation of knowledge, was better placed to integrate local action within its broader context.

We sought a rounded view of expertise, encompassing the content and relational aspects of knowledge. This meant the mutuality of substantive competencies and the social processes of attribution and selection was stressed. Rather than treating IS expertise as a well-bounded professional domain, the interaction between technical content and social context and also the fluidity and fragmentation of expertise, were emphasized. This approach underlined the need to encompass not only professional groupings but the entire range of ways in which knowledge is appropriated in social settings. Occupational and professional structures are important, but knowledge is also absorbed into organizational rules and structures, and is commodified into products and hardware (Abbott 1988). It remains a distinctive feature of IS knowledge that there are relatively few barriers to knowledge shifting between these modes. Unlike more traditional professional groups, IT workers do not have strong professional organizations, nor are their responsibilities institutionalized in any legal or regulatory framework. Also, the rate of change in the IT industry has led to continuous changes in skills and knowledge. Old skills, like coding and assembler programming, have been assimilated by the core technology and new skills have been created by the expanding frontier of applications. Nor are IS skills static at the organizational level; at the margins expertise is shaped by the acquisition of business knowledge from users, by the codification of their existing knowledge base in the form of computing standards and methodologies, and by the adoption of commodified knowledge.

The Financial Services Sector

The financial services sector provided an outstanding opportunity to explore expertise as a critical moment in industrial change. Technological innovation, as well as deregulation and market uncertainty, combined to create expectations of radical transformation. The sector led the way in IT investments—opening up visions of revolutionary change in methods of operation and in the relationship between the organization and its customers. These technological scenarios echoed the broader dynamism in products and markets stimulated by government policies of restructuring legislative barriers.

Despite some predictions, however, a decade of change seems to have done little to erase the structural characteristics of the sector. The commanding heights of financial services continued to be occupied by the same massive banks and insurance companies, and there was a high degree of continuity in product markets and institutional arrangements. Deregulation, for example, brought no major realignments in the patterns of products and services offered by the largest financial institutions. Rather, a cumulative pattern saw new products added to existing portfolios. Any large-scale strategic changes were typically undertaken through mergers or strategic alliances rather than restructuring of core businesses. Thus building societies began to offer current accounts, but they did so in a limited way, not attempting to develop the full range of banking services. Their predominant orientation towards mortgage and savings products remained intact. Similarly, most insurance companies persisted with their traditional role but added new products and sought vertical integration through alliances.

These continuities highlight persistent divisions of expertise which reflected the condensation of occupational networks and core skills. Such skill structures have been portrayed as a barrier to radical change (Abernathy and Clark 1985). But in financial services, the traditional hegemony of banking and actuarial occupations tended rather to influence the interpretation and implementation of change. True, there were pressures for new skills. Marketing skills were brought in, in response to senior management concerns that market factors should play a greater role in decision-making. And more specialized forms of expertise were acquired to meet the needs of expanding IT infrastructures and delivery systems. But it is no easy task to change the skill structures of decades or even centuries. Dominant, core skills are institutionally embedded and cannot be eliminated by regulatory or market change.

This pattern of continuity and change, then, represented the sectoral context of our study. Expansive growth and the speeding-up of product life cycles had stimulated technological innovation and seemed to demand the multi-functional integration of roles in product development and delivery. Deregulation and market dynamism called existing institutional orientations and management models into question. But growth tended to be managed through diversification or organically rather than by restructuring.

STRATEGY AND THE SECTORAL CONTEXT

Much recent research highlights 'deviations' from formalized models of strategic decision-making and rational models of strategy. Different lines of thinking have emerged here. One, based on notions of bounded rationality, analyses organizational behaviour in terms of sectional and limited kinds of rationality. Others see rationality as either cosmetic or non-existent, placing emphasis on political in-fighting as the determinant of organizational outcomes. We sought to carry forward the exploration of strategy through an account of how particular rationalities are related to the knowledges that groups articulate. Our case projects were selected on the grounds that they involved major commitments of resources and long-term implications for product markets. This gave rise to attempts to combine technical and marketing knowledges. However, it tended to be problematic to determine the nature of 'strategic IT' and precisely where initiatives were coming from. Nor was it helpful to see strategy as the preserve of top management. The rational and synoptic view of strategy we found bore little resemblance to reality. In our case organizations even 'strategic' projects were sometimes initiated by the IS function. Powerful user groups were also frequently identified as the initiators of change, though the strategic influence of users was often revealed to be more symbolic. At any rate, formal review at top management level tended to be confined to the financial aspects of projects.

Both the rational-synoptic approach and the critiques of this position unhelpfully counterpoise the rational and political aspects of organizational life. Instead rationality has to be laboriously constructed, drawing on resources of knowledge and position, rather than being a generalized potential or something eroded by political constraints. This view challenges any idea of the centralization of technical knowledge as the sole rational strategy for IT. An emphasis on the construction of rationality leads to alternative questions about the groups which are likely to get engaged in strategic projects and the incentives that motivate them.

While corporate strategy is bound up with the organization's responses to its external environment, our analysis did not stop at organizational boundaries. The environment and its attendant uncertainty do not have a direct impact on decision-making; they have strategic consequences in so far as they create problems and opportunities for groups in the organization. Thus the extent to which technological or market turbulence becomes internalized and acted on itself depends on the distribution of knowledge and the aspirations and self-images of particular groups. Environmental conditions which create a high level of uncertainty for one group or organization may actually be rather routine and unproblematic for another.

Such an approach challenges assumptions about the importance of market-driven strategies. Several of our case projects were indeed market-driven in the sense that systems managers had an acute awareness of positioning their new product in a structured market—to seek a new niche, or avoid head-on competition with a powerful rival. However, some of our findings were counter-intuitive, particularly in cases where expected strategic behaviour did not materialize. Thus Royline involved a high technology, market-oriented system which represented an important addition to the Royal Bank's product portfolio. But senior managers in the bank eschewed any 'strategic language', preferring to develop Royline within established parameters of management. At Clydesdale the development of Telebank also represented a strategic addition to the portfolio. But its immediate significance was as much to do with demonstrating the competence of the IS function to the Bank's parent company as with resolving market uncertainty.

In applying this view to the firm's relationship with the sector, we emphasized the social construction of knowledge. Rather than prioritize either the internal circumstances of the firm or dominant recipes at the level of the sector, we pointed up the interaction between sectoral and organizational factors. Dominant recipes were gaining currency at a broader level—involving precepts about new services, technologies, and organizational practices—but precisely how these were taken up in an organization reflected the history of its own systems and market situation. Knowledge of the sector was appropriated by particular groups in the process of developing projects and promoting their own positions, and its significance depended on how sectoral knowledge was selectively built into (or developed out of) problems defined by particular groups.

Negotiating the Sector

In Chapter 4 we ventured beyond dualistic conceptions of organization and environment—conceived in terms of 'subjective' internal and 'objective' external conditions, or in terms of the metaphor of the 'focal' organization. Influential research in this area has employed the 'firm-in-sector' approach (e.g. Whipp and Clark 1986; C. Smith, Child, and Rowlinson 1990) and has emphasized the emergence of sector-level recipes. However, this is not well placed to examine the fluidity of sectoral models because research was based on studies of single firms—typically very large firms which were one of a handful of dominant national exemplars in each sector. In contrast, as Clark and Staunton (1989) have stressed, emphasis needs to shift to expertise and knowledge as major factors in explaining technological change. This focus serves to carry forward the firm-in-sector perspective 'on to and into the societal filière of institutions and the consequences of those social bases for industrial innovation. The institutional filière deserves much more attention' (1989: 215). In this sense, as we discovered, sectoral boundaries can be hard to define, and the sector needs to be explored before its outlines can be established. It is important that effects at the level of the sector, such as recipes for strategy and firm interrelations, are extensively defined. Our own research in an array of firms across financial services explored how firms 'negotiate' the sector—how they position themselves and their products in the market, and how the collective outcomes of these actions shape the sector itself.

The idea of negotiation encompasses differential negotiability—features which can be negotiated by actors and those which are not immediately open to influence. In this sense, to speak of negotiating the sector is to exploit the multiple meanings of the term—of groups and organizations skilfully navigating an uncertain environment through the construction of knowledge about that environment; of the applications of power in shaping the environment; and of this happening via the interplay of knowledges constructed by groups of competing experts. Sectoral knowledge was mediated through rival forms of expertise, and continually negotiated and renegotiated amongst the shifting alliances of expert groups competing for status and resources. The relationship between sector (the 'objective' external environment) and firm (its competing internal constituents) was not one-way; it reflected the ability of firms to shape their sectoral environment, particularly where they may have direct effect. Such localized zones of influence merged with broader networks of social and economic interaction which confronted the individual firm as a seemingly fixed landscape around which it must negotiate.

Selective local construction of the sector helps to explain commonalities and differences between firms. On the one hand, prescriptions and models for organizational development generated broad concepts of industrial activity. Thus in financial services there were widespread perceptions of the need for greater market orientation involving customer-centred operations and more elaborate marketing strategies to utilize opportunities for cross-selling. Where these strategies combined with available technologies, and firms and professional groups within sub-sectors had communicated these general solutions, there existed strong cross-sectoral patterns of innovation. Thus we found the development of integrated customer databases in banks, credit-card companies, and insurance companies alike. Similarly, electronic banking was a marked feature of our banking cases, where enthusiastic uptake of some remote banking services by the public had led to certain services becoming necessary components of retail banking.

Over time some of our case firms also exhibited an ability to shift their position within the sector. For example, Bank of Scotland and the Royal Bank expanded their English customer base and Mutual Life moved into personal pensions. This formed a basis for strategy, and the capacity to be proactive, which was an invitation to expert groups to attempt to shape dominant understandings. Their success was measured by whether they were able to demonstrate competence, or even indispensability, in handling the problems and uncertainties attendant on a new sectoral position (Miles and Snow 1978). Indeed, one reason why the innovations we have analysed were strategic is that they afforded expert groups like IS functions the opportunity to develop knowledge claims and shape organizational structures of expertise, while shifting the organization's sectoral location or orientation.

Structures of Expertise

On the other hand, the strategic responses of case firms were not uniform. The context of uncertainty and persistent institutional divisions prevented the emergence of a dominant strategic recipe across the sector. Within the general pattern, firms developed specialized strategies in the light of their own sectoral location. For example, Scottish banks were early converts to the telebanking route in order to expand into the English market without the expense of developing a chain of local branches. But there were differences between, say, Bank of Scotland, which sought to establish an identity as being technologically advanced, and other banks which were happy to play a waiting game and establish the feasibility of new services before committing themselves to particular innovations. Both differed from the heavily resourced Royal Bank, which pursued the technical solution within a strategy of branch-based expansion. These differences reflected the broader configurations of expertise in organizations and the particular problems which the IS function had set for the organization. The apparent uniformity of IT applications between organizations only depended on the generic character of these technologies; the actual systems differed significantly in their technical details and functions, because of local contingencies and traditions.

This brings us to the forms of expertise and relationships between them that were examined in Chapter 5. At the organizational level, the scope of IS work was defined by 'structures of expertise' which mediated and internalized sectoral conditions. They provided an important resource for expert groups in negotiating the sector and developing strategic innovations. The position of IS work reflected tensions between tendencies to compartmentalize specialist expertise and powerful incentives to exploit technological opportunities. Such tensions were worked out not through the objective pull of task requirements but through the social construction of occupational and functional knowledge claims. Case-study evidence on the success of IS expertise, and its level of representation in management, pointed to the existence of 'player managers' within the function, representation at corporate level, and the projection of a lingua franca for the organization as a whole.

Our innovation projects contained a number that involved high degrees of technological and market uncertainty. This tended to moderate superordinate control by mainstream forms of expertise in the banking, actuarial, and accounting professions. Thus the competence of IS functions in the development process in some cases provided the necessary 'problem space' for the construction of strategic claims. None the less, even where IS expertise achieved a strategic orbit, it continued to be constrained by, and often accommodated within, other specialisms. The localized, project-based nature of IT developments constrained the ability of IS to construct strategic claims; and despite much speculation about the transformational potential of IT (e.g. Child 1987), implementation processes were often determined by existing structures of expertise. That organization structure limits the exploitation of technological knowledge is hardly a novel finding (McLoughlin 1990). But it does raise important questions about the broader relationship between the IS function and the organization.

Strategic Rationality

The innovation process itself, as we point out in Chapter 6, provides opportunities to negotiate and renegotiate the conception of the sector and the relationships between groups in the organization. We suggested that the rationalities used to justify an innovation did not simply reflect the technical features of the project, but were shaped by existing expertise structures. In some cases, projects conformed within established routines of different groups; in other cases problems were highlighted, calling into question the competence and jurisdiction of particular groups of experts. Resolving the latter often meant the articulation of a new 'strategic rationale'. Projects varied in the extent to which such rationales were developed, even for ostensibly very similar kinds of innovation.

The in-house IS function may use its growing influence and control of knowledge to develop a strategic rationale for its activities. Our cases showed some IS functions building 'strategy' into their practices and allying their specialist expertise with claims to be strategic. The structural links between IS staff and groups such as business analysts, for example, formed the basis of powerful new divisional structures, influential in the management of change. As a type of problem-solving rationality, such strategic alliances provided a framework for managing projects outside the usual routines. They also provided a means of defending IS expert control against narrow financial criteria.

IS functions in several of our case firms were engaged in constructing a strategic rationale from the bottom-up. The promotion of projects meant developing a rationality of means and ends, while much depended on the broader structure of expertise of which IS was a part. However, the ability to construct a strategic rationale depended on the political position of the IS function itself, the degree of organizational knowledge it possessed, and the nature of the project—particularly the extent to which design or implementation were dependent on other groups. For example, while formal planning failed to sustain a strategic project at Home and Auto, the powerfully-placed Management Services Division at Bank of Scotland was able to design and implement a large-scale IT project. CABINET may have had its setbacks and redefinitions, but it was developed within a strategic calculus. This type of reference to a strategic rationale might be viewed as merely ideological or rhetorical. But to do so would reflect a false distinction between the functional needs of a business and the interests of groups. Certainly the CABINET project enhanced the stature of MSD within the bank and in no way represented a functional response to organizational needs. The market context and practical implications of CABINET—its long-term, organization-wide character—were integral to the project, and implementation itself was necessarily a skilled achievement and a show of competence supporting MSD's wider knowledge claims.

The development of a clear strategic rationale towards IT may be particularly important for the IS function in negotiating lengthy and uncertain system developments. Redefinition of a project's goals between the early design and subsequent implementation was a frequent feature of large-scale and innovative projects. And such a rationale was not merely a rhetorical device; it signalled the early control of symbolic processes attached to systems development, so that when goals were redefined the same actors were potentially able to redefine the usefulness of their own specialist practices. In order to be able to resubstantiate claims of competence, actors needed to continue to deliver solutions perceived as successful by other key groups. In some of the cases studied, the IS function contributed to a redefinition of the strategic problems of the whole organization, thus renegotiating its position in the structure of expertise. The practical control exercised by the IS function provided a means of demonstrating competence and boosting knowledge claims. In these situations systems work continued to be typified by high levels of uncertainty, limiting the scope for any neat demarcation between strategic and operational issues. In short, an IT strategy could not be developed independently of the deployment of systems expertise; the development of strategy reflected the knowledge claims of the IS group, and was grounded in the uncertainty generated by innovations and the IS group's competence in handling uncertainty.

TECHNOLOGY AND EXPERTISE

The emphasis on expertise also allowed the deconstruction of technology, and the development of a more symmetrical account of 'technical' and 'social' dimensions. The techniques and practices deployed by specialist groups highlight the interaction between the knowledge embodied in technical artefacts and that in expert groups. Hence we attempt to resolve the counterposition of technology and organization; rather than see technological change as having an 'impact' on the organization, it is revealed as an integral social process. This also throws light on the broader development of IT artefacts and development methods. Our analysis highlighted the interaction between supplier offerings and user requirements in innovation.

Chapter 7 reviewed the history and state of the art in IT and its application in financial services. The chapter stressed the crucial role played by the financial service sector in the development of IT itself. From the outset the sector was one of the largest purchasers of IT products and services and played a key role in the generation of IT, including, in the early days, the construction of some of the first commercial computers. Today the IT supply industry has a virtual monopoly in the provision of hardware and universal software components such as operating systems and utilities (e.g. database systems) and is enlarging its role in the provision of applications software.

However, the finance sector also remains one of the largest employers of IS expertise. In our case firms, in-house IS functions retained a dominant role in IT acquisition; any resort to the market for the supply of hardware, software packages, and services was more than compensated by the extension and growing complexity of corporate systems. This has to be understood in the context of changes in the technology regime. As well as a general expansion in the scope and functionality of technology, there has been a shift in the focus of application from back-office transaction processing to systems that have implications for customer interfaces and management structures in the organization as a whole.

System development, and in particular software development, continue to present critical problems in the application of IT in the finance sector. Though the development issues have changed with the applications technology, there are continuing problems in managing the development process. As we pointed out in Chapter 8, almost all the firms we studied showed some level of use of structured design and development methodologies. However, in contrast to some predictions that these would be widely enforced as a means of routinizing software development, they had not been rigidly applied. Nor had Computer Aided Software Engineering (CASE) tools been widely adopted. This pointed up the importance of techniques as well as artefacts and process technologies in innovation. It was also related to pressing problems in making software development accountable to business needs, which had resulted in broadening forms of development expertise.

Implementation, as we saw in Chapter 9, is a crucial phase in development. It is a convoluted learning process, involving technical specialists and users in a struggle to get new systems to work and fulfil their strategic potential. Implementation creates uncertainties—around the technology, its development, and its outcomes. We saw that uncertainties, though endemic to implementation, were relative; their degree and form depended on the organizational distribution of knowledge. The existing internal knowledge base, the availability of different kinds of external expertise (i.e. together the structure of expertise), as well as the strategies of different groups, all bore on the extent to which uncertainties could be circumscribed.

Implementation is the process in which powerful generic knowledges (for example, of technical opportunities) are combined with local practical knowledge (for example, of the organization and its methods of operation). Successful implementation means that generic technological capabilities are adapted to meet the conditions and requirements of the user. Firm-specific knowledge becomes incorporated in IT systems—which in turn may become incorporated in future technological supply. Implementation is thus a key site of innovation (J. Fleck 1988).

The nature of the implementation process and its inherent difficulties vary according to the scope and novelty of projects and the contribution of different types of knowledge (in particular 'user' and 'technical' knowledges). Highly novel projects involve open-ended and uncertain implementation processes. In successive applications, user requirements and technical solutions will be better understood and may become stabilized around approaches that achieve wider currency; local contingent knowledge may be incorporated into artefacts made available by the supply sector. However, the trend towards stabilization is countered by the dynamism of technologies and business purposes. This was evident in our cases, where the strategic value of IT systems was reflected in the continued importance of customized solutions and the in-house IS function.

User-Led Innovation

Focusing on implementation highlights the contribution of the user to innovation. Users are highly differentiated and diverse, particularly in the context of comprehensive, integrated IT applications that support activities across the organization. Chapter 10 showed that users range from in-house IS staff, who fulfil this role as regards acquired hardware and software, to 'end-users', the clerical and administration staff who operate systems.

Our findings support Friedman's (1989) view that user relations are critical in the current phase of IT application. But the fashionable idea of the user gaining control over systems development as a result of these trends overlooks the complexity of the relationship between systems experts and users. The tensions inherent in IS–user relations were reflected in user involvement initiatives in which IS functions sought to elicit the 'commitment' of user groups, but were equally concerned to retain control of systems development. Here the systems function's interest in control was reinforced by problems in moving towards a user-driven approach; for example, in maintaining corporate IS standards and in managing multiple-user projects. As has been widely reported, users who became involved in IS projects found it difficult to acquire knowledge of technological opportunities in sufficient time to contribute to the formative stages of projects. Functional control was further sustained by occupational advantages. IS functions continued to act as the gatekeepers of external sources of knowledge; they largely determined the timing and scope of recourse to suppliers (which constrained competitive interaction between in-house and external supply). Indeed, as applications penetrated the organization more deeply, systems developers also became increasingly involved in user knowledge.

The mounting level of resources absorbed by IS functions, and the burgeoning expectations of users, created pressures for greater accountability and made the rationing of systems resources a painful task. It became increasingly important for the IS function to secure acceptance of systems across the organization and at senior levels of management. What we saw in our case studies was the development of mechanisms to cope with these proliferating and conflicting demands. The well-established 'mirror image' division of labour in IS functions—whereby systems teams would be permanently allocated to particular user groups and departments—was beginning to accommodate user involvement and structural changes in the IS function. These often involved higher levels of financial control, and sometimes the formation of quasi-market arrangements; the 'boutique' idea at Mutual Life was a specific example. Despite such mechanisms, however, tensions between systems expertise and the organization persisted in the broader pattern of IS–user relations.

To summarize, we saw the development of technology as a complex and protracted process in which expert groups, internally employed or brought in as consultants, mediated and absorbed uncertainties. Change processes and the systems that emerged were patterned by the structures of expertise; and continuous interplay between technical and non-technical knowledge was necessary for the success of systems. Technological knowledge (about information processing techniques) and organizational knowledge (about application areas and potential uses of IT) become embedded in IT systems as determinate structures of hardware and software. Thus new technological solutions represented an accumulation of earlier knowledges and patterns of expertise, with the management of expertise again lying at the heart of the analysis.

THE MANAGEMENT OF EXPERTISE

In Chapter 11 we began to examine the problems of managing complex and uncertain specialist labour with an account of the different dimensions of expertise. *Knowledge* is the technical and organizational competence which underpins the successful exercise of expertise; *power* differentially affects the ability of managerial and occupational groups to legitimate their reputation as knowledge-holders; and *tradeability* represents the opportunities to mobilize external sources through labour or product markets. Though their separate consideration may facilitate analysis, these facets of expertise are inseparable. Thus expertise comprises the knowledges possessed by different groups, coupled with their ability to claim special value for that knowledge, and based on their relative structural power in the organization and external markets.

We explored these issues, in Chapter 12, through a study of the structuring of expertise in a single organization, namely Bank of Scotland's Management Services Division. A complex pattern was revealed: technical specialists were strongly differentiated in terms of the tasks they undertook, the formal and informal collaborative networks through which they carried them out, and the experience they articulated (including universal, formal knowledge and local knowledge of the organization's business processes and technical systems). We contrasted the interpersonal and technical skills deployed by analysts, in their role of interfacing with diverse users, with the more focused division of labour of programmers, who exercised a narrower range of technical skills around particular systems. In addition, a distinctive group of 'technical interface workers' related to a range of other technical staff in maintaining the IT infrastructure.

Expertise could not be reduced to technical tasks alone, but included managerial strategies to deploy expert labour, as well as groups' own strategies for pursuing expert status. This was evident from the different presentation of skills by groups of technical workers, particularly in the relationship between expert and manager. Though IT experts deployed a range of technical and non-technical skills, they flagged particular skills to demonstrate their proximity to relevant managers (who reciprocally projected their 'membership of the tribe' and legitimacy to manage through selective emphasis on certain skilled roles).

Similarly, in the construction of expert careers, different expert segments optimized their labour-market positions by deploying particular combinations of skill. Though technical staff can assert their possession of universal, formal knowledge of the type sought on the external labour market, a much larger group was oriented towards the internal labour market. Their skill profiles were closely tied to the circumstances of the firm, including specialized technical skills, or combinations of technical skills and knowledge of in-house systems. IT experts also deployed non-technical skills, though the latter did not figure highly in their claims to be expert. This suggested that much IT expertise was already 'hybrid', and that the perceived lack of such skills may actually refer to something more complex, namely a low profile given to non-technical skills among certain expert groups. Hybrid skill configurations were best acquired through experience and may be highly firm-specific. This explained why formal technical training was less important than industrial experience. The internal labour market was far more significant than external markets for these workers.

This did not imply that economic forces could be ignored. Of course, there were limits to the effectiveness of financial controls; the integration of functions in IT systems made it especially difficult to distinguish their relative economic value. But the use of packaged systems, for example, represented a form of commodified expertise that had important implications for the status of in-house experts. Chapter 13 examined the use of packaged solutions as the means of implementing (or partially implementing) new IT systems. It showed why these attempts to purchase expertise as ready-made systems remained troublesome and partial, but still attractive to suppliers and users alike. And even where substitution between internal and external sourcing was not being considered, expertise was subject to forms of economic rationality. Indeed, the resort to a 'strategic' justification for IS itself represented an attempt to legitimate the scale of IT investment, while the use of financial controls suggested an attempt to apply an increasingly precise economic calculus to IS work.

Organizations and Markets

If technology posed problems of financial calculability, however, how much greater were the problems of costing and trading knowledge? While some kinds of knowledge can be commodified and exchanged as artefacts, much of the expertise involved in innovation projects was incorporated in groups. Such socially-embedded knowledge may more readily be tapped into through organizational forms rather than market relations. The absence of direct measures of performance when dealing with the application of new technologies means that indirect measures must be utilized, notably through the reputation of an individual or organization. Reputations are exercised through informal occupational and social networks. Reputation-building, and the successful exercise of skills and their communication via diffuse social networks, is one of the key processes by which specialist staff articulate their claims to be expert.

Nevertheless, more detailed analysis of the make–buy decision raised questions about the deployment of expertise. Why were some forms of expertise internally sourced and others obtained externally? Why was some expertise acquired as commodified hardware and some through a socially negotiated division of labour? The research approached these questions in terms of the 'black-boxing' of expertise—that is, the compartmentalization of elements of technical complexity in order to allow for simplification and standardization of the system of which they are a part. Black-boxing represents a strategy for segmenting complex technological fields and imposing a division of labour on the development and use of different parts of the system. Such strategies facilitate the convergence of a specialized supply sector and the attendant economic benefits from economics of scale (Rosenberg 1976). This has been largely achieved in the areas of hardware and basic operating systems, and utilities that tend to be independent of particular uses of IT, but is much less evident in relation to industry-specific applications—like the strategic innovations in our study. Here the importance of local knowledge of organizational practices has constrained the applicability of packaged software as black-boxed solutions, despite the cost advantages. Also, given the need to upgrade and revise packages over time, there were important issues of dependency and control. The acquisition of a package often implied a shift in the locus of control as well as an economic exchange.

While the usefulness of packages decreased with the specificity of a user's requirements, the differentiation of IT supply extended the possibilities of market provision. Almost the entire repertoire of IT skills was available as bought-in services or products—from development to maintenance, including customizing services and the supply of systems methodologies and consultancy. But the patterns of supplier deployment varied significantly. At first sight this variation seemed explicable in terms of contracting issues; where tasks were difficult to define or were highly dependent on local knowledge they tended to be carried out by the in-house function, suggesting that transaction costs were a key parameter. More detailed investigation of our case material, however, suggested that contracting problems were a second-order effect.

Economic forces still allowed a variety of solutions to the same problem; and this facilitated the exchange dynamics of IT supply by engendering trust and allowing the construction of reputation based on an informed understanding of competence. Thus the Clydesdale Telebank case was at variance with transaction cost logic, in so far as the development was managed in an informal way and reflected a shared occupational basis of trust and communication. This decision was underpinned by the creation of new sources of value that outweighed potential gains made by either side in 'cheating' on the relationship. The new gains far removed the transaction from any zero-sum conception of the exchange between the bank and the supplier. The operation of markets was thus enhanced not compromised by social networks.

Summarizing then, our study showed that the traditional dichotomy between buying systems and making them in-house is unhelpful; what emerged as a frequent *de facto* arrangement was a process of *joint development* between external suppliers and in-house systems developers, drawing on internal and external sources of expertise. This finding implicitly challenged Williamson's (1985: 73) use of the idea of 'relational transactions'. These he envisaged simply as an additional category of governance structure to markets and hierarchies. In fact, relational structures mediate internal and external sources, which are now dynamically related in implementing innovative technologies. Crucially, organizations and markets must be seen not as institutional alternatives but as differentially organized elements of the same social fabric. This view was underpinned by observations from our research on the dependence of economic exchange on social relations, the development of hybrid organizational arrangements for jointly managed innovation projects, and the transforming effects of innovation on markets and organizations alike.

Expert and Organization

Finally, we review the implications of this analysis for managerial policy and practice. Dominant traditions in industrial organization and management have emphasized the concentration of knowledge of production in managerial ranks and developed the fragmentation of work to new levels. In financial services, long-established institutional recipes produced a relatively stable set of relationships between management and employee, and critical knowledge was monopolized by a few long-established occupations in each sub-sector—the banking, actuarial, and accounting professions—whose evolution was actually coterminous with the emergence of industrial society. However, these expertise configurations, and the organizational paradigms that underpin them, were starting to break down. In particular, we saw the spread of specialist IS expertise and continued experimentation in the structural location of IS. The organizational role of IS, and the function's interaction with other powerful groups, was reflected in often contradictory trends. But change overall was evolutionary, and patterned by existing structures of expertise and the continuing dominance of core competencies. This observation supported a revision of the post-industrial thesis, namely that the expansion and increasing importance of technical forms of knowledge does not in itself equate with a new industrial order, or with the societal dominance of new knowledge-based occupations.

By the same token, managerial authority on its own proved an insufficient basis for directing innovation and deploying expertise. Management's ability to act was limited by the extent of its knowledge-base. Even in the development of strategy, the management prerogative was qualified by the claims and counter-claims of different expert groups. Management often found its strategies frustrated and curtailed by the obduracy of technology, a realm that remained opaque and unpredictable to those lacking IS expertise. In Mutual Life, for example, the problems of developing a technological reality from a strategic plan forced an early shift in emphasis to the 'softer' aspects of Customer Care. In Home and Auto the failure to implement a global information system ushered in a more pragmatic, phased methodology. Thus, while management had policy levers at their disposal, their ability to manipulate expertise proactively was constrained by the organizational allocation of tasks, power, and knowledge.

The starting-point for theorizing divisions of labour and knowledge has frequently been the 'impact' on shop- and office-floor workers. When technical knowledge is concentrated in small groups of experts the potential exists for increasing the fragmentation of work. However, when attention shifts from the point of production to the organization of expert groups, the interdependence of tasks, knowledge, and power may have quite contrary implications for managerial control. The continued segmentation of expert labour is a sign that reorganization and standardization may not be so readily applied to expert as to manual labour. While the fragmentation of manual work enhances control, specialization applied to expertise may have the effect of deepening knowledge and inhibiting simple forms of control.

This poses problems for the co-ordination of knowledge-based tasks and limits the division of labour. As a result, interdependent tasks and groups are typically arranged such that their respective knowledges overlap rather than follow a strictly sequential pattern. This is not to say that the division of technical labour is wholly fluid and 'organic'. Clearly, discrete specialisms and sequential co-ordination are still present in the organization of knowledge work. However, pressures on product life cycles and product quality tend to break down these divisions. We saw this in the lateral interactions between programmers, analysts, and users that were a typical feature of innovation in IT developments. There the role of IS experts reflected a shifting distribution of knowledge, which arose out of the linkages between the IS function and other organizational groups, as well as with external suppliers.

The distribution of knowledge represented a sometimes precarious solution to organizational dilemmas. This contrasts with expectations of the progressive routinization of IS labour (Kraft and Dubnoff 1986). Friedman (1989) has noted that the organizational role of IT, and the creation of new 'user interface roles', militate against such rationalization. We also pointed to the emergence of similar 'technical interface' roles linked to the increasingly elaborate IT infrastructure. This perspective highlighted the tension between specialization of functions, on the one hand, and, on the other, concerns about the maintenance of broad, overlapping roles and the exchange of information between groups. In this sense, there is no one solution to the problems of managing expertise; any 'solution' necessarily creates new problems or redistributes old ones. Effectiveness in the management of expertise has less to do with optimizing or minimizing the competence of a particular group than with developing the broader structures of expertise within which groups are located.

The social relations underpinning the division of knowledge applied equally to the managerial organization of systems work. As already noted, the boundary between managerial and systems work was diffuse. The pursuit of self-directed careers and the co-operative character of systems work meant that some managerial functions were internalized within specialist work groups. At the same time, IS managers frequently retained technical expertise and a technical orientation to their work. In this regard, IS management paralleled the 'player managers' of other technical functions, reinforcing the view that to some degree it takes an expert to manage an expert.

The relationship between expert and organization remains profoundly contradictory. The formation of specialized technical labour derives from organizations' efforts to exploit technology. But expert hierarchies seem never to be fully integrated into corporate objectives at the top end, nor subordinated to managerial control at the bottom. Nor are we arguing for the relative autonomy of technical workers from the institutions of capitalism. Strategies of accommodation and domination may be pursued, but remain subject to the dynamics of organizational and technological development which challenge attempts to make specialist fields transparent and accountable to those outside.

References

ABBOTT, A. (1988), *The System of Professions* (Chicago: University of Chicago Press).

ABERNATHY, W. J. (1978), *The Productivity Dilemma: Roadblock to Innovation in the Automobile Industry* (Baltimore: Johns Hopkins University Press).

—— and CLARK, K. B. (1985), 'Innovation: Mapping the winds of creative destruction', *Research Policy*, 14: 3–22.

ALVESSON, M. (1992), 'Organizations as rhetoric: Knowledge-intensive firms and the struggle with ambiguity', Conference on Knowledge Workers in Contemporary Society, Lancaster University, Sept.

ANDERSON, A. (1982), *Computing Skills* (Brighton: IMS).

ANSOFF, I. H., and STEWART, J. M. (1967), 'Strategies for a technology-based business', *Harvard Business Review*, 45 (Nov./Dec.): 71–83.

ARMSTRONG, P. (1984), 'Competition between the organizational professions and the evolution of management control strategies', in K. Thompson (ed.), *Work, Employment and Unemployment* (Milton Keynes: Open University Press).

—— (1985), 'Changing management control strategies: The role of competition between accountancy and other organisational professions', *Accounting, Organizations and Society*, 10: 129–48.

—— (1986), 'Management control strategies and inter-professional competition', in D. Knights and H. Willmott (eds.), *Managing the Labour Process* (Aldershot: Gower).

—— (1987), 'Engineers, management and trust', *Work, Employment and Society*, 1: 421–40.

—— (1989), 'Management, labour process and agency', *Work, Employment and Society*, 3: 307–22.

—— (1990), 'A comment on Murray and Knights', *Critical Perspectives on Accounting*, 1: 275–81.

—— (1991), 'Contradiction and social dynamics in the capitalist agency relationship', *Accounting, Organizations and Society*, 16: 1–25.

—— (1992), 'The engineering dimension and the management education movement', in G. L. Lee and S. Smith (eds.), *Engineers and Management: International Comparisons* (London: Routledge).

ASHWORTH, C., and GOODLAND, M. (1990), *SSADM: A Practical Approach* (New York: McGraw-Hill).

ATKINS, M. H., and GALLIERS, R. (1992), 'Human resource development for IS executives', Managing the information provider/managing the information user, SIGCPR Conference, Cincinnati.

BADARACCO, J. (1991), *The Knowledge Link: How Firms Compete through Strategic Alliances* (Boston: Harvard Business School).

BAIN, A. D. (1981), *The Economics of the Financial System* (Oxford: Martin Robertson).

BARNES, B. (1974), *Scientific Knowledge and Sociological Theory* (London: Routledge and Kegan Paul).

BARRAS, R. (1986), 'Towards a theory of innovation in services', *Research Policy*, 15: 161–73.

BARRAS, R. (1990), 'Interactive innovation in financial and business services: The vanguard of the service revolution', *Research Policy*, 19: 215–37.

——and SWANN, J. (1983), 'The adoption and impact of information technology in the UK insurance industry', London, Technical Change Centre.

BASALLA, G. (1988), *The Evolution of Technology* (Cambridge: Cambridge University Press).

BERBER, P. R. (1988), 'AI and expert systems applications in the dealing and trading environment', 4th International Expert Systems Conference, London, June.

BESSANT, J. (1985), 'The integration barrier: Problems in the implementation of advanced manufacturing technology', *Robotica*, 3: 97–103.

BIJKER, W. E., Hughes, T., and PINCH, T. (1987) (eds.), *The Social Construction of Technological Systems* (Cambridge, Mass.: MIT Press).

BILDERBEEK, R., and BUITELAAR, W. (1992), 'Bank computerization and organizational innovations: The long winding road to the bank of the future', *New Technology, Work and Employment*, 7: 54–60.

BLAKE, R. R., and MOUTON, J. S. (1984), 'Overcoming group warfare', *Harvard Business Review*, 62 (Nov./Dec.): 98–108.

BOEHM, B. (1981), *Software Engineering Economics* (New York: Prentice-Hall).

——(1986), 'A spiral model of development and enhancement', *ACM SIGSOFT Software Engineering Notes*, 11: 22–42.

BOYNTON, A. C., and ZMUD, R. W. (1987), 'Information technology planning in the 1990s: Directions for practice and research', *MIS Quarterly*, 11: 58–71.

BRADY, T. (1989), 'Users as producers: Software's silent majority', Sussex PICT Working Paper No. 3.

——(1991), *Software Purchasing Decisions* (Sutton: Computer Weekly Publications).

——TIERNEY, M., and WILLIAMS, R. (1992), 'The commodification of industry applications software', *Industrial and Corporate Change*, 1: 489–514.

BRAVERMAN, H. (1974), *Labor and Monopoly Capital* (New York: Monthly Review Press).

BRAY, P. (1992), 'The software time bomb', *Which Computer*, Sept.: 48–52.

BRIGHT, J. R. (1958), *Automation and Management* (Boston: Harvard Business School).

BRITISH COMPUTER SOCIETY (1990), 'Hybrids—A critical force in the application of information technology in the 1990s', London, BCS Task Force.

BROOKS, F. P., Jnr. (1982), *The Mythical Man-Month* (Reading, Mass.: Addison-Wesley).

BRUNSSON, N. (1982), 'The irrationality of action and action rationality', *Journal of Management Studies*, 19: 29–44.

BRYMAN, A. (1988), *Quantity and Quality in Social Research* (London: Routledge).

BUCKROYD, B., and CORNFORD, D. (1988), 'The IT skills crisis: The way ahead', Manchester, National Computer Centre.

BURNS, T., and STALKER, G. M. (1961), *The Management of Innovation* (London: Tavistock).

BUTLER, R., and CARNEY, M. G. (1983), 'Managing markets: Implications for the make–buy decision', *Journal of Management Studies*, 20: 213–31.

BYHAM, W. C., with COX, J. (1988), *Zap! The Lightning of Empowerment* (London: Business Books).

CALLON, M. (1980), 'The state and technical innovation: A case study of the electrical vehicle in France', *Research Policy*, 9: 358–76.

CAMPBELL, A., and WARNER, M. (1988), 'Organization for new forms of manufacturing operation', in R. Wild (ed.), *International Handbook of Production and Operations Management* (London: Cassels).

CAMPBELL, M. (1983), 'Career paths in a changing world', *Data Processing*, 25/9: 30–6.

CAMPBELL-KELLY, M. (1989), *ICL: A Business and Technical History* (Oxford: Clarendon Press).

CASE, A. (1985), 'Computer-aided software engineering (CASE): Technology for improving software development productivity', *Data Base*, Autumn: 35–43.

CHANDLER, A. D. (1962), *Strategy and Structure* (Cambridge, Mass.: MIT Press).

CHANNON, D. (1973), *The Strategy and Structure of British Enterprise* (London: Macmillan).

CHECKLAND, P. (1981), *Systems Thinking, Systems Practice* (Chichester: Wiley).

CHILD, J. (1972), 'Organisation structure, environment and performance: The role of strategic choice', *Sociology*, 6: 1–22.

—— (1987), 'Information technology, organization and the response to strategic challenges', *California Management Review*, 30: 33–49.

—— and SMITH, C. (1987), 'The context and process of organizational transformations—Cadbury Limited in its sector', *Journal of Management Studies*, 24: 565–93.

—— LOVERIDGE, R., HARVEY, J., and SPENCER, A. (1984), 'Microelectronics and the quality of employment in services', in P. Marstrand (ed.), *New Technology and the Future of Work and Skills* (London: Frances Pinter).

CLARK, P., and STAUNTON, N. (1989), *Innovation in Technology and Organization* (London: Routledge).

COCKBURN, C. (1983), *Brothers* (London: Pluto Press).

—— (1985), *Machinery of Dominance: Women, Men and Technical Know-How* (London: Pluto Press).

COMMONS, J. R. (1970), *The Economics of Collective Action* (Madison: University of Wisconsin Press).

CONNOR H., and PEARSON, R. (1986), *IT Manpower into the 1990s* (Brighton: IMS).

CONSTANTINE, L. (1993), 'Work organization: Paradigms for project management and organization', *Communications of the ACM*, 36: 34–43.

COOMBS, R. (1992), 'Charles Read Memorial Lecture', London, 20 May.

COUGER, J. D., and ZAWACKI, R. A. (1980), *Motivating and Managing Computer Peresonnel* (New York: Wiley).

CROMPTON, R., and JONES, G. (1988), 'Researching white-collar organizations: Why sociologists should not stop doing case studies', in A. Bryman (ed.), *Doing Research in Organizations* (London: Routledge).

CYERT, R. M., and MARCH, J. G. (1963), *A Behavioral Theory of the Firm* (Englewood Cliffs, NJ.: Prentice-Hall).

DAVIS, W. (1984), *The Corporate Infighter's Handbook: Winning the Office War* (London: Arrow Books).

DEAN, J. W. (1987), 'Building the future: The justification process for new technology', in J. M. Pennings and A. Buitendam (eds.), *New Technology as Organizational Innovation* (Cambridge, Mass.: Ballinger).

DENNIS, A., BURNS, R., and GALLUPE, R. (1987), 'Phased design: A mixed methodology for application system development', *Data Base*, Summer: 31–7.

DICKSON, D. (1974), *Alternative Technology and the Politics of Technical Change* (London: Fontana).

DIJKSTRA, E. (1968), 'Go To statement considered harmful', *Communications of the ACM*, 11: 147–8.

DRAPER, P., SMITH, I., STEWART, W., and HOOD, N. (1988), *The Scottish Financial Sector*. Edinburgh: Edinburgh University Press.

EARL, M. J. (1989), *Management Strategies for Information Technology* (London: Prentice-Hall).

EDGE, D. (1987), 'The social shaping of technology', Edinburgh PICT Working Paper No. 1, Edinburgh University.

EHN, P., and SANDBERG, A. (1979), 'Systems development: Critique of ideology and the division of labor in the computer field', in A. Sandberg (ed.), *Computers Dividing Man and Work* (Stockholm: Arbetslivcentrum).

FEENY, D., and KNOTT, P. (1988), 'IT and marketing in the UK life insurance industry', Oxford, Oxford Institute of Information Management, Templeton College.

—— EARL, M., and EDWARDS, B. (1989), 'IS arrangements to suit complex organizations: An effective IS structure', Research and Discussion Paper 89/4, Oxford, Oxford Institute of Information Management, Templeton College. .

FERNER, A. (1990), 'The changing influence of the personnel function: Privatization and organizational politics in electricity generation', *Human Resource Management Journal*, 1: 12–30.

FICHMAN, R. G., and KEMERER, C. F. (1993), 'Adoption of Software engineering process innovations: The case of object orientation', *Sloan Management Review*, 34: 7–22.

FISCHER, F. (1990), *Technocracy and the Politics of Expertise* (London: Sage).

FISHER, F., MANCKE, R., and MCKIE J. (1983), *IBM and the US Data Processing Industry: An Economic History* (New York: Praeger).

FLECK, J. (1984), 'The introduction of the industrial robot in Britain', *Robotica*, 2: 169–75.

—— (1988), 'Innofusion or diffusation? The nature of technological development in robotics', Edinburgh PICT Working Paper No. 4, Edinburgh University. Revised version of paper for workshop on Automisation programmable: Conditions d'usage du travail, Paris, Apr. 1987.

—— (1993), 'Configurations: Crystallizing contingency', *International Journal on Human Factors in Manufacturing*, 3: 15–37.

—— WEBSTER, J., and WILLIAMS, R. (1990), 'Dynamics of information technology implementation: A reassessment of paradigms and trajectories of development', *Futures*, 22: 618–40.

FLECK, L. (1979), *Genesis and Development of a Scientific Fact* (Chicago: Chicago University Press).

FOUCAULT, M. (1979), *Discipline and Punish: The Birth of the Prison* (London: Penguin).

—— (1980), *Power/Knowledge: Selected Interviews and Other Writings 1972–1977* (Brighton: Harvester Press).

FRANCIS, A., and WINSTANLEY, D. (1988), 'Managing new product development: Some alternative ways to organise the work of technical specialists', *Journal of Marketing Management*, 4: 249–60.

—— TURK, J., and WILLMAN, P. (1983) (eds.), *Power, Efficiency and Institutions: A*

Critical Appraisal of the 'Markets and Hierarchies' Paradigm (London: Heinemann).

FRANZ, C., and ROBEY, D. (1984), 'An investigation of user-led systems design: Rational and political perspectives', *Communications of the ACM*, 27: 1202–9.

FREEMAN, C. (1982), *The Economics of Industrial Innovation* (London: Frances Pinter).

——(1988), 'The factory of the future: The productivity paradox, Japanese just-in-time and information technology', PICT Policy Research Paper No. 3, Oxford.

FRIEDMAN, A. (1977), *Industry and Labour: Class Struggle at Work and Monopoly Capitalism* (London: MacMillan).

——with CORNFORD, D. (1989), *Computer Systems Development: History Organization and Implementation* (Chichester: Wiley).

FRIEDSON, E. (1986), *Professional Powers* (Chicago: University of Chicago Press).

GALBRAITH, J. R. (1977), *Organization Design* (Reading, Mass.: Addison-Wesley).

GILB, T. (1988), *Principles of Software Engineering Management* (Reading, Mass.: Addison-Wesley).

GINZBERG, M. J., and BAROUDI, J. J. (1988), 'MIS careers—A theoretical perspective', *Communications of the ACM*, 31: 586–94.

GRAMSCI, A. (1971), *Selections from the Prison Notebooks of Antonio Gramsci*, ed. Q. Hoare trans G. N. Smith (London: Lawrence and Wishart).

GREENBAUM, J. (1976), 'Division of labor in the computer field', *Monthly Review*, 28: 40–55.

——(1979), *In the Name of Efficiency* (Philadelphia: Temple University Press).

GREENHALGH, K. (1984), 'Organizational problems of new technology', paper presented to Factories in 2001 A.D. Conference, Computer Applications Consultants Ltd., Ascot, UK.

GRINDLEY, P. C. (1988), 'The UK software industry: A survey of the industry and the evaluation of policy', London, Centre for Business Strategy, London Business School.

GRONBAEK, K., KYNG, M., and MORGENSEN, P. (1993), 'CSCW challenges: Cooperative design in engineering projects', *Communications of the ACM*, 36: 67–77.

HABERMAS, J. (1973), *Legitimation Crisis* (Boston: Beacon).

HALES, M. (1980), *Living Thinkwork* (London: CSE Books).

HAMILTON, R. (1986), 'DDP—Managerial opportunities and consequences', *Omega*, 14: 475–81.

HARVEY, D. (1987), 'The boardroom breakthrough', *Business Computing and Communications*, Nov.

HAYES, R. H., and ABERNATHY, W. J. (1980), 'Managing our way to economic decline', *Harvard Business Review*, 58 (July/Aug.): 66–77.

——and GARVIN, D. A. (1982), 'Managing as if tomorrow mattered', *Harvard Business Review*, 60 (May/June): 70–9.

HEIMER, C. A. (1984), 'Organizational and individual control of career development in engineering project work', *Acta Sociologica*, 27: 283–310.

HEYDERBRAND, W. F. (1983), 'Technocratic corporatism: Towards a theory of occupational and organisational transformation', in R. Hall and R. Quinn (eds.), *Organisational Theory and Public Policy* (London: Sage).

HICKS, J. O. Jnr. (1990), *Information Systems in Business: An Introduction* (St Paul, Minn.: West).

HICKSON, D. J., HININGS, C. R., LEE, C. A., SCHNECK, R. E., and PENNINGS, J. M. (1971), 'A strategic contingencies theory of intra-organizational power', *Administrative Science Quarterly*, 16: 216–29.

HOSKIN, K. (1990), 'Using history to understand theory: A re-consideration of the historical genesis of "strategy"', EIASM Workshop on Strategy, Accounting and Control, Venice, Oct.

HOWCROFT, J. B., and LAVIS, J. (1987), 'Evolution of the payment system of London clearing banks', *Service Industries Journal*, 7: 176–94.

HOWELLS, J. (1987), 'Developments in the location, technology and industrial organization of computer services: Some trends and research issues', *Regional Studies*, 21: 493–503.

—— and HINE, J. (1990), 'Competitive strategy and the implementation of new network technology', *Technology Analysis and Strategic Management*, 3: 397–425.

—— —— (1993) (eds.), *Innovative Banking: Competition and the Management of a New Network Technology* (London: Routledge).

HUGHES, T. (1988), 'Reverse salients and critical problems', in B. Elliot (ed.), *Technology and Social Process* (Edinburgh: Edinburgh University Press).

HYMAN, R. (1987), 'Strategy or structure? Capital, labour and control', *Work, Employment and Society*, 1: 25–55.

IVES, B., and OLSON, M. H. (1984), 'User involvement and MIS success: A review of research', *Management Science*, 30: 586–603.

JAGGER, N., and BRADY, T. (1989), 'Patterns of software activity in the UK', paper presented at PICT National Workshop, Brunel University, 17–19 May.

KAPLAN, R. S. (1990) (ed.), *Measures for Manufacturing Excellence* (Boston: Harvard Business School).

KEEN, P. G. W. (1981), 'Information systems and organizational change', *Communications of the ACM*, 24: 24–33.

KING, J. L. (1983), 'Centralized versus decentralized computing: Organizational considerations and management options', *Computing Surveys*, 15: 319–49.

KING, W. R., and CLELAND, D. I. (1975), 'The design of management information systems: An information analysis approach', *Management Science*, 22: 286–97.

KLING, R. (1980), 'Social analyses of computing: Theoretical orientations in recent empirical research', *Computing Surveys*, 12: 61–110.

—— (1987), 'Computerization as an ongoing social and political process', in G. Bjerkness, P. Ehn, and M. Kyng (eds.), *Computers and Democracy: A Scandinavian Challenge* (Aldershot: Avebury).

—— (1991), 'Cooperation, coordination and control in computer supported work', *Communications of the ACM*, 34: 83–8.

KNIGHTS, D., and MORGAN, G. (1990), 'The concept of strategy in sociology: A note of dissent', *Sociology*, 24: 475–83.

—— —— (1991), 'Corporate strategy, organizations and the subject', *Organization Studies*, 12: 251–73.

KOGUT, B., and ZANDER, U. (1992), 'Knowledge of the firm, combinative capabilities and the replication of technology', *Organization Science*, 3: 383–97.

KORTH, H., and SILBERSCHATZ, A. (1986), *Database System Concepts* (New York: McGraw-Hill).

KRAFT, P. (1977), *Programmers and Managers: The Routinization of Computer Programming in the US* (New York: Springer-Verlag).

—— and DUBNOFF, S. (1986), 'Job content, fragmentation and control in computer software work', *Industrial Relations*, 25: 184–96.

KUHN, S. (1985), 'A working hypothesis: The reorganization of work in the systems department of a bank', paper presented to 27th Annual Conference of the Association of Collegiate Schools of Planning, Nov.

KUHN, T. S. (1962), *The Structure of Scientific Revolutions* (Chicago: University of Chicago Press).

KUMAR, K. (1978), *Prophecy and Progress: The Sociology of Industrial and Post-Industrial Society* (London: Allan Lane).

KYNG, M. (1991), 'Designing for cooperation: Cooperation in design', *Communications of the ACM*, 34: 65–73.

—— and MATHIASSEN, L. (1982), 'Systems development and trade union activities', in N. Bjorn-Anderson *et al.* (eds.), *Information Society: For Richer for Poorer* (Amsterdam: Elsevier).

LAND, F. (1982), 'Notes on participation', *Computer Journal*, 25: 283–5.

LARSON, M. S. (1977), *The Rise of Professionalism* (Berkeley and Los Angeles: University of California Press).

LASH, S., and URRY, J. (1987), *The End of Organized Capitalism* (Cambridge: Polity Press).

LAZONICK, W. (1991), *Business Organization and the Myth of the Market Economy* (Cambridge: Cambridge University Press).

LENZ, R. T., and LYLES, M. A. (1985), 'Paralysis by analysis: Is your planning system becoming too rational?', *Long Range Planning*, 18: 64–72.

LEONARD-BARTON, D., and KRAUS, W. A. (1985), 'Implementing new technology', *Harvard Business Review*, 63 (Nov./Dec.): 102–10.

LOVERIDGE, R. (1990), 'Incremental innovation and appropriate learning styles in direct services', in Loveridge and Pitt (1990).

—— and PITT, M. (1990), 'Introduction: Defining the field of technology and strategy', in R. Loveridge and M. Pitt (eds.), *The Strategic Management of Technological Innovation* (Chichester: Wiley).

LUCAS, H. C. (1974), *Towards Creative Systems Design* (New York: Columbia University Press).

—— (1981), *Implementation: The Key to Successful Information Systems* (New York: Columbia University Press).

LUNDVALL, B. (1988), 'Innovation as an interactive process: From user-producer interaction to the national system of innovation', in G. Dosi, K. Pavitt, and L. Sote (eds.), *Technical Change and Economic Theory* (London: Frances Pinter).

MACAULEY, S. (1963), 'Non-contractual relations in business: A preliminary study', *American Sociological Review*, 28: 55–67.

McDERMID, D. C. (1990), *Software Engineering for Information Systems* (Oxford: Blackwell Scientific Publications).

McFARLAN, F. W. (1984), 'Information technology changes the way you compete', *Harvard Business Review*, 62 (May/June): 98–103.

—— and McKENNEY, J. (1982), 'The information archipelago', *Harvard Business Review*, 60 (Sept./Oct.): 109–19.

MACHLUP, F. (1962), *The Production and Distribution of Knowledge in the US* (Princeton, NJ: Princeton University Press).

McLOUGHLIN, I. (1990), 'Management, work organisation and CAD—towards flexible automation?', *Work, Employment and Society*, 4: 217–37.

MAIDIQUE, M. A. (1980), 'Entrepreneurs, champions and technological innovation', *Sloan Management Review*, 21: 59–76.

MAILLE, A. (1990), 'Realising CASE's potential', *Computing*, 8 Feb.: 16–17.

MANTEI, M. (1981), 'The effect of programming team structure on programming tasks', *Communications of the ACM*, 24: 106–13.

MEYER, J. W., and ROWAN, B. (1977), 'Institutionalized organizations: Formal structure as myth and ceremony', *American Journal of Sociology*, 83: 340–63.

MILES, I., and GERSHUNY, J. (1986), 'The social economics of information technology', in M. Ferguson (ed.), *New Communication Technologies and the Public Interest* (London: Sage).

MILES, R. E., and SNOW, C. C. (1978), *Organizational Strategy, Structure and Process* (New York: McGraw-Hill).

MILLER, D., and FRIESEN, P. H. (1984), *Organizations: A Quantum View* (Englewood Cliffs, NJ: Prentice-Hall).

MINTZBERG, H., and WATERS, J. A. (1985), 'Of strategies, deliberate and emergent', *Strategic Management Journal*, 26: 257–72.

MINTZBERG, Y., and MINTZBERG, H. (1988), 'Strategy making as craft', in K. Urabe, J. Child, and T. Kagono (eds.), *Innovation and Management: International Comparisons* (Berlin: de Gruyter).

MUMFORD, E. (1972), *Job Satisfaction: A Study of Computer Specialists* (London: Longman).

—— (1983), *Designing Human Systems* (Manchester: Manchester Business School).

MURRAY, F., and KNIGHTS, D. (1990), 'Inter-managerial competition and capital accumulation: IT specialists, accountants and executive control', *Critical Perspectives on Accounting*, 1: 167–89.

NARDI, B., and MILLER, J. (1990), 'The spreadsheet interface: A basis for end user programming', Proceedings of the 3rd International Conference on Human-Computer Interaction, Cambridge, Aug.; Amsterdam, North-Holland.

NEWMAN, M., and ROSENBERG, D. (1985), 'Systems analysts and the politics of organizational control', *Omega*, 13: 393–406.

OFFE, C. (1984), *Contradictions of the Welfare State* (London: Hutchinson).

OWEN, D. E. (1986), 'Information systems organizations—Keeping pace with the pressures', *Sloan Management Review*, 27: 59–68.

PALMER, C. (1990), 'Hybrids—A growing initiative', *Computer Bulletin*, 2 (Aug.): 16–18.

PARNAS, D. (1972), 'On criteria to be used in decomposing systems into modules', *Communications of the ACM*, 14: 221–7.

PAWLEY, M., WINSTONE, D., and BENTLEY, P. (1991), *UK Financial Institutions and Markets* (Basingstoke: Macmillan).

PELÁEZ, E. (1988), 'A Gift from Pandora's Box: The Software Crisis.' Unpublished Ph.D. thesis (Edinburgh University).

—— (1990), 'Software copyright', paper presented to PICT Workshop on Social Perspectives on Software, Oxford, 13–14 Jan.

PETTIGREW, A. M. (1973), *The Politics of Organisational Decision Making* (London: Tavistock).

—— (1975), 'Occupational specialisation as an emerging process', in G. Esland, G. Salaman, and M.-A. Speakman (eds.), *People and Work* (Edinburgh: Holmes McDougall).

—— (1980), 'The politics of organizational change', in N. Bjorn-Anderson (ed.), *The Human Side of Information Processing* (Amsterdam: North-Holland).

—— (1985), *The Awakening Giant: Continuity and Change at ICI* (Oxford: Blackwell).

—— (1987), 'Context and action in the transformation of the firm', *Journal of Management Studies*, 24: 649–70.

PIORE, M. J., and SABEL, C. F. (1984), *The Second Industrial Divide: Possibilities for Prosperity* (New York: Basic Books).

PODOLSKY, J. (1977), 'Horace builds a cycle', *Datamation*, Nov. 162–8.

POLANYI, M. (1946), *Science, Faith and Society* (London: Oxford University Press).

—— (1967), *The Tacit Dimension* (London: Routledge and Kegan Paul).

POPPER, K. R. (1979), *Objective Knowledge: An Evolutionary Approach* (Oxford: Clarendon Press).

PORTER, M. E. (1985), 'Technology and competitive advantage', *Journal of Business Strategy*, 5: 60–78.

—— (1987), 'From competitive advantage to corporate strategy', *Harvard Business Review*, 65 (May/June): 43–59.

—— and MILLAR, V. E. (1985), 'How information gives you competitive advantage', *Harvard Business Review*, 63 (July/Aug.): 149–60.

PRAHALAD, C. K., and HAMEL, G. (1990), 'The core competence of the corporation', *Harvard Business Review*, 68 (May/June): 79–91.

PRESSMAN, R. S. (1982), *Software Engineering: A Practitioner's Approach* (New York: McGraw-Hill).

—— (1992), ibid. 3rd edn.

PRICE, D. DE SOLLA (1984), 'The science/technology relationship: the craft of experimental science and policy on the improvement of high technology innovation', *Research Policy*, 13: 3–20.

PRICE WATERHOUSE (1991), 'Information Technology Review 1990/1', London, Price Waterhouse.

QUINTAS, P. (1991), 'Engineering solutions to software problems: Some institutional factors shaping change', *Technology Analysis and Strategic Management*, 3: 359–76.

RAELIN, J. A. (1991), *The Clash of Cultures: Managers Managing Professionals* (Boston, Mass.: Harvard Business School).

RAJAN, A. (1984), *New Technology and Employment in Insurance, Banking and Building Societies* (Aldershot: Gower).

RASANEN, K., and WHIPP, R. (1992), 'National business recipes: A sector perspective', in R. Whitley (ed.), *European Business Systems: Firms and Markets in their National Contexts* (London: Sage).

RAVETZ, J. R. (1971), *Scientific Knowledge and its Social Problems* (Oxford: Clarendon Press).

REICH, R. (1993), *The Work of Nations* (London: Simon and Schuster).

RHODES, E., and WIELD, D. (1985) (eds.), *Implementing New Technologies: Choice, Decision and Change in Manufacturing* (Oxford: Blackwell).

RICHARDSON, A. J. (1987), 'Accounting as a legitimating institution', *Accounting, Organizations and Society*, 12: 341–55.

ROBEY, D., and MARKUS, M. L. (1984), 'Rituals in information system design', *MIS Quarterly*, 8: 5–15.

ROCKART, J. F. (1988), 'The line takes the leadership—IS management in a wired society', *Sloan Management Review*, 29: 57–64.

—— and FLANNERY, L. S. (1983), 'The management of enduser computing', *Communications of the ACM*, 26: 76–84.

—— and HOFMAN, J. D. (1992), 'Systems delivery: Evolving new strategies', *Sloan Management Review*, 33: 21–31.

ROSENBERG, N. (1976), *Perspectives on Technology* (Cambridge: Cambridge University Press).

ROTHWELL, R. (1986), 'Innovation and re-innovation: A role for the user', *Journal of Marketing Management*, 2: 109–23.

RUESCHEMEYER, D. (1986), *Power and the Division of Labour* (Oxford: Polity Press).

SAYER, A. (1992), *Method in Social Science: A Realist Approach*, 2nd edn. (London: Routledge).

SCARBROUGH, H., and CORBETT, J. M. (1992), *Technology and Organization: Power, Meaning and Design* (London: Routledge).

—— and LANNON, R. (1988), 'The successful exploitation of new technology in banking', *Journal of General Management*, 13: 38–51.

———— (1989), 'The management of innovation in the financial services sector: A case study', *Journal of Marketing Management*, 5: 51–62.

SCHON, D. A. (1963), 'Champions for radical inventions', *Harvard Business Review*, 41 (Mar./Apr.): 77–86.

—— (1983), *The Reflective Practitioner* (Aldershot: Avebury).

SCHUMPETER, J. A. (1975), *Capitalism, Socialism and Democracy* (New York: Harper and Row).

SCOTT MORTON, M. A. (1991), *The Corporation of the 1990s: Information Technology and Organizational Transformation* (Oxford: Oxford University Press).

SENKER, P. (1984), 'Implications of CAD/CAM for management', *OMEGA*, 12: 225–31.

SHEA, M. (1988), *Influence: How to Make the System Work for You—A Handbook for the Modern Machiavelli* (London: Century).

SHEARMAN, C., and BURRELL, G. (1987), 'The structures of industrial development', *Journal of Management Studies*, 24: 325–45.

SILVERMAN, D. (1985), *Qualitative Methodology and Sociology* (Aldershot: Gower).

SIMON, H. A. (1965), *Administrative Behavior: A Study of Decision-Making Process in Administrative Organization*, 2nd edn. (New York: The Free Press).

SIMPSON, J. (1991), 'Educating IT managers: The hybrid manager', *Computer Bulletin*, June: 26–7.

SKILLS AND ENTERPRISE BRIEFING (1991), 'Information technology skills', Skills and Enterprise Network, Aug.

SKINNER, W. (1974), 'The focused factory', *Harvard Business Review*, 52 (May/June): 113–21.

SKYRME, D. J., and EARL, M. J. (1990), 'Hybrid managers: What should you do?', *Computer Bulletin*, May: 19–21.

SLACK, J., and FEJES, F. (1987) (eds.), *The Ideology of the Information Age* (Norwood, NJ: Ablex).

SMIRCICH, L., and STUBBART, C. (1985), 'Strategic management in an enacted environment', *Academy of Management Review*, 10: 724–36.

SMITH, C. (1987), *Technical Workers: Class, Labour and Trade Unionism* (Basingstoke: Macmillan).

—— CHILD, J. and ROWLINSON, M. (1990), *Innovation in Work and Organisation—The Cadbury Experience* (Cambridge: Cambridge University Press).

SMITH, S., and WIELD, D. (1988), 'New technology and bank work: Banking on IT as an "organizational technology" ', in L. Harris (ed.), *New Perspectives on the Financial System* (Beckenham: Croom Helm).

SPENDER, J. C. (1980), 'Strategy-making in business', Unpublished Ph.D. thesis (University of Manchester).

—— (1992), 'Knowledge management: Putting your technology strategy on track', Management of Technology III, Institute of Industrial Engineers.

SPRU (Science Policy Research Unit) (1972), 'SAPPHO: Success and failure in industrial innovation', London, Centre for the Study of Industrial Innovation.

STEINER, T. D., and TEIXEIRA, D. B. (1990), *Technology in Banking: Creating Value and Destroying Profits* (Homewood, Ill.: Business One Irwin).

STONEMAN, P. (1976), *Technological Diffusion and the Computer Revolution: The UK Experience* (Cambridge: Cambridge University Press).

STOREY, J. (1985), 'The means of management control', *Sociology*, 19: 193–211.

—— (1987), 'The management of new office technology: Choice, control and social structure in the insurance industry', *Journal of Management Studies*, 24: 43–62.

SVIEBY, K. E., and LLOYD, T. (1987), *Managing Know-How: Add Value by Valuing Creativity* (London: Bloomsbury).

SWANN, P. (1990), 'Standards and the growth of a software network', in J. L. Berg and H. Schumny (eds.), *An Analysis of the Information Technology Standardisation Process* (Amsterdam: Elsevier Science/North-Holland).

—— and Lamaison, H. (1988), 'The growth of an IT network: A case study of personal computer applications software', Discussion Papers in Economics No. 8807, Brunel University.

SWANSON, E. B. (1988), *Information System Implementation: Bridging the Gap between Design and Utilization* (Homewood, Ill.: Irwin).

TEECE, D. J. (1987) (ed.), *The Competitive Challenge: Strategies for Industrial Innovation and Renewal* (Cambridge, Mass.: Ballinger).

—— (1988), 'Technological change and the nature of the firm', in G. Dosi (ed.), *Technical Change and Economic Theory* (London: Frances Pinter).

THOMPSON, P. (1989), *The Nature of Work: An Introduction to Debates on the Labour Process*, 2nd edn. (Basingstoke: Macmillan).

TIERNEY, M., and WICKHAM, J. (1989), 'Controlling software labour: Professional ideologies and the problem of control', ESRC/PICT Workshop on Critical Perspectives on Software, Manchester, July.

VON HIPPEL, E. (1976), 'The dominant role of users in the scientific instrument innovation process', *Research Policy*, 5: 212–39.

—— (1988), *The Sources of Innovation* (Oxford: Oxford University Press).

—— (1990), 'The impact of "sticky data" on innovation and problem-solving', Sloan School of Management Working Paper, 3147-90-BPS, Cambridge, Mass., MIT Press.

VOSS, C. A. (1988), 'Implementation—A key issue in manufacturing technology: The need for a field study', *Research Policy*, 17: 56–63.

WALLIS, P. J. (1979) (ed.), 'State of the Art Report: Structured Software Development: Volume 1', Maidenhead, Infotech International.

WALSHAM, G. (1993), *Interpreting Information Systems in Organizations* (Chichester: Wiley).

WALZ, D., ELAM, J., and CURTIS, B. (1993), 'Inside a software design team: Knowledge acquisition, sharing, and integration', *Communications of the ACM*, 36: 62–77.

WEBSTER, J., and WILLIAMS, R. (1993), 'The success and failure of computer-aided production management', Edinburgh PICT Research Report No. 2, Edinburgh, Edinburgh University.

WEINBERG, G. (1982), 'Overstructured management of software engineering', 6th Annual Conference on Software Engineering, Tokyo, 13–16 Sept.

WHALLEY, P. (1986), *The Social Production of Technical Work* (London: Macmillan).

WHIPP, R., and CLARK, P. (1986), *Innovation and the Auto Industry: Product, Process and Work Organization* (London: Frances Pinter).

WHITLEY, R. (1988), 'Social science and social engineering', Working Paper 171, Manchester Business School.

WHITTINGTON, R. (1990), 'The changing status of R&D', in R. Loveridge and M. Pitt (eds.), *The Strategic Management of Technological Innovation* (Chichester: Wiley).

—— (1991), 'Changing control strategies in industrial R & D', *R & D Management*, 21: 43–53.

WILLIAMS, R. (1987), 'The development of models of technology and work organisation with information and communications technologies', Edinburgh PICT Working Paper No. 7, Edinburgh University.

—— and EDGE, D. (1992), 'The social shaping of technology: A review of UK research concepts, findings and programmes in Great Britain', in M. Dierkes and U. Hoffmann (eds.), *New Technology at the Outset* (Frankfurt and New York: Campus-Verlag and Westview).

WILLIAMSON, O. E. (1975), *Markets and Hierarchies: Analysis and Antitrust Implications* (New York: The Free Press).

—— (1985), *The Economic Institutions of Capitalism* (New York: The Free Press).

WILLMAN, P. (1983), 'The organisational failures framework and industrial sociology', in Francis, Turk, and William (1983).

WILSON, T. D. (1989), 'The implementation of information systems strategies in UK companies: Aims and barriers to success', *International Journal of Information Management*, 9: 245–58.

WINKLER, C. (1986), 'Battling for new roles', *Datamation*, 15 Oct.: 82–8.

WINSTANLEY, D. (1986), 'Recruitment strategies as a means of managerial control of technological labour', paper presented to Labour Process Conference, Aston University, Birmingham.

WINTER, S. (1987), 'Knowledge and competence as strategic assets', in Teece (1987).

WOMACK, J. P., JONES, D. T., and ROOS, D. (1990), *The Machine that Changed the World* (New York: Rawson Associates).

WOOD, S., and KELLY, J. (1982), 'Taylorism, responsible autonomy and management strategy', in S. Wood, (ed.), *The Degradation of Work?* (London: Hutchinson).

ZUBOFF, S. (1988), *In the Age of the Smart Machine: The Future of Work and Power* (Oxford: Heinemann).

Index

N.B. *Page reference to charts, tables, and figures italicized.*